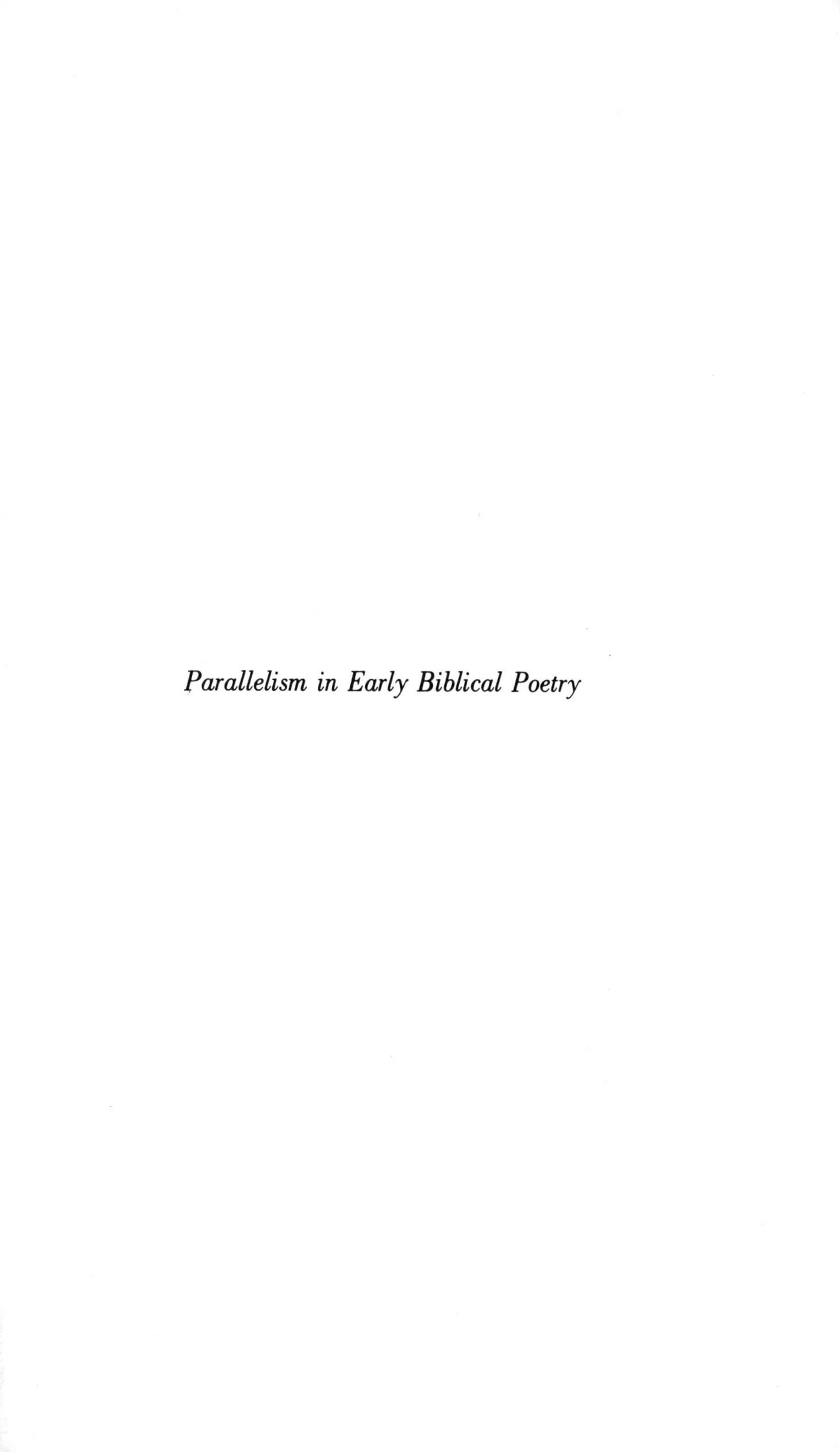

Parallelism in Early Biblical Poetry

HARVARD SEMITIC MUSEUM

HARVARD SEMITIC MONOGRAPHS

edited by
Frank Moore Cross, Jr.

Number 20

PARALLELISM IN EARLY BIBLICAL POETRY

by

Stephen A. Geller

Stephen A. Geller

PARALLELISM IN EARLY BIBLICAL POETRY

Scholars Press

Distributed by
Scholars Press
PO Box 5207
Missoula, Montana 59806

PARALLELISM IN EARLY BIBLICAL POETRY
Stephen A. Geller

Library of Congress Cataloging in Publication Data

Geller, Stephen A
Parallelism in early biblical poetry.

(Harvard Semitic monographs ; no. 20 ISSN 0073-0637)
Originally presented as the author's thesis, Harvard, 1976.
Bibliography: p.
1. Hebrew poetry, Biblical—History and criticism. 2. Hebrew language—Parallelism. 3. Bible. O.T.—Language, style. I. Title. II. Series.
BS1405.2.G44 1979 892.4'1'109 78-27255
ISBN 0-89130-275-1

Printed in the United States of America
1 2 3 4 5

Edwards Brothers, Inc.
Ann Arbor, Michigan 48104

Publication of this work was made possible
by a grant from the Abbell Publication Fund
of the Jewish Theological Seminary of America.

TO MY MOTHER

ACKNOWLEDGMENTS

This study is, with only minor revisions and expansions, a doctoral dissertation submitted to Harvard University in 1976. I wish to thank all my teachers at that institution and, especially, Professors Frank M. Cross, William L. Moran and Thomas O. Lambdin for generous hours of consultation and many useful suggestions. Professor Cross was also instrumental in the publication of this work in the series of Harvard Semitic Monographs. The special debt to him will be apparent on many pages of this study.

In addition, special thanks are due to the Jewish Theological Seminary of America and, especially, Chancellor Gerson D. Cohen. Through his understanding help I obtained funds not only toward the publication of the work but also for the preparation of the manuscript.

My thanks also to Mrs. Muriel Bennett whose contribution to the manuscript was not limited to skillful typing but extended to numerous suggestions regarding the content and format.

S.A.G.

New York, New York
July, 1978

CONTENTS

INTRODUCTION

The immediate stimulus for this study was an article by Roman Jakobson, "Grammatical Parallelism and Its Russian Facet," whose approach was provocative to one who had been dissatisfied with the treatment of parallelism in biblical literature. Most suggestive was Jakobson's recognition that semantic parallelism, in the many literatures in which it appears as a major device, must be studied in terms of all of the aspects of the poem, phonetic, semantic and, especially, grammatical:

> This focusing upon phonological, grammatical and semantic structures in their multiform interplay does not remain confined to the limits of parallel lines but expands throughout their distribution within the entire context; therefore the grammar of parallelistic pieces becomes particularly significant.[1]

Jakobson stresses that to properly understand the workings of parallelism, one must study the inter-relationships of the component features within the context of the entire poem:

> Pervasive parallelism inevitably activates all the levels of language--the distinctive features, inherent and prosodic, the morphological and syntactic categories and forms, the lexical units and their semantic classes in both their convergences and divergences acquire an autonomous poetic value.[2]

Referring to Steinitz' important study of parallelism in Finnish epic poetry,[3] Jakobson says:

> This is a pioneer work, not only in the Finno-Ugric field but also, and foremost, in the method of approach to the structural analysis of grammatical parallelism. The syntactic and morphological aspects of the poetic pattern are succinctly outlined in Steinitz' monograph, whereas their interconnections and the diverse semantic associations between the parallel lines and their components are only glimpsed. The investigator revealed the variety of grammatical relations between the paralleled verses, but the interconnection of these structurally different

---

1. Roman Jakobson, "Grammatical Parallelism and Its Russian Facet," _Language_, 42 (1966), p. 423.

2. Ibid.

3. Wolfgang Steinitz, "Der Parallelismus in der finnisch-karelischen Volksdichtung," _FF Communications_, no. 115 (Helsinki, 1934).

> distichs and their characteristic functions within a broader context calls for a self-contained and integral treatment of a given song in its entirety. . . .[4]

Jakobson's analysis of a Russian folk song and a snatch of biblical poetry along the lines described in the quotations just cited seemed a fruitful one for the analysis of biblical poetry. The careful study of a selected number of poems might reveal the complex of interweaving structures which escape the often cursory treatment of parallelism hithertofore. Especially interesting would be an examination of the relationship between semantic and grammatical parallelism. The analysis of a similar number of Ugaritic, Akkadian and biblical poems from different periods might result in laying the basis for a typology which would be most useful in the study of ancient Semitic poetic traditions.

However, it soon became apparent that a meaningful application of Jakobson's techniques to ancient poetry would be most difficult, if not impossible. In order to study the interworkings of phonetic, grammatical and semantic devices, one must have a clear understanding of each of these aspects of language. Yet each presents serious problems as regards the literatures of the ancient Near East. For example, the pronunciation of Hebrew is by no means certain for any stage of the biblical period; the language as a whole is distorted by tradition which has superimposed various diachronic levels upon each other and the whole has been refracted by the Masoretic vocalization systems. The nature of the metrical system is the object of active debate. The lexicon often presents problems, and semantic parallelism itself, although recognized as a major device since Bishop Lowth, has by no means been thoroughly studied. Little progress has been made in this area since the works of Gray,[5] Newman and Popper.[6] Biblical grammar, especially syntax, is not fully understood and, to my knowledge,

---

4. Jakobson, "Grammatical Parallelism," p. 404.

5. G. Buchanan Gray, The Forms of Hebrew Poetry, 1915. (Reprint, Ktav Publishing House, 1972, with an important Prolegomenon and useful bibliography by D. N. Freedman.)

6. Louis I. Newman and William Popper, Studies in Biblical Parallelism, Parts I and II (Berkeley: University of California Press, 1918).

grammatical parallelism in biblical literature has not been the object of systematic study. The problems are even greater for the other ancient Semitic languages.

It is clear that ancient texts are not immediately accessible to the sophisticated analysis which Jakobson and Steinitz can apply to texts in languages which are fully understood. Therefore, it is necessary to narrow the focus to one literature, biblical, and to what must be considered the most basic structures. What is required is an attempt to isolate the most significant aspects of biblical parallelism, both semantic and grammatical. What is more, the analysis of whole poems seems premature until the essential smaller structures are better understood. This study tries to establish a reasonably simple and flexible method by means of which the major semantic and grammatical structures of parallel verse can be isolated and then to examine some of the most important relationships between them. The groundwork might thereby be laid for more detailed analysis of larger structures. The phonetic aspects of poetry, excepting meter, have not been included since, important as they are, they serve as secondary means of poetic linkage. Of course, the great number of phonetic devices must play a prominent role in the more complex types of literary analysis beyond the scope of this work.

For the results of this study to be truly cohesive, a further narrowing of the focus, beyond the limitations discussed above, seems necessary. An examination of parallelism in texts from a limited period of biblical poetry would approximate a synchronic analysis; further studies of earlier and later stages would theoretically supply a diachronic understanding of the development of ancient Hebrew poetry. A chronological limitation is clearly preferable, and the logical starting point is early poetry, which is strategically situated so as to serve as a point of comparison for earlier Canaanite traditions and later biblical developments.[7]

---

7. It is also theoretically possible to start at the other end of the biblical period with examples drawn exclusively from undoubtedly late poems. However, a study of late poetry, while highly desirable in itself, would shed little light on the canons of classical parallelism which are considerably decayed in late verse.

This study aims at establishing a method for the analysis of major aspects of parallelism, with emphasis on grammatical and semantic parallelism, applying this method to a number of early poetic texts and then listing and studying the results. Accordingly, it consists of three major sections:

Part I contains necessary preliminary remarks on basic units of composition, grammatical and semantic parallelism, followed by an exposition of the method to be employed.

Part II is a collection of units drawn from early biblical poetry, the Corpus of examples, analyzed according to the method set forth in Part I.

Part III contains a series of lists and analyses dealing with selected topics raised by the methodology, with emphasis on basic patterns (the "unit formulae") and grammatical parallelism.

PART I

Preliminary Remarks

Perhaps the major intention of this study is methodological. It attempts to establish a relatively strict method which may be applied to couplets displaying parallelism or repetition. This method will be presented in this section and applied in Parts II and III. However, the method must be prefaced by a number of general remarks whose purpose is to establish a simple theoretical and practical framework for the method by stating certain principles and procedures. In both cases, no attempt at a completely comprehensive statement is intended. Discussion is limited to those general principles which are immediately relevant for the method.

The first section consists of the isolation of compositional units, emphasis being on the distinction between grammatical elements and units, metrical units, the line, couplet, triplet, and larger structures.

Next is a discussion of grammatical parallelism in general, what is termed the "reconstructed sentence" in particular, and related topics, followed by a brief introduction to the treatment of non-parallel units.

The next section deals with semantic parallelism, and attempts to outline a functional approach to this difficult problem from the point of view of "rhetorical relationships" and semantic "grades."

The final segment of Part I consists of a step-by-step exposition of the method of analysis.

Units of Composition

The compositional units of parallel verse form a pattern of interlocking relationships. Logically, one should proceed from smaller to larger units. However, due to the uncertainties which confront any analysis of Hebrew verse, a different procedure seems required. The unit of composition easiest to isolate is the couplet and its constituent A and B Lines, a structure basic to parallelism of meaning. By beginning with the couplet and line, one can keep the amount of arbitrariness, unavoidable in dealing with this topic, within reasonable bounds. One can then discuss compositional units below the level of the line and then proceed through a sequence of what might be termed compositional ranks through the line and couplet to larger structures.

The Couplet and Line

The couplet is the indispensable and necessary unit of composition for parallel verse and is, of course, isolated by semantic parallelism or repetition. The couplet itself must, of necessity, be composed of A and B Lines.[8] Non-parallel lines and couplets also occur, and are forced into the pattern of parallel verse by their relative infrequency and tendency to correspond generally to the syllable length of parallel units in their environment within a poem. What might be termed "doubly long" lines or the like must be considered couplets exhibiting enjambment between A and B Lines.

Grammatical Elements and Grammatical Units

Within the structure of the couplet, structures may be isolated by semantic parallelism or repetition. Within A and B Lines certain terms are parallel in meaning, either totally or partially. Other terms in each line may not display any degree of semantic parallelism. From the point of view of grammatical analysis, the simplest procedure would be to treat all grammatical terms alike, as equally significant. An analysis of this type is legitimate in its own terms, but would fail to take into account a goal which is basic to this study: the isolation of structures which may be considered of primary significance in the composition of parallelism. From this point of view it is hardly likely that all grammatical terms are to be assigned equal weight. For example, it is commonly accepted that the category of monosyllabic particles (*kî*, *lō(')*, *'im*, etc.) and prepositions (*ᶜal*, *'el*, *ᶜim*, etc.) are to be treated as proclitics forming a unit with the following term. This premise underlies the accentual interpretation of

8. The terms "stich" and "colon" will not be employed in this study.

Hebrew meter, but at this point will be accepted only grammatically. This line of reasoning is not entirely arbitrary but rather has some empirical support, at least in the materials of the _Corpus_ of examples. One finds that semantic parallelism is well developed for nouns and verbs. If particles were a significant factor in parallel verse, one would expect to find a rich vocabulary of parallel word pairs also for them. However, in the _Corpus_ particles and prepositions are rarely the object of parallelism (as opposed to repetition); examples like _gam_ // _ᶜim_ in Dt.32:25b are exceptions. Therefore, it is reasonable to make a distinction between two compositional units: what may be termed "grammatical elements" and "grammatical units." The former category consists of all words; the latter is the unit of composition which is more significant as a building block of the structure of parallel verse. One may establish as a rule in a working hypothesis that monosyllabic particles, including prepositions, are to be denied the status of grammatical units.[9]

Problems arise regarding the treatment of a sequence of two monosyllabic particles or disyllabic particles. Here the safest procedure seems to be to regard such elements as grammatically "anceps," so to speak; that is, capable of being awarded or denied the status of a grammatical unit according to the circumstances of the couplet in which they occur. This conditioned occurrence is not, in itself, objectionable. Anceps elements are common and proper to the sphere of meter; the transferral of the concept to grammatical structure is permissible. For example (on the orthography, see p. 44):

Dt.32:34:	hl' h' kms ᶜmdy	"Is this not stored up with me,
	ḥtm b'ṣrty	Sealed in my treasuries?"
Dt.32:30b:	'm l' ṣrm mkrm	"Unless their rock turn them over,
	(w)yhwh hsgrm	YHWH deliver them up."

The deciding factor is the line, and, beyond that, the couplet. Both units belong to a category which will be

---

9. In fact, there are two exceptions in the _Corpus_ of examples: _gam_ in Dt.32:25b and _pen_ in II Sam.1:20b. The latter example, especially, might be assigned to the metrical category 3:3.

described below as 3:2. In Dt.32:34, the A Line contains three grammatical units: *h'*, *kms*, and *^{c}mdy*. Therefore the disyllabic particle *hl'* forms no independent grammatical unit by itself, but may be treated as a single unit with *h'*. The A Line of Dt.32:30b contains only two grammatical units: *ṣrm* and *mkrm*. In this case, the sequence of two particles *'m l'* may be awarded the value of a grammatical unit. The crucial factor in each case is the over-all structure of the line and, beyond that, of the couplet. However, it will be seen below that in some cases one must proceed beyond the couplet (or triplet) to the structure of the poem as a final determinant; even then, uncertainty may still exist.

This distinction between grammatical elements and units will enable the system of notation described later to record grammatical parallelism in terms of the latter. However, many types of grammatical parallelism involving structures containing grammatical elements cannot be recorded. For example, in Num.23:8:

mh 'qb l' qbh 'l
mh 'z^{c}m l' z^{c}mh yhw

the repetition of particles is not reflected in the unit formula which represents the relationship between A and B Lines. That formula will record only the parallelism between the grammatical units *mh 'qb* // *mh 'z^{c}m*, *l' qbh* // *l' z^{c}mh* and *'l* // *yhw*.

Such devices must be the object of special study; however, they are discussed briefly in Part III of this work. Note that monosyllabic prepositions with pronominal suffix are consistently treated as grammatical units (*lî*, *lô*, *bām*, etc.). It may be advisable to treat these elements also as grammatically "anceps," a possibility that will be mentioned again in Part III.

The word *kol*, whose surface structure function is that of a noun in construct, is treated in this study as a particle as regards its function in grammatical (and metrical) units.

Metrical Units

The grammatical units described above correspond in general to the types of structures employed by the simple accentual or "stress" system of analysis of Hebrew meter. This study cannot avoid the inclusion of meter in its method if it is to attempt to deal with the major poetic devices of Hebrew verse. However, it is clear that the introduction of meter opens the door to additional uncertainty, which, of course, reflects our ignorance of the true nature of Hebrew metrics at any stage of biblical literature.

The approach taken in this study will attempt to be objective. It is becoming increasingly clearer that a syllabic approach to Hebrew (and Ugaritic) meter is the most useful one functionally;[10] that is, parallel lines often display a syllable symmetry whose frequency cannot be due merely to the natural limitations imposed by the length of the Semitic word within the framework of parallelism. It must, therefore, be a conscious concern of the poet. On the other hand, it cannot as yet be claimed that syllable symmetry is so pervasive that it clearly forms the chief determinant of Hebrew prosody. Some of the irregularities may be due to textual corruptions, particularly those caused by the failure of later scribes to understand an earlier poetic system. The safest functional approach seems to be to record the structure of each couplet in terms of both the accentual and the syllabic interpretations.

The accentual system will be recorded in the form of "metrical units," whose boundaries generally correspond to those of grammatical units; that is, usually one grammatical unit = one metrical unit. However, provision must be made for "long words" which may be assigned two accents ("stresses" or "beats") as required by the circumstances of their couplet (see below). Syllable counts, of course, play a significant role also in the Ley-Sievers system, both from the point of view of

---

10. See especially, Frank M. Cross, "Prose and Poetry in the Mythic and Epic Texts from Ugarit," _HTR_, 67 (1974), and D. N. Freedman in the _Prolegomenon_ to Gray, _Forms of Hebrew Poetry_ (Ktav reprint, 1972), pp. xxxiff.; cf. also, Freedman's "Archaic Forms in Early Hebrew Poetry," _ZAW_, 72 (1960), 101-107 and his "The Structure of Psalm 137," _Near Eastern Studies in Honor of William Foxwell Albright_, ed. H. Goedicke (Baltimore: The Johns Hopkins Press), pp. 187-205. Note also R. C. Culley, "Metrical Analysis of Classical Hebrew Poetry," _Essays on the Ancient Semitic World_, ed. J. W. Wevers and D. B. Redford (Toronto: University of Toronto Press), pp. 12-28.

the allowable number of unaccented syllables between stresses, and also in the assignment of more than one stress to polysyllabic words.[11] In this study, only the latter aspect will play a role.

The Line and the Couplet

One may now return to the line and the couplet, which may be classified according to the ratio of metrical to grammatical units: 2:2, 3:3, 4:4, the most common types, but also 3:2, 4:2, 2:3, 4:3, 2:4, 3:4 and 4:5. This is a full inventory of the patterns which appear in the *Corpus*.

However, as noted above, just as the couplet and line determine the basic parameters of the grammatical and metrical units, so also must the over-all structure of the poem be referred to as a final determinant in isolating the structure of the couplet, line, and all smaller constituents. Reference to the poem's structure will be necessary only in cases of doubt, where the rules stated above offer no clear solution; most especially when dealing with grammatically anceps elements. The difficulty, of course, is that this highest instance, so to speak, is itself often uncertain, a situation which does not face the student of literatures whose basic structures are fixed and well known. For example, some poems in the *Corpus* seem to display a metrical pattern 3:3 throughout; so, Dt.32 and II Sam.22, to name only the longest poems. Others clearly display mixed meter; that is, an alternation between 3:3 and 4:4; so, for example Ex.15 and Jud.5. The use of mixed meter is well attested for Ugaritic and early Hebrew poetry, and occurs clearly also in Akkadian.[12] The practical result of the employment of mixed meter in a poem is that no certain decision

---

11. For a clear statement of the problem, see Gray, *Forms of Hebrew Poetry*, ch. 4.

12. On mixed meters in Ugaritic and Hebrew, see especially Frank M. Cross and David N. Freedman, *Studies in Ancient Yahwistic Poetry* (Baltimore, 1950. Microfilm-reprint, Ann Arbor, 1961), p. 25; and William F. Albright, *Yahweh and the Gods of Canaan* (Garden City, New York: Doubleday and Company, 1968), pp. 9ff.

can be achieved regarding the value in grammatical and metrical units to be awarded structures containing grammatically anceps elements. The structure of the line cannot here be of service as it is in lines in poems with a single metrical pattern. For example, in Jud.5:23b:

k l' b' l^{c}zrt yhw "For they did not come to the aid of YHWH"

is k l' b' (kî lō(') bâ'û) to be assigned the value of one or two grammatical and metrical units? The sequence of two particles k l' is grammatically anceps, and since the poem exhibits mixed meter, one may legitimately assign either three or four grammatical and metrical units to the line in question. Nor is the structure of the couplet of any assistance. The B Line (l^{c}zrt yhw bgbrm, "To the aid of YHWH with (their) warriors") is certainly 3:3; however, it can be demonstrated that couplets with the ratio of grammatical to metrical units in A and B Lines 4:4::3:3 occur in the *Corpus*; so, for example, Ps.68:14b. In effect, this means that considerable uncertainty exists in the delineation of the primary units of composition which any analysis of parallelism based on an accentual interpretation of Hebrew verse must accept. It should be pointed out that the unit discussed above does display syllabic symmetry (9:9).

However, reasonable clarity, at least for the materials of the *Corpus*, can be achieved on one important issue: the function of lines with the ratio of grammatical to metrical units 2:2. They may be termed "short lines," and are well attested in early Semitic poetic structure, appearing prominently also in Ugaritic and, especially, Akkadian poetry. Here the structural approach is most rewarding. In the *Corpus* 2:2 lines display a feature not shared by lines with the structure 3:3, 4:4, etc.; namely, they never appear as independent units of composition in a couplet (i.e., as lines) but only in combination with another short line. Equally significant is the fact that this composition of two short lines appears in conjunction with another line of the same structure or lines of the type 3:3, 4:4, etc. to form couplets. The only exceptions seem to be two lines in Ex.15, vv.12 and 18.[13]

It is clear that the combination of two short lines may be viewed as the structural equivalent of the line composed of four metrical units. Confirming this conclusion is the fact that not only do short lines not appear singly in the Corpus, but also no sequence of three short lines is found; i.e., 2:2:2. The simplest procedure is to distinguish between two types of four metrical unit lines, determined structurally: a line composed of two short lines, displaying internal parallelism and, therefore, a clear caesura between the two halves; and a line without such a clear caesura, which may therefore be viewed as a sequence of two short lines connected by enjambment. The former type may be symbolized by the schema -- // -- and the latter by -- / --; the double virgule (//) indicates a strong caesura, the single virgule (/), the absence of a caesura. Supporting the conclusion that the latter type of line is composed of two enjambed short lines is the fact that no example exists in the Corpus in which the virgule divides a closely bound grammatical structure like, for example, the construct relationship.

It is admissible to include in the category of four metrical unit lines exhibiting a clear caesura other types of strongly disjunctive structures: repetition, vocatives, and, perhaps also, elements in apposition and casus pendens. The following is a list of the types of 4:4 lines occurring in the Corpus, with an example of each:

1. -- // --
   a. Internal parallelism
      Ex.: mm š'l // ḥlb ntn (Jud.5:25a)
   b. Repetition
      Ex.: 'nk lyhw // 'nk 'šr (Jud.5:3b)
   c. Vocative
      Ex.: mqdš yhw // knn ydk (Ex.15:17c)

---

13. Both lines follow clearly marked triplets to which they can scarcely be attached--v.18 is liturgical in nature and may be a later addition to the poem; v.12 has, most probably, been displaced and, so far as meaning is concerned, might be attached quite naturally to vv.5, 6 or 10. Its present position may be due to the similarity between nṭt and nḥt, which begins the following unit.

d. Apposition

Ex.: 'zmr lyhw // 'lh yśr'l (Jud.5:3c)

e. <u>Casus pendens</u>

Ex.: 'l m'b // y'ḥzm r^c^d (Ex.15:15b)

2. -- / -- (enjambed)

Ex.: bspl 'drm / hqrb ḥm' (Jud.5:25b)

The short line is therefore a significant compositional element, but not, in the examples of the <u>Corpus</u>, an independent one. The latter are limited to lines of 3 and 4 metrical units, with varying ratios of grammatical units.

In general, it is apparent that one must strictly distinguish between the independent, and therefore basic, compositional units, and those whose use must be considered optional. The basic compositional units may be listed as a series of ranks, from lesser to more inclusive: the grammatical element, the grammatical unit, the metrical unit, the line and, of course, the couplet. Optional compositional elements are the short line and the larger units to be discussed below: the triplet, the quatrain, the strophe, and chains of verses.

Couplets are composed of lines of three or four metrical units. The number of possible combinations of grammatical and metrical units is large; however, most A and B Lines consist of the ratios of metrical and grammatical units 3:3 and 3:3, 3:3 and 3:2, 4:4 and 4:4, 4:3 and 4:3, or 3:4 and 3:4. It is more convenient to refer to the ratios of metrical and grammatical units in the lines forming the couplet separately. Therefore, reference will henceforth be to couplets with the ratio of grammatical units 3:3, 4:4, 3:2, etc., and of metrical units 3:3, 4:4, 3:4, etc. Since four metrical unit lines are combinations of short lines 2:2, it will be useful to record that fact. Therefore, in the relevant steps in the method employed in the <u>Corpus</u> (nos.3-5; see below) grammatical and metrical units will be represented doubly as 4:4(2:2::2:2), 3:4(2:2), etc.

The number of possible couplet structures in terms of metrical units may be symbolically illustrated by the following list. The sign - - - represents the line of three metrical units; -- // -- and -- / -- reflect the four metrical unit patterns mentioned above:

3:3 $\frac{- - -}{- - -}$; 3:4 $\frac{- - -}{\text{-- // --}}$ and $\frac{- - -}{\text{-- / --}}$; 4:3 $\frac{\text{-- // --}}{- - -}$

and $\frac{\text{-- / --}}{- - -}$; 4:4 $\frac{\text{-- // --}}{\text{-- // --}}$ $\frac{\text{-- / --}}{\text{-- // --}}$ $\frac{\text{-- // --}}{\text{-- / --}}$ $\frac{\text{-- / --}}{\text{-- / --}}$

Of course, not all of the nine possible combinations are equally well represented in the Corpus.

The Triplet

The sequence of three lines is not a compositional unit of the obligatory nature of the couplet, but is common in Hebrew and Ugaritic and occurs in Akkadian. Triplets must in all cases be analyzed as a sequence of interlocking couplets; i.e., A-B Lines and B-C Lines. They will be so treated in the Corpus.[14] Triplets fall into two basic categories: those in which a non-parallel line forms the A or C Line (never the B Line in the Corpus), and those composed of three parallel lines. The former type may be symbolized as A B B' or A A' B, the latter as A A' A". Of course, the theoretical number of line combinations in terms of metrical and especially grammatical units is large.

The Quatrain, Chain and Strophe

Couplets very frequently fall together in pairs determined semantically or grammatically by subordination. One of the couplets may be non-parallel. However, the structure of the quatrain is less tightly bound than that of the triplet since the primary relationship is between the individual couplets. In only one example in the Corpus (Ps.29:1-2) has the quatrain seemed so tightly interwoven as to require analysis as three couplets: A-B, B-C, and C-D. The Corpus contains no example of alternating parallelism which would require analysis of the relationship between A-C and B-D Lines, and so attest to the quatrain as a compositional unit on the level of the triplet. Several examples approach alternating parallelism; for example:

---

14. This is not to deny that the relationship between the A and C Lines of the triplet is not also important and must be studied as part of the detailed analysis of a poem.

Dt.32:21

hm qn'ny bl' 'l	"They made me jealous with a non-god;
k^csny bhblhm	They angered me with their nothings;
'ny 'qn'm bl' ^{c}m	I shall make them jealous with a non-people;
bgy nbl 'k^{c}sm	I shall anger them with a brutish nation."

Yet even in this case, analysis of the separate couplets is possible and the couplet is probably the dominant unit, alternating parallelism being a secondary, if significant, device. However, genuine alternating parallelism does occur between short lines:

Ex.15:9b-c

'ḥlq šll // tml'm npš	"I shall divide the spoil; my greed will be sated;
'rq ḥrb // tršm yd	I shall whet my sword; my hand will destroy."

Even examples displaying no clear caesura between short lines may be considered as variations of alternating parallelism:

Ex.15:4

mrkbt pr^c / yr bym	"He cast the chariots of Pharaoh into the sea;
(w)mbḥr šlšw / ṭb^c bym sp	His best troops drowned in the Reed Sea."

Larger compositional units ("strophes") are often difficult to isolate unless clearly delineated by sense or grammar. The most tightly bound larger structure is what might be termed the "chain" of lines, for example, Dt.33:13-16a. Such longer sequences are certainly worthy of careful analysis. This study, however, is concerned primarily with the basic compositional units, the parallel couplet and, beyond it, the triplet.

Grammatical Parallelism: The Reconstructed Sentence and Related Topics

Parallelism in all cases involves a primarily binary relationship, that between the A and B Lines of the couplet. To be sure, secondary poetic devices cross the boundaries of the couplets and supply numerous types of phonetic, grammatical, and semantic "coupling"[15] to the larger environment of the poem. However, the primary determinant is the couplet. In all cases of strict parallelism (and repetition) it should be possible to reduce the couplet to a single statement which has been restated binarily. For each example, one can restore, or "reconstruct," the hypothetical unitary statement by arranging A and B Lines in such a way that semantically parallel units appear in the same positions and in a sequential syntagmatic structure which also includes non-parallel elements. Units in the same position in this "reconstructed sentence" should ideally belong to the same "semantic paradigm" (see <u>Semantic Parallelism</u>). From the point of view of grammar, units in the same position will, in many cases, also be grammatically strictly parallel; in other cases, they will be what may be termed grammatically "compatible." This distinction requires further discussion.

Strict grammatical parallelism may be said to exist between semantically parallel members of the reconstructed sentence when they display full syntactic congruence; that is, belong to the same grammatical paradigm. For example, the subject of a nominal sentence in the A Line must be parallel to the subject of a nominal sentence in the B Line, the direct object of a transitive verb to the same, etc.

Members of the same semantic paradigm in the reconstructed sentence should, by reason of that fact, be considered to be grammatically compatible. The simplest type of compatible elements are those which are annexed to grammatically congruent elements; so, for example, the <u>nomen rectum</u> attached to a noun grammatically parallel to its A Line member, or forms with pronominal suffixes parallel to unsuffixed forms. Many types of grammatical compatibility are more complex, ranging from single words to whole phrases, and displaying numerous grammatical relationships. These are listed and discussed in Part III. The introduction of the concept of the reconstructed sentence will allow even grammatical elements which are directly incongruent to be considered compatible,

---

15. On "coupling," see Samuel R. Levin, <u>Linguistic Structures in Poetry</u> (The Hague: Mouton & Co., 1962), ch. 4.

especially when an idiomatic expression or "compound verb"[16] is involved. So, for example, II Sam.22:14:

yr^{c}m mn šmm yhwh "YHWH thundered from heaven;
(w)^{c}lyn ytn qlh Elyon sent forth his voice."

The reconstructed sentence may be represented as follows:[17]

yr^{c}m yhwh
mn šmm
ytn qlh ^{c}lyn

yr^{c}m and *ytn qlh* are grammatically incongruent (intransitive verb // transitive verb + object), but are compatible because *ytn qlh* forms, of course, an indivisible idiomatic unit and occupies the same position as *yr^{c}m* in the reconstructed sentence.

The reconstructed sentence is an application of the concept of grammatical paradigm to the framework of the parallel couplet. It must be remembered that it is a hypothetical construct. Terms in the same position belong to the same paradigm of parallelism and should be interchangeable. So, in the example given above, there are four inherent hypothetical sentences:

1. yr^{c}m mn šmm yhwh
2, yr^{c}m mn šmm ^{c}lyn
3. ytn qlh mn šmm yhwh
4. ytn qlh mn šmm ^{c}lyn

Note that word order is not significant for analysis.[18]

---

16. Compound verbs are those which, from the point of view of their "deep structure" syntactic functioning in the sentence, must be considered as consisting of verb + preposition; see the sub-line unit analyses in Part III.

17. The reconstructed sentence will be presented with semantically and grammatically parallel units in vertical columns, occupying equivalent positions in the sentence. Sub-unit grammatical elements are joined by a line to the A or B Line grammatical unit to which they belong.

18. The reconstructed sentence should not require a lexical replacement. There is one possible exception in the *Corpus*, *timmas* in Ps.68:3a-b. Yet even here, one cannot say that the lexical replacement is a grammatical or even semantic necessity.

So far the reconstructed sentence has been discussed only from the point of view of grammar. However, the rigid application of the concept soon makes it apparent that for the analysis of certain types of significant structures one must refer also to aspects of semantic parallelism. The latter topic will be discussed in general in a following section. Here reference will be only to those issues which involve the application of semantic parallelism to the reconstructed sentence.

The key to the problem is the treatment of what may be termed "compound" units. For example, in the unit cited above (II Sam.22:14) it is clear that ytn qlh is a compound idiomatic unit parallel to the simple $yr^{c}m$. In fact, the parallelism of simple and compound units (or the reverse), of compounds with other compounds, or even double and triple compounds, are very common in the *Corpus* of examples. The application of the principle of the reconstructed sentence enables one to isolate several major categories.

For a purely grammatical approach, all that is required of the hypothetical sentences inherent in the reconstructed sentence is that they be grammatical (although in some cases minor adjustments must be made; see the following sections). However, if the system of analysis is to deal with truly significant compositional elements, it must take into account also semantic acceptability. An examination of the reconstructed sentences of the examples in the *Corpus* soon reveals that units may form compounds of two basic types: those which are purely grammatical in nature, and those in which semantic relationships are also crucial. Semantic compounds exhibit a significant degree of semantic contiguity[19] between the grammatical (and metrical) units of which they are composed. In grammatical compounds, on the other hand, the constituent grammatical units of A and B Lines are essentially interchangeable in the reconstructed sentence. It is also clear that there are some compounds of which the parts are interchangeable

---

19. Compounds formed by semantic attraction, or contiguity, reflect the type of relationship termed "metonymic" by Roman Jakobson and Morris Halle, *Fundamentals of Language* (The Hague: Mouton and Co., 1956), ch. 5.

neither grammatically nor semantically, and which therefore must be considered indivisible. One may therefore posit the following categories of compounds isolated by the reconstructed sentence:

1. Divisible compounds
   a. Grammatical
   b. Semantic
2. Indivisible compounds (both grammatical and semantic)

These categories are fully applicable only to the parallelism of compounds to other compounds. Compounds parallel to simple units, or the reverse, are by nature indivisible. The differences between these types of compounds may be illustrated by a few examples. Reference to the lists of sub-line units in Part III will provide a full repertoire for the Corpus.

II Sam.1:22b-c

qšt yntn / l' nśg 'ḥr	"Jonathan's bow did not turn back;
(w)ḥrb š'l / l' tšb rqm	Saul's sword did not return empty."

Dt.32:38a

ḥlb zbḥmw y'klw	"Who ate the fat of their sacrifices;
yštw yn nskmw	Who drank the wine of their libations?"

Dt.32:22b

t'kl 'rṣ wyblh	"It devours the earth and its produce;
(w)tlhṭ msdy hrm	It sets aflame the foundations of the mountains."

In II Sam.1:22b-c, the units qšt yntn and ḥrb š'l are fully interchangeable grammatically and semantically in the reconstructed sentence; hypothetically, qšt š'l and ḥrb yntn are equally acceptable (although, of course, the sequence qšt-ḥrb might be shown to be due to culturally determined factors like the fixed sequence of parallel word pairs, etc.). These units clearly form a purely grammatical, and divisible, compound.

In Dt.32:38a, however, although all the hypothetical sentences are grammatical, only the two which actually appear in the couplet are semantically acceptable; i.e., y'klw yn nskmw, yštw ḥlb zbḥmw, y'klw ḥlb nskmw and yštw yn zbḥmw are equally nonsensical. Both lines form compounds which are grammatically divisible, but semantically indivisible due to the degree of semantic contiguity between the units.

On the other hand, in Dt.32:22b the hypothetical combinations 'rṣ hrm and msdy wyblh are unacceptable either grammatically or semantically. The parallel compounds 'rṣ wyblh and msdy hrm are indivisible in the context of the reconstructed sentence.

It should be pointed out that units whose relationship is truly autonomous need not be treated as semantic compounds. For example, in Num.24:9:

mbrkk brk "Blessed is everyone who blesses you,
'rrk 'rr Cursed is everyone who curses you!"

the hypothetical sentences mbrkk 'rr and 'rrk brk, while directly opposed to the poet's intention, are by no means nonsensical.

The distinctions discussed above seem necessary to any meaningful attempt to understand the structure of parallel verse since one is, after all, attempting to isolate the structures the poet worked with. This is not to claim that serious problems of interpretation do not remain, or that all ambiguities have been removed.

The manner of presentation of these different types of compounds will be outlined in step 10 of the method. However, at this point a few more remarks must be made concerning the nature of grammatical compounds in particular.

Most grammatical compounds consist of nouns in construct. However, other grammatical structures have been admitted into the system. These include:

1. Periphrastic equivalents of constructs
   Ex.: Ex.15:17: mkn lšbtk (so also Ps.68:5a; lrkb b^{c}rbt)
2. Relatives parallel to constructs
   Ex.: Dt.32:15b: 'lh ^{c}śhw // ṣr yš^{c}th (so also Dt.32:35a: lym nqm wšlm // l^{c}t tmṭ rglm)

Note in this context also II Sam.22:23: ky kl drkw,

where *kl* (here strengthened by *ky*) has been awarded the value of a metrical unit.

3. Coordinated nouns or verbs

   Ex.: Jud.5:30: rḥm rḥmtm

   II Sam.22:8a: tg^{c}š wtr^{c}š

4. Noun plus attributive

   Ex.: Ex.15:10: bmm 'drm

5. Compounds formed by two units, one of which is a monosyllable. The largest group consists of monosyllabic forms of prepositions with pronominal suffix; specifically, *l*:

   Ex.: Dt.32:7b: wygdkh // wy'mrw lkh

   So also one example in the *Corpus* with *b*:

   Dt.32:20: bnm l' 'mn bm

   Also included in this class are pronouns; so *my*: Ex.15:11a-b: m kmk; *zh*: Ex.15:2b: z 'l; *hmh*: Dt.32:28: 'bd ^{c}ṣt hmh; *mh*: Dt.32:20a: mh 'ḥrtm; and *z't*: Dt.32:27b: p^{c}l kl z't.

6. Compounds formed by "quasi-verbal"[20] sentences

   Ex.: Gen.49:15b: yhy lms ^{c}bd

7. Particles plus noun

   Ex.: Num.24:17a: wl' ^{c}t // wl' qrb

Transformations

There remain a number of couplets which contain semantic parallelism between one or more units, but for which no reconstructed sentence can be written. Specifically, the semantically parallel units are in syntactic positions which do not "line up" paradigmatically. In such cases a reconstructed sentence must be produced by subjecting the B Line to one or more grammatical transformations which will place semantically parallel units in grammatically compatible positions. Of course, reconstructed sentences which require transformation are doubly hypothetical. For example, II Sam.22:37:

trḥb ṣ^{c}dy tḥtny	"You lengthen my stride under me;
(w)l' m^{c}dw qrsly	My ankles do not stumble."

The A Line contains a transitive verb with object, the B Line an intransitive verb. No reconstructed sentence can be

20. On "quasi-verbal" sentences, see note 23.

composed with the couplet as it stands. The B Line must be transformed: negative particle + intransitive verb + subject --→ negative particle + transitive verb + object.

The transformation produces a <u>hiphil</u> form <u>tam^c^îd</u>; the theoretical transformed sentence is, then, <u>l'</u> <u>tam^c^îd</u> <u>qrsly</u> "You do not let my ankles stumble" (note also the necessary change in person). The reconstructed sentence would then be:

trḥb s^c^dy

thṭny

l' tm^c^d qrsly

Part III contains a list of the transformations which occur in the materials of the <u>Corpus</u>.

<u>Required Grammatical Adjustments in Reconstructed Sentences</u>

All the hypothetical sentences inherent in the structure of the reconstructed sentence, varying in number according to its pattern, should be grammatical. In many cases, however, adjustments must be made to allow full grammaticality. All of these must be below the level of incongruence which necessitates a grammatical transformation, although they sometimes must be made in a sentence which already has been transformed. Not included in this category are the rearrangements made in the case of a "compound verb"; i.e., a verb + preposition which must, in the framework of the reconstructed sentence, be considered a unit (see Part III). For example:

y^c^r qnh

Dt.32:11a: knšr

yrḥp ^c^l gzlw

So also, <u>inter</u> <u>alia</u>, <u>hbw</u> <u>gdl</u> l (Dt.32:3); <u>ybnw</u> <u>l</u> (Dt.32:29); <u>ytnḥm</u> <u>^c^l</u> (Dt.32:36); <u>'šw^c^</u> <u>'l</u> (II Sam.22:7a); <u>sl</u> <u>l</u> (Ps.68:5a); and <u>mšl</u> <u>b</u> (Ps.89:10). Also not included in the category of adjustments in the reconstructed sentence are examples involving "double-duty" suffixes only (although, in such cases, the suffix is parenthesized). For example:

Ex.15:16b: ^c^d y^c^br ^c^m(k) z qnt yhw

Excluded also are all cases of <u>waw</u> at the beginning of the B Line, which are simply omitted from the reconstructed sentence.

The following is a list of what must be considered necessary adjustments, arranged in a generally hierarchical order from less to more consequential examples. Both deleted and added elements are parenthesized. The pattern of the couplet will clarify the nature of the parenthesized elements. If forms are not immediately understandable from the orthography, they are vocalized (so Gen.49:7a, etc.). In addition, this section contains a discussion of two special patterns requiring comment, as well as a few final remarks on the reconstructed sentence in general.

1. Some examples require adjustments which may be considered relatively insignificant. In each case at least one of the hypothetical sentences of the reconstructed sentence necessitates the ellipsis or rearrangement of a morphological element, a replacement in number or gender, or both. All of these are categories which are among those which play no role in the system of analysis and are not registered by the grammatical notation system which will be outlined below. The replacement or deletion may be from either the A or the B Line of the couplet.

a. A particle of the B Line is intrusive in the reconstructed sentence:

<u>Examples</u>:

Ps.68:17b-c:
l'hm lšbt
hr ḥmd lnṣḥ
('p) yhw yškn

Ps.89:6:
šmym pl'kh
ydw yhwh
bqhl qdšm ('p) 'mntkh

So also Dt.4a (<u>ky</u>), perhaps, the <u>waw</u> of <u>w'ny</u> (from the A Line) in Dt.32:39c-d.

b. A preposition in the B Line is intrusive in the reconstructed sentence:

<u>Examples</u>:

Num.23:9a:
ṣrm 'r'n
k mr'š
(m)gb^{c}t 'šrn

Dt.33:13:
šmm m^{c}l
mmgd
(m)thm rbṣt tḥt

In both examples the regens of the construct has been deleted from the B Line of the couplet.

Also:

Dt.32:24b: šn bhmt
'šlḥ bm
(ᶜm) ḥmt zḥly ᶜpr

The preposition here is the functional equivalent of a coordinating conjunction.

c. A change of gender and/or number is required:

Examples:

Gen.49:7a: 'pm k ᶜz (ᶜazzā(h))
'rr (gender)
ᶜbrtm k qšt (qš)

II Sam.22:8a: tgᶜš wtrᶜš (ygᶜšw wyrᶜšw) 'rṣ
(gender and number)
yrgzn (trgz) msdy hrm

Other examples:

Gender only

Num.24:7b	Dt.33:29c
Dt.32:2a	Hab.3:3b

Number only

Dt.32:7b
Dt.32:30a
Jud.5:28b

Gender and number

Dt.32:1	Dt.33:13
Dt.32:4a	II Sam.22:8a
Dt.32:27b	II Sam.22:23

d. A pronominal suffix in the B Line must be removed:

Num.24:8b: y'kl gym
ṣrw
ygrm ᶜṣmt(hm)

This is the sole example of this category in the Corpus.

2. More significant are the examples in which a change of syntax is involved, sometimes requiring a morphological replacement.

a. Examples requiring morphological change:

Ps.68:17a-b: lm trṣdn hrm (hārê) gbnnm ḥmd 'lhm lšbt
Jud.5:19a: b' mlk (mlkm) knᶜn 'z nlḥm
Ps.29:5: ql yhw (y)šbr 'rz ('rzm) (h)lbnn

Ps.29:8: ql yhw yḥl mdbr qdš

Ex.15:4: mrkbt pr^{c} yr bym sp

mbḥr šlšw ṭb^{c}

Ps.68:17a-b involves the removal of the construct (itself an emendation) from the reconstructed sentence. Since it, like the following three examples, is a repetition unit, there is only one hypothetical sentence inherent in the reconstructed sentence. Jud.5:19a and Ps.29:5 require the opposite: the suspension of the absolute status of the _regens_ of the construct. The same is true of Ps.29:8 and Ex.15:4, where, however, the morphological replacement involves only a change in vocalization.[21]

b. Examples not requiring a morphological change:

Dt.32:28: ky gy 'bd ^{c}ṣt / 'n bhm tbnh hmh

In this example, the "quasi-verbal" sentence in the B Line becomes, in the reconstructed sentence, a relative clause; so also Ps.89:13.

In Dt.32:32b, a nominal sentence is transformed by its placement in the reconstructed sentence into a clause displaying the typical _casus_ _pendens_ structure:

^{c}nbmw ^{c}nby rš / 'šklt mrrt lmw

3. Most serious are those examples which require the insertion in the reconstructed sentence of a grammatical element not found in either A or B Lines of the couplet, even after transformation.

---

21. Note that all are examples of "climactic parallelism" and contain at least partial repetition. For a linguistic analysis of this type, see Samuel E. Loewenstamm, "The Expanded Colon in Ugaritic and Biblical Verse," _JSS_, 14 (1969), 176-196, and Edward L. Greenstein, "Two Variations of Grammatical Parallelism in Canaanite Poetry and Their Psycholinguistic Background," _JANES_, 6 (1974), 87-105.

<u>Examples</u>:

Dt.33:28b: ^{c}l 'rṣ dgn wtrš
'p (m)šmw n^{c}rp ṭl

In this case, the B Line has been transformed and requires the insertion of the preposition <u>m</u> before <u>šmw</u> according to the rules of standard prose grammar, although prepositions are often omitted in poetry.

II Sam.22:38: 'rdp w'šmdm
'yby
l' 'šb (m) ^{c}d kltm

The reconstructed sentence requires the placement of <u>m</u>, here as a complement to the verb <u>šwb</u>. The following unit is similar:

II Sam.22:39: wl' yqmn (m)
'mḥṣm tḥt rgly
yplw

One example seems to require the insertion of conjunctive <u>waw</u>:

Dt.32:39c-d: 'mt w'ḥyh
(w)'ny
mḥṣty (w)'rp'

Reference is to the second <u>waw</u>; the first should perhaps be removed in the reconstructed sentence.

A significant replacement occurs in Dt.32:20. In this example a pronominal suffix must be replaced by <u>'eṯ</u> + suffix:

'strh pny m hm ('ōṯām)
'r'h (mh) 'ḥrtm

Here <u>'strh pny m</u> must be viewed as a compound; and <u>mh</u> of the B Line probably must be deleted. The hypothetical sentences would then be:

1. 'strh pny mhm
2. 'strh pny m'ḥrtm
3. 'r'h mh 'ḥrtm
4. 'r'h 'tm ('ōṯām)

A lexical replacement may be required by the pattern of Ps.68:3a-b: khndp ^{c}šn
tndp (tms)
khms dng mpn 'š

Additional Remarks

A number of examples display a special pattern whose treatment in the reconstructed sentence requires comment. Characteristic of these examples is that the A Line contains a definite syntactic caesura (in all but Jud.5:3, two independent clauses). For illustration, the A Line caesura is represented by // (double virgule) in three unit examples.

Ex.15:14: šm^c ^{c}mm // yrgzn
ḥl 'ḥz yšb plšt

Dt.32:11b: yprś knpw // yqḥw
yś'hw ^{c}l 'brth

Dt.32:39c-d: 'ny 'mt // w'ḥyh
mḥṣty w'ny 'rp'

Jud.5:3b-c: 'nk lyhw // 'nk 'šr
'zmr lyhw / 'lh yśr'l

Jud.5:19a: b' mlkm // nlḥm
'z nlḥm mlk kn^{c}n

Ps.77:17b-c: r'k mym // yḥlw
'p yrgzw thmt

Ps.114:3: (h)ym r'h // wyns
(h)yrdn ysb l'ḥr

In each case the reconstructed sentence must violate the boundaries of the syntactic break because of semantic parallelism (or repetition). Only in this way can the semantically parallel units be properly arranged. Note that some of the examples in the following list display one of the types of adjustments in the reconstructed sentence discussed in the preceding pages:

Ex.15:14:
^{c}mm yrgzn
šm^c
yšb plšt (b)ḥl n'ḥz

Dt.32:11b:
knpw yqḥw
yprś
'brth yś'hw ^{c}l

Dt.32:39c-d:
'mt w'ḥyh
(w)'ny
mḥṣty (w)'rp'

Jud.5:3b-c:
'šr
'nk lyhw 'lh yśr'l
'zmr

Jud.5:19a: b' mlk(m) kn^{c}n nlḥm

Ps.77:17b-c: r'kh mym yḥlw
thmt 'p yrgzw

Ps.114:3: r'h (h)ym wyns
(h)yrdn ysb l'ḥr

The only problems from the point of view of grammatical parallelism are in Dt.32:11b and Ex.15:14. Perhaps in the former example *yś'hw ^{c}l* should not be viewed as a compound (see below). In Ex.15:14 the reconstructed sentence is the result of a transformation (see the *Corpus*).

One further pattern concerning procedure in the method of analysis requires comment. It involves only three examples in the *Corpus*:

Ps.68:5a: šr lyhw // zmr šm
sl lrkb b^{c}rbt

Ps.68:6: 'b ytmm // (w)dyn 'lmnt
yhwh bm^{c}n qdš

Ps.89:12: lkh šmym // 'p lkh 'rṣ
tbl wml'h // 'th ysdtm

None of these examples, especially the last, is without problems. However, as interpreted in the *Corpus*, the structure of each may be represented loosely as A A' A''. In each example the short lines of the A Line are not only parallel to each other (internal parallelism), but each is parallel to the B Line. The procedure in such cases will be to treat the first short line as an addition (see step 8 in the exposition of the method, below). For example, the reconstructed sentence for Ps.68:5a is:

šr lyhw zmr šm
sl l rkb b^{c}rbt

Note that *sl l* is treated as a compound.

The adjustments and patterns discussed above do not affect the legitimacy of the concept of the reconstructed sentence, although many individual examples may involve problems of interpretation. Mention must be made of a special case:

Num.23:9b: hn ^{c}m lbdd yškn
bgym l' ytḥšb

Peculiar here is the fact that the common semantic pair ^{c}amm and goy are not in grammatically parallel positions; nor is there any transformation which can produce grammatical compatibility between them. Dt.32:11b, discussed above, may present similar problems:

knpw yqḥw
yprś
'brth yś'hw ^{c}l

The treatment of yś'hw ^{c}l as a compound is clumsy, although not impossible. A much smoother reconstructed sentence would be:

yqḥw
yprś knpw ^{c}l 'brth
yś'hw

Not enough units of this type are present in the *Corpus* to determine whether, in such cases, we are dealing with an intentional poetic device.

Non-parallel Units

Twenty-eight units in the Corpus (ca. 12%) are non-parallel; that is, display no significant degree of semantic parallelism or repetition. Non-parallel units form couplets (17 examples) or the A-B Lines (7 examples) or the B-C Lines (4 examples) of triplets. Only two examples of single lines occur; that is, lines which do not clearly belong to the preceding or following unit: Ex.15:12, which may be misplaced, and Ex.15:18.[22] The fact that the latter line is liturgical, or, as noted, even a later addition to the poem may account for its isolation. Otherwise, non-parallel lines which do not form couplets can be assigned by meaning to a contiguous unit in their environment.

Non-parallel units fall into the following general grammatical categories as regards the structure of A and B Lines:

1. Verbal sentence-verbal sentence (VS-VS)
2. Nominal sentence-nominal sentence (NS-NS)
3. Verbal sentence-nominal sentence (VS-NS)
4. Nominal sentence-verbal sentence (NS-VS)
5. "Quasi-verbal" sentence-nominal sentence (QVS-NS)[23]
6. Verbal sentence-"quasi-verbal" sentence (VS-QVS)
7. Enjambed units

Only those units are to be considered enjambed in which A and B Lines of necessity form a complete sentence. Such units must be considered couplets rather than doubly long lines.

Part III contains a list of the examples of the Corpus which fall into the grammatical categories listed above, as well as a discussion of the types of non-parallel semantic relationships which can occur between non-parallel lines.[24]

---

22. See above, note 13.

23. "Quasi-verbal" sentences are nominal sentences with hyh, to which category one may conveniently add sentences with the copula, the existential adverbs yš and 'yn; cf. Francis Anderson, The Hebrew Verbless Clause in the Pentateuch (Journal of Biblical Literature Monograph Series, vol. 14. Nashville: Abingdon Press, 1970), p. 23.

24. See also Joachim Begrich, "Der Satzstil im Fünfer," ZSem, 9 (1933.34), 374-382, especially 194ff.

Semantic Parallelism

Since the beginning of modern study of biblical poetry, semantic parallelism has been considered one of its major devices, if not the chief one.[25] The topic is a difficult one. Hence it is not surprising that studies of biblical parallelism have largely left untreated the problem of the nature and various types of semantic relationship between parallel units beyond the generalities covered by terms like "antithetical" or "synonymous" parallelism (let alone the essentially useless category of so-called "synthetic" parallelism).[26] Recent studies in parallelism have emphasized the isolation of formulaic "word-pairs" and have been invaluable in demonstrating the cultural continuity between Canaanite and later biblical poetic traditions. However, they have not been concerned with the general semantic relationship between parallel formulae, although rhetorical devices like "step parallelism" have long been recognized for Hebrew and have been well documented for Ugaritic. There are few exceptions; the main one is the recognition by Albright and Cross of what the latter terms "impressionistic" parallelism; on which, more below.[27]

The main problem lies not only in the limited amount of material at our disposal but also in the inherent difficulty of setting up semantic categories for the classification of parallel terms. What is desirable is a relatively simple, but flexible, method for dealing with semantic parallelism which will isolate poetically significant patterns. It seems to me that such a functional approach is possible through the application to this topic of the concept of the semantic paradigm and the combination of this concept with that of what may be termed "rhetorical relationships."

The concept of paradigm has been extended from grammar to semantics by S. Levin. A grammatical paradigm, which he

---

25. David N. Freedman in the Prolegomenon to Gray, Forms of Hebrew Poetry, suggests that semantic parallelism is merely a secondary poetic device (p. xxvi).

26. See Appendix B.

27. Also so-called "emblematic" parallelism and S. Gevirtz's "epithetic"; see Patterns in the Early Poetry of Israel (Chicago: The University of Chicago Press, 1963), p. 26.

labels "Type I," he defines as:

> . . . equivalence classes; that is, classes whose members are equivalent in respect to some feature or features, these features always to be understood as lying outside the form in question--as constituting a *tertium comparationis*.[28]

He then extends this concept to a form of paradigm he calls "Type II" which is, in fact, a semantic paradigm:

> The features defining membership in this new type of paradigm will again be features external to the members of the class (as was true for our Type I classes) but, whereas the external features there were linguistic (environment), the external features defining our Type II classes will be extralinguistic. One such type of class is that involving meaning. We choose to say in this treatment that two forms are semantically equivalent as they overlap in cutting up the general "thought-mass"--which lies outside individual languages, but which the forms of individual languages refer to. Synonyms are therefore regarded as being equivalent in respect to this extralinguistic reference. In the same way, words constituting semantic fields are also equivalent and form paradigms; e.g., names of animals, sets of abstract terms, or even a group of words like *moon*, *star*, *sea*, *time*, and *sun*, between which semantic affinities may be said to exist. Moreover, it is not necessary that semantic paradigms be organized only on the basis of meaning similarity; such paradigms may be and are organized on the basis of meaning opposition. . . .[29]

The simple application of the concept of semantic paradigms will result in the setting up of conceptual categories (Steinitz' *Begriffskategorien*). This is in itself not entirely useful in analyzing semantic parallelism. After all, in parallelism we are dealing in every case with the relationship between two terms, and, specifically, in a fixed sequence: B Line to A Line. It is necessary to combine the concept of semantic paradigm with the recognition that the relationship of the B Line term to its A Line parallel involves in every case what might be called a "rhetorical relationship," that is, one which is intended to produce a certain literary effect. This approach, close to that of K. Krohn cited (critically) by Steinitz,[30] provides the key to an economical method of

---

28. Levin, *Linguistic Structures in Poetry*, p. 21.

29. Ibid., p. 25.

30. The work of K. Krohn is known to me only through the work of Steinitz, who rejects it in his *Parallelismus*, pp. 180ff. He discusses Krohn's attempt to establish laws for word parallelism, some of which he summarizes as follows:

classifying parallelism with a relatively small amount of arbitrariness. So, for example, *yyn* ("wine"), *dm ^{c}nbym* ("blood of grapes"), *ḥlb* ("milk"), *mym* ("water"), *nzlym* ("flowing things" = "fluid") are all members of a semantic paradigm which also includes words like *škr* ("strong drink"), *tyrš* ("new wine"), etc. The *tertium comparationis*, or common denominator, is "potables" or the like. Of course, *mym* and *nzlym* also belong to another common paradigm which includes such terms as *ym* ("sea"), *thm* ("deep"), *nhr* ("river"), etc.; the common denominator here is "bodies of water" or the like. In fact, most words belong to a number of semantic paradigms. However, in the context of parallelism only two members of a given paradigm can be present, and what is most significant is the rhetorical relationship between them. For example, the pair *yyn* // *škr* are by no means interchangeable; the relationship of *škr* to *yyn* may be termed enumerative or distributive.

Law of Equality (*Gesetz der Gleichheit*)

- Identity (parallel words are derived from the same root)
- Synonymity (ex.: *Stute* : *Mutterpferd*)
- Similarity (ex.: *Vater* : *Mutter*)
- Contrast (ex.: *Finger* : *Zehe*)
- Abstract : concrete (ex.: *Sinn* : *Herz*)
- Concept (*Begriff*) : metaphor (ex.: *Braut* : *Vogel*)
- General : specific (ex.: *Kind* : *Junge*)
- Specific : general (ex.: *Birkhuhn* : *Fuchs*)
- Whole : part (ex.: *Wald* : *Baum*)
- Material : product (ex.: *Eisen* : *Schwert*)
- Concept (*Begriff*) : a characteristic (*Eigenschaft*) (ex.: *Mutter* : *Gebärerin*)

Law of Contiguity (*Gesetz der Berührung*)

- Spatial (örtliche) contiguity (ex.: *Stein* : *Baumstumpf*)
- Temporal contiguity (ex.: *Weihnachten* : *Stephanstag*)
- Causal contiguity (ex.: *Freude* : *Lied*)

Steinitz criticizes this type of classification for its arbitrariness and for that fact that it fails to take into account his own (sometimes hazy) distinction between "synonymous" and "analogous" parallelism. To some extent his criticism is justified; but Krohn's approach is basically similar to the one taken in this study, although the categories correspond to his only in part. It must be stressed, however, that the categories are not to be understood as logical ones (against Krohn), but strictly rhetorical.

The literary effect is what Cross calls "impressionistic" when the parallel terms are placed in their context: "he drank wine/strong drink" is not intended to mean "he drank wine and strong drink" but something like "he drank whatever it was he drank; wine, strong drink, etc."[31]

The parallelism of *yyn* // *dm ^{c}nbym* produces a quite different effect. The terms are logically interchangeable; the rhetorical effect is repetition, the echoing of the A Line term by its B Line parallel. Simultaneously, however, one cannot overlook the fact that *dm ^{c}nbym* is a metaphorical description, or, better, epithet of *yyn*; so also the relationship between *mym* and *nzlym*.

Proceeding along these lines it is possible to isolate a number of rhetorical relationships in the materials of the *Corpus*. The various categories will be presented in the following manner:

1. Simple Categories
2. Categories modified for proper noun (PN) and pronoun (PR)
3. Compound Categories

Each type is preceded by a term, usually an abbreviation, by which it is identified in the *Corpus* and Part III.

Simple Categories

1. *Syn* = synonym

A large class of parallel units belong to this group, whose rhetorical effect may be described as variational repetition (to be distinguished from repetition = identity, below). This is the effect described above for the relationship between *yyn* and *dm ^{c}nbym* (where a metaphorical, epithetical nuance is also involved). The members of this category may be termed synonymous, proper. They belong to semantic paradigms the numbers of which are essentially interchangeable logically. One may temporarily overlook secondary features such as

---

31. See Appendix B; also, Cross, "Prose and Poetry," pp. 7-8; and Popper, *Studies in Biblical Parallelism*, pp. 436ff. This kind of relationship, termed "List" below, is basically the same as Steinitz' "analogous parallelism." For an interesting Chinese equivalent, see James R. Hightower, "Some Characteristics of Parallel Prose" in *Studia Serica Bernhard Karlgren Dedicata*, ed. S. Egerod and E. Glahn, p. 62.

differences in "tone." So, in English, "house," "home," "residence," "palace," and "domicile" may be considered basically synonymous, despite the fact that one might commonly say, "I am going home" but is much less likely to say, "I am going to my domicile," let alone, "I am going to my palace" (unless facetiously, ironically, etc.).

Examples:

Num.23:21a: 'n // ᶜml ("crime" // "fault")

Gen.4:23a: ql // 'mrt ("my voice" // "my word")

2. List

Another large class is labelled simply "List." Members of this category exhibit the type of relationship described above for the parallelism of yyn and škr; that is, they belong to a type of paradigm whose members are related by an understood common denominator and are not logically interchangeable, even in the most general way. The rhetorical effect is, as noted above, enumerative or impressionistic.

Examples:

Dt.32:38a: y'klw // yštw ("eat" // "drink")

Dt.32:2a: kmṭr // kṭl ("like rain" // "like dew")

Gen.4:23b: 'š // yld ("man" // "youth")

Two smaller classes both display a rhetorical effect which may be called contrastive:

3. Ant = antonym

This category is related to number (1) above; that is, the members belong to a paradigm in which (basic) identity is replaced by (basic) non-identity.

Examples:

Dt.32:25a: mḥṣ // mḥdrm ("outside" // "inside")

II Sam.22:28: tšᶜ // tšpl ("you save" // "you humble")

4. Mer = merism

The type of contrast displayed by this category is in the framework of the rhetorical relationship termed "List"; the impressionistic effect is the statement of extremes, which may imply everything that is between.[32]

---

32. On this device in general, see A. M. Honeyman, "Merismus in Biblical Hebrew," JBL, 71 (1952), 11-18.

Examples:

Dt.32:1: (h)šmym // (h)'rṣ ("O heavens!" // "O earth!")

Dt.33:13b-c: šmm // mthm ("(from . . .) the heavens" // "from the deep")

Several other categories can also be related directly either to Syn or List:

Syn

5. Epith = epithet

The B Line parallel is a description of or circumlocution for the A Line parallel. This is the relationship illustrated above for the pair yyn // dm ᶜnbym ("wine" // "blood of grapes")

6. PN = proper noun

The B Line parallel is a proper noun parallel to a common noun in the A Line. The rhetorical effect is close to that of WP, discussed below; that is, specification.

Example:

Gen.49:16: ᶜm // šbṭ yśr'l ("his people" // "the tribes of Israel")

7. PR = pronoun

In this class the B Line parallel is a pronoun; the A Line term is its antecedent.

Example:

Jud.5:29: ḥkmt śrth // ('p) h' ("The wisest of her ladies" // "she")

The rhetorical meaning of this small class is unclear.

List

8. WP = whole-part PW = part-whole

The characteristic of this class is that one parallel member may be considered the common denominator of the semantic paradigm of which the other parallel member is an individual constituent. The rhetorical effect in the case of WP is specificiation; in the case of PW, generalization.

Examples:

WP: Dt.33:29c: 'ybk // ᶜl bmtm ("your enemies" // "(on) their backs")

PW: Ps.114:4: k'lm // kbny ṣ'n ("like rams" // "like sheep")

9. Concr.-Abstr. = concrete-abstract[33]
   Abstr.-Concr. = abstract-concrete

This category is similar to the preceding one in that its rhetorical sense is generalizing or specifying, depending on whether the abstract term is in the B Line or A Line, respectively. Here also, the general (= abstract) term is the common denominator of the semantic paradigm of which the parallel term is a member; in this case, however, the general term is an abstract noun.

Examples:

Concr.-Abstr.: Dt.32:25a: ḥrb // 'mh ("the sword" // "terror")

Abstr.-Concr.: Dt.32:23: r^{c}t // ḥṣy ("disasters" // "my arrows")

10. Num = numerical

This is a simple variation of List; both A and B terms are numbers. Its rhetorical meaning is the same.

Example:

Dt.32:30a: 'ḥd // šnym ("one" // "two")

Two categories are to be differentiated from those listed up to this point by the fact that the parallel members cannot belong to the same semantic paradigm and are not semantically parallel:

11. D = identity
    "D" = virtual identity

This class is composed of terms which are identical, that is, total repetition. This is also the rhetorical meaning, which must be distinguished from that of Syn, whose variational repetition produces an "echoing" effect. By "virtual identity" is meant a relationship between A and B Line terms which are different forms of the same root; for example, Num.24:7b: mlk // mlkt. The signs D and "D" are employed for this class because it is similarly used in the semantic "grades" to be discussed below (and for deletions from the A Line which appear in the B Line as repetition).

---

33. On concrete-abstract, cf. Mitchell Dahood, Psalms I. Anchor Bible, vol. 17a (Garden City, N. Y.: Doubleday and Company, 1970), pp. 411ff.

12. Met = metaphor

Terms in this class are related metaphorically; that is, by a figure or image meaningful in a specific context established by the individual couplets.

Example:

Ps.68:3b-c: dng // rš^{c}m ("wax" // "the wicked")

Modified Categories

The categories which have been described so far may be termed "simple," in that only one type of rhetorical relationship dominates in each case. It is necessary to add a number of categories which are basically similar, but which also display certain types of modification. The system of grammatical notation employed in Part II includes the status of pronoun (PR) and proper noun (PN). It is useful to introduce these factors also into the notation of semantic categories, since proper nouns, especially, play an important role in semantic "formulae"; that is, standard formulaic expressions characteristic above all of oral literature. Many parallel units display a proper noun or, less commonly, a pronoun in either A or B Lines or both. The rhetorical meaning when both A and B Line parallels contain PN or PR is the same as for the simple rhetorical grade which dominates. When only one parallel member exhibits PN or PR, an added nuance is implied, which in the case of PN is the same as for the simple rhetorical class PN discussed above; i.e., a type of specification.

When both A and B Line units contain proper nouns or pronouns, that modification will be indicated by placing the sign (PN) or (PR) after the simple rhetorical sign; so, Syn(PN), List(PN), etc. Only one class in which the modification in both A and B Lines is pronominal (PR) is present in the Corpus: Syn(PR). Note that this modification also includes prepositions with pronominal suffixes.

The following types of this non-rhetorical modification for PN and PR occur in the Corpus:

Syn(PN): Num.23:7b: y^{c}qb // yśr'l ("Jacob" // "Israel")
List(PN): Gen.4:24: qn // lmk ("Cain" // "Lamech")
Epith(PN): Num.23:18: blq // bn ṣpr ("Balak" // "Son of Sippor")

WP(PN): Ps.114:3: (h)ym // (h)yrdn ("Sea" // "Jordan")

D(PN): yhwh // yhwh (often)

Syn(PR): Dt.32:23: ^{c}lmw // bm ("to (upon) them" // "against them")

The other major class of modification for PN and PR involves sequence, in that the modification is present either in the A or B Line parallel units. (Note that sequence is also a factor in the simple rhetorical categories WP and PW, Concr.-Abstr., and Abstr.-Concr.). Rhetorical meaning is also involved, at least in the case of PN, as noted above. Sequence is indicated by a hyphen; it is to be understood that the first sign represents the A Line unit and the sign after the hyphen the B Line parallel. The following classes appear in the Corpus:

1. Rhetorical category-PN and the reverse:
   a. PN-Syn: II Sam.22:29: yhwh // 'lhy ("YHWH" // "my God")

      This class is merely the opposite of the simple rhetorical category PN.

   b. PN-PW: Ps.89:11: rhb // 'ybkh ("Rahab" // "your enemies")
   c. WP-PN: Ex.15:14: ^{c}mm // yšb plšt ("the peoples" // "the enthroned of Canaan")
   d. PN-WP: Gen.49:10a: myhd // mbn dglw ("from Judah" // "from his banners")
   e. Epith-PN: Ps.68:6: dyn 'lmnt // yhw ("the judge of widows" // "YHWH")
   f. PN-Epith: Gen.4:23a: ^{c}d wṣl // nš lmk ("Adah and Sillah" // "wives of Lamech")
   g. PN-Ant: Dt.32:12: yhwh // 'l nkr ("YHWH" // "strange god")
   h. Met.-PN: Ps.68:3b-c: 'š // yhwh ("fire" // "YHWH")

2. Rhetorical category-PR and the reverse:
   a. PR-Syn: Dt.32:34: ^{c}mdy // b'ṣrty ("with me" // "in my treasuries")

      This category is the reverse of the simple rhetorical class PR, above.

   b. PW-PR: II Sam.22:9b-c: mphw // mmnw ("from his mouth" // "from him")

c. PR-WP: Dt.32:20a: mhm // mh 'ḥrtm ("(from) them" // "their end")

One category requires special comment, because it seems to be composed of two rhetorical categories plus the modification for PN:

Epith-WP-PN: Ps.29:3: 'l (h)kbd // ql yhw ("the God of glory" // "the voice of YHWH")

However, the unit which contains these parallel terms exhibits difficulties of interpretation, especially as regards its arrangement (see the Corpus).

Finally, one category displays the characteristic of sequence, although the factors PN and PR are not involved:

Epith-Syn: Ex.15:17b-c: mkn lšbtk // mqdš ("the dais of your throne" or, "your dwelling place" // "the shrine")

This, of course, is the reverse of the simple category Epith, above.

Compound Categories

A very small group of parallel units displays a semantic relationship which must be considered truly compound from the point of view of rhetorical meaning. The units in question belong simultaneously to two rhetorical categories. This situation will be symbolized by the sign = placed between the rhetorical signs. In addition, one of the classes also involves the modification for PN described above:

1. Ant=WP: II Sam.22:28: ᶜm ᶜny // ᶜnm rmt ("poor people" // "haughty eyes")
2. Epith="D": Ex.15:2b: (z)'l // 'lh 'b ("(this is) my God" // "the God of my father")
3. WP="D": Jud.5:28b: rkb // pᶜm mrkbtw ("his chariotry" // "the hooves of his chariots")

This approach to the issue of the semantic relationship between parallel units certainly does not remove all problems. In particular, one may legitimately question the rhetorical category to which individual units are assigned in the Corpus. In many cases nuances are present which cannot be captured by the system of notation and the categories it represents.

However, the system outlined above is at least a beginning for the analysis of what seems to be a most significant aspect of semantic parallelism as a literary device, the rhetorical relationship between A and B Line parallel units. It should be clear from the multitude of categories that one cannot make do with only three or four types of semantic relationships between parallel terms. The system is, in fact, extremely varied and complex.

The rhetorical relationship of A and B Lines is the total of the relationships represented by the sub-line units. For example, a unit with the semantic values Syn; List; PW may be loosely described as displaying variational repetition, impressionistic parallelism, and generalization.

Semantic Grades

It will be useful to introduce into the system of analysis another type of semantic distinction: what may be termed "semantic grades." By this term is meant inherent degree of parallelism; for example, "house" is felt by most speakers of English to be closer to terms like "home," "residence," "domicile," and also "door," "wall," "roof," than terms which also belong to one of the possible semantic paradigms of the word, like "street," "insurance," "contract," "plumber." Of course, since no procedure exists for hierarchical classification within semantic paradigms, any dogmatism on such matters is misplaced: rather, the distinction described above is useful only from that most shifting of bases, common sense, to which may be added literary sense. An empirical basis for discrimination may be partially established for biblical Hebrew by recourse to the concordance or to related literatures; however, this is by no means a safe guide, in view of the limited extent of surviving ancient Hebrew literature and its distribution over a period of approximately a thousand years. Nevertheless, a distinction between closer and more distant synonyms may have functional value, and has been adopted in this study, which recognizes four "grades" of parallelism. These are labelled neutrally as simply A, B, C, and D. What seem to be close synonyms are assigned to grade A, more distant synonyms in the paradigm to grade B. However, grade B is employed also for another purpose: in some cases it indicates philological uncertainty regarding the relationship of parallel units which present difficulties, but which, however, do not seem to be so corrupt as to impede analysis.

In general, the assigning of a parallel relationship to grade B will serve as a convenient device for isolating what seem to be problems in regard to parallelism. It may be pointed out that the distinction between A and B might be put to a specific use in later studies; namely, to distinguish between parallel terms which are firmly attested as formulaic "word pairs" and those which are not.

In addition, this study recognizes two further semantic grades, which are labelled C and D (and "D"). Grade D indicates total repetition, i.e., identity; "D", substantial identity through the parallelism of terms formed from the same root. Grade C is employed for terms which are grammatically parallel and which occupy the same rank in the reconstructed sentence, but which display either no or very little degree of inherent semantic parallelism; that is, which do not seem to belong to the same semantic paradigm. This sign is employed for all metaphorical rhetorical relationships; for example, assigned to grade C is the parallelism of dng (wax) and rš^{c}m (the wicked) in Ps.68:3b-c. Also assigned to grade C are pronominal relationships; that is, cases in which parallelism is between a pronoun and its antecedent.

The function of the signs representing the semantic grades A, B, C, and D in the method is to replace the semantically neutral sign "x" in the unit formulae; that is, the grammatical and metrical relationship of a B Line to its A Line represented by, for example, x x x may be replaced by A A B, A C B, A B D, etc. In this way the unit formulae can bear basic semantic information as well as the grammatical and metrical data conveyed by the sign "x". Also, as noted above, uncertainties regarding synonymity can be marked by use of the sign B.

Method of Analysis

The examples of the Corpus are examined by means of a method which, for parallel units, contains eleven steps:

1. Text
2. Translation
3. Metrical units
4. Grammatical units
5. Syllabic symmetry
6. Grammatical structure
7. Transformation
8. Addition
9. Reconstructed sentence
10. Comparison
11. Result
    a. Formula
    b. Deletion-Compensation
    c. Semantic parallelism
    d. Transformation

Triplets are analyzed as a sequence of two couplets. A, B, and C Lines are treated as a unit for steps 1-6, separately for steps 7-11. Non-parallel units are analyzed only for steps 1-6 and 11, which contain the simple statement: non-parallel unit followed by, in parentheses, a characterization of the basic structure in abbreviation: (NS-NS), (VS-VS), etc.

The steps may be assigned to three groups: 1-6 are preparatory, stating the basic data which form the object of analysis; 7-10 comprise the analysis itself, the key step being No. 10, the comparison; No. 11 presents the results of analysis, and itself consists of four sections, as listed above. The following is an exposition of the method:

1. Text
2. Translation

The first two steps may be treated together: the presentation of the biblical text to be analyzed. This study is not intended to be a philological one. Its main textual interest is in finding examples of early poetry as free as possible from textual corruption. The text follows, in the main, the works of Albright, Cross and Freedman listed at the beginning of Part II. For a full philological discussion, one must refer to the work of these scholars. Each example has, however, been carefully examined textually from the point of view of its soundness for analysis. Clearly, a text which involves extensive philological discussion and emendation cannot be subjected to the system of analysis employed in this study. Only those emendations which seem to the writer to be virtually above suspicion by reason of convincing inner-biblical parallels, strong support from the ancient versions, or the compelling logic of the context have been accepted for analysis. This procedure, in dealing with the philological studies on which this work is based, does not reflect an ideological position, but a practical necessity. To make use only of completely sound texts, assuming there are such, would reduce the number of examples below the point where analysis of any kind would be useful. Therefore, a certain number of restored texts must be admitted to the Corpus. However, limits must be set if the study is to avoid the suspicion of attempting to isolate patterns in heavily emended texts, in whose restoration poetic form is often a significant factor. Even minor emendations have often not been included if they do not have any relevance for the system of analysis.

The text is presented in the orthography appropriate to its probable period of composition. It also appears in this spelling throughout the study. Of course, orthography is not a factor which is in any way essential for analysis. However, it is an important aspect of the method of philological study of ancient poetry initiated by Albright, is employed in the works on which this study is based, and has been continued here.[34]

---

34. In general, see Frank M. Cross and David N. Freedman, Early Hebrew Orthography. A Study of the Epigraphic Evidence. American Oriental Series, vol. 36 (New Haven: American Oriental Society, 1952). Poems not included, or only partially included in the base studies listed at the beginning of Part II follow either the older, purely consonantal, orthography or the later one employing final matres, depending on the assessment of their date. So, Gen.4 and Ps.29 have been assigned to the earlier spelling (that of, for example, Num.23 and 24, Ex.15, and Ps.68); Ps.77, 89, 114 and Dt.32, to the later orthography (that of, for example, II Sam.22). It must be stressed again that orthography itself is not significant for the method of analysis.

3. Metrical units
4. Grammatical units
5. Syllabic symmetry

These three steps present basic structural and metrical information about the unit. Grammatical and metrical units have been defined above. Steps 3 and 4 display the ratio of these units in A and B Lines; step 5 the presence or absence of syllabic symmetry. Lines are syllabically symmetrical when A and B Lines contain the same number of syllables, or when either line exceeds the other by one syllable. Four metrical unit lines may also contain a statement of the internal syllabic relationship between the short lines of which they are composed, as well as the external relationship between the A and B Lines of the couplet. Hence the references to "external" or "internal" symmetry or asymmetry in such cases.

Syllable counts are based on a system of syllabification which, in the main, follows the accepted rules for the Tiberian vocalization; so for example, the syncope required by the rule of _shwa_, and the treatment of so-called _shwa medium_ as non-vocalic; i.e., as the phonetic equivalent of _shwa quiescens_ (= zero). Since evidence is lacking for the specific date when these syncopes took place, as well as the related phenomenon of spirantization,[35] it seems preferable to apply them even to the early materials of the _Corpus_. On the other hand, adjustments are made in the Masoretic vocalization for developments which seem clearly to be late. Specifically, all anaptyctic vowels in segholates and elsewhere, _patah furtivum_, and _hateph_ vowels which replace _shwa quiescens_, are eliminated. In fact, it is unlikely that a single system of vocalization would suffice even for the relatively limited time range covered by the _Corpus_. It is not impossible that earlier examples like Jud.5, Ex.15, and Ps.29 preserved case endings, perhaps in the form of a neutral vowel. Certainly the process of differentiation between Canaanite and Hebrew was still taking place during the time span represented by the examples in the _Corpus_, and poetry, of course, tends to be more

---

35. See, especially, Zellig Harris, _The Development of the Canaanite Dialects_, American Oriental Series, vol. 16 (Microfilm-reprint, Ann Arbor, 1965).

conservative than prose in preserving earlier stages of a language. The system of syllabification outlined above is not free from arbitrariness, but should not affect the viability of the general results as regards syllabic symmetry since the system allows for a margin of one syllable before declaring a unit asymmetrical.

Special comment is required on the treatment of the definite article and conjunctive waw. The definite article seems to have no place in early poetry; its presence must be ascribed to scribal activity. In this study it is consistently parenthesized and never included in the syllable counts. As demonstrated by Cross and Freedman, the placement of waw at the beginning of sentences in poetry is often due to scribal practice.[36] Uncertainty as to the originality of initial waw has led to the adoption of the following practice for this work:

1. waw is omitted at the beginning of all A Lines.
2. waw at the beginning of the B Line and, internally, at the beginning of a short line is parenthesized and not included in the syllable counts. Other conjunctive particles ('ap, gam, etc.) are not eliminated.

Again, this somewhat arbitrary procedure should not affect the general results in any significant way. For example, as regards waw, it can be demonstrated that consistently retaining waw sometimes increases syllable asymmetry and sometimes removes it, with little result on the overall statistics.

---

36. On initial waw, see especially, Cross and Freedman, Studies in Ancient Yahwistic Poetry, pp. 54ff. Note that, for the reasons stated there, the nota accusativi 'et and the prose relative pronoun 'ăšer have also been eliminated. One may retain the definite article, as Cross and Freedman suggest, where it preserves its supposedly older demonstrative use (so, for example, in Dt.32:1: (h)šmym, (h)'rṣ (vocatives)), but the date of the introduction of the definite article as well as its origin are in doubt; hence the treatment in this study (see Thomas O. Lambdin, "The Junctural Origin of the West Semitic Definite Article," Near Eastern Studies in Honor of William Foxwell Albright, pp. 315-333).

6. Grammatical structure

The grammatical structure of the couplet or triplet is recorded in the form of a system of grammatical notation whose sole function is to facilitate analysis in the following steps by supplying an economical means of representing major aspects of morphology and syntax. The system consists of a series of signs (letters and numerals), symbols (punctuation marks and diacritical marks), and abbreviations. The full list will be found at the beginning of Part II before the *Corpus* of examples.

7. Transformation

With this step the process of analysis begins. B Lines which contain semantically parallel units but in grammatically incompatible positions, must be transformed to a structure which will allow the formation of a reconstructed sentence.

8. Addition

This step also is preparatory to the formation of the reconstructed sentence. Since A and B Lines theoretically form a single statement, each metrical unit present in the A Line but absent from the B Line must be "added" to the latter. This procedure is represented in the form of the grammatical notation system. There may, of course, be more than one addition or none at all.

9. Reconstructed sentence

The reconstructed sentence is presented in a columnar format which should make the procedure employed in the following stage, the comparison, clearer and easier to analyze.

10. Comparison

This is the critical step, the exact comparison of semantically and grammatically parallel metrical units. The procedure consists of the following stages:

a. First, metrical units which have been added to the B Line in step 8, if any, are treated as if they were present in that line. Since the comparison in this case is of metrical units which are, in fact, hypothetical, it is parenthesized. The result is, in every case, repetition and so is indicated by the semantic sign for repetition, D: (x : x :: D). The sign D is doubly appropriate, since one is dealing with units which have been deleted from the A Line in the formation of the B Line.

b. The next step consists of the comparison of metrical units in the same position in the reconstructed sentence. The result is a formula sign which contains grammatical, metrical, and semantic information. The relationship between parallel metrical units may be indicated by the neutral formula sign "x", which represents the parallelism of one metrical unit in the B Line to one metrical unit in the A Line. Basic grammatical data is expressed by the sign in that it attests to grammatical congruence or compatibility between the units, that is, general grammatical parallelism.[37] However, additional grammatical semantic and metrical information is also conveyed by the formula sign. This must be outlined in some detail.

<u>Grammatical Information</u>. The formula signs distinguish between simple and compound relationships. The latter category is subdivided along the lines described above in the section dealing with the reconstructed sentence; i.e., grammatical, semantic and indivisible compounds. Compounds are represented in the notation system by the symbol / (virgule). It is employed for grammatical and indivisible compounds. In the case of the latter, the virgule is placed through the formula sign: x̸. For semantic compounds, the virgule is hyphenated: ⌿. The following is a partial list of compound relationships, which will illustrate the use of these symbols. A full inventory will be found in the section on sub-line units in Part III.

a. /x : simple // compound;

ex.: rkb // p^{c}m mrkbtw (Jud.5:28b)

b. x/ : compound // simple;

ex.: mkn lšbtk // mqdš (Ex.15:17b-c)

c. */x̸: simple // double compound;

ex.: bg^{c}rtkh // mnšmt rḥ 'pkh (II Sam.22:16b)

---

37. Much of this information is also conveyed by the standard A B C A' B' C' notation system, but in a less systematic way. Note, however, that the unit formulae cannot indicate sequence, a significant, if secondary, poetic device, which plays a key role in any detailed literary analysis. Especially important are the differences in word order between prose and poetic language.

d. /x̸̲ : simple // triple compound;

ex.: yqdmny // yhy yhwh mš^{c}n ly (II Sam.22:19)

e. x/x : compound // compound (grammatical);

ex.: 'lp 'dm // 'l m'b (Ex.15:15a-b)

f. x≠x : compound // compound (semantic);

ex.: ṣpn wymn // tbr wḥrmn (Ps.89:13)

g. x̸ : compound // compound (indivisible);

ex.: 'rṣ wyblh // msdy hrm (Dt.32:22b)

h. x/x/x : double compound // double compound (grammatical).

ex.: mmgd hrr qdm // mmgd gb^{c}t ^{c}lm (Dt.33:15)

i. x≠x≠x : double compound // double compound (semantic);

ex.: ḥlb zbḥmw y'klw // yštw yn nskmw (Dt.32:38a)

j. x/x̸ : compound // double compound (grammatical)

ex.: l'r ḥṣk // lngh brq ḥntk (Hab.3:11b)

k. x≠x̸ : compound // double compound (semantic);

ex.: šn bhmt // ^{c}m ḥmt zḥly ^{c}pr (Dt.32:24b)

Other types of compounds occur in the Corpus. In some cases the symbolization is, admittedly, arbitrary. It must be stressed that the only common relationships are simple // compound and the reverse, compound // compound, and compound // double compound. The others are infrequent and, in some cases, unique.

Metrical Information. The formula signs are also capable of displaying the relationship between grammatical and metrical units through the employment of two symbols: * (asterisk) and _ (underline). The former symbol indicates that the number of metrical units in parallel terms exceeds the number of grammatical units by one; the latter symbol indicates the reverse. In addition, position can be represented by the placement of the symbols, in the case of * to the right or left of the formula sign, in the case of _, under the relevant sign. The following list will illustrate the use of these symbols. In each case, the formula sign will be followed by a representation in chart form of the relationship between grammatical units (GU) and metrical units (MU), and an example drawn from the Corpus.

a. Examples of * :

		A Line	B Line	
1. x*	<u>GU</u>	1	1	Ex.: 'hlk // mškntk (Num.24:5)
	<u>MU</u>	1	2	
2. *x	<u>GU</u>	1	1	Ex.: w'rmmnhw // w'nwhw (Ex.15:2b)
	<u>MU</u>	2	1	
3. *x*	<u>GU</u>	1	1	Ex.: mbrkk // 'rrk (Num.24:9)
	<u>MU</u>	2	2	
4. x/*	<u>GU</u>	2	1	Ex.: lḥp ymm // ^{c}l mprṣw (Jud.5:17c-d)
	<u>MU</u>	2	2	
5. */x	<u>GU</u>	1	2	Ex.: ^{c}l krbm // ^{c}l knpy rh (II Sam.22:11)
	<u>MU</u>	2	2	
6. */x̸	<u>GU</u>	1	3	Ex.: bg^{c}rtkh // mnšmt rḥ 'pkh (II Sam.22:16b)
	<u>MU</u>	2	3	

b. Examples of _ :

		A Line	B Line	
1. /x̲	<u>GU</u>	1	2	Ex.: blq // bn ṣpr (Num.23:18)
	<u>MU</u>	1	1	
2. x̲/	<u>GU</u>	2	1	Ex.: 'r ly // z^{c}m (Num.23:7b)
	<u>MU</u>	1	1	
3. x̲/̲x̲	<u>GU</u>	2	2	Ex.: m mn // m spr (Num.23:10a)
	<u>MU</u>	1	1	
4. x/x̸̲	<u>GU</u>	2	3	Ex.: ymt ^{c}lm // šnt dr wdr (Dt.32:7a)
	<u>MU</u>	2	2	
5. x̲/̵x	<u>GU</u>	2	2	Ex.: ^{c}m ^{c}ny // ^{c}nm rmt (II Sam.22:28)
	<u>MU</u>	1	2	
6. /x̲/	<u>GU</u>	3	3	Ex.: 'bd ^{c}ṣt hmh // 'n bhm tbnh (Dt.32:28)
	<u>MU</u>	2	3	
7. /x̸̲	<u>GU</u>	1	3	Ex.: t^{c}nn // tšb 'mrh lh (Jud.5:29)
	<u>MU</u>	1	2	
8. /x̸̲	<u>GU</u>	1	4	Ex.: yqdmny // yhy yhwh mš^{c}n ly (II Sam.22:19)
	<u>MU</u>	1	3	

Of these signs, only x* is common in the <u>Corpus</u>; many are unique examples posing special problems. Note that *x* represents an unusual situation, the symbol * being used to indicate a metrical augment in both A and B Lines.

By means of these signs one can display the various relationships between grammatical and metrical units, although the system is by no means free of difficulties. In addition, one possesses a practical means of contrasting the syllabic and accentual (represented by the metrical units) interpretations of Hebrew verse. In general, a high frequency of signs containing * or _ indicates a considerable degree of incongruity between grammatical and metrical units (= "beats" or "stresses") which may point to a weakness in the accentual interpretation; on this, see Appendix A.

In the formula signs the neutral sign "x" is replaced by the signs for the semantic grades A, B, C, and D. Semantic information is thus superimposed on the metrical and grammatical data. For example, the sign x/x̸ may appear as A/A̸, B/A̸, D/A̸, etc. In fact, the use of the sign C is much restricted and B is employed only relatively infrequently. Since D indicates repetition, it is, by its nature, excluded from the sign x̸ or its variations.

The type of semantic relationship termed "rhetorical" does not form part of the formula, but follows it in parentheses. It is indicated by its abbreviation (Syn, Epith, etc.) in most cases. To incorporate the rhetorical meaning into the formula sign would perhaps make it bear more information than it conveniently can.

c. The final stage in the comparison is the listing of any metrical unit in the reconstructed sentence present in the B Line but absent from the A Line. Since, in fact, this addition generally represents compensation for a unit deleted from the A Line, it seems useful to state simply + compensation when the latter does not consist of an independent grammatical unit, but rather of additional syllables added by means of the parallelism of a shorter term in the A Line with a longer one in the B Line or of a simple term with a compound. The various types of compensation are listed in Part III.

11. Result

This is a summary of steps 7-10 and consists of four parts:

a. The "unit formula": The unit formula is simply the sum of the parallel relationships of the reconstructed sentence, as represented by the formula signs of step 10. It is, therefore, a symbolic presentation of the relationship of the B Line of the parallel or repetition couplet to its A Line. Deletions from the A Line, listed in the first stage of the comparison, are added to the formula signs. The formula signs are listed in the order they occur in step 10, except that simple signs generally precede compound ones. So, for example, the formula x x x (which may be realized semantically according to any of the four semantic "grades": A A A, D A A, A A B, etc.) represents the parallelism of three simple metrical units in the B Line to three in the A Line; the unit formula x /x (D), the parallelism of a simple metrical unit in the B Line to one such unit in the B Line, the parallelism also of a simple unit in the A Line to a compound in the B Line, and the deletion of one metrical unit from the A Line. Note that compensation is not indicated in the unit formulae, since they represent only a statement of the B Line in terms of its A Line. A full list of the unit formulae forms the first section of Part III.

b. Deletion-Compensation: This is a statement of the B Line in relation to the A Line in terms of step 8 and the last stage of step 10; that is, units hypothetically added to the B Line in the reconstructed sentence (and which, therefore, represent deletions from the A Line), and units added to the B Line by way of compensation, respectively. Many examples, of course, display neither deletion nor compensation.

c. Semantic parallelism: At this point all the rhetorical semantic relationships in step 10 are listed.

d. Transformation: If the unit required one or more transformations in step 7, they are here listed in reverse and thereby represent a hypothetical generation of the B Line by its A Line. The theoretical grammatical form of the B Line which was employed for the purpose of comparison is thereby restored to its actual form.

PART II

The Corpus of Examples

The materials which form the basis of analysis consist of units of verse, couplets and triplets, drawn from early Hebrew poetry. As noted in Part I, the text for most of these examples is directly based on the method pioneered by Albright's model study of the Oracles of Balaam and, especially, *Studies in Ancient Yahwistic Poetry* by Frank M. Cross and David N. Freedman. These studies and later works by these scholars have placed the study of old Hebrew verse on a footing sufficiently firm to enable the gathering of a body of poetic materials which can serve as the object of analysis for a work of this kind. The basic principles regarding the treatment of text were discussed in the exposition of the method. The following is a list of the examples to be analyzed in the *Corpus*:

1. The Song of Lamech (Gen.4:23-24)
2. The Blessing of Jacob (Gen.49)
3. The Song of the Sea (Ex.15)
4. The Song of the Ark (Num.10:35)
5. The Oracles of Balaam (Num.23-24)
6. The Song of Moses (Dt.32)
7. The Blessing of Moses (Dt.33)
8. The Song of Deborah (Jud.5)
9. David's Lament (II Sam.1)
10. II Sam.22 = Ps.18
11. The Psalm of Habakkuk (Hab.3)
12. Ps.24
13. Ps.29
14. Ps.68
15. Ps.77 (only v.17)
16. Ps.89
17. Ps.114

Because of the strict criteria for selection applied, most of the poems are represented only partially. Textual interpretation for the bulk of them is based on the following studies (followed by the abbreviation employed in the Corpus to identify them):

1. Gen.49, Dt.33, Jud.5, II Sam.1: Cross and Freedman, Studies in Ancient Yahwistic Poetry (C-F)
2. Ex.15: Cross and Freedman, Studies in Ancient Yahwistic Poetry (C-F); Cross and Freedman, "The Song of Miriam" (SMir); Cross, "The Song of the Sea and Canaanite Myth"; and Cross, Canaanite Myth and Hebrew Epic, pp. 112-144 (CMHE)
3. Num.23-24: Albright, "The Oracles of Balaam" (OBal)
4. II Sam.22=Ps.18: Cross and Freedman, Studies in Ancient Yahwistic Poetry (C-F); Cross and Freedman, "A Royal Song of Thanksgiving"
5. Hab.3: Albright, "The Psalm of Habakkuk" (PHab)
6. Ps.68: Albright, "A Catalogue of Early Hebrew Lyric Poems" (Cat)

On many points of text and interpretation one must now consult Cross' Canaanite Myth and Hebrew Epic and Albright's Yahweh and the Gods of Canaan.

All of the poems represented in the Corpus must be taken as dating from the twelfth through the tenth centuries (or perhaps earlier in the case of Gen.4:23-24 and Ps.29) with the exception of Dt.32, an early example of the ribh, for which a ninth-century date seems preferable.[38]

The limited number of texts available for analysis, and their further reduction by the process of selection for the Corpus, means, of course, that only the most general results can be considered as having even relative validity. One must remember that Steinitz had several thousand lines of Finnish poetry composed by a single poet to work with; and that Parry points out that "the small quantity of Homer's work which we possess" prevents the establishment of a clear system for analyzing his poetry![39] This caveat will often be repeated in Part III.

---

38. So also Frank M. Cross, Canaanite Myth and Hebrew Epic (Cambridge, Mass.: Harvard University Press, 1973), p. 264, n. 193. The dating of the poems follows that of the base studies, which should be consulted for details.

39. The Making of Homeric Verse. The Collected Papers of Milman Parry (Oxford, Adam Parry, ed., 1971), p. 103.

Grammatical Notation

The following is a list of the signs, symbols, and abbreviations used for the representation of grammatical structure:

1	Subject of the verbal sentence
2	(Direct) object
3	Adverbial relationships (adverbs, prepositional phrases)
a	Transitive verb
b	Intransitive verb
c	Intransitive verb which has been produced by transformation to passive and reflexive conjugations
part.	Participle
S	Subject of the nominal sentence
P	Predicate of the nominal sentence
pr	Independent pronoun
-s	Pronominal possessive and object suffix
,-R	Relative phrase or clause
rel.pr.	Relative pronoun
inf.abs.	Infinitive absolute
inf.const.	Infinitive construct
-C	*Nomen rectum* of the construct relationship
pn	Proper noun
ptcl	Particle
neg	Negative particle
&	Coordinating conjunction
prep	Preposition
!	After vocatives, precatives, imperatives and emphatic particles
?	After interrogative particles and pronouns
,-	Before attributives
,=	Before elements in apposition
" "	To facilitate analysis, certain forms are enclosed by apostrophes; specifically, the infinitive absolute when its function is adverbial, the preposition of comparison *k^{ə}(mô)* and similar elements, cognate accusatives, and the verbal element or "existential" adverbs in "quasi-verbal" sentences. Its use in the *Corpus* is limited and will be apparent from the examples in which it is employed.

_ -s The initial element and resumptive pronominal suffix of the casus pendens structure are underlined.

In general, involved syntactic structures are simplified, when possible, in the comparison and following steps of the analysis.[40]

40. Number, gender, and tense are among those grammatical features not indicated by the notation system which might be included in more detailed analysis.

The Corpus of Examples

Gen.4

Text: v.23a — ^{c}d wṣl // šm^{c}n ql
nš lmk // h'zn 'mrt

Translation: Adah and Zillah, hear my voice;
Wives of Lamech, heed my word!

Met. units: 4:4(2:2::2:2)

Gram. units: 4:4(2:2::2:2)

Syll. symmetry: 5:5::3:6 (B line internally asymmetrical)

Gram. structure: lpn! &lpn! // a! 2-s
l-Cpn! // a! 2-s

Transformation: none

Addition: none

Reconstr. sent.: ^{c}d wṣl šm^{c}n ql
nš lmk h'zn 'mrt

Comparison: lpn! &lpn! :: l-Cpn! :: A̸ (PN-Epith)
a! : a! :: A (Syn)
2-s : 2-s :: A (Syn)

Result: Formula: A A A̸
Del.-Comp.: none
Semantic parallelism: PN-Epith; Syn
Transformation: none

Gen.4

Text: v.23b — k 'š hrgt lp$š^{c}$
(w)yld lḥbrt

Translation: I have killed a man for striking me.
A youth for wounding me.

Met. units: 3:3

Gram. units: 3:3

Syll. symmetry: 8:6 (asymmetrical)

Gram. structure: ptcl 2 a 3-s
,2 3-s

Transformation: none

Addition: + a

Reconstr. sent.: k / 'š hrgt lp$š^{c}$
yld lḥbrt

Comparison: (a : a :: D)
ptcl-2: 2 :: A (List)
3-s : 3-s :: A* (Syn)
+ compensation

Result: Formula: A A* (D)
Del.-Comp.: - a + compensation
Semantic parallelism: List; Syn
Transformation: none

<u>Gen.4</u>

Text: v.24 k šb^{c}tm yqm qn
(w) lmk šb^{c}m wšb^{c}

Translation: Cain was avenged sevenfold,
Lamech seventy and sevenfold!

Met. units: 3:3

Gram. units: 3:3

Syll. symmetry: 7:6 (symmetrical)

Gram. structure: ptcl 3 c lpn
,lpn 3 &3

Transformation: none

Addition: + c

Reconstr. sent.:
šb^{c}tm qn
k / yqm
šb^{c}m wšb^{c} lmk

Comparison: (c : c :: D)
ptcl-3 : 3 &3 :: /"D" ("D"=Num)
lpn : lpn :: A (List(PN))
+ compensation

Result: Formula: A /"D"(D)
Del.-Comp.: - a + compensation
Semantic parallelism: "D"=Num; List(PN)
Transformation: none

Gen.49

Text: v.5 — šm^{c}n wlw 'ḥm
kl ḥms mkrthm

Translation: Simeon and Levi are brothers;
Weapons of violence are their merchandise.

Comment: The translation of mkrthm is unclear; however, the unit is certainly non-parallel.

Met. units: 3:3

Gram. units: 3:3

Syll. symmetry: 7:9 (asymmetrical)

Gram. structure: Spn &Spn P
P-C S-s

Result: Non-parallel unit (NS-NS)

Gen.49

Text: v.6a — bsdm 'l tb' npš
bqhlm 'l tḥd kbd

Translation: Do not share their council, my soul;
Do not join their assembly, my heart (liver)!

Comment: Interpretation following C-F.
This seems to be the best way of solving the problem of the prefix of tḥd.

Met. units: 3:3

Gram. structure: 3-s neg b! l-s!
3-s neg b! l-s!

Transformation: none

Addition: none

Reconstr. sent.: bsdm 'l tb' npš
bqhlm 'l tḥd kbd

Comparison: 3-s : 3-s :: A (Syn)
neg-b! : neg-b! :: B (Syn)
l-s! : l-s! :: A (List)

Result: Formula: A A B
Del.-Comp.: none
Semantic parallelism: Syn; List
Transformation: none

Gen.49

Text: v.6b — k b'pm hrg 'š
brṣnm ᶜqr šr

Translation: In their anger they killed a man;
Willingly they hamstrung an ox.

Met. units: 3:3

Gram. units: 3:3

Syll. symmetry: 8:7 (symmetrical)

Gram. structure: ptcl 3-s a 2
3-s a 2

Transformation: none

Addition: none

Reconstr. sent.: k / b'pm hrg 'š
brṣnm ᶜqr šr

Comparison: ptcl-3-s : 3-s :: B (Syn)
a 2 : a 2 :: B≠B (List)

Comment: It is unlikely that a specific individual is in mind, which would require the rhetorical category Epith.
Possible also is Met (metaphor).

Result: Formula: B B≠B
Del.-Comp.: none
Semantic parallelism: Syn; List
Transformation: none

Gen.49

Text: v.7a — 'rr 'pm k ᶜz
(w)ᶜbrtm k qšt

Translation: Cursed is their wrath, which is (so) powerful,
Their anger, which is (so) harsh.

Met. units: 3:3

Gram. units: 3:2

Syll. symmetry: 6:7 (symmetrical)

Gram. structure: P(part.c) S-s ,-R(ptcl b)
,S-s ,-R(ptcl b)

Transformation: none

Addition:	+ P(part.c)
Reconstr. sent.:	'rr 'pm k ^{c}z (^{c}azzā(h))
	^{c}brtm k qšt (qš)
Comparison:	(P(part.c) : P(part.c) :: D)
	S-s : S-s :: A (Syn)
	,-R(ptcl-b) : ,-R(ptcl-b) :: A* (Syn)
	+ compensation
Result:	Formula: A A* (D)
	Del.-Comp.: - P(part.c) + compensation
	Semantic parallelism: Syn
	Transformation: none

<u>Gen.49</u>

Text: v.7b	'ḥlqm by^{c}qb
	(w)'pṣm byśr'l
Translation:	I shall divide them among Jacob;
	I shall scatter them among Israel.
Met. units:	3:3
Gram. units:	2:2
Syll. symmetry:	7:7 (symmetrical)
Gram. structure:	a-s 3pn
	a-s 3pn
Transformation:	none
Addition:	none
Reconstr. sent.:	'ḥlqm by^{c}qb
	'pṣm byśr'l
Comparison:	a-s : a-s :: *A (Syn)
	3pn : 3pn : A* (Syn(PN))
Result:	Formula: *A A*
	Del.-Comp.: none
	Semantic parallelism: Syn; Syn(PN)
	Transformation: none

Gen.49

Text: v.9a	gr 'ry yhd
	mṭrp bn ᶜlt
Translation:	Judah is a lion's whelp.
	You depart from the prey, my son!
Met. units:	3:3
Gram. units:	3:3
Syll. symmetry:	6:7 (symmetrical)
Gram. structure:	P-C Spn
	3 lpn! b
Result:	Non-parallel unit (NS-VS)

Gen.49

Text: v.9b	krᶜ rbṣ k'ry
	(w)klb' m yqmn
Comment:	Num.24:9 is similar to this unit. It will be analyzed here.
Translation:	He crouches, lies down like a lion,
	Like a lion which none would dare arouse.
Comment:	On lb' as "lion," cf. Speiser, Genesis, ad locem.
	The suffix of yqmn refers to lb'.
Met. units:	3:3
Gram. units:	3:3
Syll. symmetry:	7:8 (symmetrical)
Gram. structure:	b b "3"
	,"3" ,-R(lpr? a-s)
Comment:	The relative clause is a rhetorical question.
Transformation:	none
Addition:	+ b
	+ b
Reconstr. sent.:	krᶜ rbṣ k'ry / klb' m yqmn

Comparison: (b : b :: D)
(b : b :: D)
"3" : "3" :: A (Syn)
+ ,-R(lpr?
+ a-s)

Result: Formula: A (D D)
Del.-Comp.: - b + ,-R(lpr?
- b + a-s)
Semantic parallelism: Syn
Transformation: none

<u>Gen.49</u>

Text: v.10a l' ysr špṭ myhd
(w)mḥqq mbn dglw

Comment: Text and interpretation following C-F.

Translation: Judah will never lack a ruler,
Its standards, a leader.

Met. units: 3:3

Gram. units: 3:3

Syll. symmetry: 8:8 (symmetrical)

Gram. structure: neg b l 3pn
,l 3-C-s

Transformation: none

Addition: + neg-b

Reconstr. sent.: špṭ myhd
l' ysr
mḥqq mbn dglw

Comparison: (neg-b : neg-b :: D)
l : l :: A (Syn)
3pn : 3-C-s :: /A (PN-WP)
+ compensation

Result: Formula: A /A (D)
Del.-Comp.: - neg-b + compensation
Semantic parallelism: Syn; PN-WP
Transformation: none

Gen.49

Text: v.11a 'sr lgpn ^{c}r
(w)lśrq bn 'tn

Translation: He ties his ass to a vine,
His purebred, to a choice vine.

Comment: This translation follows the usual meaning of *gpn* and, by parallelism, an appropriate meaning for *śrq*. On *bn 'tn*, see Speiser, *Genesis*, *ad locem*. C-F's interpretation would produce no significant change in the analysis.

Met. units: 3:3

Gram. units: 3:3

Syll. symmetry: 7:9 (asymmetrical)

Gram. structure: a(inf.abs.) 3 2-s
,3 2-C-s

Comment: On *'sr* = *'āsôrî* (infinitive absolute + -î) see Moran, "The Hebrew Language in Its Northwest Semitic Background," p. 67.

Transformation: none

Addition: + a(inf.abs.)

Reconstr. sent.:
lgpn ^{c}r
'sr
lśrq bn 'tn

Comparison: (a(inf.abs.) : a(inf.abs.) :: D)
3 : 3 :: A (List)
2-s : 2-C-s :: /A (Epith)
+ compensation

Result: Formula: A /A (D)
Del.-Comp.: - a(inf.abs.) + compensation
Semantic parallelism: List; Epith
Transformation: none

Gen.49

Text: v.11b kbs byn lbš
(w)bdm ^{c}nbm swt

Translation: He washes his garment in wine,
In the blood of grapes, his mantle.

Met. units: 3:3

Gram. units: 3:3

Syll. symmetry: 7:7 (symmetrical)

Gram. structure: a 3 2-s
,3-C 2-s

Transformation: none

Addition: + a

Reconstr. sent.: kbs byn lbš / bdm ᶜnbm swt

Comparison: (a : a :: D)
3 : 3-C :: /A (Epith)
2-s : 2-s :: A (Syn)
+ compensation

Result: Formula: A /A (D)
Del.-Comp.: - a + compensation
Semantic parallelism: Epith; Syn
Transformation: none

<u>Gen.49</u>

Text: v.12a ḥkll ᶜnm myn
lbn šnm mḥlb

Translation: (His) darkness of eyes is more than (that of) wine;
(His) whiteness of teeth is more than (that of) milk.

Comment: That is, "His eyes are darker than wine; his teeth are whiter than milk." Alternatively, one may take both lines as exclamations. In any case, no change will be produced in the final formula.

Met. units: 3:3

Gram. units: 3:3

Syll. symmetry: 7:7 (symmetrical)

Gram. structure: S-C P(3)
S-C P(3)

Transformation: none

Addition: none

Reconstr. sent.: ḥkll ᶜnm myn
lbn šnm mḥlb

Comparison: S-C P(3) : S-C P(3) :: A/A≠A (Ant/List)

Result: Formula: A/A≠A
Del.-Comp.: none
Semantic parallelism: Ant; List
Transformation: none

Gen.49

Text: v.14 yśśkr ḥmr grm
rbṣ bn mšptm

Translation: Issachar is a castrated (?) ass,
Crouching between the saddlebags.

Comment: The translation of mšptm following Speiser, Genesis, ad locem. The uncertainties of translation will not affect analysis in this non-parallel unit.

Met. units: 3:3

Gram. units: 3:2

Syll. symmetry: 6:6 (symmetrical)

Gram. structure: Spn P ,-P
,P(part.b) 3

Result: Non-parallel unit (NS-NS)

Gen.49

Text: v.15a yr' mnḥ k ṭb
(w)'rṣ k nᶜm

Comment: Accepting C-F's emendations yir'ê(h), mᵊnūḥô and 'arṣô; the insertion of ybṭ in the B Line, while attractive, is not necessary from the point of view of the system of analysis employed in this study.

Translation: When he saw that his resting place was (so) good,
His land was (so) pleasant,

Met. units: 3:3

Gram. units: 3:2

Syll. symmetry: 7:6 (symmetrical)

Gram. structure: a 2-s ,=2(ptcl b)
,2-s ,=2(ptcl b)

Transformation: none

Addition: + a

Reconstru. sent.:
'rṣ k ṭb
yr'
mnḥ k n^cm

Comparison: (a : a :: D)
2-s : 2-s :: A (Syn)
,=2(ptcl-b) : ,=2(ptcl-b) :: A* (Syn)
+ compensation

Result: Formula: A A* (D)
Del.-Comp.: - a + compensation
Semantic parallelism: Syn
Transformation: none

Gen.49

Text: v.15b
yṭ škm lsbl
(w)yh lms ^cbd

Translation: He bent his shoulder to carry;
He became a corvée worker.

Met. units: 3:3

Gram. units: 3:3

Syll. symmetry: 6:6 (symmetrical)

Gram. structure: a 2-s 3(inf.const.a)
"b" P(3) ,-P((3) part.a)

Transformation: none

Addition: + a
+2-s

Reconstr. sent.:
lsbl
yṭ škm
yh lms ^cbd

Comment: Note that the infinitive in the A Line is the functional equivalent of the "quasi-verbal" sentence in the B Line.

Comparison: (a : a :: D)
(2-s : 2-s :: D)
3(inf.const.a) :: "b" P(3) ,-P((3) part.a) :: /X̸ (WP)
+ compensation

Result: Formula: /X̸ (D D)
Del.-Comp.: - a + compensation
- 2-s
Semantic parallelism: Syn; WP
Transformation: none

Gen.49

Text: v.16 dn ydn ᶜm
k'ḥd šbṭ yśr'l

Comment: C-F's insertion of dn before ᶜm (dîn ᶜammô) is most attractive. However, it eases but does not remove the syllable asymmetry.

Translation: Dan judges his people,
Together, the tribes of Israel.

Comment: Speiser's translation of k'ḥd ("like(any other)"), following Ehrlich, obstructs the analysis of this unit. Clearly ᶜm and šbṭ yśr'l are semantically parallel terms and should be grammatically parallel as well.

Met. units: 3:3

Gram. units: 3:3

Syll. symmetry: 5:8 (asymmetrical)

Gram. structure: lpn a 2-s
,3 2-Cpn

Transformation: none

Addition: + lpn
+ a

Reconstr. sent.:

		ᶜm	
dn	ydn		k'ḥd
		šbṭ yśr'l	

Comparison: (lpn : lpn :: D)
(a : a :: D)
2-s : 2-Cpn :: /A (PN)
+ 3
+ compensation

Result: Formula: /A (D D)
Del.-Comp.: - lpn + 3
- a + compensation
Semantic parallelism: PN
Transformation: none

<u>Gen.49</u>

Text: v.17a dn nḥš ^{c}l drk
šppn ^{c}l 'rḥ

Comment: Omitting MT's <u>yhy</u>; see C-F.

Translation: Dan is a snake on the road,
A horned snake on the path,

Met. units: 3:3

Gram. units: 3:2

Syll. symmetry: 6:6 (symmetrical)

Gram. structure: Spn P 3
,P 3

Transformation: none

Addition: + Spn

Reconstr. sent.: dn nḥš ^{c}l drk
dn šppn ^{c}l 'rḥ

Comparison: (Spn : Spn :: D)
P : P :: A* (WP)
3 : 3 :: A (Syn)
+ compensation

Result: Formula: A A* (D)
Del.-Comp.: - Spn + compensation
Semantic parallelism: WP; Syn
Transformation: none

Gen.49

Text: v.17b (h)nšk ᶜqb ss
(w)ypl rkb 'ḥr

Translation: Who bites the heels of the horse
So that its rider falls backward.

Met. units: 3:3

Gram. units: 3:3

Syll. symmetry: 6:7 (symmetrical)

Gram. structure: P(part.a) 2-C
b 1-s 3

Result: Non-parallel unit (NS-VS)

Gen.49

Text: v.19 gd gdd ygdn
(w)h' ygd ᶜqbm

Comment: Attaching mem to MT's ᶜqb (dittography); see C-f.

Translation: Gad is a band which raids;
He raids from the rear.

Comment: Translation and interpretation following C-F. The Peshitta's interpretation of the A Line seems to be similar: gd bgys' ypwq; so also the Targum's paraphrase; cf. Rashi, ad locem, who, following Onkelos, interprets ygdnw as "raids from him." The suffix of ygdn is "emphatic."

Met. units: 3:3

Gram. units: 3:3

Syll. symmetry: 6:6 (symmetrical)

Gram. structure: Spn P ,-R(a)
lpr a 3

Transformation: lpr a 3 --→ Spr P(part.a) 3

Comment: The transformation produces a participle, gād (root: gwd).

Addition: + ,-R(a)

Reconstr. sent.: gd {gdd / gd} ygdn ᶜqbm

Comment:	The sentence gd gd ygdn ^{c}qbm, "Gad is a raider who raids from the rear" is clumsy; however, the sentence is, of course, hypothetical.
Comparison:	(,-R(a) : ,-R(a) :: D)
	Spn : Spr :: C (PR)
	P : P(part.a) :: "D"
	+ 3
Result:	Formula: C "D" (D)
	Del.-Comp.: - ,-R(a) + 3
	Semantic parallelism: PR; "D"
	Transformation: Spr P(part.a) 3--→ lpr a 3

Gen.49

Text: v.20	'šr šmn lḥm
	(w)ytn m^{c}dn mlk
Comment:	Of the A Line variants suggested by C-F (šāmēn laḥmô and šəmēnā(h) 'arṣô), the variant closer to MT has been chosen. In the B Line MT's hw' has been omitted. In this non-parallel unit, these changes have little significance for the method of analysis.
Translation:	Asher's food is rich;
	He provides kingly delicacies.
Met. units:	3:3
Gram. units:	3:3
Syll. symmetry:	6:6 (symmetrical)
Gram. structure:	-Cpn P(part.b) S-s
	a 2-C
Result:	Non-parallel unit (NS-VS)

Gen.49

Text: v.25a	m'l 'bk wy^{c}zrk
	(w)'l šdy wybrkk
Comment:	Emending MT's 't to 'l (C-F).

Translation: From the God of your father who helps you,
El Shadday, who blesses you.

Met. units: 3:3

Gram. units: 3:3

Syll. symmetry: 10:9 (symmetrical)

Gram. structure: 3-C-s ,-R(&a-s)
,3pn ,=3pn ,-R(&a-s)

Comment: Perhaps 'l in the A Line should be treated as a PN also.

Transformation: none

Addition: none

Reconstr. sent.:
m / 'l 'bk wy^{c}zrk .
m \ 'l šdy wybrkk

Comparison: 3-C-s : 3pn ,=3pn :: D≠A (Epith-PN)
,-R(&a-s) : ,-R(&a-s) :: A (Syn)

Result: Formula: A D≠A
Del.-Comp.: none
Semantic parallelism: Epith-PN; Syn
Transformation: none

Comment: This unit narrowly misses being refractory on several counts. Metrically, it is a good argument for an exclusively syllabic analysis of early Hebrew verse, since it is bizarre to award m'l 'bk and 'l šdy (5 and 3 syllables, respectively) two metrical units and wy^{c}zrk and wybrkk (5 and 6 syllables) only one.

Gen.49

Text: v.27 bnymn z'b yṭrp
bbqr y'kl ^{c}ḋ
(w)l^{c}rb yḥlq šll

Translation: Benjamin is a wolf which preys,
In the morning devours booty,
In the evening divides the spoil.

Met. units: 3:3:3

Gram. units: 3:3:3

Syll. symmetry: 6:5:7 (B and C Lines asymmetrical)

Gram. structure: Spn P ,-R(a)
,-R(3 a 2)
,-R(3 a 2)

<u>A-B</u> <u>Lines</u>

Transformation: none

Addition: + Spn
+ P

Reconstr. sent.: bnymn z'b ytṛp / y'kl ^{c}d bbqr

Comment: It seems likely that <u>y'kl ^{c}d</u> is to be treated as an indivisible unit. Possibly, however, <u>^{c}d</u> is to be considered a separate unit which could also be the object of <u>yṭrp</u>.

Comparison: (Spn : Spn :: D)
(P : P :: D)
,-R(a) : ,-R(...a 2) :: /A (List)
+ 3
+ compensation

Result: Formula: /A (D D)
Del.-Comp.: - Spn + 3
- P + compensation
Semantic parallelism: List
Transformation: none

<u>B-C</u> <u>Lines</u>

Transformation: none

Addition: none

Reconstr. sent.: bbqr y'kl ^{c}d
l^{c}rb yḥlq šll

Comparison: 3 : 3 :: A (Mer)
a : a :: B (Syn)
2 : 2 :: A (Syn)

Result: Formula: A B A
Del.-Comp.: none
Semantic parallelism: Mer; Syn
Transformation: none

<u>Ex.15</u>

Text: v.1b   šr lyhw // k g' g'
ss wrkb / rm bym

Translation: Sing to YHWH, for he is truly exalted;
Horse and chariotry he has thrown into the sea!

Met. units: 4:4(2:2::2:2)

Gram. units: 4:4(2:2::2:2)

Syll. symmetry: 5:5::3:4 (external asymmetry; internally symmetrical)

Gram. structure: a! 3pn // ptcl "3"(inf.abs.b) b
2 &2 / a 3

Result: Non-parallel unit (VS-VS)

<u>Ex.15</u>

Text: v.2a ^{c}z wzmrt yhw
(w)yh ly lyš^{c}

Comment: This unit is probably an interpolation; however, this fact need not affect its antiquity; see C-F.

Translation: YHWH is my strength and my protection;
He has become my help.

Met. units: 3:3

Gram. units: 3:3

Syll. symmetry: 8:6 (asymmetrical)

Gram. structure: P-s &P-s Spn
"b" 3-s P(3)

Transformation: none

Addition: + Spn

Reconstr. sent.: ^{c}z wzmrt
yhw
yh ly lyš^{c}

Comparison: (Spn : Spn :: D)
P-s &P-s : "b" 3-s P(3) :: /A/ (List)
+ compensation

Result: Formula: /A/ (D)
Del.-Comp.: - Spn + compensation
Semantic parallelism: List
Transformation: none

Ex.15

Text: v.2b
z 'l w'rmmnh
'lh 'by w'nwh

Comment: Text rearrangement following C-F, *metri causa*.

Translation:
This is my God whom I exalt,
The God of my father whom I admire.

Met. units: 3:3

Gram. units: 2:3

Syll. symmetry: 9:9 (symmetrical)

Gram. structure:
Ppr S-s ,-R(&a-s)
,S-C-s ,-R(&a-s)

Transformation: none

Addition: none

Reconstr. sent.:
z / 'l w'rmmnh
'lh 'by w'nwh

Comparisons:
Ppr-S-s : S-C-s :: /A (Epith-"D")
,-R(&a-s) : ,-R(&a-s) :: *A (Syn)

Result: Formula: *A /A
Del.-Comp.: none
Semantic parallelism: Epith-"D"; Syn
Transformation: none

Ex.15

Text: vv.3-4
yhw gbr // yhw šm
mrkbt pr^{c} / yr bym
(w)mbḥr šlšw / ṭb^{c} bym sp

Comment: One of the variants suggested by C-F for the A Line and B Line of this unit has been selected. The others (*'š mlḥm* and *pr^{c} wḥl*, respectively) would produce only minor changes in the final results.

Translation: YHWH is a warrior; YHWH is his name;
He cast the chariots of Pharaoh into the sea;
His best troops drowned in the Reed Sea.

Met. units: 4:4:4(2:2::2:2::2:2)

Gram. units: 4:4:5(2:2::2:2::2:3)

Syll. symmetry: 4:4::5:4::5:6 (B and C Lines externally asymmetrical)

Gram. structure: Spn P // Spn P-s
2-Cpn / a 3
1-C-s / a 3-Cpn

<u>A-B</u> <u>Lines</u>

Result: Non-parallel unit (NS-VS)

<u>B-C</u> <u>Lines</u>

Transformation: 1-C-s c 3-Cpn ---→ 2-C-s a 3-Cpn

Comment: The transformation produces a transitive verb: <u>ṭibba^{c}</u>. As noted by C-F, this seems to be the reading of the Peshitta and some witnesses of the LXX.

Addition: none

Reconstr. sent.: mrkbt pr^{c} yr
bym sp
mbḥr šlšw ṭb^{c}

Comparison: 2-Cpn : 2-C-s :: A̸ (List)
a : a :: B (Syn)
3 : 3- :: D
\+ -Cpn

Comment: Note the compensation (<u>sp</u>) without deletion. On the parallelism of <u>yr</u> and <u>ṭb^{c}</u>, see also Job 38:6.

Result: Formula: B D A̸
Del.-Comp.: - Ø + -Cpn
Semantic parallelism: List; Syn D
Transformation: 2-C-s a 3-Cpn ---→ 1-C-s c 3-Cpn

Ex.15

Text: v.5 thmt yksym
yrd bmṣlt km 'bn

Translation: The deeps covered them;
They went down into the depths like stone.

Met. units: 3:3

Gram. units: 2:3

Syll. symmetry: 7:9 (asymmetrical)

Gram. structure: 1 a-s
b 3 "3"

Transformation: b 3 "3" --→ a-s 1 "3"

Comment: The hypothetical form resulting from the transformation would be *tôradnēm(ô)* *(hiphil)*.

Addition: none

Reconstr. sent.: thmt yksym (tksnm)
km 'bn
mṣlt trdnm (yrdm)

Comment: A theoretical masculine plural has been supplied in the reconstructed sentence (*yrdm* = *yôrîdûm*), despite the fact that *thmt* can be feminine.

Comparison: 1 : 1 :: A (Syn)
a-s : a-s :: *B (Syn)
\+ "3"

Result: Formula: A *B
Del.-Comp.: - Ø + "3"
Semantic parallelism: Syn
Transformation: a-s 1 "3" --→ b 3 "3"

Comment: Note the compensation without deletion.

Ex.15

Text: v.6 ymnk yhw // n'dr bkḥ
ymnk yhw // tr^{c}ṣ 'yb

Translation: Your right hand, O YHWH, is fearful in strength;
Your right hand, O YHWH, smashes the enemy!

Comment: This translation follows the VSS and the interpretation of <u>n'dr</u> as infinitive absolute; cf. <u>Smir</u>, p. 245 and Moran, "The Hebrew Language in Its Northwest Semitic Background," p. 67.

Met. units: 4:4(2:2::2:2)

Gram. units: 4:4(2:2::2:2)

Syll. symmetry: 6:5::6:4 (B Line internally asymmetrical)

Gram. structure: l-s lpn! // b(inf.abs.) 3
l-s lpn! // a 2

Transformation: none

Addition: + b(inf.abs.)
+ 3

Reconstr. sent.: ymnk yhw n'dr bkḥ trᶜṣ 'yb

Comparison: (b(inf.abs.) : b(inf.abs.) :: D)
(3 : 3 :: D)
l-s : l-s :: D
lpn! : lpn! :: D(PN)
+ a
+ 2

Result: Formula: D D (D D)
Del.-Comp.: -b(inf.abs.) + a
-3 + 2
Semantic parallelism: D; D(PN)
Transformation: none

<u>Ex.15</u>

Text: v.7 brb g'nk / thrs qmk
tšlḥ ḥrnk // y'klm kqš

Comment: Omitting <u>waw</u> from the beginning of the A Line.

Translation: By your great majesty you destroyed your adversaries;
You sent forth your wrath, which consumed them like chaff.

Met. units: 4:4(2:2::2:2)

Gram. units: 4:4(2:2::2:2)

Syll. symmetry: 6:5::7:6 (internal symmetry; external asymmetry)

Gram. structure: 3-C-s / a 2-s
a 2-s // ,-R(a-s "3")
Result: Non-parallel unit (VS-VS)

Ex.15

Text: v.8
brḥ 'pk / n^{c}rm mm
nṣb km nd nzlm
qp' thmt blb ym

Comment: Omitting *waw* at the beginning of the A Line.

Translation: By the blast of your nostrils the waters piled up;
The floods stood like a heap;
The deeps churned in the midst of the sea.

Comment: On the translation of *qp'*, see C-F. The first line has been attached to this unit, to which it belongs semantically.

Met. units: 4(2:2):3:3
Gram. units: 4(2:2):3:4
Syll. symmetry: 5:4::9:9 (symmetrical)
Gram. structure: 3-C-s / c l
c "3" l
b l 3-C

A-B Lines

Transformation: none
Addition: + 3-
+ -C-s
Reconstr. sent.:
n^{c}rm mm
brḥ 'pk km nd
nṣb nzlm
Comparison: (3-C-s : 3-C-s :: D/D)
c : c :: A (Syn)
l : l :: A (Syn)
+ "3"
+ compensation

Result:	Formula: A A (D/D)
	Del.-Comp.: - 3 + "3"
	- -C-s + compensation
	Semantic parallelism: Syn
	Transformation: none

<u>B-C Lines</u>

Transformation:	none
Addition:	+ "3"
Reconstr. sent.:	nṣb / qp' km nd nzlm / thmt blb ym
Comparison:	("3" : "3" :: D)
	c : b :: B (Syn)
	l : l :: A (Syn)
	+ 3-C
Result:	Formula: B A (D)
	Del.-Comp.: - "3" + 3-C
	Semantic parallelism: Syn
	Transformation: none

<u>Ex.15</u>

Text: v.9	'mr 'yb // 'rdp 'śg
	'ḥlq šll // tml'm npš
	'rq ḥrb // tršm yd
Translation:	The foe said, "I shall pursue; I shall overtake;
	I shall divide the spoil; my greed will be sated;
	I shall whet my sword; my hand will destroy."
Comment:	The suffixes of <u>tml'm</u> and <u>tršm</u> are taken, with C-F, to be enclitic; cf. also LXX.
Met. units:	4:4:4(2:2::2:2::2:2)
Gram. units:	4:4:4(2:2::2:2::2:2)
Syll. symmetry:	4:4::5:5::4:5 (A and B Lines externally asymmetrical)
Gram. structure:	a 1 // 2(a a)
	,2(a 2 // b-encl.<u>mem</u> 1-s)
	,2(a 2-s // a-encl.<u>mem</u> 1-s)

A-B Lines

Result: Non-parallel unit (VS-VS)

B-C Lines

Transformation: none

Addition: none

Reconstr. sent.: 'ḥlq šll tml'm npš
'rq ḥrb tršm yd

Comparison: 2(a 2 : 2(a 2-s :: B≠B (List)
b-encl.*mem* 1-s) : a-encl.*mem* 1-s :: B≠B (List)

Result: Formula: B≠B B≠B
Del.-Comp.: none
Semantic parallelism: List
Transformation: none

Ex.15

Text: v.10 nšpt brḥk // ksm ym
ṣll k^{c}prt / bmm 'drm

Translation: You blew with your wind; Sea covered them;
They sank like a lead weight in the terrible waters.

Comment: On *ṣll* as "sink," see the parallel *yrd* in v.5 and the comments in C-F.

Met. units: 4:4(2:2::2:2)

Gram. units: 4:4(2:2::2:2)

Syll. symmetry: 7:4::6:5 (A Line internally asymmetrical)

Gram. structure: b 3-s // a-s 1
b "3" / 3 ,-3

Transformation: b "3" 3 ,-3 ---→ a-s "3" 1 ,-1

Comment: The transformation produces a hypothetical transitive form *ṣill^{ə}lûm(ô)* (*piel*) (// *kissāmô*). Note the similarity to the transformation in v.5. A *hiphil* form would, of course, also be possible; neither is attested in the O.T.

Addition: + b
+ 3-s

Reconstr. sent.:		ksm (kissûm(ô))	ym	
	nšpt brḥk			k^{c}prt
		ṣlmm (ṣill^{ə}lām(ô))	mm 'drm	

Comparison: (b : b :: D)
(3-s : 3-s :: D)
a-s : a-s :: B (Syn)
l : l ,-l :: /A (Epith)
+ "3"
+ compensation

Result: Formula: B /A (D D)
Del.-Comp.: - b + "3"
- 3-s + compensation
Semantic parallelism: Syn; Epith
Transformation: a-s "3" l ,-l ---→ b "3" 3 ,-3

<u>Ex.15</u>

Text: v.11
m kmk b'lm yhw
m kmk n'dr bqdš
nr' thlt // ^{c}ś pl'

Translation: Who like you among the gods, O YHWH,
Who like you is terrible among the holy ones,
Feared for praiseworthy acts, performing wonders?

Comment: On <u>qdš</u> as a collective noun, see Cross, <u>CMHE</u>, p. 129, note 61.

Met. units: 3:3:4(2:2)

Gram. units: 4:4:4

Syll. symmetry: 9:8::5:3 (C Line internally asymmetrical)

Gram. structure: Spr? "3-s" 3 lpn!
,Spr? "3-s" P(part.c) 3
,=P(part.c)-C ,=P(part.a)-C

Comment: Also possible is the interpretation:
Spr? P("3")-s 3 lpn!
Spr? P("3")-s l(part.c)! 3
,=l(part.c)-C! ,=l(part.a)-C!
"Who is like you among the gods, O YHWH;
Who is like you, O terrible among the holy ones,

(One) feared for praiseworthy acts,
performer of wonders?"

In this common interpretation, n'dr bqdš, nr' thlt and ᶜś pl' are vocatives, paralleling yhw in the A Line. The analysis followed above has the advantage of allowing direct grammatical parallelism between b'lm and bqdš.

A-B Lines

Transformation: none

Addition: + lpn!

Reconstr. sent.:

```
                 b'lm
m kmk  n'dr            yhw
                 bqdš
```

Comparison: (lpn! : lpn! :: D)
Spr?-"3-s" : Spr?-"3-s" :: D/D
3 : 3 :: A (Epith)
+ P(part.c)

Result: Formula: A D/D (D)
Del.-Comp.: - lpn! + P(part.c)
Semantic parallelism: Epith; D
Transformation: none

B-C Lines

Transformation: none

Addition: + Spr?-"3-s"
+ 3

Reconstr. sent.:

```
       n'dr
m kmk              ᶜś pl'  bqdš
       nr' thlt
```

Comment: More accurately:

```
          n'dr
   m kmk  nr' thlt  bqdš
          ᶜś pl
```

However, the system requires the treatment of ᶜś pl' as an addition. This is similar to the treatment of units with the structure A A' A'' discussed in Part I.

Comparison: (Spr?-"3-s" : Spr?-"3-s" :: D/D)
(3 : 3 :: D)
Part(part.c) : P(part.c)-C :: /A (Syn)
+ ,=P(part.a)
+ -C

Result: Formula: /A (D D/D)
Del.-Comp.: - Spr?-"3-s" + ,=P(part.a)
- 3 + -C
Semantic parallelism: Syn
Transformation: none

Ex.15

Text: v.13 nḥt bḥsdk / ^{c}m z g'lt
nhlt b^{c}zk / 'l nw qdšk

Translation: By your faithfulness you led the people you redeemed;
With your strength you guided them to your holy encampment.

Met. units: 4:4(2:2::2:2)

Gram. units: 4:4(2:2::2:2)

Syll. symmetry: 7:5::7:6 (A Line internally asymmetrical)

Gram. structure: a 3-s / 2 ,-R(rel.pr. a)
a 3-s / 3-C-s

Transformation: none

Addition: + 2
+ ,-R(rel.pr.-a)

Reconstr. sent.: nḥt bḥsdk
^{c}m z g'lt 'l nw qdšk
nhlt b^{c}zk

Comparison: (2 : 2 :: D)
(,-R(rel.pr.-a) : ,-R(rel.pr.-a) :: D)
a : a :: A (Syn)
3-s : 3-s :: A (List)
+ 3
+ -C-s

Result: Formula: A A (D D)

Del.-Comp.: - 2 + 3

- ,-R(rel.pr.-a) + -C-s

Semantic parallelism: Syn; List

Transformation: none

<u>Ex.15</u>

Text: v.14 šm^c ^{c}mm yrgzn

ḥl 'ḥz yšb plšt

Translation: When the peoples heard, they trembled;

Pangs seized the inhabitants of Philistia.

Comment: Or: "the enthroned of Philistia"; see Cross, <u>CMHE</u>, p. 130, note 65.

Met. units: 3:3

Gram. units: 3:4

Syll. symmetry: 8:8 (symmetrical)

Gram. structure: a 1 b

1 a 2-Cpn

Transformation: 1 a 2-Cpn ---→ 3 c 1-Cpn

Comment: The transformation results in a <u>niphal</u> verb: <u>nôḥăzû</u>.

Addition: + a

Reconstr. sent.: šm^c ^{c}mm yrgzn

yšb plšt (b)ḥl n'ḥz

Comparison: (a : a :: D)

1 : 1-Cpn :: /A (WP-PN)

b : 3-c :: /<u>A</u> (Syn)

+ compensation

Result: Formula: /<u>A</u> /A (D)

Del.-Comp.: - a + compensation

Semantic parallelism: WP-PN; Syn

Transformation: 3 c 1-Cpn ---→ 1 a 2-Cpn

Comment: The formula is a variant of x /x (D), produced by the awarding of the value of one MU to the idiom <u>ḥl 'ḥz</u>. A treatment of the unit as 3:4 would result in the formula /x /x (D).

Ex.15

Text: v.15 — 'z nbhl 'lp 'dm
'l m'b // y'ḥzm r^{c}d
nmg kl yšb kn^{c}n

Translation: The leaders of Edom were terrified;
Trembling seized the mighty men of Moab;
All the inhabitants of Canaan melted away.

Met. units: 3:4(2:2):3

Gram. units: 3:4(2:2):3

Syll. symmetry: 9::4:5::9 (symmetrical)

Comment: The metrical analysis is based on several considerations. As regards the A Line, one may read, as C-F suggest, 'ăzê, thereby facilitating a scansion of 4(2:2). The unit as a whole would then be 4:4:3(2:2::2:2::3). Moreover, C-F suggest reading adverbial kullā or the like in the C Line, resulting in an overall scansion of 4:4:4(2:2::2:2::2:2). In both cases, however, it is methodologically preferable from the point of view of the system of analysis to retain the vocalizations of MT. Both kl and 'z are monosyllables of the types which, as explained in Part I, are not awarded the value of a full metrical unit. kl occurs frequently with yšb. In Josh.2:9, 24 nmg appears with kl yšby and in Ps.75:4 with kl (cf. also Amos 9:13 and Isa.14:31). Therefore, the C Line on this unit is most safely treated as a 3:3 line, since one can hardly permit a caesura after kl. The A Line's 'z is more difficult to analyze metrically. The rarity of 'ăzê in MT in no way argues against its acceptability in this unit. Moreover, assigning 3 metrical units to the A Line produces the metrical pattern 3:4:3 which is unique in the examples of the Corpus. Nevertheless, the analysis suggested above conforms more closely to the method employed in this study.

Gram. structure: 3 c 1-Cpn
2-Cpn a-s 1
c "1"-C-Cpn

A-B Lines

Transformation: 1. 2-Cpn a-s 1 --→ 2-Cpn a 1
2. 2-Cpn a 1 --→ 1-C c 3

Comment: The first transformation removes the *casus pendens*; the second produces an intransitive verb (*niphal*): *nôḥăzû* (cf. v.14).

Addition: none

Reconstr. sent.: 'z ⟋ nbhl 'lp 'dm
⟍ n'ḥz (b)r^{c}d 'l m'b

Comparison: 3-c : c 3 :: /A (Syn)
1-Cpn : 1-Cpn :: A/A (List(PN))
+ compensation

Comment: Whatever the etymology of *'ēlê* (cf. Dahood, *Psalms* I, pp. 9f.), it is unlikely that it is a simple synonym of *'lp*; hence its assignment to "List."

Result: Formula: /A A/A
Del.-Comp.: - ∅ + compensation
Semantic parallelism: Syn; List (PN)
Transformation:
1. 1-Cpn c 3 --→ 2-Cpn a 1
2. 2-Cpn a 1 --→ 2-Cpn a-s 1

B-C Lines

Transformation: 1. c "1"-C-Cpn --→ a "2"-C-Cpn
2. a "2"-C-Cpn --→ "2"-C-Cpn a-s

Comment: The first transformation produces a transitive verb, probably a *polel* which actually is attested in the O.T. (Ps.65:11 and Job 30:22; cf. Isa.64:6, reading *tmggnw*): y^{ə}*mōgēg*, with archaic suffix: *y^{ə}mōg^{ə}gēmô*. However, it must be stressed that the hypothetical form required by a transformation need not be lexically attested. The second transformation changes the structure to that of a sentence with *casus pendens*. A causative transformation of *y'ḥzm r^{c}d* does not seem necessary.

Addition:	none
Comment:	The B Line's <u>y'ḥzm</u> <u>r^{c}d</u> is an idiomatic unit (cf., with <u>r^{c}dh</u>, Isa.33:14 and Ps.48:7). The theoretical subject of the transformed verb is probably YHWH.
Reconstr. sent.:	'l m'b y'ḥzm r^{c}d kl yšb kn^{c}n ymggm
Comparison:	<u>2-Cpn</u> : <u>"2"-C-Cpn</u> :: A/A (List-PW) a-s l : a-s :: A/(Syn)
Result:	Formula: A/A A/ Del.-Comp.: none Semantic parallelism: List-PW; Syn Transformation: 1. <u>"2"-C-Cpn</u> <u>a-s</u> --→ a "2"-C-Cpn 2. a "2"-C-Cpn --→ c "1"-C-Cpn

---

<u>Ex.15</u>

Text: v.16a	tpl ^{c}lhm / 'mt wpḥd bgdl zr^{c}k / ydm k'bn
Translation:	You made panic and fear fall upon them; By your great power they were made dumb like stone.
Comment:	Reading <u>tappîl</u>; see C-F. This may also be the understanding reflected by Targum's <u>tappēl</u>). In addition, read, with C-F, <u>gōdel</u> and <u>yiddammû</u>.
Met. units:	4:4(2:2::2:2)
Gram. units:	4:4(2:2::2:2)
Syll. symmetry:	5:4::6:5 (external asymmetry)
Gram. structure:	a 3-s / 2 &2 3-C-s / c "3"
Result:	Non-parallel unit of the type VS-VS
Comment:	If one reads <u>tappîl</u> one obtains a (perhaps accidental) sequence of alternation between transitive and intransitive verbs from v.14 to 16a: šm^{c} yrgzn 'ḥz nbhl y'ḥzm nmg tpl ydm a b a c a c a c

<u>Ex.15</u>

Text: v.16b	^{c}d y^{c}br ^{c}mk yhw
	^{c}d y^{c}br ^{c}m z qnt
Translation:	While your people crossed over, O YHWH,
	While the people you created crossed over,
Met. units:	3:3
Gram. units:	3:3
Syll. symmetry:	8:8 (symmetrical)
Gram. structure:	3(prep. b 1-s) lpn!
	,3(prep. b 1 ,-R(rel.pr. a))
Transformation:	none
Addition:	+ lpn!
Reconstr. sent.:	^{c}d y^{c}br ^{c}m(k) z qnt yhw
	(lpn! : lpn! :: D)
	prep.-b : prep.-b :: D
	1-s : 1 :: "D"
	+ ,-R(rel.pr.-a)
Result:	Formula: D "D" (D)
	Del.-Comp.: - lpn! + ,-R(rel.pr.-a)
	Semantic parallelism: D
	Transformation: none

<u>Ex.15</u>

Text. v.17	tb^{c}m ṭṭ^{c}m / bhr nḥltk
	mkn lšbtk / p^{c}lt yhw
	mqdš yhw // knn ydk
Comment:	Omitting the <u>waw</u> of MT's <u>wṭṭ^{c}m</u> and reading <u>yhw</u> for MT's <u>'dny</u> in the C Line; see C-F.
Translation:	You brought them, you planted them in the mountain of your possession.
	The dais of your throne which you made, O YHWH,
	The shrine, O YHWH, which your hands established.
Met. units:	4:4:4(2:2::2:2::2:2)
Gram. units:	4:4:4(2:2::2:2::2:2)

Syll. symmetry: 8:6::6:5::4:6 (A and B Lines externally asymmetrical; A and C Lines internally asymmetrical)

Comment: Retaining MT's <u>'dny</u> in the C Line would make that unit internally symmetrical.

Gram. structure: a-s a-s / 3-C-s
,=3 3-s / ,-R(a) lpn!
,=3 lpn! // ,-R(a l-s)

<u>A-B Lines</u>

Transformation: none

Addition: + a-s
+ a-s

Reconstr. sent.:
bhr nḥltk
tb'm tt^{c}m p^{c}lt yhw
mkn lšbtk

Comparison: (a-s : a-s :: D)
(a-s : a-s :: D)
3-C-s : 3 3-s :: A≠A (Epith)
+ ,-R(a)
+ lpn!

Result: Formula: A≠A (D D)
Del.-Comp.: - a-s + ,-R(a)
- a-s + lpn!
Semantic parallelism: Epith
Transformation: none

<u>B-C Lines</u>

Transformation: none

Addition: none

Reconstr. sent.:
mkn lšbtk p^{c}lt
yhw
mqdš knn ydk

Comparison: 3-3-s : 3 :: A/ (Epith-Syn)
,-R(a) : ,-R(a l-s) :: /A (Syn)
lpn! : lpn! :: D(PN)

Result: Formula: A/ /A D
Del.-Comp.: none
Semantic parallelism: Eptih-Syn; Syn; D(PN)
Transformation: none

Num.10

Text: v.35 — qm yhw // (w)ypṣ 'bk
(w)yns mśn'k mpnk

Translation: — Rise, O YHWH, let your enemies be scattered;
Let your foes flee before you!

Met. units: — 4(2:2):3

Gram. units: — 4(2:2):3

Syll. symmetry: — 4:7::11 (A Line internally asymmetrical)

Gram. structure: — b! lpn! // b! l-s
b! l-s 3-s

Transformation: — none

Addition: — + b!
+ lpn!

Reconstr. sent.:

```
          ypṣ  'bk
qm  yhw                 mpnk
          yns  mśn'k
```

Comparison: — (b! : b! :: D)
(lpn! : lpn! :: D)
b! : b! :: A (Syn)
l-s : l-s :: A (Syn)
+ 3-s

Result: — Formula: A A (D D)
Del.-Comp.: - b!   + 3-s
- lpn!
Semantic parallelism: Syn
Transformation: none

Num.23

Text: v.7a — mn 'rm ynḥn blq
mlk m'b mhrr qdm

Translation — Balak has brought me from Aram,
Moab's king, from the mountains of Qedem.

Met. units: — 3:3

Comment: — The fact that the poem seems to be 3:3 throughout is the chief factor in assigning only 3 metrical units to this unit.

Gram. units: — 3:4

Syll. symmetry: — 8:8 (symmetrical)

Gram. structure: 3pn a-s lpn
,l-Cpn 3-Cpn
Transformation: none
Addition: + a-s
Reconstr. sent.: mn 'rm ynḥn blq
mhrr qdm mlk m'b
Comparison: (a-s : a-s :: D)
3pn : 3-Cpn :: /A (Syn(PN))
lpn : l-Cpn :: /$\underline{A}$ (Epith(PN))
+ compensation
Result: Formula: /$\underline{A}$ /A (D)
Del.-Comp.: - a-s + compensation
Semantic parallelism: Syn(PN); Epith(PN)
Transformation: none

<u>Num.23</u>
Text: v.7b lk 'r ly y^{c}qb
lk z^{c}m yśr'l
Translation: Go curse Jacob for me;
Go execrate Israel!
Met. units: 3:3
Gram. units: 4:3
Syll. symmetry: 7:7 (symmetrical)
Gram. structure: b! a! 3-s 2pn
b! a! 3pn
Transformation: none
Addition: none
Reconstr. sent.: 'r y^{c}qb
lk ly
z^{c}m yśr'l
Comparison: b! : b! :: D
a! 3-s : a! :: $\underline{A}$/ (Syn)
2pn : 2pn :: A (Syn(PN))
Result: Formula: D A $\underline{A}$/
Del.-Comp.: none
Semantic parallelism: Syn; Syn(PN)
Transformation: none

Num.23

Text: v.8	mh 'qb l' qbh 'l (w)mh 'z^{c}m l' z^{c}mh yhw
Comment:	Following Albright's restoration of the suffix of MT's z^{c}mh in the B Line; see OBal.
Translation:	Shall I curse whom God has not cursed; Shall I execrate whom YHWH has not execrated?
Met. units:	3:3
Gram. units:	3:3
Syll. symmetry:	7:8 (symmetrical)
Gram. structure:	3? a 2(,-R(neg a-s lpn)) 3? a 2(,-R(neg a-s lpn))
Transformation:	none
Addition:	none
Reconstr. sent.:	mh 'qb l' qbh 'l mh 'z^{c}m l' z^{c}mh yhw
Comparison:	3?-a : 3?-a :: A (Syn) neg-a-s : neg-a-s :: A (Syn) lpn : lpn :: A (Syn (PN))
Result:	Formula: A A A Del.-Comp.: none Semantic parallelism: Syn; Syn(PN) Transformation: none

---

Num.23

Text: v.9a	k mr'š ṣrm 'r'n (w)mgb^{c}t 'šrn
Translation:	From the peak of the mountains I see; From the hills I look.
Comment:	Following Albright's interpretation of the suffix of 'r'n and 'šrn, although the retention of MT's pronominal suffixes would affect analysis only in a minor way.
Met. units:	3:3
Gram. units:	3:2
Syll. symmetry:	7:7 (symmetrical)

Gram. structure: ptcl 3-C a
, 3 a

Transformation: none

Addition: + ptcl-3-

Reconstr. sent.: k mr'š ṣrm 'r'n / (m)gb^c t 'šrn

Comparison: (ptcl-3- : ptcl-3- :: D)
-C : 3 :: A* (Syn)
a : a :: A (Syn)
+ compensation

Result: Formula: A A* (D)
Del.-Comp.: - ptcl-3- + compensation
Semantic parallelism: Syn
Transformation: none

Num.23

Text: v.9b hn ^c m lbdd yškn
(w)bgym l' ytḥšb

Comment: Vocalizing hinnê for MT's hēn (Albright, OBal), although analysis is not affected.

Translation: Here is a people that dwells apart,
That does not reckon itself to the nations!

Comment: bdd can have the meaning "securely" or the like, parallel to (l)bṭḥ; so, in the Corpus, Dt.33:28 and, elsewhere, Jer.49:31, Ps.4:9, etc. Here such a meaning is possible, but due to the semantic parallel l' ytḥšb, is unlikely. On the latter idiom in the niphal, cf. Dt.2:11, 20; Josh.13:3 and II Sam 4:2.

Met. units: 3:3

Gram. units: 3:2

Syll. symmetry: 8:7 (symmetrical)

Gram. structure: P! S ,-R(3 b)
,-R(3 neg c)

Transformation: none

Addition: + P!-S

Reconstr. sent.: lbdd yškn
hn ^{c}m
bgym l' ytḥšb

Comparison: (P!-S : P!-S :: D/D)
3 : 3 :: A (Ant)
b : neg-c :: B*(Ant)
+ compensation

Result: Formula: A B* (D/D)
Del.-Comp.: - P!-s + compensation
Semantic parallelism: Ant.
Transformation: none

Comment: A peculiar feature of this unit is that the terms ^{c}amm and gōy, so often parallel, are not only not in grammatically parallel positions, but do not need to be, and cannot be, made grammatically parallel by transformation.

Num.23

Text: v.10a m mn ^{c}pr y^{c}qb
(w)m spr trb^{c}t yśr'l

Comment: On text and interpretation, see Albright, OBal.

Translation: Who has counted the dust of Jacob;
Who has numbered the dust cloud of Israel?

Met. units: 3:3

Gram. units: 4:4

Syll. symmetry: 7:8 (symmetrical)

Gram. structure: lpr? a 2-Cpn
lpr? a 2-Cpn

Transformation: none

Addition: none

Reconstr. sent.: m mn ^{c}pr y^{c}qb
m spr trb^{c}t yśr'l

Comparison: lpr?-a : lpr?-a :: D/A (Syn)
2-Cpn : 2-Cpn :: A/A (Syn/Syn(PN))

Result: Formula: D/A A/A
Del.-Comp.: none
Semantic parallelism: Syn; Syn(PN)
Transformation: none

Num.23

Text: v.10b tmt npš mt yšrm
(w)th 'ḥrt kmh

Translation: May I die an upright man's death;
May my end be like his!

Comment: Albright's suggestion that this expression is a "misunderstood oath" is persuasive (OBal). If so, yšrm may be a circumlocution or a textual error for rš^{c}m.

Met. units: 3:3

Gram. units: 4:3

Syll. symmetry: 8:8 (symmetrical)

Gram. structure: b! 1-s "2-C"
"b"! S-s P("3")-s

Comment: Note the apostrophization of mt yšrm as a "cognate accusative."

Transformation: none

Comment: No transformation is required since the B Line forms a "quasi-verbal" sentence.

Addition: none

Reconstr. sent.: tmt npš mt yšrm
th 'ḥrt kmh

Comparison: b! 1-s : "b"! S-s :: A⌿A (Syn)
"2-C" : P("3")-s :: C/ (PR)

Result: Formula: C/ A⌿A
Del.-Comp.: none
Semantic parallelism: Syn; PR
Transformation: none

Num.23

Text: v.18 — qm blq wšm^{c}
h'zn ^{c}d bn ṣpr

Comment: Following Albright's emendation <u>^{c}ēdî</u>, "my testimony," although the effect on the analysis is minimal (OBal). This emendation is supported by LXX and Sam and perhaps also Job 32:12.

Translation: Arise, Balak, and hear;
Heed my testimony, Son of Sippor!

Met. units: 3:3

Gram. units: 3:4

Syll. symmetry: 6:9 (asymmetrical)

Gram. structure: b! lpn! &a!
a! 2-s l-Cpn!

Transformation: none

Addition: + b!

Reconstr. sent.:

```
    blq      wšmᶜ
qm                  ᶜd
    bn ṣpr   h'zn
```

Comparison: (b! : b! :: D)
lpn! : l-Cpn! :: /<u>A</u> (Epith (PN))
&a! : a! :: A (Syn)
+ 2-s

Result: Formula: A /<u>A</u> (D)
Del.-Comp.: - b! + 2-s
Semantic parallelism: Epith(PN); Syn
Transformation: none

Num.23

Text: v.19b — hh' 'mr wl' y^{c}ś
dbr wl' yqmn

Translation: Does he promise, but not do,
Speak, but not perform?

Met. units: 3:3

Gram. units: 3:2

Syll. symmetry: 8:8 (symmetrical)

Gram. structure: ptcl? lpr a &neg a
,a &neg a-s

Transformation: none

Addition: + ptcl?-lpr

Reconstr. sent.: 'mr wl' y^{c}ś́
hh'
dbr wl' yqmn

Comparison: (ptcl?-lpr : ptcl?-lpr :: D)
a : a :: A (Syn)
&neg-a : &neg-a-s :: A* (Syn)
+ compensation

Result: Formula: A A* (D)
Del.-Comp.: - ptcl?-lpr + compensation
Semantic parallelism: Syn
Transformation: none

<u>Num.23</u>

Text: v.21a l' hbṭ 'n by^{c}qb
(w)l' r' ^{c}ml byśr'l

Translation: No crime has been revealed in Jacob;
No fault has been seen in Israel.

Comment: With Albright, the verbs have been treated as passives; see OBal.

Met. units: 3:3

Gram. units: 3:3

Syll. symmetry: 7:9 (asymmetrical)

Gram. structure: neg c l 3pn
neg c l 3pn

Transformation: none

Addition: none

Reconstr. sent.: l' hbt 'n by^{c}qb
l' r' ^{c}ml byśr'l

Comparison: neg-c : neg-c :: A (Syn)
l : l :: A (Syn)
3pn : 3pn :: A (Syn (PN))

Result:	Formula: A A A
	Del.-Comp.: none
	Semantic parallelism: Syn; Syn(PN)
	Transformation: none

Num.23

Text: v.21b	yhw 'lhw ^{c}m
	(w)tr^{c}t mlk b
Translation:	YHWH his God is with him
	(Who) has royal majesty.
Comment:	Translation following Albright, OBal.
Met. units:	3:3
Gram. units:	3:3
Syll. symmetry:	7:5 (asymmetrical)
Gram. structure:	Spn ,=S-s P(3)-s
	S-C P(3)-s
Result:	Non-parallel unit (NS-NS)

Num.23

Text: v.22	'l mṣ'h mmṣrm
	k t^{c}pt r'm l
Comment:	The participial form in MT has been retained, against OBal.
Translation:	It was El who brought him out of Egypt
	Storming (?) like a wild bull.
Comment:	Translation following Albright, OBal.
Met. units:	3:3
Gram. units:	3:3
Syll. symmetry:	7:6 (symmetrical)
Gram. structure:	Spn P(part.a)-s 3pn
	ptcl S-C P(3)-s
Result:	Non-parallel unit (NS-NS)

<u>Num.23</u>

Text: v.23a	k l' nḥš by^{c}qb
	(w)l' qsm byśr'l
Translation:	There is no divining against Jacob;
	There is no conjuring against Israel.
Comment:	Translation and interpretation following Albright, OBal.
Met. units:	3:3
Gram. units:	2:2
Syll. symmetry:	7:7 (symmetrical)
Gram. structure:	ptcl neg c 3pn
	neg c 3pn
Comment:	Following Albright's suggestion that <u>nḥš</u> and <u>qsm</u> are passives. In any case, the effect on analysis is minimal.
Transformation:	none
Addition:	none
Reconstr. sent.:	l' nḥš by^{c}qb
	k /
	l' qsm byśr'l
Comparison:	ptcl-neg-c : neg-c :: *A (Syn)
	3pn : 3pn :: A* (Syn(PN))
Result:	Formula: *A A*
	Del.-Comp.: none
	Semantic parallelism: Syn; Syn(PN)
	Transformation: none

<u>Num.23</u>

Text: v.23b	k ^{c}t y'mr ly^{c}qb
	(w)lyśr'l mh p^{c}l 'l
Translation:	Now shall be said to Jacob,
	To Israel, "What God has accomplished!"
Met. units:	3:3
Gram. units:	3:4
Syll. symmetry:	9:8 (symmetrical)
Gram. structure:	ptcl 3 c 3pn
	,3pn 1(2pr! a 1pn)
Transformation:	none

Addition: + ptcl-3
+ c

Reconstr. sent.:
k ^{c}t y'mr ly^{c}qb / lyśr'l mh p^{c}l 'l

Comparison: (ptcl-3 : ptcl-3 :: D)
(c : c :: D)
3pn : 3pn :: A (Syn(PN))
+ l(2pr!-a
+ lpn)

Result: Formula: A (D D)
Del.-Comp.: - ptcl-3 + l(2pr!-a
-c + lpn)
Semantic parallelism: Syn(PN)
Transformation: none

Num.23

Text: v.24b l' yškb ^{c}d y'kl ṭrp
(w)dm ḥllm yšt

Translation: He does not lie down until he devours prey,
Drinks the blood of the slain.

Met. units: 3:3

Gram. units: 3:3

Syll. symmetry: 7:6 (symmetrical)

Gram. structure: neg b 3(prep a 2)
,=3(2-C a)

Transformation: none

Addition: + neg-b

Reconstr. sent.:
l' yškb ^{c}d / y'kl ṭrp / yšt dm ḥllm

Comparison: (neg-b : neg-b :: D)
prep-a 2 : 2-C a :: A/Ⱥ(D) (List)
+ compensation

Result: Formula: A/Ⱥ (D)
Del.-Comp.: - neg-b + compensation
Semantic parallelism: List
Transformation: none

Num.24

Text: v.5 — mh ṭb 'hlk y^{c}qb
(w)mškntk yśr'l

Translation: How beautiful are your tents, O Jacob,
Your encampments, O Israel!

Met. units: 3:3

Gram. units: 3:2

Syll. symmetry: 9:8 (symmetrical)

Gram. structure: ptcl! b 1-s lpn!
,1-s lpn!

Transformation: none

Addition: + ptcl!-b

Reconstr. sent.:
'hlk y^{c}qb
mh ṭb
mškntk yśr'l

Comparison: (ptcl!-b : ptcl!-b :: D)
1-s : 1-s :: A* (Syn)
lpn! : lpn! :: A (Syn (PN))
+ compensation

Result: Formula: A A* (D)
Del.-Comp.: - ptcl!-b + compensation
Semantic parallelism: Syn; Syn(PN)
Transformation: none

Num.24

Text: v.6b — k'rzm nṭ^{c} yhw
k'hlm ^{c}l mm rbm

Translation: Like cedars YHWH has planted,
Like aloes by abundant waters.

Comment: Interpretation following Albright, OBal.

Met. units: 3:3

Gram. units: 3:3

Syll. symmetry: 9:8 (symmetrical)

Gram. structure: "3" ,-R(a lpn)
,"3" 3 ,-3

Transformation: none

Addition: + ,-R(a
+ lpn)

Reconstr. sent.: k'rzm
nṭ^{c} yhw ^{c}l mm rbm
k'hlm

Comparison: (,-R(a : ,-R(a :: D)
(1pn) : 1pn) :: D)
"3" : "3" :: A (List)
+ 3
+ ,-3

Result: Formula: A (D D)
Del.-Comp.: - ,-R(a + 3
- 1pn) + ,-3
Semantic parallelism: List
Transformation: none

<u>Num.24</u>

Text: v.7b yrm m'gg mlk
(w)ttnś' mlkt

Comment: Omitting the waw at the beginning of the A Line.

Translation: May his kingship be higher than Agag's;
May his kingship be exalted!

Met. units: 3:3

Gram. units: 3:2

Syll. symmetry: 7:6 (symmetrical)

Gram. structure: b! 3pn 1-s
c! 1-s

Transformation: none

Addition: + 3pn

Reconstr. sent.: yrm (trm) mlk
m'gg
ttnś' (ytnś') mlkt

Comparison: (3pn : 3pn :: D)
b! : c! :: A* (Syn)
1-s : 1-s :: "D"
+ compensation

Result: Formula: "D" A (D)
Del.-Comp.: - 3pn + compensation
Semantic parallelism: Syn; "D"
Transformation: none

Comment: Alternatively, one may compare 1-s : 1-s (mlk : mlkt) :: "D". The formula would, of course, be the same, but this type of example illustrates the practical difficulty one often encounters in applying the accentual interpretation of Hebrew verse.

Num.24

Text: v.8b — y'kl gym ṣrw
(w)ᶜṣmthm ygrm

Translation: He devours the nations, his enemies;
He crushes their bones.

Met. units: 3:3

Gram. units: 3:2

Syll. symmetry: 6:7 (symmetrical)

Gram. structure: a 2 ,=2-s
2-s a

Transformation: none

Addition: + ,=2-s

Reconstr. sent.: y'kl gym
ygrm ᶜṣmt(hm) ṣrw

Comment: Possibly gym ṣrw should be treated as a unit. As it stands the addition produces a non-grammatical sentence. The suffix of ᶜṣmthm would have to be replaced by a construct: ᶜṣmt ṣrw.

Comparison: (,=2-s : ,=2-s :: D)
a : a :: A (List)
2 : 2-s :: A* (WP)
+ compensation

Result: Formula: A A* (D)
Del.-Comp.: - ,=2-s + compensation
Semantic parallelism: List; WP
Transformation: none

Num.24

Text: v.9 mbrkk brk
(w)'rrk 'rr

Translation: Blessed is everyone who blesses you;
Cursed is everyone who curses you!

Met. units: 3:3

Gram. units: 2:2

Syll. symmetry: 7:6 (symmetrical)

Gram. structure: S-s P
S-s P

Transformation: none

Addition: none

Reconstr. sent.: mbrkk brk
'rrk 'rr

Comparison: S-s : S-s :: *A* (Ant)
P : P :: A (Ant)

Result: Formula: A *A*
Del.-Comp.: none
Semantic parallelism: none
Transformation: none

Num.24

Text: v.17a 'r'n wl' ^{c}t
'šrn wl' qrb

Translation: I see, but not now;
I envision, but it is not near.

Comment: The suffixes of the verbs are taken to be "energetic nun" (OBal). Their retention as pronominal suffixes would affect analysis only in a minor way.

Met. units: 3:3

Gram. units: 3:3

Syll. symmetry: 6:7 (symmetrical)

Gram. structure: a &neg 3
a &neg 3

Transformation: none

Addition: none

Reconstr. sent.: 'r'n wl' ^{c}t
'šrn wl' qrb
Comparison: a : a :: A (Syn)
&neg 3 : &neg 3 :: D/A (Syn)
Result: Formula: A D/A
Del.-Comp.: none
Semantic parallelism: Syn; D
Transformation: none

<u>Num.24</u>

Text: v.17c mḥṣ p't m'b
(w)qdqd kl bn št
Comment: Omitting <u>waw</u> at the beginning of the A Line.
Translation: It smites the temples of Moab,
The pate of all the Sons of Sheth.
Met. units: 3:3
Gram. units: 3:3
Syll. symmetry: 6:6 (symmetrical)
Gram. structure: a 2-Cpn
,2-"2"-2-Cpn
Transformation: none
Addition: + a
Reconstr. sent.: p't m'b
mḥṣ
qdqd kl bn št
Comparison: (a : a :: D)
2-Cpn : 2-"2"-2-Cpn :: A/A̸ (List(PN))
+ compensation
Result: Formula: A/A̸ (D)
Del.-Comp.: - a + compensation
Semantic parallelism: List(PN)
Transformation: none

Dt.32

Text: v.1 h'znw (h)šmym w'dbrh
(w)tšm^c (h)'rṣ 'mry py

Translation: Heed, O heavens, what I shall speak;
Hear, O earth, the words of my mouth!

Comment: Or, alternatively for the B Line: "Let the earth hear the words of my mouth!"

Met. units: 3:3

Gram. units: 3:4

Syll. symmetry: 10:6 (asymmetrical)

Comment: The syllable asymmetry is extreme. A simple solution would be to reverse w'dbrh and 'mry py (cf. Ex.15:2b, also for metrical reasons). The resulting sentences are as natural as the above and the syllable symmetry is restored.

h'znw (h)šmym 'mry py (8)
(w)tšm^c (h)'rṣ w'dbrh (8)

Note Ps.50:7: šm^{c}h ^{c}my w'dbrh; and, for h'zn with a direct object, see Gen.4:23 and Isa. 32:9 (both with 'mrh). However, the unit is analyzable as it stands; therefore the received text can serve as the basis of analysis.

Gram. structure: a! lpn! 2(,-R(&a))
a! lpn! 2-c

Transformation: none

Addition: none

Reconstr. sent.: h'znw (h'znh) (h)šmym w'dbrh
tšm^c (yšm^{c}w) (h)'rṣ 'mry py

Comment: Alternatively, and more strictly from the point of view of the system of analysis:

Addition: + 2(,-R(&a))

h'znw (h)šmym
'mry py w'dbrh
tšm^c (h)'rṣ

However, it seems more likely that w'dbrh and 'mry py are clearly intended to be both semantically parallel and grammatically compatible.

Comparison:	a! : a! :: A (Syn)
	lpn! : lpn! :: A (Mer)
	2(,-R(&a)) : 2-C :: /$\underline{A}$ (Syn)
Result:	Formula: A A /$\underline{A}$
	Del.-Comp.: none
	Semantic parallelism: Syn; Mer
	Transformation: none

<u>Dt.32</u>

Text: v.2a	y^{c}rp kmṭr lqḥy
	tzl kṭl 'mrty
Translation:	Let my teaching drop like rain;
	Let my word drip like dew!
Met. units:	3:3
Gram. units:	3:3
Syll. symmetry:	7:7 (symmetrical)
Gram. structure:	a! "3" 1-s
	a! "3" 1-s
Transformation:	none
Addition:	none
Reconstr. sent.:	y^{c}rp (t^{c}rp) kmṭr lqḥy
	tzl (yzl) kṭl 'mrty
Comparison:	a! : a! :: A (Syn)
	"3" : "3" :: A (List)
	1-s : 1-s :: A (Syn)
Result:	Formula: A A A
	Del.-Comp.: none
	Semantic parallelism: Syn; List
	Transformation: none

<u>Dt.32</u>

Text: v.2b	kś^{c}rm ^{c}ly dš'
	(w)krbbm ^{c}ly ^{c}śb
Translation:	Like rain on herbs;
	Like showers on grass.

Met. units: 3:3

Gram. units: 3:3

Syll. symmetry: 6:6 (symmetrical)

Gram. structure: "3" 3-C
"3" 3-C

Transformation: none

Addition: none

Reconstr. sent.: kś^{c}rm ^{c}ly dš'
krbbm ^{c}ly ^{c}śb

Comparison: "3" : "3" :: A (Syn)
3-C : 3-C :: D/A (Syn)

Comment: It does not seem that dš' differs sufficiently from ^{c}śb to be classified rhetorically as "List."

Result: Formula: A D/A
Del.-Comp.: none
Semantic parallelism: Syn
Transformation: none

Dt.32

Text: v.3 ky šm yhwh 'qr'
hbw gdl l'lhnw

Translation: I proclaim the name of YHWH;
Ascribe greatness to our God!

Met. units: 3:3

Gram. units: 3:3

Syll. symmetry: 6:7 (symmetrical)

Gram. structure: ptcl 2-Cpn a
a! 2 3-s

Transformation: none

Addition: none

Reconstr. sent.: 'qr' šm yhwh
ky /
hbw gdl l 'lhnw

Comment: qr' šm is taken to be a variant of the commoner qr' bšm, "to proclaim" or, better, "to acclaim"; cf. qr'w bšmw // hwdw lyhwh in Isa.12:4 = Ps.105:1 = I Chron.16:8 and

	Ps.116:13, 17. Like hbw qdl l- it is an idiomatic unit.
Comparison:	ptcl-a 2- : a! 2 :: A̸ (Syn)
	-Cpn : 3-s :: A (Epith)
Result:	Formula: A A̸
	Del.-Comp.: none
	Semantic parallelism: Syn; Epith
	Transformation: none

Dt.32

Text: v.4a	(h)ṣr tmm p^{c}lh
	ky kl drkw mšpṭ
Translation:	The Rock's work is perfect;
	All his ways are right.
Met. units:	3:3
Gram. units:	3:3
Syll. symmetry:	6:7 (symmetrical)
Gram. structure:	-C P S-s
	,ptcl "S"-C-s P
Transformation:	none
Addition:	+ -C
Reconstr. sent.:	(h)ṣr p^{c}lh tmm (tmmm/tmmt) (h)ṣr (ky) kl drkw mšpṭ
Comparison:	(-C : -C :: D)
	P : P :: A (Syn)
	S-s : ptcl-"S"-C-s :: /A (Syn)
	+ compensation
Result:	Formula: A /A (D)
	Del.-Comp.: - -C = compensation
	Semantic parallelism: Syn
	Transformation: none

Dt.32

Text: v.6a — hlyhwh tgmlw z't
^{c}m nbl wl' ḥkm

Translation: Will you recompense YHWH in this way,
O brutish and stupid people?

Met. units: 3:3

Gram. units: 3:3

Syll. symmetry: 8:7 (symmetrical)

Gram. structure: ptcl?-3pn a 2pr
l! ,-l! &neg l!

Result: Non-parallel unit (enjambment)

Dt.32

Text: v.7a — zkr ymt ^{c}lm
bnh šnt dr wdr

Comment: Reading *bînā(h)* for MT's *bînû*; cf. the VSS, which attest to symmetry of number in A and B Lines. The difference is, however, not reflected in the grammatical notation system.

Translation: Remember the days of old;
Consider the years of antiquity!

Met. units: 3:3

Gram. units: 3:4

Syll. symmetry: 6:7 (symmetrical)

Gram. structure: a! 2-C
a! 2-C &,-C

Transformation: none

Addition: none

Reconstr. sent.: zkr ymt ^{c}lm
bnh šnt dr wdr

Comparison: a! : a! :: A (Syn)
2-C : 2-C &,-C :: A/Ⱥ (Syn)

Result: Formula: A A/Ⱥ
Del.-Comp.: none
Semantic parallelism: Syn
Transformation: none

Dt.32

Text: v.7b	š'l 'bkh wygdkh
	zqnkh wy'mrw lkh
Translation:	Ask your father to tell you,
	Your elders, to relate to you!
Met. units:	3:3
Gram. units:	3:3
Syll. symmetry:	10:10 (symmetrical)
Gram. structure:	a! 2-s &a-s
	,2-s &a 3-s
Transformation:	none
Addition:	+ a!
Reconstr. sent.:	'bkh wygdkh (wəyaggîdûkā(h))
	š'l
	zqnkh wy'mrw lkh (wy'mr lkh)
Comparison:	(a! : a! :: D)
	2-s : 2-s :: A(Syn)
	&a-s : &a-s 3-s :: /A (Syn)
	+ compensation
Result:	Formula: A /A (D)
	Del.-Comp.: - a! + compensation
	Semantic parallelism: Syn
	Transformation: none

Dt.32

Text: v.8a	bhnḥl ᶜlyn gym
	bhprdh bny 'dm
Translation:	When Elyon gave the inheritances of the nations,
	When he set the divisions of mankind,
Met. units:	3:3
Gram. units:	3:3
Syll. symmetry:	7:8 (symmetrical)
Gram. structure:	3(inf.const.a-Cpn 2)
	3(inf.const.a-s 2-C)
Transformation:	none
Addition:	none

Reconstr. sent.: bhnḥl ^{c}lyn gym
bhprdh bny 'dm

Comparison: 3(inf.const.a-Cpn) : 3(inf.const.a-s) ::
A/ (PN-Syn)
2 : 2-C :: /A (Syn)

Result: Formula: A/ /A
Del.-Comp.: none
Semantic parallelism: PN-Syn; Syn
Transformation: none

Dt.32

Text: v.8b yṣb gblt ^{c}mm
lmspr bny 'lhm

Comment: The B Line follows the reading of LXX as confirmed now by Qumran.

Translation: He established the territories of the peoples
According to the number of the lesser gods.

Met. units: 3:3

Gram. units: 3:3

Syll. symmetry: 7:8 (symmetrical)

Gram. structure: a 2-C
3-C-Cpn

Result: Non-parallel unit (enjambment)

Dt.32

Text: v.9 ky ḥlq yhwh ^{c}mh
y^{c}qb ḥbl nḥlth

Translation: YHWH's own portion was his people;
Jacob was his own apportioned possession.

Met. units: 3:3

Gram. units: 3:3

Syll. symmetry: 6:6 (symmetrical)

Gram. structure: ptcl S-Cpn P-s
Ppn S-C-s

Transformation: none

Addition:	none
Reconstr. sent.:	ky / ḥlq yhwh ᶜmh ḥbl nḥlth yᶜqb
Comparison:	ptcl-S-Cpn : S-C-s :: A≠A (PN-Syn)
	P-s : Ppn :: A (PN)
Result:	Formula: A A≠A
	Del.-Comp.: none
	Semantic parallelism: PN-Syn; PN
	Transformation: none

<u>Dt.32</u>

Text: v.10a	ymṣ'hw b'rṣ mdbr
	(w)bthw yll yšmn
Translation:	He found him in the desert,
	In the desolation of a howling wilderness.
Met. units:	3:3
Gram. units:	3:3
Syll. symmetry:	8:8 (symmetrical)
Gram. structure:	a-s 3-C
	,3-C-C
Comment:	Alternatively, for the B Line, ,=3 ,=3-C
Transformation:	none
Addition:	+ a-s
Reconstr. sent.:	ymṣ'hw b'rṣ mdbr bthw yll yšmn
Comparison:	(a-s : a-s :: D)
	3-C : 3-C-C :: A≠Ⱥ (Epith)
	+ compensation
Result:	Formula: A≠Ⱥ (D)
	Del.-Comp.: - a-s + compensation
	Semantic parallelism: Epith
	Transformation: none

Dt.32

Text: v.10b — ysbbnhw ybnnhw
yṣrnhw k'šn ^{c}nh

Translation: He surrounded him, cared for him;
He guarded him as the apple of his eye.

Comment: The translation of *ybnnhw* is uncertain, but should not impede analysis.

Met. units: 3:3

Gram. units: 2:3

Syll. symmetry: 10:9 (symmetrical)

Comment: This unit, like several others in the *Corpus*, is more amenable to a syllabic than an accentual metrical analysis. *ysbbnhw* and *ybnnhw* have the same number of syllables and the awarding of two metrical beats to the one or the other is arbitrary; see the appendix to Part III.

Gram. structure: a-s a-s
a-s "3-C-s"

Transformation: none

Addition: + a-s

Reconstr. sent.:

```
            ybnnhw
ysbbnhw              k'šn ᶜnh
            yṣrnhw
```

Comparison: (a-s : a-s :: D)
a-s : a-s :: *B (Syn)
+ "3-
+ -C-s

Result: Formula: *B (D)
Del.-Comp.: - a-s + "3-
+ -C-s
Semantic parallelism: Syn
Transformation: none

Comment: If one awards two metrical units to *ysbbnhw*, the resulting formula is B (D*).

Dt.32

Text: v.11a — knšr y^{c}r qnh
^{c}l gzlw yrḥp

Translation: Like an eagle which protects its nest,
Which hovers over its chicks,

Comment: The translation of y^{c}r follows the LXX. Alternatively for y^{c}r and yrḥp, "stirs up" and "soars over," respectively. Analysis will not be affected by the alternate meanings.

Met. units: 3:3

Gram. units: 3:2

Syll. symmetry: 6:7 (symmetrical)

Gram. structure: "3" ,-R(a 2-s)
,=R(3-s b)

Transformation: none

Addition: + "3"

Reconstr. sent.:

```
      y^cr      qnh
knšr
      yrḥp ^cl  gzlw
```

Comment: yrḥp ^{c}l is a compound; therefore, no transformation is required.

Comparison: ("3" : "3" :: D)
a : b :: B(Syn)
2-s : 3-s :: A* (List)
+ compensation

Result: Formula: B A* (D)
Del.-Comp.: - "3" + compensation
Semantic parallelism: Syn; List
Transformation: none

Dt.32

Text: v.11b — yprś knpw yqḥw
yś'hw ^{c}l 'brth

Translation: He spread his wings; took him up;
He lifted him on his pinions.

Met. units: 3:3

Gram. units: 3:2

Syll. symmetry: 9:8 (symmetrical)

Gram. structure: a 2 a-s
a-s 3-s

Transformation: none

Addition: + a

Reconstr. sent.: yprś knpw yqḥw / 'brth yś'hw ᶜl

On the problem posed by this (and similar) units, see the section on the reconstructed sentence in Part I.

Comparison: (a : a :: D)
2 : 3-s :: A* (Syn)
a-s : a-s :: A (List)
+ compensation

Result: Formula: A A* (D)
Del.-Comp.: -a + compensation
Semantic parallelism: Syn; List
Transformation: none

Dt.32

Text: v.12 yhwh bdd ynḥnw
(w)'n ᶜmh 'l nkr

Translation: YHWH alone led him;
No strange god was with him.

Comment: The analysis assumes, with the Vulgate and the Peshitta, that bdd and the suffix of ᶜmh both refer to YHWH. The Targum's paraphrase refers both to Israel; while the LXX applies the former term to God and the latter to Israel.

Met. units: 3:3

Gram. units: 3:3

Syll. symmetry: 7:6 (symmetrical)

Gram. structure: lpn 3 a-s
"neg b" P(3)-s S ,-S

Transformation: none

Comment: Since the B Line is a "quasi-verbal" sentence, no transformation is required.

Addition: + a-s

Reconstr. sent.: yhwh bdd

'l nkr 'n ^{c}mh ynḥnw

Comment: An unusual feature of the addition is that it makes ynḥnw, as regards the B Line, a relative clause:

"neg b" P(3)-s S ,-S ,-R(a-s)

Comparison: (a-s : a-s :: D)

lpn : S ,-S :: /A (PN-Ant)

3 : "neg-b"-P(3)-s :: A (Syn)

+ compensation

Result: Formula: A /A (D)

Del.-Comp.: - a-s + compensation

Semantic parallelism: PN-Ant; Syn

Transformation: none

Dt.32

Text: v.13a yrkbhw ^{c}l bmty 'rṣ

(w)y'klhw tnbt śdy

Comment: Reading wᵊya'ăk̲îlēhû for MT's wᵊyō(')k̲al; cf. LXX, Sam., Peshitta and Targum. Note also Isa.58:14 and wynqhw in 13b, following. MT's text would require a simple transformation to causative which would, in any case, produce the required form.

Translation: He mounted him on the high places of the earth;

He fed him the produce of the field.

Met.units: 3:3

Gram.units: 3:3

Syll.symmetry: 9:9 (symmetrical)

Gram.structure: a-s 3-C

a-s 2-C

Comment: Both lines contain idioms; moreover, yrkbhw ^{c}l is to be considered a compound. Therefore, no transformation is necessary for comparison. The only question is whether A and B Lines are to be considered semantically indivisible units. It seems to me that each may be broken after the second term, as in the reconstructed sentence below.

Transformation: none

Addition: none

Reconstr. sent.: yrkbhw ^{c}l bmty 'rṣ
y'klhw tnbt śdy

Comparison: a-s : a-s :: B (WP)
3-C : 2-C :: A≠A (WP/Syn)

Result: Formula: B A≠A
Del.-Comp.: none
Semantic parallelism: WP; Syn
Transformation: none

Dt.32

Text: v.13b ynqhw dbš msl^{c}
(w)šmn mḥlmš ṣr

Comment: Omitting waw at the beginning of the A Line.

Translation: He let him suck honey from rock,
Oil from flinty stone.

Met. units: 3:3

Gram. units: 3:3

Syll. symmetry: 7:5 (asymmetrical)

Comment: Even treating dbš as a segholate, the unit is asymmetrical. Note that the metrical difficulty is removed if one follows the Vulgate, which reads w^{ə}yînaq, as in the B Line of the previous unit it supports MT's w^{ə}yō(')ḵal.

Gram. structure: a-s 2 3
,2 3-C

Transformation: none

Addition: + a-s

Reconstr. sent.: dbš msl[c]
ynqhw
šmn mḥlmš ṣr

Comparison: (a-s : a-s :: D)
2 : 2 :: A (List)
3 : 3-C :: /A (Syn)
+ compensation

Result: Formula: A /A (D)
Del.-Comp.: - a-s + compensation
Semantic parallelism: List; Syn
Transformation: none

Dt.32

Text: v.15b ytš 'lh [c]śhw
(w)ynbl ṣr yš[c]th

Translation: He cast off the God who made him;
He treated brutishly the rock of his help.

Met. units: 3:3

Gram. units: 3:3

Syll. symmetry: 7:8 (symmetrical)

Gram. structure: a 2 ,-R(a-s)
a 2-C-s

Transformation: none

Addition: none

Reconstr. sent.: ytš 'lh [c]śhw
ynbl ṣr yš[c]th

Comparison: a : a :: A (List)
2 ,-R(a-s) :: 2-C-s :: A/A (Epith/List)

Result: Formula: A A/A
Del.-Comp.: none
Semantic parallelism: List; Epith
Transformation: none

Dt.32

Text: v.18 sr yldkh tšh
(w)tškḥ 'l mḥllkh

Comment: Reading tiššê(h) for MT's tešî.

Translation: You forgot the rock who conceived you;
You ignored the God who engendered you.

Met. units: 3:3

Gram. units: 3:3

Syll. symmetry: 7:8 (symmetrical)

Gram. structure: 2 ,-R(a-s) a
a 2 ,=2(part.a)-s

Transformation: none

Addition: none

Reconstr. sent.: ṣr yldkh tšh
'l mḥllkh tškḥ

Comparison: 2 : 2 :: A (Epith-Syn)
,-R(a-s) : ,=2(part.a)-s :: A (Syn)
a : a :: A (Syn)

Result: Formula: A A A
Del.-Comp.: none
Semantic parallelism: Epith-Syn; Syn
Transformation: none

Dt.32

Text: v.20a 'strh pny mhm
'r'h mh 'ḥrtm

Comment: Omitting hypermetrical wy'mr at the beginning of the A Line.

Translation: I shall hide my face from them;
I shall see what their end will be.

Met. units: 3:3

Gram. units: 3:3

Syll. symmetry: 7:6 (symmetrical)

Gram. structure: a 2-s 3
a 2(Ppr? S-s)

Transformation: none

Addition: none

Reconstr. sent.: 'strh pny m hm ('tm)
'r'h (mh) 'ḥrtm

Comparison: a 2-s : a :: B/ (Ant)
3-s : 2(Ppr? S-s) :: /C (PR-WP)

Result: Formula: B/ /C
Del.-Comp.: none
Semantic parallelism: Ant; PR-WP
Transformation: none

Dt.32

Text: v.20b ky dr thpkt hmh
bnm l' 'mn bm

Translation: There are a rebellious generation,
Children who have no faithfulness.

Met. units: 3:3

Gram. units: 3:3

Syll. symmetry: 7:6 (symmetrical)

Gram. structure: ptcl P-C Spr
,P ,-R(neg S P(3)-s)

Transformation: none

Addition: + Spr

Reconstr. sent.:
```
      dr   thpkt
ky /                 hmh
      bnm l' 'mn bm
```

Comparison: (Spr : Spr :: D)
ptcl-P-C : ,P ,-R(neg-S P(3)-s) :: A/Ⱥ (Syn)
+ compensation

Result: Formula: A/Ⱥ (D)
Del.-Comp.: - Spr + compensation
Semantic parallelism: Syn
Transformation: none

Dt.32

Text: v.21a hm qn'ny bl' 'l
k^{c}sny bhblhm

Translation: They made me jealous with a non-god;
They angered me with their nothings;

Comment:	This unit forms a close quatrain with the following unit, which could be analyzed as alternating parallelism.
Met. units:	3:3
Gram. units:	3:2
Syll. symmetry:	7:8 (symmetrical)
Gram. structure:	lpr a-s 3 a-s 3-s
Transformation:	none
Addition:	+ lpr
Reconstr. sent.:	qn'ny bl' 'l hm k^{c}sny bhblhm
Comparison:	(lpr : lpr :: D) a-s : a-s :: A (Syn) 3 : 3 :: A* (Syn) + compensation
Result:	Formula: A A* (D) Del.-Comp.: - a-s + compensation Semantic parallelism: Syn Transformation: none

---

<u>Dt.32</u>

Text: v.21b	'ny 'qn'm bl' ^{c}m bgy nbl 'k^{c}sm
Comment:	<u>waw</u> at the beginning of the A Line has been omitted.
Translation:	I shall make them jealous with a non-people; I shall anger them with a brutish nation.
Met. units:	3:3
Gram. units:	3:3
Syll. symmetry:	8:7 (symmetrical)
Gram. structure:	lpr a-s 3 3 ,-3 a-s
Transformation:	none
Addition:	+ lpr
Reconstr. sent.:	'qn'm bl' ^{c}m 'ny 'k^{c}sm bgy nbl

Comparison: (lpr : lpr :: D)
a-s : a-s :: A (Syn)
3 : 3 ,-3 :: /A (Syn)
+ compensation

Result: Formula: A /A (D)
Del.-Comp.: - lpr + compensation
Semantic parallelism: Syn
Transformation: none

Dt.32

Text: v.22a
ky 'š qdḥh b'py
(w)tqd ^{c}d š'l tḥtt

Translation:
A fire has ignited from my nostrils;
It devours down to lowest Sheol.

Comment: Translating the preposition *b* of *b'py* as "from"; cf. *b'pw* II Sam.22:9.

Met. units: 3:3

Gram. units: 3:3

Syll. symmetry: 8:6 (asymmetrical)

Comment: The asymmetry is produced by the treatment of *š'l* as a monosyllabic word.

Gram. structure: ptcl 1 b 3-s
b 3 ,-3

Transformation: none

Addition: + ptcl-1

Reconstr. sent.:
ky 'š qdḥh b'py
tqd ^{c}d š'l tḥtt

Comparison: (ptcl-1 : ptcl-1 :: D)
b : b :: A (Syn)
3-s : 3 ,-3 :: /B (Mer)
+ compensation

Comment: This analysis is based on the assumption that the image presented by the unit is that of the fire of YHWH's wrath proceeding from him in his heavenly abode to the most distant (and, therefore, lowest) extremity of the universe. The picture is similar to that of II Sam.22.

Result:	Formula: A /B (D)
	Del.-Comp.: - ptcl-l + compensation
	Semantic parallelism: Syn; Mer
	Transformation: none

<u>Dt.32</u>

Text: v.22b	t'kl 'rṣ wyblh
	(w)tlhṭ msdy hrm
Comment:	<u>waw</u> is omitted at the beginning of the A Line.
Translation:	It devours the earth and its produce;
	It sets aflame the foundations of the mountains.
Met. units:	3:3
Gram. units:	3:3
Syll. symmetry:	6:8 (asymmetrical)
Gram. structure:	a 2 &2-s
	a 2-C
Transformation:	none
Addition:	none
Reconstr. sent.:	t'kl 'rṣ wyblh
	tlhṭ msdy hrm
Comparison:	a : a :: A (Syn)
	2 &2-s : 2-C :: Ⱥ (List)
Comment:	It is unlikely that merism is intended as in the previous unit.
Result:	Formula: A Ⱥ
	Del.-Comp.: none
	Semantic parallelism: Syn; List
	Transformation: none

<u>Dt.32</u>

Text: v.23	'sph ^{c}lmw r^{c}t
	ḥṣy 'klh bm

Comment: Revocalizing MT's 'aspê(h) as 'ōsîpā(h). Alternatively, one may vocalize 'ōsᵊpā(h) (root: 'sp); cf. Micah 4:6 (parallel to qbṣ). In either case, syllable asymmetry is produced.

Translation: I shall add disasters to them;
I shall use up my arrows against them.

Met. units: 3:3

Gram. units: 3:3

Syll. symmetry: 8:6 (asymmetrical)

Gram. structure: a 3-s 2
2-s a 3-s

Transformation: none

Addition: none

Reconstr. sent.: 'sph ᶜlmw rᶜt
'klh bm ḥṣy

Comparison: a : a :: B (List)
3-s : 3-s :: A (Syn(PR))
2 : 2-s :: A (Abst.-Concr.)

Result: Formula: A A B
Del.-Comp.: none
Semantic parallelism: List; Syn(PR); Abst.-Concr.
Transformation: none

Dt.32

Text: v.24b šn bhmt 'šlḥ bm
ᶜm ḥmt zḥly ᶜpr

Comment: Omitting waw at the beginning of the A Line.

Translation: The fang of beasts I shall send against them,
Along with the venom of gliders in the dust.

Met. units: 3:3

Gram. units: 4:3

Syll. symmetry: 8:8 (symmetrical)

Gram. structure: 2-C a 3-s
,&(prep) 2-C-C

Comment: Since the preposition ^{c}m functions here as a coordinator, it has been marked as &(prep).

Transformation: none

Addition: + a-3-s

Reconstr. sent.:
        šn bhmt
'šlḥ bm
        (^{c}) ḥmt zḥly ^{c}pr

Comparison: (a-3-s : a-3-s :: D/D)
2-C : &(prep)-2-C-C :: A≠Ⱥ (List)
+ compensation

Result: Formula: A≠Ⱥ (D/D)
Del.-Comp.: - a-3-s + compensation
Semantic parallelism: List
Transformation: none

Dt.32

Text: v.25a
mḥṣ tškl ḥrb
(w)mḥdrm 'mh

Translation: Outside the sword will bereave,
Inside, terror.

Met. units: 3:3

Gram. units: 3:2

Syll. symmetry: 6:6 (symmetrical)

Gram. structure: 3 a 1
,3 1

Transformation: none

Addition: + a

Reconstr. sent.:
mḥs   ḥrb
      tškl
mḥdrm   'mh

Comparison: (a : a :: D)
3 : 3 :: A* (Ant)
1 : 1 :: A (Concr.-Abstr.)
+ compensation

Result: Formula: A A* (D)
Del.-Comp.: -a + compensation
Semantic parallelism: Ant; Concr.-Abstr.
Transformation: none

<u>Dt.32</u>

Text: v.25b — gm bḥr gm btlh
ynq ^{c}m 'š śbh

Translation: Both young men and women,
Infants along with old men.

Comment: The nouns are the objects of <u>tškl</u> of the previous unit, with which this one forms a quatrain. The LXX and Vulgate read there <u>tšklm</u>, which is perhaps superior to MT's unsuffixed form.

Met. units: 3:3

Gram. units: 2:3

Comment: The phrase <u>gm</u> <u>btlh</u> has been assigned the value of 2 metrical units.

Syll. symmetry: 7:6 (symmetrical)

Gram. structure: & 2 & 2
,2 &(prep) 2-C

Comment: On the treatment of <u>^{c}m</u> as a coordinator, see v.24b.

Transformation: none

Addition: none

Reconstr. sent.: gm bḥr gm btlh
ynq ^{c}m 'š śbh

Comparison: & 2 & 2 : 2 &(prep) 2-C :: *A/A̸ (List)

Comment: This unit is perhaps refractory as regards the system of analysis. The rather baroque formula is the result of a number of factors: it seems necessary to treat both lines as semantic compounds; the A Line contains only two grammatical units; two metrical units have been assigned the phrase <u>gm</u> <u>btlh</u>. The formula cannot capture the parallelism of the two particles <u>gam</u> and <u>^{c}im</u>, rare in the examples of the <u>Corpus</u>. Note that the unit is syllabically symmetrical.

Result: Formula: *A/A̸
Del.-Comp.: none
Semantic parallelism: List
Transformation: none

Dt.32

Text: v.27b — pn y'mrw ydnw rmh
(w)l' yhwh $p^{c}l$ kl z't

Translation: Lest they say, "Our hand is powerful;
It was not YHWH who did all this."

Met. units: 3:3

Gram. units: 3:3

Syll. symmetry: 9:7 (asymmetrical)

Gram. structure: ptcl a 2(l-s b)
,2(neg lpn a "2"-Cpr)

Transformation: none

Comment: No transformation is required since, in the case of ydnw rmh, we are dealing with an idiom.

Addition: + ptcl-a

Reconstr. sent.:
ydnw rmh (rm)
pn y'mrw
l' yhwh $p^{c}l$ ($p^{c}lw$) kl z't

Comparison: (ptcl-a : ptcl-a :: D)
l-s : neg-lpn :: B (WP-PN)
b : a "2"-Cpr :: /B (Syn)
+ compensation

Result: Formula: B /B (D)
Del.-Comp.: - ptcl-a + compensation
Semantic parallelism: WP-PN; Syn
Transformation: none

Dt.32

Text: v.28 — ky gy 'bd ^{c}ṣt hmh
(w)'n bhm tbnh

Translation: They are a nation without counsel,
In whom there is no understanding.

Met. units: 3:3

Gram. units: 4:3

Syll. symmetry: 8:6 (asymmetrical)

Gram. structure: ptcl P ,-R(part.b)-C Spr
, ,-R("neg b" P(3)-s l)

Comment: This grammatical analysis will facilitate the process of comparison.

Transformation: none

Reconstr. sent.:

```
        'bd ᶜṣt
ky gy                 hmh
        'n bhm tbnh
```

Comparison: (ptcl-P : ptcl-P :: D)
,-P(part.b)-C-Spr : ,-R("neg'b"-P(3)-s 1) ::
/A/ (Syn)
+ compensation

Result: Formula: /A/ (D)
Del.-Comp.: - ptcl-P + compensation
Semantic parallelism: Syn
Transformation:none

Dt.32

Text: v.29 lw ḥkmw yśklw z't
ybnw l'ḥrtm

Translation: If they were wise they would comprehend this;
They would have concern for their end.

Comment: LXX takes lw as negative l' (cf. I Sam.20:2); the Vulgate continues its force throughout the rest of the unit. This interpretation would not affect the basic formula.

Met. units: 3:3

Gram. units: 3:2

Syll. symmetry: 8:7 (symmetrical)

Gram. structure: ptcl b a 2pr
,a 3-s

Comment: ybnw l is a compound verb. No transformation is necessary to line up parallel terms.

Transformation: none

Addition: + ptcl-b

Reconstr. sent.:

```
          yśklw  z't
lw ḥkmw
          ybnw l 'ḥrtm
```

Comparison:	(ptcl-b : ptcl-b :: D)
	a : a :: A (Syn)
	2pr : 3-s :: C* (PR-Syn)
	+ compensation
Result:	Formula: A C* (D)
	Del.-Comp.: - ptcl-b + compensation
	Semantic parallelism: Syn; PR-Syn
	Transformation: none

<u>Dt.32</u>

Text: v.30a	'kh yrdp 'ḥd 'lp
	(w)šnym ynsw rbbh
Translation:	How can one pursue a thousand,
	Or two give chase to ten thousand,
Met. units:	3:3
Comment:	<u>'kh</u> has not been awarded the value of a metrical unit (or grammatical unit) despite the fact that it is not a monosyllable.
Gram. units:	3:3
Syll. symmetry:	7:7 (symmetrical)
Gram. structure:	ptcl? a 1 a
	,1 a 2
Transformation:	none
Addition:	none
Reconstr. sent.:	yrdp (yrdpw) 'ḥd 'lp 'kh ynsw (yns) šnym rbbh
Comparison:	ptcl?-a : a :: A (Syn)
	1 : 1 :: A (Num)
	2 : 2 :: A (Num)
Result:	Formula: A A A
	Del.-Comp.: none
	Semantic parallelism: Syn; Num
	Transformation: none

Dt.32

Text: v.30b 'm l' ṣrm mkrm
(w)yhwh hsgrm

Comment: Omitting ky.

Translation: Unless their rock turn them over,
YHWH deliver them up.

Comment: This unit forms a quatrain with the preceding one.

Met. units: 3:3

Gram. units: 3:2

Comment: The particles 'm l' have been awarded together the value of one metrical and grammatical unit. Note the contrast with the treatment of 'kh in the previous unit.

Syll. symmetry: 7:5 (asymmetrical)

Comment: The unit remains asymmetrical even with the omission of ky in the A Line. The VSS do not seem to ease the situation.

Gram. structure: ptcl neg l-s a-s
,lpn a-s

Transformation: none

Addition: + ptcl-neg

Reconstr. sent.: 'm l' ṣrm mkrm / yhwh hsgrm

Comparison: (ptcl-neg : ptcl-neg :: D)
l-s : lpn :: A (Epith-PN)
a-s : a-s :: A* (Syn)
+ Ø

Result: Formula: A A* (D)
Del.-Comp.: - ptcl-neg + Ø
Semantic parallelism: Epith-PN; Syn
Transformation: none

Dt.32

Text: v.32a ky mgpn sdm gpnm
(w)mšdmt ^{c}mrh

Translation:	Their vine is from the vines of Sodom, From the terraces of Gomorrah.
Met. units:	3:3
Gram. units:	3:2
Syll. symmetry:	7:6 (symmetrical)
Gram. structure:	ptcl P(3)-Cpn S-s ,P(3)-Cpn
Transformation:	none
Addition:	+ S-s
Reconstr. sent.:	ky ⟨ mgpn sdm / mšdmt ᶜmrh ⟩ gpnm
Comparison:	(S-s : S-s :: D) ptcl-P(3)-Cpn : P(3)-Cpn :: A/A*(D) (List; List(PN)) + compensation
Result:	Formula: A/A* (D) Del.-Comp.: -S-s + compensation Semantic parallelism: List; List(PN) Transformation: none

---

Dt.32

Text: v.32b	ᶜnbmw ᶜnby rš 'šklt mrrt lmw
Translation:	Their grapes are venomous grapes Which have bitter clusters.
Met. units:	3:3
Gram. units:	3:3
Syll. symmetry:	8:8 (symmetrical)
Gram. structure:	S-s P-C ,S ,-S P(3)-s
Transformation:	none
Addition:	+ S-s
Reconstr. sent.:	ᶜnbmw ⟨ ᶜnby rš / 'šklt mrrt lmw ⟩
Comment:	This is the simplest way of lining up the parallel terms. Note that in the reconstructed sentence the B Line has become part

of a sentence with casus pendens. In effect, a type of transformation has taken place. In other cases, where the A Line has casus pendens, it was necessary to perform a transformation of the B Line to a sentence with the same structure. In this example, however, where the casus pendens structure in the reconstructed sentence results from the addition, it is unnecessary to perform such a transformation. The structure of the B Line must now be understood to be:

ᶜnbmw 'šklt mrrt lmw: 3-s S ,-S P(3)-s

However, the larger structure is S(3-s) P(S ,-S p(3)-s); hence, it is possible to compare ᶜnby rš and 'šklt mrrt lmw directly; cf. Ps.89:12.

Comparison:	(S-s : S-s :: D) P-C : S ,-S P(3)-s :: A/A̸ (List/Syn) + compensation
Result:	Formula: A/A̸ (D) Del.-Comp.: -S-s + compensation Semantic parallelism: List; Syn Transformation: none

---

Dt.32

Text: v.33	ḥmt tnnm ynm (w)r'š ptnm 'kzr
Translation:	Their wine is the poison of serpents, The harsh venom of vipers.
Met. units:	3:3
Gram. units:	3:3
Syll. symmetry:	7:6 (symmetrical)
Gram. structure:	P-C S-s ,P-C ,-P
Transformation:	none
Addition:	+ S-s

Reconstr. sent.: ḥmt tnnm / ynm / r'š ptnm 'kzr

Comparison: (S-s : S-s :: D)
P-C : P-C ,-P :: A/A̸ (Syn)
+ compensation

Result: Formula: A/A̸ (D)
Del.-Comp.: - S-s + compensation
Semantic parallelism: Syn
Transformation: none

Comment: Alternatively, one may posit the following reconstructed sentence:
ḥmt tnnm / ynm 'kzr ('kzrh) / r'š ptnm
The resulting formula would be: A/A (D) with deletion-compensation: - S-s + ,-P.

Dt.32

Text: v.34 hl' h' kms ᶜmdy
ḥtm b'ṣrty

Translation: Is this not stored up with me,
Sealed in my treasuries,

Met. units: 3:3

Gram. units: 3:3

Syll. symmetry: 8:7 (symmetrical)

Gram. structure: ptcl? Spr P(part.c) 3-s
,P(part.c) 3-s

Transformation: none

Addition: + ptcl?-Spr

Reconstr. sent.: kms ᶜmdy / hl' h' / ḥtm b'ṣrty

Comparison: (ptcl?-Spr : ptcl?-Spr :: D)
P(part.c) : P(part.c) :: A (Syn)
3-s : 3-s :: C* (PR-Syn)
+ compensation

Result: Formula: A C* (D)
Del.-Comp.: - ptcl?-Spr + compensation
Semantic parallelism: Syn; PR-Syn
Transformation: none

<u>Dt.32</u>

Text: v.35a lym nqm wšlm
l^{c}t tmṭ rglm

Comment: MT's <u>ly</u> emended to <u>lym</u>, following the LXX.

Translation: For the day of vengeance and recompense,
For the time when their foot stumbles.

Comment: This unit forms a quatrain with the preceding unit.

Met. units: 3:3

Gram. units: 3:3

Syll. symmetry: 7:6 (symmetrical)

Gram. structure: 3-C &-C
,3 ,-R(b l-s)

Transformation: none

Addition: none

Reconstr. sent.: lym nqm wšlm
l^{c}t tmṭ rglm

Comparison: 3-C &-C : 3 ,-R(b l-s) :: A//Ø (Syn/Met)

Result: Formula: A//Ø
Del.-Comp.: none
Semantic parallelism: Syn; Met
Transformation: none

<u>Dt.32</u>

Text: v.35b ky qrb ym 'dm
(w)ḥš ^{c}tdt lmw

Translation: The day of their destruction is near;
That which will happen to them hastens.

Met. units: 3:3

Gram. units: 3:3

Syll. symmetry: 6:6 (symmetrical)

Gram. structure: ptcl P(part.b) S-C-s
P(part.b) S 3-s

Transformation: none

Addition: none

Reconstr. sent.: ky / qrb ym 'dm
ḥš ᶜtdt lmw

Comparison: ptcl-P(part.b) : P(part.b) :: A (Syn)
S-C-s : S 3-s :: B̸ (PW)

Comment: ᶜtdt lmw is a hapax. This analysis assumes that the phrase is the functional equivalent of ᶜtdthm.

Result: Formula: A B̸
Del.-Comp.: none
Semantic parallelism: Syn
Transformation: none

Comment: Alternatively, one may posit the following reconstructed sentence:

ky / qrb ym 'dm lmw
ḥš ᶜtdt

The resulting formula will be A B/ with no deletion but with compensation: + 3-s.

Dt.32

Text: v.36a ky ydn yhwh ᶜmh
(w)ᶜl ᶜbdw ytnḥm

Translation: YHWH will judge his people;
He will consider mercy for his servants.

Comment: Or, for ytnḥm, "consider redress" or the like; cf. Speiser's comments in the Anchor Genesis on Gen.27:42. Possibly even "avenge" is not inappropriate here; cf. Isa.1:24 where nḥm (niphal) is parallel to nqm. This seems to be also the sense of Targum's paraphrase of this verse.

Met. units: 3:3

Gram. units: 3:2

Syll. symmetry: 7:7 (symmetrical)

Gram. structure: ptcl a lpn 2-s
3-s c

Comment: No transformation is necessary since <u>yt̮nḥm</u> <u>^{c}l</u> is a compound verb.

Transformation: none

Addition: + lpn

Reconstr. sent.:

```
       ydn        ᶜmh
ky⁄                        yhwh
       ytnḥm ᶜl   ᶜbdw
```

Comparison: (lpn : lpn :: D)
ptcl-a : c :: B (Syn)
2-s : 3-s :: A* (Syn)
+ compensation

Result: Formula: B A* (D)
Del.-Comp.: - lpn + compensation
Semantic parallelism: Syn
Transformation: none

<u>Dt.32</u>

Text: v.37 'mr 'y 'lhmw
ṣr ḥsyw bh

Comment: Omitting <u>waw</u> at the beginning of the A Line.

Translation: He will say, "Where is their god;
The rock in whom they trusted,

Met. units: 3:3

Gram. units: 3:3

Syll. symmetry: 7:5 (asymmetrical)

Gram. structure: a 2(P(3?) S-s)
,2(S ,-R(b 3-s))

Transformation: none

Addition: + a
+ P(3?)

Reconstr. sent.:

```
           'lhmw
'mr 'y              ḥsyw bh
           ṣr
```

Comparison: (a : a :: D)
(P(3?) : P(3?) :: D)
S-s : S :: A (Epith)
+ ,-R(b
+ 3-s)

Result: Formula: A (D D)
Del.-Comp.: -a + ,-R(b
-P(3?) + 3-s)
Semantic parallelism: Epith
Transformation: none

Dt.32

Text: v.38a ḥlb zbḥmw y'klw
yštw yn nskmw

Comment: 'šr is omitted as a prosaic addition. Read plural nskmw (nᵊsîkēmô) with the VSS.

Translation: Who ate the fat of their sacrifices;
Who drank the wine of their libations?"

Comment: This unit forms a quatrain with the preceding one.

Met. units: 3:3

Gram. units: 3:3

Syll. symmetry: 8:7 (symmetrical)

Gram. structure: ,-R(2-C-s a)
,-R(a 2-C-s)

Transformation: none

Addition: none

Reconstr. sent.: y'klw ḥlb zbhmw
yštw yn nskmw

Comparison: a 2-C-s : a 2-C-s :: A≠A≠A (List)

Result: Formula: A≠A≠A
Del.-Comp.: none
Semantic parallelism: List
Transformation: none

Dt.32

Text: v.38b — yqmw wy^{c}zrkm
yhyw ^{c}lkm strh

Comment: Read plural yhyw with the VSS.

Translation: Let them arise to help you;
Let them be your protection!

Met. units: 3:3

Gram. units: 3:3

Syll. symmetry: 8:7 (symmetrical)

Gram. structure: b! &a!-s
"b!" 3-s P

Transformation: none

Comment: No transformation is necessary since the B Line is a "quasi-verbal" sentence.

Addition: + b!

Reconstr. sent.:
      wy^{c}zrkm
yqmw
      yhyw ^{c}lkm strh

Comparison: (b! : b! :: D)
&a!-s : "b!" 3-s P :: */A̸ (Syn)
+ compensation

Result: Formula: */A̸ (D)
Del.-Comp.: - b! + compensation
Semantic parallelism: Syn
Transformation: none

Dt.32

Text: v.39c-e — 'ny 'mt w'ḥyh
mḥṣty w'ny 'rp'
(w)'n mydy mṣl

Translation: I kill and make well;
I smite and I heal;
No one can save from my hand.

Met. units: 3:3:3

Gram. units: 3:3:3

Syll. symmetry: 8:8:6 (B and C Lines asymmetrical)

Gram. structure: lpr a &a
a &lpr a
"neg b" P(3)-s S

A-B Lines

Transformation: none

Addition: none

Reconstr. sent.: (w)'ny 'mt w'ḥyh / mḥṣty (w)'rp'

Comment: This arrangement probably requires the placing of a waw before 'rp'.

Comparison: lpr : &lpr :: D
a : a :: A (Syn)
&a : a :: A (Syn)

Result: Formula: D A A
Del.-Comp.: none
Semantic parallelism: D; Syn
Transformation: none

B-C Lines

Result: Non-parallel unit (VS-QVS)

Dt.32

Text: v.41b 'šb nqm lṣry
(w)lmśn'y 'šlm

Translation: I shall punish my foes;
I shall pay back my enemies.

Met. units: 3:3

Gram. units: 3:2

Syll. symmetry: 7:6 (symmetrical)

Gram. structure: a 2 3-s
3-s a

Transformation: none

Addition: none

Reconstr. sent.: 'šb nqm lṣry
'šlm lmśn'y

Comparison: a 2 : a :: A/ (Syn)
3-s : 3-s :: A* (Syn)

Result: Formula: A/ A*
Del.-Comp.: none
Semantic parallelism: Syn
Transformation: none

<u>Dt.32</u>

Text: v.42a 'škr ḥṣy mdm
(w)ḥrby t'kl bśr

Translation: I shall make my arrows drunk with blood;
My sword will devour flesh.

Met. units: 3:3

Gram. units: 3:2

Syll. symmetry: 6:6 (symmetrical)

Gram. structure: a 2-s 3
1-s a 2

Transformation: 1-s a 2 --→ 2-s a 2

Comment: The result of the transformation is a sentence with causative verb with two objects:
ḥarbî 'a'ăk̲îl bāśār

Addition: none

Reconstr. sent.: 'škr m/dm ḥṣy
''kl bśr ḥrby

Comparison: a 3 : a 2 :: A≠A (List)
2-s : 2-s :: A (List)

Result: Formula: A A≠A
Del.-Comp.: none
Semantic parallelism: List
Transformation: 2-s a 2 --→ 1-s a 2

<u>Dt.33</u>

Text: v.2a-c yhw mśn b'
(w)zrḥ mś^{c}r lm
hp^{c} mhr pr'n

Comment: Whether one reads in the B Line <u>ln</u> with the VSS or <u>lm</u> with MT does not affect analysis.

Translation: YHWH came from Sinai;
He shone from Seir to them;
He beamed forth from Mount Paran.

Met. units: 3:3:3

Gram. units: 3:3:3

Syll. symmetry: 6:7:6 (symmetrical)

Gram. structure: 1pn 3pn b
b 3pn 3-s
b 3-Cpn

A-B Lines

Transformation: none

Addition: + 1pn

Reconstr. sent.:

```
     mśn    b'
yhw               lm
     mś^cr  zrḥ
```

Comparison: (1pn : 1pn :: D)
3pn : 3pn :: A (List(PN))
b : b :: C (Met)
+ 3-s

Result: Formula: A C (D)
Del.-Comp.: - 1pn + 3-s
Semantic parallelism: List(PN); Met
Transformation: none

B-C Lines

Transformation: none

Addition: + 3-s

Reconstr. sent.:

```
zrḥ  mś^cr
                lm
hp^c  mhr pr'n
```

Comparison: (3-s : 3-s :: D)
b : b :: A (Syn)
3pn : 3-Cpn :: /A (List(PN))
+ compensation

Result: Formula: A /A (D)
Del.-Comp.: - 3-s + compensation
Semantic parallelism: Syn; List(PN)
Transformation: none

Dt.33

Text: v.6 — yḥ r'bn w'l ymt
(w)yhy mtw mspr

Translation: May Reuben live and not die;
May his men (not) be few!

Comment: This translation assures that the force of the negative particle '1 continues in the B Line. On the idiom involved in mtw mspr, see C-F.

Met. units: 3:3

Gram. units: 3:3

Syll. symmetry: 9:6 (asymmetrical)

Gram. structure: b! lpn &neg b!
"b!" S-s P

Transformation: none

Comment: No transformation is necessary since the B Line is a "quasi-verbal" sentence and, in any case, forms an idiomatic unit.

Addition: + b!
+ lpn

Reconstr. sent.: yḥ r'bn w'l ⟨ ymt / yhy mtw mspr ⟩

Comparison: (b! : b! :: D)
(lpn : lpn :: D)
&neg-b! : "b!" S-s P :: /∅ (Syn)
+ compensation

Result: Formula: /∅ (D D)
Del.-Comp.: - b! + compensation
- lpn
Semantic parallelism: Syn
Transformation: none

Dt.33

Text: v.11a — brk yhw ḥl
(w)p^{c}l ydw trṣ

Translation: Bless, O YHWH, his strength;
Accept the work of his hands!

Met. units: 3:3
Gram. units: 3:3
Syll. symmetry: 6:5 (symmetrical)
Gram. structure: a! lpn! 2-s
2-C-s a!
Transformation: none
Addition: + lpn!
Reconstr. sent.: brk ḥl
yhw
trṣ p^cl ydw
Comparison: (lpn! : lpn! :: D)
a! : a! :: A (List)
2-s : 2-C-s :: /A (Abstr.-Concr.)
+ compensation
Result: Formula: A /A (D)
Del.-Comp.: - lpn! + compensation
Semantic parallelism: List; Abstr.-Concr.
Transformation: none

Dt.33
Text: v.11b mḥṣ mtnm qmw
(w)mś́n'w mn yqmn
Translation: Smite the loins of his adversaries,
Of his enemies, whoever attacks him!
Comment: Text and interpretation following C-F.
Met. units: 3:3
Gram. units: 3:3
Syll. symmetry: 7:8 (symmetrical)
Gram. structure: a! 2-encl.mem-C-s
,-C-s ,-R(lpr? a-s)
Transformation: none
Addition: + a!
+ 2-encl.mem-
Reconstr. sent.: qmw
mḥṣ mtnm mn yqmn
mś́n'w

Comparison: (a! : a! :: D)
(2encl.<u>mem</u>- : 2encl.<u>mem</u>- :: D)
-C-s : -C-s :: A (Syn)
+ ,-R(1pr?
+ a-s)

Result: Formula: A (D D)
Del.-Comp.: - a! + ,-R(1pr?
- 2encl.-<u>mem</u>- + a-s)
Semantic parallelism: Syn
Transformation: none

<u>Dt.33</u>

Text: v.13 mbrkt yhw 'rṣ
mmgd šmm m^{c}l
(w)mthm rbṣt tḥt

Comment: Reading <u>m^{c}l</u> for MT's <u>mṭl</u>; see C-F.

Translation: Blessed by YHWH is his land,
From the abundance of the heavens above,
From the deep crouching below.

Met. units: 3:3:3

Gram. units: 3:3:3

Syll. symmetry: 7:6:6 (symmetrical)

Gram. structure: P(part.c)-Cpn S-s
3-C ,-R(3)
, 3 ,-R(part.b 3)

<u>A-B Lines</u>

Result: Non-parallel unit (enjambment)

<u>B-C Lines</u>

Transformation: none

Addition: + 3-

Reconstr. sent.:
šmm m^{c}l
mmgd
(m)thm rbṣt (rbṣm) tḥt

Comparison: (3- : 3- :: D)
-C : 3 :: A (Mer)
,-R(3) : ,-R(part.b 3) :: /A (Ant)
+ compensation

Result: Formula: A /A (D)
Del.-Comp.: - 3- + compensation
Semantic parallelism: Mer; Ant
Transformation: none

Text: v.14 mmgd tb't šmš
mmgd grš yrḥ

Comment: <u>mem</u> of MT's <u>yrḥm</u> omitted; <u>grš</u> is taken as plural with Sam (C-F).

Translation: From the abundance of the crops of the sun,
From the abundance of the produce of the moon,

Met. units: 3:3

Gram. units: 3:3

Syll. symmetry: 6:5 (symmetrical)

Gram. structure: 3-C-C
,3-C-C

Transformation: none

Addition: none

Reconstr. sent.: mmgd tb't šmš
mmgd grš yrḥ

Comparison: 3-C-C : 3-C-C :: D/A/A (Syn; List)

Result: Formula: D/A/A
Del.-Comp.: none
Semantic parallelism: D; Syn; List
Transformation: none

<u>Dt.33</u>

Text: v.15 mmgd hrr qdm
mmgd gb^{c}t ^{c}lm

Comment: Text following C-F.

Translation: From the abundance of the ancient mountains,
From the abundance of the eternal hills,

Met. units: 3:3

Gram. units: 3:3

Syll. symmetry: 5:6 (symmetrical)

Gram. structure: 3-C-C
,3-C-C

Transformation: none

Addition: none

Reconstr. sent.: mmgd hrr qdm
mmgd gb^{c}t ^{c}lm

Comparison: 3-C-C : 3-C-C : D/A/A (Syn)

Result: Formula: D/A/A
Del.-Comp.: none
Semantic parallelism: none
Transformation: none

<u>Dt.33</u>

Text: v.16a mmgd 'rṣ wml'h
(w)rṣn škn sn

Comment: Omitting <u>waw</u> at the beginning of the A Line.

Translation: From the abundance of the earth and its fullness,
The favor of the Dweller at Sinai.

Comment: Interpretation following C-F.

Met. units: 3:3

Gram. units: 3:3

Syll. symmetry: 7:7 (symmetrical)

Gram. structure: ,3-C-&-C-s
,-C-C-Cpn

Result: Non-parallel unit (enjambment)

<u>Dt.33</u>

Text: v.16b th lr'š ysp
(w)lqdqd nzr 'ḥw

Comment: Reading <u>th</u>, which is closer to the parallel text in Gen.49.

Translation: Let it be on the head of Joseph,
On the pate of the leader of his brothers!

Met. units: 3:3

Gram. units: 3:3

Syll. symmetry: 6:7 (symmetrical)
Gram. structure: "b!" P(3)-Cpn
,P(3)-C-C-s
Transformation: none
Addition: + "b!"
Reconstr. sent.: lr'š ysp
th
lqdqd nzr 'ḥw
Comparison: ("b!" : "b!" :: D)
P(3)-Cpn : P(3)-C-C-s :: A/A̸ (WP; PN-Epith)
+ compensation
Result: Formula: A/A̸ (D)
Del.-Comp.: - "b!" + compensation
Semantic parallelism: WP; PN-Epith
Transformation: none

<u>Dt.33</u>
Text: v.17c hm rbbt 'prm
(w)hm 'lp mnš
Comment: <u>waw</u> omitted before the A Line.
Translation: Behold the multitudes of Ephraim;
Behold the thousands of Manasseh!
Comment: <u>hm</u> as in Ugaritic (C-F).
Met. units: 3:3
Gram. units: 3:3
Syll. symmetry: 6:6 (symmetrical)
Gram. structure: P(ptcl!) S-Cpn
P(ptcl!) S-Cpn
Transformation: none
Addition: none
Reconstr. sent.: rbbt 'prm
hm
'lp mnš
Comparison: P(ptcl!) : P(ptcl!) :: D
S-Cpn : S-Cpn :: A/A (Num/List(PN))
Result: Formula: D A/A
Del.-Comp.: none
Semantic parallelism: Num; List(PN)
Transformation: none

Dt.33

Text: v.18 — śmḥ zbln bṣ'tk
(w)yśśkr b'hlk

Comment: The unit is syllabically symmetrical and needs no addition to the B Line.

Translation: Rejoice, O Zebulon, in your going forth,
Issachar, in your tents!

Met. units: 3:3

Gram. units: 3:2

Syll. symmetry: 9:8 (symmetrical)

Gram. structure: b! lpn! 3(inf.const.b)-s
,lpn! 3-s

Transformation: none

Addition: + b!

Reconstr. sent.:
```
     zbln   bṣ'tk
śmh
     yśśkr  b'hlk
```

Comparison: (b! : b! :: D)
lpn! : lpn! :: A (List(PN))
3(inf.const.b)-s : 3-s :: B* (Ant)
+ compensation

Result: Formula: A B* (D)
Del.-Comp.: - b! + compensation
Semantic parallelism: List(PN); Ant
Transformation: none

Dt.33

Text: v.20b — gd klb' škn
(w)ṭrp zr[c] 'p qdqd

Comment: Adding gd to the A Line; see C-F.

Translation: Gad lies in wait like a lion;
He tears arm and head.

Comment: On the translation of lb', see Speiser, *Genesis*, to Gen.49:9.

Met. units: 3:3

Gram. units: 3:3

Syll. symmetry: 6:7 (symmetrical)

Gram. structure: Spn "3" P(part.b)
P(part.a) 2 &2
Result: Non-parallel unit (NS-NS)

<u>Dt.33</u>
Text: v.22 dn gr 'ry
yznq mn (h)bšn
Comment: Retaining MT's <u>mn</u>.
Translation: Dan is a lion's whelp
Which springs away from a viper.
Comment: Translation of <u>bšn</u> following C-F.
Met. units: 3:3
Gram. units: 3:2
Syll. symmetry: 4:6 (asymmetrical)
Gram. structure: Spn P-C
b 3
Result: Non-parallel unit (NS-VS)

<u>Dt.33</u>
Text: v.23 nptl śb^{c} rṣn
(w)ml' brkt yhw
ym wdrm yrš
Comment: Reading <u>yîraš</u>; see C-F.
Translation: Naphtali is sated with favor,
Full of the blessings of YHWH;
He shall take possession of the West and the South.
Met. units: 3:3:3
Gram. units: 3:3:3
Syll. symmetry: 7:6:6 (symmetrical)
Gram. structure: Spn P(part.b)-C
,P(part.b) 2-Cpn
2 &2 a

<u>A-B Lines</u>
Transformation: none
Addition: + Spn

Reconstr. sent.: śb^c rṣn / nptl / ml' brkt yhw

Comparison: (Spn : Spn :: D)
P(part.b)-C : P(part.b) 2-Cpn :: A/A̸ (Syn-PN)
+ compensation

Result: Formula: A/A̸ (D)
Del.-Comp.: - Spn + compensation
Semantic parallelism: Syn-PN

B-C Lines

Result: Non-parallel unit (NS-VS)

Dt.33

Text: v.24
brk mbnm 'šr
yhy rṣy 'ḥw
ṭbl bšmn rglw

Translation:
Asher is the most blessed of the sons;
He is the most favored of his brothers,
Dipping his feet in oil.

Comment: Alternatively, one may retain MT's yhy as precative and make the necessary adjustments in the grammatical notation. The meter, however, is not affected.

Met. units: 3:3:3

Gram. units: 3:3:3

Syll. symmetry: 7:6:6 (symmetrical)

Gram. structure:
P(part.c) 3 Spn
"b" P(part.c)-C-s
,P(part.a) 3 2

A-B Lines

Transformation: none

Addition: + Spn

Reconstr. sent.: brk mbnm / 'šr / yhy rṣy 'ḥw

Comparison: (Spn : Spn :: D)
P(part.c) 3 : "b" P(part.c)-C-s :: A/A̸ (Syn)
+ compensation

Result: Formula: A/Ⱥ (D)
Del.-Comp.: - Spn + compensation
Semantic parallelism: Syn
Transformation: none

<u>B-C Lines</u>

Result: Non-parallel unit (QVS-NS)

<u>Dt.33</u>

Text: v.28a yškn yśr'l bṭḥ
bdd ^{c}n y^{c}qb

Comment: Following the emendation of MT's <u>^{c}yn</u> to <u>^{c}n</u> ("dwell"), despite the lack of support from the VSS; see C-F.

Translation: Israel encamps in safety;
Jacob dwells securely.

Met. units: 3:3

Gram. units: 3:3

Syll. symmetry: 6:5 (symmetrical)

Gram. structure: b 1pn 3
3 b 1pn

Transformation: none

Addition: none

Reconstr. sent.: yškn yśr'l bṭḥ
^{c}n y^{c}qb bdd

Comparison: b : b :: A (Syn)
1pn : 1pn :: A (Syn(PN))
3 : 3 :: A (Syn)

Result: Formula: A A A
Del.-Comp.: none
Semantic parallelism: Syn(PN); Syn
Transformation: none

<u>Dt.33</u>

Text: v.28b ^{c}l 'rṣ dgn wtrš
'p šmw y^{c}rp ṭl

Comment: Reading ^c^l with Sam. for MT's 'l and 'arṣô (C-F).

Translation: On his land are grain and wine;
His heavens drip dew.

Met. units: 3:3

Gram. units: 3:3

Syll. symmetry: 8:7 (symmetrical)

Gram. structure: P(3)-s S &S
ptcl 1-s a 2

Transformation: 1. ptcl 1-s a 2 --→ ptcl S-s P(part.a) 2
2. ptcl S-s P(part.a) 2 --→ ptcl 3-s P(part.c) S

Comment: The first transformation produces a nominal sentence, the second a passive participle, with rearrangement of subject and object: "From his heavens dew is dropped" ('p mšmw n^c^rp ṭl). It is possible that the transformed sentence, if it existed in fact, would be 'p mšmw m^c^rp ṭl, "From his heavens is a dripping of dew"; cf. the phrase m^c^rp ^c^nn in Ecclesiasticus 43:22.

Addition: none

Reconstr. sent.: ^c^l 'rṣ dgn wtrš
('p) (m)šmw n^c^rp ṭl

Comparison: P(3)-s S &S : ptcl-3-s P(part.c) 2 :: A//A (Mer/List)

Result: Formula: A//A
Del.-Comp.: none
Semantic parallelism: Mer; List
Transformation:
1. ptcl 3-s P(part.c) S --→ ptcl S-s P(part.a) 2
2. ptcl S-s P(part.a) 2 --→ ptcl 1-s a 2

Dt.33

Text: v.29c ykḥš 'ybk lk
(w)'t ^c^l bmtm tdrk

Comment: Omitting *waw* at the beginning of the A Line.

Translation: Your enemies shall cringe before you;
You shall tread upon their backs.

Met. units: 3:3

Gram. units: 3:3

Syll. symmetry: 10:9 (symmetrical)

Gram. structure: c 1-s 3-s
lpr 3-s b

Transformation: lpr 3-s b --→ 3-s 1-s c

Comment: The result of the transformation is a passive sentence *bmtm lk tdrkn*, "Their backs are trod upon by you" or the like. Often a transformation is not necessary when a passive verb is parallel to an intransitive one. In this case, however, the parallel terms must be lined up for analysis. *drk* ^{c}*l* is a unit which, in any case, is equivalent to a transitive verb. In fact, *drk* in its meaning of "to tread" is sometimes treated as a transitive verb; cf. Job 24:11; Amos 9:13; Micah 6:15.

Addition: none

Reconstr. sent.:

ykḥš (tkḥšn)		'ybk
	lk	
tdrkn (ydrk)		bmtm

Comment: The hypothetical sentence *ykḥš lk bmtm* "their backs cringe before you" or the like is forced, but analysis shall proceed nevertheless. It does not seem necessary to treat *tdrkn bmtm* as an indivisible idiomatic unit.

Comparison: c : c :: A (List)
1-s : 1-s :: A (WP)
3-s : 3-s :: C (Syn(PR))

Result: Formula: A A C
Del.-Comp.: none
Semantic parallelism: WP; List; Syn(PR)
Transformation: 3-s 1-s c --→ lpr 3-s b

Jud.5

Text: v.3 — šm^{c} mlkm // h'zn rznm
'nk lyhw // 'nk 'šr
'zmr lyhw / 'lh yśr'l

Translation: Hear, O kings; heed, O rulers;
I to YHWH, I shall sing;
I shall hymn YHWH, the God of Israel!

Met. units: 4:4:4(2:2::2:2::2:2)

Gram. units: 4:4:4(2:2::2:2::2:2)

Syll. symmetry: 5:6::6:6::6:6 (symmetrical)

Gram. structure: a! 1! // a! 1!
lpr 3pn // lpr a
a 3pn / ,=3-Cpn

A-B Lines

Result: Non-parallel unit (VS-VS)

B-C Lines

Transformation: none

Addition: + lpr
+ lpr

Reconstr. sent.:
      'šr
'nk   lyhw 'lh yśr'l
      'zmr

Comparison: (lpr : lpr :: D)
(lpr : lpr :: D)
3pn : 3pn :: D(PN)
a : a :: A (Syn)
+ ,=3-
+ -Cpn

Result: Formula: D A (D D)
Del.-Comp.: - lpr + ,=3-
- lpr + -Cpn
Semantic parallelism: D(PN); Syn
Transformation: none

Jud.5

Text: v.17c-d — yšb lḥp ymm
(w)^{c}l mprṣw yškn

Comment: Omitting the tribal name <u>'šr</u> at the beginning of the A Line; see C-F.

Translation: He dwells at the coast of the sea;
He encamps along its bays.

Met. units: 3:3

Gram. units: 3:2

Syll. symmetry: 6:6 (symmetrical)

Gram. structure: b 3-C
3-s b

Transformation: none

Addition: none

Reconstr. sent.: yšb lḥp ymm
yškn ᶜl mprṣw

Comparison: b : b :: A (Syn)
3-C : 3-s :: A/* (Syn)

Result: Formula: A A/*
Del.-Comp.: none
Semantic parallelism: Syn
Transformation: none

<u>Jud.5</u>

Text: v.19a b' mlkm nlḥm
'z nlḥm mlk knᶜn

Comment: It is unnecessary for analysis to remove <u>'z</u> from the beginning of the B Line.

Translation: The kings came; they fought;
Then the kings of Canaan fought.

Met. units: 3:3

Gram. units: 3:3

Syll. symmetry: 8:8 (symmetrical)

Gram. structure: b l c
3 c l-Cpn

Transformation: none

Addition: + b

Reconstr. sent.: b' mlk(m) knᶜn 'z nlḥm

Comparison:	(b : b :: D)
	1 : 1- :: "D"
	c : 3-c :: D
	+ -Cpn
Result:	Formula: "D" D (D)
	Del.-Comp.: -b + -Cpn
	Semantic parallelism: "D"; D
	Transformation: none

<u>Jud.5</u>

Text: v.19b	bt^{c}nk ^{c}l m mgd
	bṣ^{c} ksp l' lqḥ
Translation:	At Taanach by the waters of Megiddo
	They did not take booty of silver.
Met. units:	3:3
Gram. units:	3:3
Syll. symmetry:	8:6 (asymmetrical)
Gram. structure:	3pn ,-R(3-Cpn)
	2-C neg a
Result:	Non-parallel unit (enjambment)

<u>Jud.5</u>

Text: v.20	mn šmm nlḥm (h)kkbm
	mmzltm nlḥm ^{c}m ssr'
Comment:	On the text, see C-F.
Translation:	From heaven the stars fought;
	From their courses they fought with Sisera.
Met. units:	3:3
Gram. units:	3:3
Syll. symmetry:	9:12 (asymmetrical)
Gram. structure:	3 c 1
	3-s c 3pn
Transformation:	none
Addition:	+ 1

Reconstr. sent.: mn šmm
nlḥm (h)kkbm ^{c}m ssr'
mmzltm

Comparison: (1 : 1 :: D)
3 : 3-s :: A (WP)
c : c :: D
+ 3pn

Result: Formula: A D (D)
Del.-Comp.: - 1 + 3pn
Semantic parallelism: WP; D
Transformation: none

Jud.5

Text: v.23b k l' b' l^{c}rzt yhw
l^{c}zrt yhw bgbrm

Translation: For they did not come to the aid of YHWH,
To the aid of YHWH with their warriors.

Comment: On the interpretation of bgbrm, see C-F. One may vocalize with them bəgibbōrēmô or leave the form unsuffixed: "with warriors."

Met. units: 3:3

Gram. units: 3:3

Syll. symmetry: 9:10 (symmetrical)

Gram. structure: ptcl neg b 3-Cpn
,3-Cpn 3-s

Transformation: none

Addition: + ptcl-neg-b

Reconstr. sent.: k l' b' l^{c}zrt yhw bgbrm

Comparison: (ptcl-neg-b : ptcl-neg-b :: D)
3-Cpn : 3-Cpn :: D/D (D(PN))
+ 3-s

Result: Formula: D/D (D)
Del.-Comp.: - ptcl-neg-b + 3-s
Semantic parallelism: D; D(PN)
Transformation: none

Jud.5

Text: v.24 — tbrk mnšm y^{c}l
mnšm b'hl tbrk

Comment: Omitting 'št ḥbr hqny as a gloss, with most commentators; see C-F.

Translation: May Jael be most blessed of women;
May she be most blessed of women in the tent!

Met. units: 3:3

Gram. units: 3:3

Gram. structure: 2 a // 2 a
3-C / a 2

Transformation: none

Addition: + 2
+ a

Reconstr. sent.: mm š'l ḥlb ntn / ḥm'h hqrb bspl 'drm

Comparison: (2 : 2 :: D)
(a : a :: D)
2 : 2 :: A (List)
a : a :: A (Syn)
+ 3-
+ -C

Result: Formula: A A (D D)
Del.-Comp.: - 2 + 3-
- a + -C
Semantic parallelism: List; Syn
Transformation: none

Jud.5

Text: v.26a — ydh lytd tšlḥn
(w)ymnh lhlmt ^{c}mlm

Comment: Vocalizing tišlaḥanna with C-F.

Translation: She stretched out her hand to a peg,
Her right hand, to a worker's mallet.

Met. units:	3:3
Gram. units:	3:3
Syll. symmetry:	9:9 (symmetrical)
Gram. structure:	2-s 3 a
	,2-s 3-C
Transformation:	none
Addition:	+ a
Reconstr. sent.:	ydh lytd tšlḥn
	ymnh lhlmt ^{c}mlm
Comparison:	(a : a :: D)
	2-s : 2-s :: A (WP)
	3 : 3-C :: /A (List)
	+ compensation
Result:	Formula: A /A (D)
	Del.-Comp.: - a + compensation
	Semantic parallelism: WP; List
	Transformation: none

Jud.5

Text: v.28b	md^{c} bšš / rkb lb'
	md^{c} 'ḥr / p^{c}m mrkbtw
Translation:	Why does his chariotry delay in coming;
	Why do the hooves of his chariots (i.e., chariot horses) tarry?
Met. units:	4:4(2:2::2:2)
Gram. units:	4:4(2:2::2:2)
Syll. symmetry:	5:4::5:6 (A and B Lines externally asymmetrical)
Gram. structure:	ptcl? b / 1-s 3(inf.const.b)
	ptcl? b / 1-C-s
Transformation:	none
Addition:	+ 3(inf.const.b)
Reconstr. sent.:	md^{c} bšš rkb lb'
	'ḥr p^{c}m mrkbtw

Comparison: (3(inf.const.b) : 3(inf.const.b) :: D)
ptcl? : ptcl? :: D
b : b :: A (Syn)
l-s : l-C-s :: /A (WP="D")
\+ compensation

Result: Formula: D A /A (D)
Del.-Comp.: - 3(inf.const.b) + compensation
Semantic parallelism: Syn; WP="D"
Transformation: none

<u>Jud.5</u>

Text: v.29 ḥkmt śrth t^{c}nn
'p h' tšb 'mrh lh

Comment: <u>ḥkmt</u> is singular; cf. VSS and C-F.

Translation: The wisest of her ladies answers her;
She responds with words to her.

Met. units: 3:3

Gram. units: 3:4

Syll. symmetry: 9:8 (symmetrical)

Gram. structure: l-C-s a-s
ptcl lpr a 2-s 3-s

Transformation: none

Addition: none

Reconstr. sent.: ḥkmt śrth t^{c}nn
'p h' tšb 'mrh lh

Comparison: l-C-s : ptcl-lpr :: C/ (PR)
a-s : a 2-s-3-s :: /A̲ (Syn)

Result: Formula: C/ /A̲
Del.-Comp.: none
Semantic parallelism: PR; Syn
Transformation: none

Jud.5

Text: v.30 — hl' ymṣ' // yḥlq šll
rḥm rḥmtm / lr'š gbr

Translation: Have they not found, divided the spoil,
One girl, two girls for each warrior?

Met. units: 4:4(2:2::2:2)

Gram. units: 4:4(2:2::2:2)

Syll. symmetry: 5:6::4:3 (A and B Lines externally asymmetrical)

Gram. structure: ptcl? a // a 2
,2 2 / 3-C

Transformation: none

Addition: + ptcl?
+ a
+ a

Reconstr. sent.:
šll
hl' ymṣ' yḥlq lr'š gbr
rḥm rḥmtm

Comparison: (ptcl? : ptcl? :: D)
(a : a :: D)
(a : a :: D)
2 : 2 2 :: /A (WP)
+ 3-
+ -C

Result: Formula: /A (D D D)
Del.-Comp.: - ptcl? + 3-
- a + -C
- a
Semantic parallelism: WP
Transformation: none

II Sam.1

Text: v.20b — pn tśmḥn / bnt plštm
pn t^{c}lzn / bnt (h)^{c}rlm

Translation: Lest the daughters of the Philistines rejoice;
Lest the daughters of the uncircumcised exult.

Met. units: 4:4(2:2::2:2)

Gram. units: 4:4(2:2::2:2)

Comment: The possibility of a metrical and grammatical structure of 3:3 cannot be excluded.

Syll. symmetry: 4:5::4:5 (symmetrical)

Gram. structure: neg b / l-Cpn
neg b / l-C

Transformation: none

Addition: none

Reconstr. sent.: pn tśmḥn / t^{c}lzn bnt plštm / (h)^{c}rlm

Comparison: neg : neg :: D
b : b :: A (Syn)
l-Cpn : l-C :: D/A (PN-Epith)

Result: Formula: D A D/A
Del.-Comp.: none
Semantic parallelism: D; Syn; PN-Epith
Transformation: none

Comment: If the unit consists of 3 metrical units, the formula would be *D/A* D/A.

II Sam.1

Text: v.21b k šm ng^{c}l / mgn gbrm
mgn š'l / bl mšḥ bsmn

Comment: Following C-F's readings of *bal* and *gal* passive *mušaḥ*; the latter is suggested also by the LXX.

Translation: There the heroes' shield was befouled;
The shield of Saul was not anointed with oil.

Met. units: 4:4(2:2::2:2)

Gram. units: 4:4(2:2::2:2)

Syll. symmetry: 4:5::4:5 (symmetrical)

Gram. structure: ptcl 3 c / l-C
l-C / neg c 3

Transformation: none

Addition: ptcl-3

Reconstr. sent.: k šm ng^{c}l mgn gbrm
bl mšḥ bšmn mgn š'l

Comparison: (ptcl-3 : ptcl-3 :: D)
c : neg-c 3 :: /A (Syn)
l-C : l-Cpn :: D/A (WP-PN)
+ compensation

Result: Formula: D/A /A (D)
Del.-Comp.: - ptcl-3 + compensation
Semantic parallelism: Syn; WP-PN
Transformation: none

II Sam.1

Text: v.22 mdm ḥllm // mḥlb gbrm
qšt yntn / l' nśg 'ḥr
(w)ḥrb š'l / l' tšb rqm

Comment: On yntn for MT's yhntn, see C-F.

Translation: From the blood of the slain, from the fat of warriors
Jonathan's bow did not turn back;
Saul's sword did not return empty.

Met. units: 4:4:4(2:2::2:2::2:2)

Gram. units: 4:4:4(2:2::2:2::2:2)

Syll. symmetry: 5:5::4:5::3:5 (A and C Lines externally asymmetrical; C Line internally asymmetrical)

Gram. structure: 3-C // 3-C
l-Cpn / neg b 3
l-Cpn / neg b 3

A-B Lines

Result: Non-parallel unit (enjambment)

B-C Lines

Transformation: none

Addition: none

Reconstr. sent.: qšt yntn l' nśg 'ḥr
(w)ḥrb š'l l' tšb (yšb) rqm

Comparison: l-Cpn : l-Cpn :: A/A (List; List(PN))
neg-b 3 : neg-b 3 :: A/A (Syn)

Result: Formula: A/A A/A
Del.-Comp.: none
Semantic parallelism: List; List(PN); Syn
Transformation: none

II Sam.1

Text: v.27 'k npl gbrm
(w)y'bd kl mlḥm

Translation: How have the warriors fallen,
The weapons of war perished!

Met. units: 3:3

Gram. units: 3:3

Syll. symmetry: 7:8 (symmetrical)

Gram. structure: ptcl! b l
,b l-C

Transformation: none

Addition: + ptcl!

Reconstr. sent.: 'k npl gbrm / y'bd kl mlḥm

Comparison: (ptcl! : ptcl! :: D)
b : b :: B (Syn)
l : l-C :: /A (List)
+ compensation

Result: Formula: B /A (D)
Del.-Comp.: - ptcl! + compensation
Semantic parallelism: Syn; List
Transformation: none

II Sam.22

Text: v.5 'ppny mšbry mt
nḥly bly^{c}l yb^{c}tny

Comment: Omitting ky at the beginning of the A Line with C-F, an omission, however, which makes the unit syllabically asymmetrical.

Translation: The breakers of Death enveloped me;
The rivers of Belial overwhelmed me;
Comment: This unit forms a quatrain with the following unit.
Met. units: 3:3
Gram. units: 3:3
Syll. symmetry: 8:10 (asymmetrical)
Gram. structure: a-s 1-Cpn
1-Cpn a-s
Transformation: none
Addition: none
Reconstr. sent.: 'ppny mšbry mwt
yb^{c}tny nḥly bly^{c}l
Comparison: a-s : a-s :: B (Syn)
1-Cpn : 1-Cpn :: A/A (List/Syn(PN))
Result: Formula: B A/A
Del.-Comp.: none
Semantic parallelism: Syn; List; Syn(PN)
Transformation: none

<u>II Sam.22</u>
Text: v.6 ḥbly š'l sbbny
qdmny mqšy mt
Translation: The bonds of Sheol surrounded me;
The snares of Death confronted me.
Met. units: 3:3
Gram. units: 3:3
Syll. symmetry: 7:8 (symmetrical)
Gram. structure: 1-Cpn a-s
a-s 1-Cpn
Transformation: none
Addition: none
Reconstr. sent.: sbbny ḥbly š'l
qdmny mqšy mt
Comparison: 1-Cpn : 1-Cpn :: A/A (List; List(PN))
a-s : a-s :: B (Syn)

Result: Formula: B A/A
Del.-Comp.: none
Semantic parallelism: List; List(PN); Syn
Transformation: none

II Sam.22

Text: v.7a — bṣr ly 'qr' yhwh
(w)'l 'lhy 'šw^{c}

Translation: When in distress I called out, "YHWH!";
I cried for help to my God.

Met. units: 3:3

Gram. units: 4:2

Syll. symmetry: 7:7 (symmetrical)

Gram. structure: 3 3-s a 2(lpn!)
3-s a

Transformation: none

Comment: No transformation is needed since 'šw^{c} 'l is a compound.

Addition: + 3-3-s

Comment: bṣr l is a replacement for bṣrty and might be treated as a single grammatical unit for that reason. However, the usual procedure called for by the system of analysis will be followed even though it will produce a variant formula.

Reconstr. sent.:
'qr' yhwh
bṣr ly
'šw^{c} 'l 'lhy

Comparison: (3-3-s : 3-3-s :: D/D)
a : b : A (Syn)
2(lpn!) : 3-s :: A* (PN-Syn)
+ compensation

Result: Formula: A A* (D/D)
Del.-Comp.: - 3-3-s + compensation
Semantic parallelism: Syn; PN-Syn
Transformation: none

II Sam.22

Text: v.7b — yšm^c mhklh qly
(w)šw^{c}ty tb' b'znw

Comment: Omitting *waw* at the beginning of the A Line. One of the variants of the B Line has been chosen; see C-F. The other, *šw^{c}ty lpnw tb'*, would produce no significant change in analysis.

Translation: He heard my voice from (inside) his palace;
My cry for help entered his ears.

Met. units: 3:3

Gram. units: 3:3

Syll. symmetry: 8:8 (symmetrical)

Gram. structure: a 3-s 2-s
1-s b 3-s

Transformation: 1-s b 3-s --→ 2-s a 3-s

Comment: A transformation may not be necessary, since *tb' b'znw* is certainly an idiomatic unit. However, the transformation, which produces a causative verb (*yābî(')*), lines up the parallel terms grammatically in the manner required by the system.

Addition: + 3-s

Reconstr. sent.: yšm^c qly
mhklh
yb' b'znw šw^{c}ty

Comment: It is less likely that b'znw is intended as a parallel to *mhklh*.

Comparison: (3-s : 3-s :: D)
a : a 3-s :: /A (Syn)
2-s : 2-s :: A (Syn)
+ compensation

Result: Formula: A /A (D)
Del.-Comp.: - 3-s + compensation
Semantic parallelism: Syn
Transformation: 2-s a 3-s --→ 1-s b 3-s

II Sam.22

Text: v.8a — tg^{c}š wtr^{c}š 'rṣ
msdy hrm yrgzw

Comment: Omitting waw at the beginning of the A Line. The C Line will not be analyzed. The repetition of the root g^{c}š in MT's ytg^{c}šw is suspicious (C-F). The evidence of the VSS is unclear; but a difference between the two verbs seems to be supported by the LXX and Vulgate in the II Samuel passage, and by the Targum and Peshitta of both II Samuel and Psalm 18. Perhaps a form of r^{c}d or a like verb should replace ytg^{c}šw or even the repetition of a form of rgz.

Translation: The earth trembled and shook;
The supports of the mountains trembled.

Met. units: 3:3

Gram. units: 3:3

Syll. symmetry: 6:8 (asymmetrical)

Gram. structure: b &b l
l-C b

Transformation: none

Addition: none

Reconstr. sent.: tg^{c}š wtr^{c}š (ytg^{c}šw wyr^{c}šw) 'rṣ
yrgzw (trgz) msdy hrm

Comparison: b &b : b :: A/ (Syn)
l : l-C :: /A (List)

Result: Formula: A/ /A
Del.-Comp.: none
Semantic parallelism: Syn; List
Transformation: none

II Sam.22

Text: v.9 — ^{c}lh ^{c}šn b'pw
(w)'š mphw t'kl
gḥlm b^{c}rw mmnw

Translation: Smoke went forth from his nostrils;
Fire consumed from his mouth;
Coals burned forth from him.

Met. units: 3:3:3

Gram. units: 3:3:3

Syll. symmetry: 7:6:8 (B and C Lines asymmetrical)

Gram. structure: b l 3-s
l 3-s a
l b 3-s

A-B Lines

Transformation: none

Comment: No transformation is required because ^{c}lh ^{c}šn and 'š t'kl are idiomatic units.

Addition: none

Reconstr. sent.: ^{c}lh ^{c}šn b'pw
t'kl 'š mphw

Comment: The semantic compounds ^{c}lh ^{c}šn and t'kl 'š require grammatical adjustment:
^{c}lh (^{c}lth) ^{c}šn
t'kl (y'kl) 'š

Comparison: b l : a l :: A/A (List)
3-s : 3-s :: A (List)

Result: Formula: A A/A
Del.-Comp.: none
Semantic parallelism: List
Transformation: none

B-C Lines

Transformation: none

Comment: 'š t'kl and gḥlm b^{c}rw must be considered semantic compounds indivisible in this context. No transformation is necessary.

Addition: none

Reconstr. sent.: 'š t'kl mphw
gḥlm b^{c}rw mmnw

Comment: As in the A-B Lines, the semantic compounds must be adjusted grammatically:

'š t'kl (y'klw)

gḥlm bᶜrw (bᶜrh)

Comparison: 1 a : 1 b :: A≠A (List)

3-s : 3-s :: A (PW-PR)

Result: Formula: A A≠A

Del.-Comp.: none

Semantic parallelism: List; PW-PR

Transformation: none

II Sam.22

Text: v.10 yṭh šmm wyrd

(w)ᶜrpl tḥt rglw

Comment: Omitting waw at the beginning of the A Line and reading yaṭṭê(h) for MT's wayyēṭ.

Translation: He spread apart the heavens and descended,

A storm-cloud under his feet.

Met. units: 3:3

Gram. units: 3:3

Syll. symmetry: 7:6 (symmetrical)

Gram. structure: a 2 &b

S P(3)-C-s

Result: Non-parallel unit (VS-NS)

II Sam.22

Text: v.11 yrkb ᶜl krbm

(w)yd'h ᶜl knpy rḥ

Comment: Omitting waw at the beginning of the A Line. Of the two B Line variants, yᶜp and yd'h, the latter has been chosen. It is the rarer of the terms and the more likely one to have been glossed. Also reading krbm with VSS (C-F).

Translation: He was mounted on the Cherubim;
He swooped on the wings of the wind.

Met. units: 3:3

Comment: Note that ^{c}l in the A Line has been awarded the value of one metrical unit, but not ^{c}l in the B Line. Reading ^{c}ălê in A or B Lines, or both, would not affect the metrical situation.

Gram. units: 2:3

Syll. symmetry: 6:6 (symmetrical)

Gram. structure: b 3
b 3-C

Transformation: none

Addition: none

Reconstr. sent.: yrkb ^{c}l krbm
yd'h ^{c}l knpy rḥ

Comparison: b : b :: A (List)
3 : 3-C :: */A (Epith)

Result: Formula: A */A
Del.-Comp.: none
Semantic parallelism: List; Epith
Transformation: none

II Sam.22

Text: v.12 yšt ḥšk sbbtw
skth ḥšrt mm

Comment: Omitting waw at the beginning of the A Line.

Translation: He placed darkness around him (lit.: as his surroundings);
The rain cloud as his covering.

Met. units: 3:3

Gram. units: 3:3

Syll. symmetry: 7:6 (symmetrical)

Gram. structure: a 2 "2-s"
,"2-s" 2-C

Comment: yšt takes two objects; on the construction, G.K.117ii.

Transformation: none

Addition: + a

Reconstr. sent.:

```
     ḥšk      sbbtw
yšt
     ḥšrt mm  skth
```

Comparison: (a : a :: D)
2 : 2-C :: /A (List)
"2-s" : "2-s" :: B (WP)
+ compensation

Result: Formula: B /A (D)
Del.-Comp.: - a + compensation
Semantic parallelism: List; WP
Transformation: none

II Sam.22

Text: v.14 yr^c^m mn šmm yhwh
(w)^c^lyn ytn qlh

Translation: YHWH thundered from heaven;
Elyon sent forth his voice.

Met. units: 3:3

Gram. units: 3:3

Syll. symmetry: 7:6 (symmetrical)

Gram. structure: b 3 lpn
lpn a 2-s

Transformation: none

Comment: No transformation is necessary since ytn qlh is a semantic compound.

Addition: + 3

Reconstr. sent.:

```
yrᶜm      yhwh
                 mn šmm
ytn qlh  ᶜlyn
```

Comparison: b : a 2-s : /A (Epith)
lpn : lpn :: A (Syn(PN))

Comment: Alternatively, the rhetorical relationship between yr^c^m and ytn qlh may be classified as metaphorical.

Result: Formula: A /A (D)
Del.-Comp.: - 3 + compensation
Semantic parallelism: Epith; Syn(PN)
Transformation: none

II Sam.22

Text: v.15 — yšlḥ ḥṣm wypṣm
brqm ybrq wyhmm

Comment: Omitting waw at the beginning of the A Line. The insertion of ybrq in the B Line is by no means necessary for the analysis of the unit; nor does it affect the syllabic symmetry of the unit (8:7 without ybrq, 8:9 with it). However, its presence in some significant LXX MSS (boc_2e_2) and, especially, the similarity to Ps.144:6 increase the probability of its originality here (C-F).

Translation: He sent forth arrows to scatter them;
He shot forth lightning(s) to panic them.

Met. units: 3:3

Gram. units: 3:3

Syll. symmetry: 8:9 (symmetrical)

Gram. structure: a 2 &a-s
2 a &a-s

Transformation: none

Addition: none

Reconstr. sent.: yšlḥ ḥṣm wypṣm
ybrq brqm wyhmm

Comparison: a 2 : 2 a :: C≠C (Met)
&a-s : &a-s :: A (Syn)

Result: Formula: A C≠C
Del.-Comp.: none
Semantic parallelism: Met; Syn
Transformation: none

II Sam.22

Text: v.16a — yr'w 'pqm ym
yglw msdt tbl

Comment: Omitting waw at the beginning of the A Line. On the enclitic mem of 'pqm, see C-F.

Translation: The bed of the sea became visible;
The foundations of the world were revealed,

Met. units: 3:3
Gram. units: 3:3
Syll. symmetry: 7:8 (symmetrical)
Gram. structure: c l-encl.<u>mem</u>-C
c l-C
Transformation: none
Addition: none
Reconstr. sent.: yr'w 'pqm ym
yglw msdt tbl
Comparison: c : c :: A (Syn)
l-encl.<u>mem</u>-C : l-C :: A≠A (List)
Result: Formula: A A≠A
Del.-Comp.: none
Semantic parallelism: Syn; List
Transformation: none

<u>II Sam.22</u>
Text: v.16b bg^{c}rtkh yhwh
mnšmt rḥ 'pkh
Comment: On the text, see C-F. This unit forms a quatrain with the preceding one.
Translation: At your rebuke, O YHWH;
At the blast of the breath of your nostrils.
Met. units: 3:3
Gram. units: 2:3
Syll. symmetry: 7:7 (symmetrical)
Gram. structure: ,3-s lpn!
,3-C-C-s
Transformation: none
Addition: + lpn!
Reconstr. sent.: bg^{c}rtkh
yhwh
mnšmt rḥ 'pkh
Comparison: (lpn! : lpn! :: D)
3-s : 3-C-C-s :: */¢ (Met)
+ compensation

Result: Formula: */¢ (D)
Del.-Comp.: - lpn! + compensation
Semantic parallelism: Met
Transformation: none

II Sam.22

Text: v.17 yšlḥ ydh mmrm
ymšny mmm rbm

Comment: The text of the A Line is based on the common idiom šlḥ yd and the close parallel in Ps.144:7 (C-F). However, it should be noted that the text of MT is by no means impossible (šlḥ followed by lqḥ; i.e., šlḥ wyqḥ, etc. is also common. Note the similar verse Ps.57:4: yšlḥ mšmym wywšy^{c}ny). It has the additional advantage of being simple to analyze. MT's text is, however, syllabically asymmetrical.

Translation: He stretched out his hand from the heights;
He drew me from the mighty waters.

Met. units: 3:3

Gram. units: 3:3

Syll. symmetry: 7:7 (symmetrical)

Gram. structure: a 2-s 3
a-s 3 ,-3

Transformation: none

Addition: none

Reconstr. sent.: yšlḥ ydh mmrm
ymšny mmm rbm

Comparison: a 2-s : a-s :: B/ (Ant)
3 : 3,-3 :: /B (Mer)

Comment: This analysis assumes that the poet intends to contrast mm rbm and mrm as the extremities of the universe. On the association of waters with Sheol, the depths, etc., see, *inter alia*, Jonah 2.

Result: Formula: B/ /B
Del.-Comp.: none
Semantic parallelism: Ant; Mer
Transformation: none

II Sam.22

Text: v.18 yṣlny m'yby ky ᶜzw
mśn'y ky 'mṣw mmny

Comment: On the text, see C-F

Translation: He saved me from my enemies when they were powerful,
From my foes when they were stronger than I.

Met. units: 3:3

Gram. units: 3:3

Syll. symmetry: 11:11 (symmetrical)

Gram. structure: a-s 3-s ,-R(ptcl b)
,3-s ,-R(ptcl b 3-s)

Transformation: none

Addition: + a-s

Reconstr. sent.: yṣlny { m'yby ky ᶜzw / mśn'y ky 'mṣw } mmny

Comparison: (a-s : a-s :: D)
3-s : 3-s :: A (Syn)
ptcl-b : ptcl-b :: A (Syn)
+ 3-s

Result: Formula: A A (D)
Del.-Comp.: - a-s + 3-s
Semantic parallelism: Syn
Transformation: none

II Sam.22

Text: v.19 yqdmny bym 'dy
(w)yhy yhwh mšᶜn ly

Translation: They confronted me on the day of my disaster,
But YHWH was my support.

Met. units:	3:3
Gram. units:	3:4
Syll. symmetry:	9:7 (asymmetrical)
Gram. structure:	a-s 3-C-s "b" Spn P 3-s
Transformation:	none
Comment:	No transformation is required because the B Line is a "quasi-verbal" sentence which forms an idiomatic unit.
Addition:	+ 3- + -C-s
Reconstr. sent.:	yqdmny bym 'dy yhy yhwh mš^{c}n ly
Comparison:	(3- : 3- :: D) (-C-s : -C-s :: D) a-s : "b" Spn P-3-s :: /B̸ (Ant) + compensation
Result:	Formula: /B̸ (D D) Del.-Comp.: - 3- + compensation - -C-s Semantic parallelism: Ant Transformation: none
Comment:	This analysis is metrically troublesome since <u>bym 'dy</u> (4 syllables) has been awarded two metrical units while <u>yqdmny</u> (5 syllables) has been awarded only one. If one reverses the metrical units, the resulting formula would be */B (<u>D/D</u>).

<u>II Sam.22</u>

Text: v.21	ygmlny yhwh kṣdqy kbr ydy yšb ly
Translation:	YHWH rewarded me according to my righteousness; He recompensed me according to my blamelessness.

Met. units: 3:3
Gram. units: 3:4
Syll. symmetry: 9:7 (asymmetrical)
Gram. structure: a-s lpn "3-s"
"3-C-s" a 3-s
Transformation: none
Addition: + lpn
Reconstr. sent.: ygmlny yhwh kṣdqy
yšb ly kbr ydy
Comparison: (lpn : lpn :: D)
a-s : a-3-s :: /A (Syn)
"3-s" : "3-C-s" :: /A (Syn)
+ compensation
Result: Formula: /A /A (D)
Del.-Comp.: - lpn + compensation
Semantic parallelism: Syn
Transformation: none

II Sam.22

Text: v.22 ky šmrty drky yhwh
(w)l' pš^{c}ty m'lhy
Comment: Reading pš^{c}ty with the Peshitta for MT's rš^{c}ty; see C-F.
Translation: I have kept the ways of YHWH;
I have not rebelled against my God.
Met. units: 3:3
Gram. units: 3:2
Syll. symmetry: 8:8 (symmetrical)
Gram. structure: ptcl 2 2-Cpn
neg b 3-s
Transformation: none
Comment: No transformation is necessary since pš^{c}ty m may be considered a compound verb.
Addition: + 2-
Reconstr. sent.: ky šmrty drky yhwh
l' pš^{c}ty m 'lhy

Comparison: (2- : 2- :: D)
ptcl-a : neg-b :: A (Syn)
-C : 3-s :: A* (PN-Syn)
+ compensation
Result: Formula: A A* (D)
Del.-Comp.: - 2- + compensation
Semantic parallelism: Syn; PN-Syn
Transformation: none

II Sam.22

Text: v.23 ky kl mšpṭw lngdy
ḥqtw l' 'sr mmny

Comment: Following Ps.18 in the B Line and restoring a *mem* to MT's *mny*; see C-F. Note also the parallel in Job 27:5 and the readings of the Vulgate and Peshitta.

Translation: All his rules are before me;
I do not remove his laws from myself.

Met. units: 3:3

Gram. units: 3:3

Syll. symmetry: 8:9 (symmetrical)

Gram. structure: ptcl "S"-C-s P(3)-s
2-s neg a 3-s

Transformation: 1. 2-s neg a 3-s --→ 2-s "neg b" P(part.a) 3-s
2. 2-s "neg b" P(part.a) 3-s --→ S-s "neg b" P(part.c) 3-s

Comment: The first transformation produces a nominal sentence with a negated participle: *'ēnennî mēsîr*. The second transformation produces an intransitive sentence with a passive participle: *'ēnān mûsārôṯ*.

Addition: none

Reconstr. sent.: ky kl / mšpṭw lngdy
ḥqtw 'nn msrt mmny ('nm msrm mmny)

Comparison: ptcl-"S"-C-s : S-s :: A/ (Syn)
P(3)-s :: "neg-b"-P(part.c) 3-s :: /B (Syn)

Result: Formula: A/ /B
Del.-Comp.: none
Semantic parallelism: Syn
Transformation:
1. S-s "neg b" P(part.c) 3-s --→ 2-s "neg b" P(part.a) 3-s
2. 2-s "neg b" P(part.a) 3-s --→ 2-s neg a 3-s

II Sam.22

Text: v.28 'th ^{c}m ^{c}ny tš^{c}
(w)^{c}nm rmt tšpl

Comment: Following the text of Ps.18, but omitting ky at the beginning of the A Line. On the textual problems, see C-F.

Translation: You save the lowly people;
But you humble haughty eyes.

Met. units: 3:3

Gram. units: 4:3

Syll. symmetry: 7:6 (symmetrical)

Gram. structure: 1pr 2 ,-2 a
2 ,-2 a

Transformation: none

Addition: + 1pr

Reconstr. sent.: 'th ^{c}m ^{c}ny tš^{c}
^{c}nm rmt tšpl

Comparison: (1pr : 1pr :: D)
2 ,-2 : 2 ,-2 :: B/B (Ant=WP)
a : a :: A (Ant)
+ Ø

Result: Formula: A B/B (D)
Del.-Comp.: - 1pr + Ø
Semantic parallelism: Ant=WP; Ant
Transformation: none

Comment: The semantic compound requires grammatical adjustments for number and gender of the type

encountered in the reconstructed sentence
(see Part I):

^{c}m ^{c}ny(^{c}nyt)
^{c}nm rmt(rm)

II Sam.22

Text: v.29 — ky 'th nry yhwh
'lhy tgh ḥšky

Comment: Following C-F's restoration of the text, and reading nry with II Sam. However, read the second person tgh for MT's ygh, with Vulgate and LXX miniscules (boc_2e_2).

Translation: You are my lamp, O YHWH;
My God, you brighten my darkness!

Met. units: 3:3

Gram. units: 3:3

Syll. symmetry: 7:7 (symmetrical)

Gram. structure: ptcl Spr P-s lpn!
1-s! a 2-s

Transformation: 1-s! a 2-s --→ 1-s! P(part.a) 2-s

Addition: + ptcl-Spr

Reconstr. sent.:
ky 'th nry yhwh
mgh ḥšky 'lhy

Comparison: (ptcl-Spr : ptcl-Spr :: D)
P-s : P(part.a) 2-s :: /A (Epith)
lpn! : 1-s! :: A (PN-Syn)
+ compensation

Result: Formula: A /A (D)
Del.-Comp.: - ptcl-Spr + compensation
Semantic parallelism: Epith; PN-Syn
Transformation: 1-s! P(part.a) 2-s --→ 1-s! a 2-s

II Sam.22

Text: v.32 ky my 'l mbl^{c}dy yhwh
(w)my ṣr zlty 'lhnw

Comment: *zlty* following Ps.18; see C-F.

Translation: Who except YHWH is God;
Who except our God is a rock?

Met. units: 3:3

Gram. units: 4:4

Syll. symmetry: 9:9 (symmetrical)

Gram. structure: ptcl Spr? P 3-Cpn
Spr? P 3-C-s

Transformation: none

Addition: none

Reconstr. sent.: ky my ⁄ 'l mbl^{c}dy yhwh
ṣr zlty 'lhnw

Comparison: ptcl-Spr?-P : Spr?-P :: *D/A* (Epith)
3-Cpn : 3-C-s :: A/A (Syn/PN-Syn)

Result: Formula: *D/A* A/A
Del.-Comp.: none
Semantic parallelism: Epith; Syn; PN-Syn
Transformation: none

II Sam.22

Text: v.34 mšwh rgly k'ylt
(w)^{c}l bmtw y^{c}mdny

Comment: The simplest solution to the problem of MT's *bmty* is to read *bmtw* (note the confusion between *rgly* and *rglw* in the A Line). In both places where the phrase occurs it is followed by a word beginning with *yod* (Hab.3:19: *ydrkny*). The image is certainly a military one, here referring to sure-footedness and speed (cf. v.37-38) in war. Compare also Jud.5:18. The image could be transferred to other pursuits, cf. Cant.2:8-9 and 8:14.

Translation: He makes my feet like the does';
He lets me stand on his heights.

Met. units: 3:3

Comment: ^{c}l bmtw and y^{c}mdny both have 4 syllables. The latter has been awarded two metrical units.

Gram. units: 3:2

Syll. symmetry: 9:8 (symmetrical)

Gram. structure: P(part.a) a "3"
3-s a-s

Transformation: 3 a-s --→ 3 P(part.a)-s

Addition: + "3"

Reconstr. sent.: mšwh rgly
k'ylt ^{c}l bmtw
m^{c}mdny

Comparison: ("3" : "3" :: D)
P(part.a) 2-s : P(part.a)-s :: A/* (Syn)
+ 3-s

Result: Formula: A/* (D)
Del.-Comp.: - "3" + 3-s
Semantic parallelism: Syn
Transformation: 3 P(part.a) --→ 3 a-s

Comment: Had ^{c}l bmty been awarded two metrical units the result would be:
Formula: A/ (D)
Del.-Comp.: - "3" + prep
+ -C

II Sam.22

Text: v.37 trḥb ṣ^{c}dy tḥtny
(w)l' m^{c}dw qrsly

Translation: You lengthen my stride under me;
My ankles do not stumble.

Met. units: 3:3

Gram. units: 3:2

Syll. symmetry: 7:6 (symmetrical)

Gram. structure: a 2-s 3-s
neg b 1-s

Transformation: neg b 1-s --→ neg a 2-s

Comment:	The result of the transformation would be the <u>hiphil</u> of <u>m^{c}d</u>, which, in fact, occurs twice with <u>mtnym</u> as object.
Addition:	+ 3-s
Reconstr. sent.:	trḥb s^{c}dy thtny l' tm^{c}d qrsly
Comparison:	(3-s : 3-s :: D) a : neg-a :: B* (Syn) 2-s : 2-s :: A (List) + compensation
Result:	Formula: A B* (D) Del.-Comp.: - 3-s + compensation Semantic parallelism: Syn; List Transformation: neg a 2-s --> neg b 1-s

---

<u>II Sam.22</u>

Text: v.38	'rdp 'yby w'šmdm l' 'šb ^{c}d kltm
Comment:	The variant <u>'šmdm</u> has been chosen over <u>'śgm</u> of Ps.18. Since <u>hśg</u> is common after <u>rdp</u>, <u>'šmdm</u> may be <u>lectio</u> <u>difficilior</u>.
Translation:	I pursued my enemies and destroyed them; I did not desist until I had annihilated them.
Met. units:	3:3
Gram. units:	3:2
Syll. symmetry:	9:7 (asymmetrical)
Comment:	The syllable asymmetry may be removed if one reads simple <u>'šmdm</u>; cf. the staccato style of Ex.15:9; see C-F.
Gram. structure:	b 2-s &a-s neg b 3(inf.const.a)-s
Transformation:	none
Addition:	+ 2-s
Reconstr. sent.:	'rdp (m)'yby w'šmdm l' 'šb ^{c}d kltm
Comment:	Note that the reconstructed sentence requires that one read <u>mē'ōyᵊbay</u> for the B Line.

Comparison: (2-s : 2-s :: D)
b : neg-b :: B (Syn)
&a-s : 3(inf.const.a)-s :: A* (Syn)
+ compensation

Result: Formula: B A* (D)
Del.-Comp.: - 2-s + compensation
Semantic parallelism: Syn
Transformation: none

<u>II Sam.22</u>

Text: v.39 'mḥṣm wl' yqmn
yplw tḥt rgly

Comment: Omitting <u>waw</u> at the beginning of the A Line. <u>'mḥṣm</u> seems preferable to <u>'klm</u>, which may be influenced by the end of the preceding unit; see C-F.

Translation: I smashed them so that they could not rise,
So that they fell under my feet.

Met. units: 3:3

Gram. units: 2:3

Syll. symmetry: 8:6 (asymmetrical)

Gram. structure: a-s &neg b
b 3-C-s

Transformation: none

Addition: + a-s

Reconstr. sent.:
wl' yqmn
'mḥṣm (m)tḥt rgly
yplw

Comment: Note that the reconstructed sentence requires that one read <u>mittaḥ(a)t</u> in the A Line; cf. the preceding unit.

Comparison: (a-s : a-s :: D)
&neg b :: b :: *B (Syn)
+ 3-
+ -C

Result: Formula: *B (D)
Del.-Comp.: - a-s + 3-
+ -C
Semantic parallelism: Syn
Transformation: none

II Sam.22

Text: v.40 t(')zrny ḥl lmlḥmh
tkr^{c} qmy tḥtny

Comment: Omitting waw at the beginning of the A Line. On the probable pronunciation of MT's tzrny (tazrēnī) as "popular," see C-F.

Translation: You have girded me for war with valor;
You have made my foes crouch beneath me.

Met. units: 3:3

Gram. units: 3:3

Syll. symmetry: 8:7 (symmetrical)

Gram. structure: a-s 2 3
a 2-s 3-s

Result: Non-parallel unit (VS-VS)

II Sam.22

Text: v.41 'yby ntth ly ^{c}rp
mśn'y w'ṣmtm

Comment: Omitting waw at the beginning of the A Line. Rearrangement of the unit is not necessary for analysis in this system.

Translation: You have given me the neck of my enemies,
Of my foes, whom I exterminate.

Comment: Or: "My foes, I exterminate them." However, the interpretation above will facilitate analysis.

Met. units: 3:3

Gram. units: 4:2

Syll. symmetry: 8:7 (symmetrical)

Gram. structure: -C-s a 3-s 2-
,-C-s, ,-R(&a-s)

Comment: Note the lack of resumptive suffix of ^crp, made possible by the fact that ntn ^crp is an idiom: cf. Ex.23:27, etc.

Transformation: none

Addition: + a-3-s
+ 2-

Reconstr. sent.: 'yby
ntth ly ^crp w'smtm
mśn'y

Comparison: (a-3-s : a-3-s :: (D/D)
(2- : 2- :: D)
-C-s : -C-s :: A (Syn)
+ ,-R(a-s)

Result: Formula: A (D/D D)
Del.-Comp.: - a-3-s + ,-R(&a-s)
- 2-
Semantic parallelism: Syn
Transformation: none

II Sam.22

Text: v.42 yšw^cw w'n mš^c
'l yhwh wl' ^cnm

Comment: Reading yšw^cw with Ps.18; see C-F.

Translation: They cried for help, but there was none to save,
To YHWH, but he did not answer them.

Met. units: 3:3

Gram. units: 3:3

Syll. symmetry: 8:7 (symmetrical)

Gram. structure: a &"neg b" P(part.a)
,3pn &neg a-s

Transformation: none

Addition: + a

Reconstr. sent.: w'n (wl') mš^c
yšw^cw 'l yhwh
wl' (w'n) ^cnm (^cōnām)

Comment: Note the adjustments required by the semantic compound.

Comparison: (a : a :: D)

&"neg b" P(part.a) : &neg a-s :: A≠A (Syn)

+ 3pn

Result: Formula: A≠A (D)

Del.-Comp.: - a + 3pn

Semantic parallelism: Syn

Transformation: none

<u>II Sam.22</u>

Text: v.43 'śḥqm k^{c}pr 'rṣ

kṭṭ ḥṣt 'dqm

Comment: Omitting <u>waw</u> at the beginning of the A Line.

Translation: I crushed them like the dust of the ground;

Like the dirt of the streets I pulverized them.

Met. units: 3:3

Gram. units: 3:3

Syll. symmetry: 7:7 (symmetrical)

Gram. structure: a-s "3-C"

"3-C" a-s

Transformation: none

Addition: none

Reconstr. sent.: 'śḥqm k^{c}pr 'rṣ

'dqm kṭṭ ḥṣt

Comparison: a-s : a-s :: A (Syn)

"3-C" : "3-C" :: A/A (Syn/List)

Result: Formula: A A/A

Del.-Comp.: none

Semantic parallelism: Syn; List

Transformation: none

<u>II Sam.22</u>

Text: v.44b-c — tśmny lr'š gym
^{c}m l' yd^{c}ty y^{c}bdny

Comment: Reading <u>tśmny</u> with Ps.18.

Translation: You set me at the head of nations,
A people I did not know serve me.

Met. units: 3:3

Gram. units: 3:3

Syll. symmetry: 8:9 (symmetrical)

Comment: This unit is one of those which strongly supports a syllabic interpretation of Hebrew meter. Note that in the B Line each of the following has been awarded the value of one metrical unit: <u>^{c}m</u> (1 syllable); <u>l' yd^{c}ty</u> (4 syllables); <u>y^{c}bdny</u> (4 syllables).

Gram. structure: a-s 3-C
1 ,-R(neg a) a-s

Transformation: 1 ,-R(neg a) a-s --→ 2 ,-R(neg a) a 3-s

Comment: The result of the transformation is a sentence with causative verb and in which the pronominal object suffix has been replaced with a preposition with suffix:
^{c}amm lō(') yāḏa^{c}tî ta^{c}ăḇîḏ lî

Addition: none

Reconstr. sent.: tśmny lr'š gym
l' yd^{c}ty
t^{c}bd ly ^{c}m

Comment: Note that <u>tśmny lr'š</u> is an idiomatic unit.

Comparison: a-s 3- : a 3-s :: A/ (Syn)
-C : 2 :: A (Syn)
\+ ,-R(neg-a)

Result: Formula: A A/
Del.-Comp.: - Ø + ,-R(neg a)
Semantic parallelism: Syn
Transformation: 2 ,-R(neg a) a 3-s --→ 1 ,-R(neg a) a-s

Comment: Alternatively, one may posit the following reconstructed sentence:

tśmny lr'š gym / ^{c}m l' yd^{c}ty y^{c}bdny

In this sentence y^{c}bdny may be understood as a coordinated or, possibly, a relative clause ("who serve me"). No transformation would be required; and the result would be:

Formula: A (D D)

Del.-Comp.: - a-s + ,-R(neg a)
- 3- + a-s

II Sam.22

Text: v.45 — bny nkr ytkḥšw ly
lšm^{c} 'zn yšm^{c}w ly

Comment: MT's text may need rearranging (see C-F), but will serve for the purposes of this analysis.

Translation: Foreigners fawn upon me;
At the report (of me) they obey me.

Met. units: 3:3

Gram. units: 4:4

Syll. symmetry: 9:8 (symmetrical)

Comment: The same metrical comments made on the preceding unit apply here also, particularly as regards the B Line.

Gram. structure: 1-C c 3-s
3-C c 3-s

Transformation: none

Addition: + 1-
+ -C

Reconstr. sent.:
ytkḥšw ly
bny nkr lšm^{c} 'zn
yšm^{c}w ly

Comparison: (1- : 1- :: D)
(-C : -C :: D)
c-3-s : c-3-s :: A/D (Syn)
+ 3-
+ -C

Result: Formula: *A/D* (D D)
Del.-Comp.: - 1- + 3-
- -C + -C
Semantic parallelism: Syn
Transformation: none

II Sam.22

Text: v.47 ḥy yhwh brk ṣry
yrm 'lhy yš^{c}y

Comment: Omitting *waw* before *brk* and vocalizing jussive *yārōm*; see C-F.

Translation: As YHWH lives, may my rock be blessed;
Exalted be my saving God!

Met. units: 3:3

Gram. units: 4:3

Syll. symmetry: 7:7 (symmetrical)

Gram. structure: 1-Cpn! P(part.c)! S-s
b! 1-C-s

Transformation: none

Comment: No transformation is necessary since both *brk* and *yrm* are intransitive precatives, as, indeed, *ḥy* may be; cf. Dahood, *Psalms*, *ad locem*.

Addition: + 1-Cpn!

Reconstr. sent.:
brk ṣry
ḥy yhwh
yrm 'lhy yš^{c}y

Comparison: (1-Cpn! : 1-Cpn! :: *D/D*)
P(part.c)! : b! :: A (List)
1-s : 1-C-s :: /A (Syn(Epith))
+ compensation

Result: Formula: A /A (*D/D*)
Del.-Comp.: - 1-Cpn! + compensation
Semantic parallelism: List; Syn(Epith)
Transformation: none

Hab.3

Text: v.2a — yhwh šm^{c}ty šm^{c}kh
r'ty yhwh p^{c}lkh

Comment: Reading r'ty for MT's yr'ty; see Albright, PHab.

Translation: YHWH, I have heard your fame;
I have seen, O YHWH, your deeds.

Met. units: 3:3

Gram. units: 3:3

Syll. symmetry: 8:8 (symmetrical)

Gram. structure: lpn! 2 2-s
a lpn! 2-s

Transformation: none

Addition: none

Reconstr. sent.:
šm^{c}ty šm^{c}kh
yhwh
r'ty p^{c}lkh

Comment: It seems necessary to treat šm^{c}ty šm^{c}kh and r'ty p^{c}lkh as semantic compounds; šēma^{c} is regularly used with the verb šm^{c}, and pō^{c}al occurs several times as the object of a verb of seeing (r'h: Ps.66:5, 90:16; 95:9; hbṭ // r'h, Isa.5:12; mp^{c}lt with ḥzh, Ps.46:9).

Comparison: lpn! : lpn! :: D(PN)
a 2-s : a 2-s :: A≠A (List)

Result: Formula: A A≠A
Del.-Comp.: none
Semantic parallelism: D(PN); List
Transformation: none

Hab.3

Text: v.3a — 'lh mtmn yb'
(w)qdš mhr pr'n

Translation: God came from Teman,
The Holy One, from Mount Paran.

Met. units: 3:3

Gram. units: 3:3

Syll. symmetry: 7:6 (symmetrical)

Gram. structure: 1 3pn b
,1 3-Cpn
Transformation: none
Addition: + b
Reconstr. sent.: 'lh mtmn
yb'
qdš mhr pr'n
Comparison: (b : b :: D)
1 : 1 :: A (Epith)
3pn : 3-Cpn :: /A (WP(PN))
+ compensation
Result: Formula: A /A (D)
Del.-Comp.: -b + compensation
Semantic parallelism: Epith; WP(PN)
Transformation: none

Hab.3

Text: v.3b ksh šmym hdh
(w)thlth ml'h (h)'rṣ
Translation: His majesty covered the heavens;
His praise filled the earth.
Met. units: 3:3
Gram. units: 3:3
Syll. symmetry: 6:8 (asymmetrical)
Gram. structure: a 2 1-s
1-s a 2
Transformation: none
Addition: none
Reconstr. sent.: ksh (ksth) šmym hdh
ml'h (ml') 'rṣ thlth
Comparison: a : a :: A (List)
2 : 2 :: A (Mer)
1-s : 1-s :: A (List)
Result: Formula: A A A
Del.-Comp.: none
Semantic parallelism: List; Mer
Transformation: none

Hab.3

Text: v.5 lpnw ylk dbr
(w)yṣ' ršp lrglw

Translation: Plague went before him;
Pestilence went ahead of him.

Met. units: 3:3

Gram. units: 3:3

Syll. symmetry: 6:6 (symmetrical)

Gram. structure: 3-s b l
b l 3-s

Comment: *dbr* and *ršp* should perhaps be marked PN as personified, as, indeed, *ršp* is derived from the name of the Canaanite god.

Transformation: none

Addition: none

Reconstr. sent.: lpnw ylk dbr
lrglw yṣ ršp

Comparison: 3-s : 3-s :: A (Syn)
b : b :: A (Syn)
l : l :: A (Syn)

Result: Formula: A A A
Del.-Comp.: none
Semantic parallelism: Syn
Transformation: none

Hab.3

Text: v.6a-b ^{c}md wymdd 'rṣ
r'h wytr gym

Translation: He stood and shook the earth;
He looked and made the nations leap.

Comment: On the problems posed by *ymdd*, see Albright, PHab.

Met. units: 3:3

Gram. units: 3:3

Syll. symmetry: 6:7 (symmetrical)

Gram. structure: b &a 2
a &a 2

Transformation: none

Addition: + b

Reconstr. sent.:

                    wymdd 'rṣ
^{c}md r'h
                    wytr   gym

Comparison: (b : b :: D)

&a : &a :: B (Syn)

2 : 2 :: A (WP)

+ a

Result: Formula: B A (D)

Del.-Comp.: - b + a

Semantic parallelism: Syn; WP

Transformation: none

Hab.3

Text: v.6c-d

ytpṣṣw hrry ^{c}d

šḥw gb^{c}t ^{c}lm

Comment: Albright's suggested reconstruction of the C Line of this triplet is tempting, but will not be used for analysis (see PHab). waw has been omitted from the beginning of the A Line.

Translation: Primeval mountains shattered;

Ancient hills flattened;

Met. units: 3:3

Gram. units: 3:3

Syll. symmetry: 7:6 (symmetrical)

Gram. structure: c 1-C

b 1-C

Transformation: none

Addition: none

Reconstr. sent.: ytpṣṣw (ttpṣṣn) hrry ^{c}d

šḥw   gb^{c}t ^{c}lm

Comparison: c : b :: A (List)

1-C : 1-C :: A/A (Syn)

Result: Formula: A A/A
Del.-Comp.: none
Semantic parallelism: List; Syn
Transformation: none

<u>Hab.3</u>

Text: v.11b
l'r ḥṣkh yhlkw
lngh brq ḥntkh

Translation:
They go forth by the light of your arrows,
By the radiance of your flashing spear.

Met. units: 3:3

Gram. units: 3:3

Syll. symmetry: 9:8 (symmetrical)

Gram. structure:
3-C-s b
,3-C-C-s

Transformation: none

Addition: + b

Reconstr. sent.:
l'r ḥṣkh
yhlkw
lngh brq ḥntkh

Comparison:
(b : b :: D)
3-C-s : 3-C-C-s :: A/Ⱥ (Syn/List)
+ compensation

Result:
Formula: A/Ⱥ (D)
Del.-Comp.: -b + compensation
Semantic parallelism: Syn; List
Transformation: none

<u>Hab.3</u>

Text: v.12
bz^{c}m tṣ^{c}d 'rṣ
b'p tdš gym

Translation:
In fury you trample the earth;
In wrath you tread on the nations.

Met. units: 3:3

Gram. units: 3:3

Gram. structure: 3 a 2
3 a 2
Transformation: none
Addition: none
Reconstr. sent.: bz^{c}m ṣ^{c}d 'rṣ
bp' tdš gym
Comparison: 3 : 3 :: A (Syn)
a : a :: A (Syn)
2 : 2 :: A (List-WP)
Result: Formula: A A A
Del.-Comp.: none
Semantic parallelism: Syn; List-WP
Transformation: none

<u>Ps.24</u>

Text: v.7 ś' š^{c}rm r'škm
(w)hnś' ptḥ ^{c}lm
(w)yb' mlk (h)kbd
Translation: Raise your heads, O gates;
Raise yourselves, O ancient doors;
Let the glorious king enter!
Met. units: 3:3:3
Gram. units: 3:3:3
Syll. symmetry: 8:8:5 (B-C Lines asymmetrical)
Gram. structure: a lpn! 2-s
c 1-C!
b! 1-C

<u>A-B Lines</u>

Transformation: none
Comment: No transformation is necessary since <u>ś' r'škm</u> is an idiomatic unit.
Addition: none

Reconstr. sent.: ś' r'škm š^{c}rm
hnś' pṭḥ ^{c}lm
Comparison: a 2-s : c :: A/ (Syn)
l! : l-C! :: /A (Epith)
Result: Formula: A/ /A
Del.-Comp.: none
Semantic parallelism: Syn; Epith
Transformation: none

<u>B-C</u> <u>Lines</u>
Result: Non-parallel unit (VS-VS)

<u>Ps.24</u>

Text: v.8 m z mlk (h)kbd
yhw ^{c}zz wgbr
yhw gbr mlḥm
Translation: Who is the glorious king?
YHWH, mighty and war-like,
YHWH, the hero in warfare!
Met. units: 3:3:3
Gram. units: 3:3:3
Syll. symmetry: 5:7:7 (A-B Lines asymmetrical)
Comment: The syllabic problems of this and the preceding unit would be eliminated by treating as a couplet:
yb' mlk (h)kbd (5)
m z mlk (h)kbd (5)
Gram. structure: Spr? Ppr ,=P-C
Spn ,-S ,-&S
,=Spn ,=S-C

<u>A-B</u> <u>Lines</u>
Result: Non-parallel unit (enjambment)

<u>B-C</u> <u>Lines</u>
Transformation: none
Addition: + ,=S
Reconstr. sent.: yhwh ^{c}zz wgbr mlḥm
Comment: This procedure seems necessary to catch the repetition of <u>gbr</u>. Note the absence of <u>waw</u> in the B Line.

Comparison: (,=S : ,=S :: D)
Spn : ,=Spn :: D(PN)
,-&S : ,=S- :: "D"
+ -C

Result: Formula: D "D" (D)
Del.-Comp.: - ,=S + -C
Semantic parallelism: D(PN); D
Transformation: none

Ps.29

Text: vv.1-2
hb lyhw // bn 'lm
hb lyhw / kbd w^{c}z
hb lyhw / kbd šm
hštḥw lyhw / bhdrt qdš

Comment: It seems clearly necessary to treat this unit as a quatrain.

Translation:
Give YHWH, O Sons of El,
Give YHWH glory and strength;
Give YHWH the glory due his name;
Bow to YHWH in his holy appearance!

Comment: On the translation of bn 'l and hdrt qdš, see, most recently, Cross, CMHE, p. 152, notes 25 and 28. Read also qodšô, following Cross, ibid., note 29.

Met. units: 4:4:4:4(2:2::2:2::2:2::2:2)

Gram. units: 4:4:4:4(2:2::2:2::2:2::2:2)

Syll. symmetry: 5:4::5:4::5:4::6:5 (internally symmetrical; C and D Lines externally asymmetrical)

Gram. structure:
a! 3pn // 1-Cpn!
a! 3pn / 2 &2
a! 3pn / 2-C-s
c! 3pn / 3-C-s

A-B Lines

Transformation: none

Addition:
+ 1-
+ -Cpn!

Reconstr. sent.: hbw lyhw bn 'lm kbd w^{c}z

Comparison: (1-Cpn! : 1-Cpn! :: D/D)
a! : a! :: D
3pn : 3pn :: D (D(PN))
+ 2
+ &2

Result: Formula: D D (D/D)
Del.-Comp.: - 1- + 2
- -Cpn! + &2
Semantic parallelism: D; D(PN)
Transformation: none

<u>B-C Lines</u>

Transformation: none
Addition: + &2
Reconstr. sent.: hb lyhw kbd šm w^{c}z
Comparison: (&2 : &2 :: D)
a! : a! :: D
3pn : 3pn :: D (D(PN))
2 : 2- :: "D"
+ -C-s

Result: Formula: D D "D" (D)
Del.-Comp.: - &2 + -C-s
Semantic parallelism: D; D(PN); "D"
Transformation: none

<u>C-D Lines</u>

Transformation: none
Addition: none
Reconstr. sent.: hbw kbd šm
lyhw bhdrt qdš
hštḥw
Comparison: a! 2-C-s : c :: A̸/ (Syn)
3pn : 3pn :: D (D(PN))
+ 3-
+ -C-s

Result: Formula: D A̸/
Del.-Comp.: - Ø + 3-
+ -C-s
Semantic parallelism: Syn; D(PN)
Transformation: none

<u>Ps.29</u>

Text: v.3	'l (h)kbd hr^{c}m
	ql yhw ^{c}l (h)mym
	yhw ^{c}l mym rbm
Comment:	The first and second lines have been reversed; cf. Cross, <u>CMHE</u>, p. 153.
Translation:	The God of glory thunders;
	The voice of YHWH, over the waters;
	YHWH, over the mighty waters.
Met. units:	3:3:3
Gram. units:	3:3:3
Syll. symmetry:	5:5:6 (symmetrical)
Gram. structure:	l-C b
	S-Cpn P(3)
	Spn P(3) ,-P(3)

<u>A-B Lines</u>

Transformation:	S-Cpn P(3) --→ l-Cpn 3
Comment:	Note that P(3) becomes simple 3 in the transformation.
Addition:	+ b
Reconstr. sent.:	'l (h)kbd
	hr^{c}m ^{c}l (h)mym
	ql yhw
Comparison:	(b : b :: D)
	l-C : l-Cpn :: A≠A (Epith-WP-PN)
	+ 3
Result:	Formula: A≠A (D)
	Del.-Comp.: - b + 3
	Semantic parallelism: Epith-WP-PN
	Transformation: l-Cpn 3 --→ S-Cpn P(3)
Comment:	Alternatively, one may reverse the second and third lines. Analysis would proceed along the following lines (B-C Lines same as A-B Lines above)
Transformation:	l-C b --→ S-C P(part.b)
Addition:	+ P(3)
	+ ,-P(3)
Reconstr. sent.:	yhw
	mr^{c}m ^{c}l mym rbm
	'l (h)kbd

Comparison: (3 : 3 :: D)
(,-3 :: ,-3 :: D)
Spn : S-C :: /A (Epith)
+ P(part.b)

Result: Formula: /A (D D)
Del.-Comp.: - 3 + P(part.b)
-3 ,-3
Semantic parallelism: Epith
Transformation: S-C P(part.b) --→ 1-C b

<u>B-C</u> <u>Lines</u>

Transformation: none

Addition: + S-

Reconstr. sent.: ql yhw ^{c}l mym rbm

Comment: Such seems to be the procedure required by the system of analysis; cf. vv.5 and 8 below. Note that (<u>h</u>) has been ignored in the reconstructed sentence in this case.

Comparison: (S- : S- :: D)
-Cpn : Spn :: "D" ("D"(PN))
P(3) : P(3) :: D
+ ,-P(3)

Result: Formula: "D" D (D)
Del.-Comp.: - S- + ,-P(3)
Semantic parallelism: D; "D"(PN)
Transformation: none

<u>Ps.29</u>

Text: v.4 ql yhw bkḥ
ql yhw bhdr

Comment: A type of chain begins with v.3 which extends through v.9. However, it is not necessary to depart from the procedure of analysis by basic units; i.e., couplets and triplets.

Translation: The voice of YHWH is powerful;
The voice of YHWH is majestic.

Met. units: 3:3

Comment: Or 4(2:2), in which case this unit is the A Line of a triplet 4:3:4(2:2::3::2:2) (so Cross, CMHE, p. 154):

ql yhw bkḥ // ql yhw bhdr
ql yhw šbr 'rzm
yšbr yhw / 'rz (h)lbnn

However, while the unit is short, it can, I believe, stand as 3:3.

Gram. units: 3:3

Syll. symmetry: 5:6 (symmetrical)

Gram. structure: S-Cpn P(3)
S-Cpn P(3)

Transformation: none

Addition: none

Reconstr. sent.: ql yhw bkḥ / bhdr

Comparison: S-Cpn : S-Cpn :: D/D (D/D(PN))
P(3) : P(3) :: A (Syn)

Result: Formula: A D/D
Del.-Comp.: none
Semantic parallelism: D; D(PN); Syn
Transformation: none

Ps.29

Text: v.5 ql yhw / šbr 'rzm
(w)yšbr yhw / 'rz (h)lbnn

Translation: The voice of YHWH breaks the cedars;
YHWH shatters the cedars of Lebanon.

Met. units: 4:4(2:2::2:2)

Gram. units: 4:4(2:2::2:2)

Syll. symmetry: 3:5::5:5 (A and B Lines asymmetrical; A Line internally asymmetrical)

Gram. structure: S-Cpn P(part.a) 2
a 1pn 2-Cpn

Comment: This analysis follows MT's šōbēr and so will require a transformation of the B Line. Cross suggests reading yəšabbēr for metrical reasons and on the pattern of yhl...yhl in v.8 (CMHE, p. 154). Dahood (Psalms) rejects Held's suggestion to read šibbēr and takes the alternation of šōbēr-yəšabbēr as an example of the interchange in conjugations one finds, for example, in Ps.24's śə'û-hinnāśə'û. A reading šābar would be equally possible. All of these suggestions have, from the point of view of this system, the advantage of requiring no transformation. However, this alone does not justify emendation of MT. Cross' suggestion has the advantage of making the unit syllabically symmetrical; but this advantage is lessened by a treatment of the line as 4(2:2), since the syllable count would then be an unbalanced 3:6, increasing the syllable asymmetry.

Transformation: a lpn 2-Cpn --→ P(part.a) Spn 2-Cpn

Addition: + S-

Reconstr. sent.: ql yhw šbr / mšbr 'rz(m) (h)lbnn

Comparison: (S- : S- :: D)
-Cpn : Spn :: "D" ("D"(PN))
P(part.a) : P(part.a) :: "D"
2 : 2- :: "D"
+ - Cpn

Result: Formula: "D" "D" "D" (D)
Del.-Comp.: - S- + -Cpn
Semantic parallelism: "D"; "D"(PN)
Transformation: P(part.a) Spn --→ a lpn 2-Cpn

Ps.29

Text: v.6 yrqdm km ᶜgl lbnn
(w)śryn km bn r'mm

Comment: The initial waw of the A Line has been omitted. The verse has been divided as commonly now (so also the treatment of the mem of yrqdm as enclitic).

Translation: He makes Lebanon dance like a calf; Sirion, like a young wild ox.

Met. units: 3:3

Gram. units: 3:3

Syll. symmetry: 9:8 (symmetrical)

Gram. structure: a-encl.mem "3" 2pn
,2pn "3-C"

Transformation: none

Addition: + a-encl.mem

Reconstr. sent.: yrqdm km ^{c}gl lbnn
km bn r'mm śryn

Comparison: (a-encl.mem : encl.mem :: D)
"3" : "3-C" :: /A (List)
2pn : 2pn :: A (List(PN))
+ compensation

Result: Formula: A /A (D)
Del.-comp.: - a-encl.mem + compensation
Semantic parallelism: List; List(PN)
Transformation: none

Ps.29

Text: v.8 ql yhw / yḥl mdbr
yḥl yhw / mdbr qdš

Translation: The voice of YHWH makes the desert tremble;
YHWH makes the desert of Qadesh tremble.

Met. units: 4:4(2:2::2:2)

Gram. units: 4:4(2:2::2:2)

Syll. symmetry: 3:4::4:4 (symmetrical)

Gram. structure: 1-Cpn / a 2
a 1pn / 2-Cpn

Transformation: none

Addition: + 1-

Reconstr. sent.: ql yhw yḥl mdbr qdš

Comparison:	(1- : 1- :: D)
	-Cpn : 1pn :: "D" ("D"(PN))
	a : a :: D
	2 : 2- :: "D"
	+ -Cpn
Result:	Formula: "D" D "D" (D)
	Del.-Comp.: - 1- + -Cpn
	Semantic parallelism: D; "D"(PN); "D"
	Transformation: none

<u>Ps.29</u>

Text: v.10	yhw lmbl yšb
	(w)yšb yhw / mlk l^{c}lm
Translation:	YHWH sits enthroned on the Flood-dragon;
	YHWH sits enthroned as king forever.
Comment:	On the translation of <u>mabbūl</u>, see Cross, <u>CMHE</u>, p. 155, note 42.
Met. units:	3:4(2:2)
Gram. units:	3:4(2:2)
Syll. symmetry:	7:8 (symmetrical)
Gram. structure:	1pn 3pn b
	b 1pn / "3" 3
Transformation:	none
Addition:	+ 3pn
Reconstr. sent.:	yhw yšb lmbl mlk l^{c}lm
Comparison:	(3pn : 3pn :: D)
	1pn : 1pn :: D (D(PN))
	b : b :: D
	+ "3"
	+ 3
Result:	Formula: D D (D)
	Del.-Comp.: - 3pn + "3"
	+ 3
	Semantic parallelism: D; D(PN)
	Transformation: none

<u>Ps.68</u>

Text: v.3	khndp ᶜšn tndp khms dng / mpn 'š y'bd ršᶜm / mpn yhw
Comment:	This triplet is retained as in MT, but follows Albright's vocalization and interpretation, including that of <u>tndp</u> as fem. collective (Cat); but see Dahood, <u>Psalms</u>, <u>ad locem</u>.
Translation:	They shall be dispersed as smoke is dispersed, As wax melts away before flame, The wicked shall perish before YHWH.
Met. units:	3:4:4(3::2:2::2:2)
Gram. units:	3:4:4(3::2:2::2:2)
Comment:	It is clearly necessary to award the preposition <u>mippᵊnê</u> the value of a full metrical unit, despite the complications this will produce in the formula.
Syll. symmetry:	9::5:4::6:5 (B and C Lines externally asymmetrical)
Gram. structure:	"3"(inf.const.c-C) c ,"3"(inf.const.c-C) / 3-C b 1 / 3-Cpn

<u>A-B Lines</u>

Transformation:	none
Addition:	+ c
Reconstr. sent.:	khndp ᶜšn tndp (tms) khms dng mpn 'š
Comment:	An unusual feature of this addition is that it probably requires a lexical replacement of <u>tinnādēp</u> by <u>timmas</u>. It does not seem likely that the phrase <u>mpn 'š</u> is to be considered a substitution addition to the B Line. The reconstructed sentence which would result from such an addition is: khndp ᶜšn mpn 'š tndp (tms) khms dng While it is true that flame does drive smoke away, it is unlikely that that is the image

here. Therefore, <u>hms</u> <u>dnq</u> <u>mpn</u> <u>'š</u> is to be treated as a semantic compound.

Comparison: (c : c :: D)
"3"(inf.const.c-C) : "3"(inf.const.c-C 3-C)
:: A≠≠≠A (Syn; List)
+ compensation

Result: Formula: A≠≠≠A (D)
Del.-Comp.: - c + compensation
Semantic parallelism: Syn; List
Transformation: none

<u>B-C Lines</u>

Transformation: none

Addition: none

Reconstr. sent.: khms dng mpn 'š
y'bd rš^{c}m mpn yhw

Comparison: "3"(inf.const.c-) : b :: C (Met)
-C : l :: C (Met)
3-C : 3-Cpn :: D/C (D/Met-PN)

Result: Formula: C C D/C
Del.-Comp.: none
Semantic parallelism: Met; Met-PN; D
Transformation: none

<u>Ps.68</u>

Text: v.5a šr lyhw // zmr šm
sl lrkb b^{c}rbt

Comment: Dahood's suggestions (<u>Psalms</u>, <u>ad</u> <u>locem</u>) are ingenious but accepted here is only his retention of MT's spelling of <u>^{c}rbt</u>, based on the attested, if unexplained and infrequent, interchange of <u>b</u> and <u>p</u> in Northwest (and East) Semitic.

Translation: Sing to YHWH; hymn his name;
Make a road for the rider in the clouds!

Comment: The translation of <u>sl</u> is uncertain. It seems safest to follow the attested meaning of the word in Hebrew since it is a not impossible semantic parallel to <u>šr</u> and <u>zmr</u>.

Met. units: 4(2:2):3

Gram. units: 4(2:2):3

Syll. symmetry: 5:5::9 (symmetrical)

Gram. structure: a 3pn // a 2
a 3 3

Transformation: none

Addition: + a
+ 3pn

Reconstr. sent.: zmr šm
šr lyhw
sl l rkb b^{c}rbt

Comparison: (a : a :: D),
(3pn : 3pn :: D)
a : a :: B (Syn)
2-s : 3 3 :: /A (Epith)
+ compensation

Result: Formula: B /A (D D)
Del.-Comp.: - a + compensation
- 3pn
Semantic parallelism: Syn; Epith
Transformation: none

<u>Ps.68</u>

Text: v.6 'b ytmm // (w)dyn 'lmnt
yhw bm^{c}n qdš

Translation: The father of orphans, the judge of widows,
YHWH is in his holy abode.

Met. units: 4(2:2):3

Gram. units: 4(2:2):3

Syll. symmetry: 5:5::6 (asymmetrical)

Gram. structure: S-C // ,=S-C
,=Spn P(3)-C-s

Comment: Also possible is the following interpretation of the unit:
P-C // ,=P-C
Spn 3-C-s

The father of orphans, the judge of widows
Is YHWH in (or: from) his holy abode.

Other interpretations are also feasible. The one chosen, however, is the only one which will allow the unit to be analyzed readily as a parallel unit.

Transformation: none

Addition: + S-
+ -C

Reconstr. sent.: 'b ytmm (w)dyn 'lmnt / yhw bm^{c}n qdš

Comparison: (S-C : S-C :: D/D)
,=S-C : ,=Spn :: A/ (Epith-PN)
+ P(3)-
+ -C-s

Result: Formula: A/ (D/D)
Del.-Comp.: - S- + P(3)-
- -C-s + -C-s
Semantic parallelism: Epith-PN
Transformation: none

Ps.68

Text: v.14b knp yn / nḥp bksp
(w)'brth byrqrq ḥrṣ

Translation: The wings of the dove are covered with silver,
Its pinions with yellow gold.

Met. units: 4(2:2):3

Gram. units: 4(2:2):3

Syll. symmetry: 4:4::8 (symmetrical)

Gram. structure: 1-C // c 3
,1-s 3-C

Transformation: none

Addition: + c

Reconstr. sent.: knp yn / 'brth nḥp bksp / byrqrq ḥrṣ

Comparison: (c : c :: D)
1-C : 1-s :: A/ (Syn)
3 : 3-C :: /A (List)
+ compensation

Result: Formula: A/ /A (D)
Del.-Comp.: -c + compensation
Semantic parallelism: Syn; List
Transformation: none

Ps.68

Text: v.16 hr 'lhm // hr bšn
hr gbnnm // hr bšn

Translation: O mighty mountains, mountains of Bashan,
O jagged (?) mountains, mountains of Bashan!

Comment: Following Albright's vocalization of *hr* as plural (*hārê*), despite the fact that it disturbs the syllable symmetry in a minor way (see Cat). The translation of *gbnnm* is uncertain, but it must mean something like "jagged, rough." It is taken to be a grade B synonym of *'lhm*, here probably "mighty."

Met. units: 4:4(2:2::2:2)

Gram. units: 4:4(2:2::2:2)

Syll. symmetry: 5:4::5:4 (symmetrical)

Gram. structure: 1-Cpn! // ,=1-Cpn!
,=1-Cpn! // ,=1-Cpn!

Comment: The phrases are analyzed as vocatives. Nominal sentences are also possible.

Transformation: none

Addition: none

Reconstr. sent.: hr 'lhm
hr bšn
hr gbnnm

Comparison: 1-Cpn! : ,=1-Cpn! :: D/B (Syn)
,=1-Cpn! : ,=1-Cpn! :: D/D (D(PN))

Result: Formula: D/B D/D
Del.-Comp.: none
Semantic parallelism: D(PN); Syn
Transformation: none

Ps.68

Text: v.17 lm trṣdn // hrm gbnnm
hr ḥmd / 'lhm lšbt
'p yhw yškn lnṣḥ

Translation: Why do you look (?), O jagged (?) mountains,
O mountains which God desired for his habitation,
YHWH, to dwell forever.

Comment: On gbnnm, see the preceding unit. The translation of trṣdn is also uncertain, but, fortunately, will not in any way impede analysis because of the structure of the unit.

Met. units: 4:4:3(2:2::2:2::3)

Gram. units: 4:4:3(2:2::2:2::3)

Syll. symmetry: 6:5::4:6::7 (B Line internally asymmetrical; C Line externally asymmetrical)

Gram. structure: 3? b // 1! ,-1!
,=1!-CR(a 1pn 3(inf.const.b)-s
ptcl 1pn 2(b) 3)

Comment: The grammatical analysis is complicated in a minor way by following Albright's reading hārê (Cat). A relative clause in construct, indicated by the sign -CR, is itself unproblematic. Certainly the relative clause continues into the C Line. The staircase effect of the unit can better be presented by the following arrangement:

lm trṣdn hrm gbnnm
hr ḥmd 'lhm lšbt
'p yhw yškn lnṣḥ

<u>A-B Lines</u>

Transformation: none

Addition: + 3?
+ b
+ ,-l!

Reconstr. sent.: lm trṣdn hrm (hārê) gbnnm ḥmd 'lhm lšbt

Comparison: (3? : 3? :: D)
(b : b :: D)
(,-l! : ,-l! :: D)
l! : =l!- :: "D"
+ ,-CR(a
+ lpn
+ 3(inf.const.b)-s

Result: Formula: "D" (D D D)
Del.-Comp.: - 3? + ,-CR(a
- b + lpn
- ,-l! + 3(inf.const.b)-s
Semantic parallelism: "D"
Transformation: none

<u>B-C Lines</u>

Transformation: none

Addition: + ,=l!-
+ -CR(a

Reconstr. sent.:

```
        'lhm      lšbt
hr ḥmd                    lnṣḥ
        ('p) yhw  yškn
```

Comment: The particle <u>'p</u> is, of course, intrusive in the reconstructed sentence.

Comparison: (,=l!- : ,=l!- :: D)
(a : a :: D)
lpn : ptcl-lpn :: A (PN)
3(inf.const.b)-s : 2(b) :: A (Syn)
+ 3

Result: Formula: A A (D D)
Del.-Comp.: - ,=l!- + 3
- a
Semantic parallelism: Syn; PN
Transformation: none

Ps.68

Text: v.18 rkb yhw rbtm
'lpm šnn 'dny

Translation: The chariots of YHWH are tens of thousands;
Thousands are the warriors of the Lord.

Comment: The A and B Lines of the triplet, as emended by Albright, seem serviceable for analysis; see Cat.

Met. units: 3:3

Gram. units: 3:3

Syll. symmetry: 7:9 (asymmetrical)

Gram. structure: S-Cpn P
P S-Cpn

Transformation: none

Addition: none

Reconstr. sent.: rkb yhw rbtm
šnn 'dny 'lpm

Comparison: S-Cpn : S-Cpn :: A/A (List; PN-Epith)
P : P :: A (Num)

Result: Formula: A A/A
Del.-Comp.: none
Semantic parallelism: List; PN-Epith; Num
Transformation: none

Ps.68

Text: v.19 ᶜlt lmrm // šbt šb
lqḥt mtnt b'rm

Comment: Albright's emendation of b'dm to b'rm (Cat) seems satisfactory; in any case, it will not affect the analysis of the unit significantly. Note the pun mrm-'rm.

Translation: You went north (or: to the heights); you took captives;
You received gifts from Aram.

Met. units: 4(2:2):3

Gram. units: 4(2:2):3

Syll. symmetry: 6:5::9 (asymmetrical)

Gram. structure: b 3 // a 2
a 2 3pn
Transformation: none
Addition: + b
+ 3
Reconstr. sent.: ^{c}lt lmrm [šbt šb / lqḥt mtnt] b'rm
Comparison: (b : b :: D)
(3 : 3 :: D)
a 2 : a 2 :: A≠A (List)
+ 3pn
Result: Formula: A≠A (D D)
Del.-Comp.: - b + 3pn
- 3
Semantic parallelism: List
Transformation: none

<u>Ps.77</u>

Text: v.17
r'kh mym yhwh
r'kh mym yḥlw
'p yrgzw thmt

Translation:
The waters saw you, O YHWH,
The waters saw you and shook;
The deeps trembled.

Met. units: 3:3:3
Gram. units: 3:3:2
Syll. symmetry: 6:7:7 (symmetrical)
Gram. structure: a-s 1 lpn!
a-s 1 b
ptcl b 1

<u>A-B Lines</u>

Transformation: none
Addition: lpn!
Reconstr. sent.: r'kh mym yhwh yḥlw
Comparison: (lpn! : lpn! :: D)
a-s : a-s :: D
+ b

Result: Formula: D D (D)
Del.-Comp.: - lpn! + b
Semantic parallelism: D
Transformation: none

<u>B-C</u> <u>Lines</u>

Transformation: none
Addition: + a-s
Reconstr. sent.: r'kh mym yḥlw / thmt ('p) yrgzw
Comparison: (a-s : a-s :: D)
l : l :: A* (Syn)
b : ptcl-b :: A (Syn)
+ compensation
Result: Formula: A A* (D)
Del.-Comp.: - a-s + compensation
Semantic parallelism: Syn
Transformation: none

<u>Ps.89</u>

Text: v.6 ydw šmym / pl'kh yhwh
'p 'mntkh / bqhl qdšm
Translation: In the heavens they praise your wonderful deeds, O YHWH,
Your faithfulness, in the assembly of the holy ones.
Met. units: 4(2:2):3
Gram. units: 4(2:2):3
Syll. symmetry: 4:5::6:5 (externally asymmetrical)
Gram. structure: a 3 / 2-s lpn!
ptcl 2-s / 3-C
Comment: Only the interpretation of <u>šmym</u> as sharing the preposition of <u>bqhl</u> (cf. Dahood, <u>Psalms</u>, <u>ad</u> <u>locem</u>) will allow a simple analysis of this unit. Note also <u>bšḥq</u> // <u>bbny</u> <u>'lm</u> in the following unit.
Transformation: none
Addition: + a
+ lpn!

Reconstr. sent.: šmym pl'kh / ydw yhwh / bqhl qdšm ('p) 'mntkh

Comparison: (a : a :: D)
(lpn! : lpn! :: D)
3 : 3-C :: /A (Syn)
2-s : ptcl-2-s :: A* (Syn)
+ compensation

Result: Formula: A* /A (D D)
Del.-Comp.: - a + compensation
- lpn!
Semantic parallelism: Syn
Transformation: none

Ps.89

Text: v.7 ky my bšḥq / y^c rk lyhwh
ydmh lyhwh / bbny 'lm

Translation: Who in the sky can compete with YHWH,
Can compare to YHWH among the lesser gods?

Met. units: 4:4(2:2::2:2)

Gram. units: 4:4(2:2::2:2)

Syll. symmetry: 4:5::5:4 (symmetrical)

Gram. structure: ptcl lpr? 3 / b 3pn
,b 3pn / 3-C

Transformation: none

Addition: + ptcl-lpr?

Reconstr. sent.: bšḥq y^c rk / ky my lyhwh / bbny 'lm ydmh

Comparison: (ptcl-lpr? : ptcl-lpr? :: D)
3 : 3-C :: /A (Syn)
b : b :: A (Syn)
3pn : 3pn :: D (D(PN))
+ compensation

Result: Formula: D A /A (D)
Del.-Comp.: - ptcl-lpr? + compensation
Semantic parallelism: Syn; D(PN)
Transformation: none

Ps.89

Text: v.8	'l n^{c}rṣ / bsd qdšm rb wnr' / ^{c}l kl sbbw
Comment:	The VSS, including the Targum's paraphrase, place rb (MT: rbh) in the B Line.
Translation:	God is terrible in the assembly of the holy ones, Great and feared over all who surround him.
Met. units:	4:4(2:2::2:2)
Gram. units:	4:4(2:2::2:2)
Syll. symmetry:	3:5::4:5 (A Line internally asymmetrical)
Gram. structure:	Spn P(part.c) / 3-C ,P(part.b) &P(part.c) / "3"-C-s
Transformation:	none
Addition:	+ Spn
Reconstr. sent.:	n^{c}rṣ bsd qdšm 'l rb wnr' ^{c}l kl sbbw
Comparison:	(Spn : Spn :: D) P(part.c) : P(part.b) &P(part.c) :: /A (Syn) 3-C : "3"-C-s :: A≠A (Epith) + compensation
Result:	Formula: A≠A /A (D) Del.-Comp.: - Spn + compensation Semantic parallelism: Syn; Epith Transformation: none

---

Ps.89

Text: v.10	'th mšl / bg't (h)ym bnś' glw // 'th tšbḥm
Comment:	MT's bś' should probably be emended either to binśō' or bᵊśē'ṯ; the former has been chosen as closer to MT, although the effect on analysis is nil.
Translation:	You are the one who rules over Sea's pride; When his waves rose up, you subdued them.
Comment:	The translation of tšbḥm as "subdue" or the like seems assured by the context of similar

	passages; cf. Dahood, Psalms, ad locem. Taking g't as "back" (cf. Cross, CMHE, p. 160, n. 67 and Dahood, ad locem) will not seriously affect analysis.
Met. units:	4:4(2:2::2:2)
Gram. units:	4:4(2:2::2:2)
Syll. symmetry:	4:4::4:6 (B Line externally and internally asymmetrical)
Gram. structure:	Spr P(part.a) / 3-Cpn 3(inf.const.b)-C-s / lpr a-s
Comment:	Note the treatment of the temporal clause with resumptive suffix in the pattern of casus pendens.
Transformation:	1. 3(inf.const.b)-C-s lpr a-s --→ 3(inf.const.b)-C-s Spr P(part.a)-s 2. 3(inf.const.b)-C-s Spr P(part.a)-s --→ 2(inf.const.b)-C-s Spr P(part.a)
Comment:	The result of the first transformation is a nominal sentence: binśō' gallāw 'attā(h) məšabbəḥēm The second transformation eliminates the adverbial clause, and, therefore, the resumptive suffix: nəśō' gallāw 'attā(h) məšabbēaḥ It may be noted that the texts of LXX, Vulgate and Peshitta would require no transformation since the temporal clauses are direct objects, as if already reflecting a Hebrew nəśō' gallāw. Moreover, the verbs in both lines are already parallel in form (finite in LXX and Vulgate, participles in the Peshitta). Perhaps we should read tmšl for MT's mšl (simple dittography in the oldest orthography).
Addition:	none
Reconstr. sent.:	mšl b g't (h)ym 'th mšbḥ nś' glw

Comparison:	Spr : Spr :: D
	P(part.a) : P(part.a) :: A (Syn)
	3-Cpn : 2(inf.-const.b)-C-s :: A/A (Met; WP)
Result:	Formula: D A A/A
	Del.-Comp.: none
	Semantic parallelism: Met; WP
	Transformation:
	1. 2(inf.const.b)-C-s Spr P(part.a) --→ 3(inf.const.b)-C-s Spr P(part.a)-s
	2. 3(inf.const.b)-C-s Spr P(part.a)-s --→ 3(inf.const.b)-C-s lpr a-s

---

Ps.89

Text: v.11	'th dk'th / kḥll rhb
	bzr^c ^{c}zkh / pzrth 'ybkh
Translation:	You crushed Rahab like a corpse;
	With your mighty arm you scattered your foes.
Met. units:	4:4(2:2::2:2)
Gram. units:	4:4(2:2::2:2)
Syll. symmetry:	5:5::5:7 (A and B Lines asymmetrical; B Line internally asymmetrical)
Gram. structure:	lpr a / "3" 2pn
	3-C-s / a 2-s
Transformation:	none
Addition:	+ lpr
	+ "3"
Reconstr. sent.:	'th [dk'th / pzrth] kḥll [rhb / 'ybkh] bzr^c ^{c}zkh
Comment:	The addition of kḥll is admissible only if one assumes that the meaning of the B Line is that YHWH scatters the corpses of his foes (cf. pzrt ^{c}ṣmt in Ps.63:6 and 141:7). ḥll, when added to the B Line, must be understood as a collective noun, as often; or one may take 'ybkh as singular (cf. Cross, CMHE, p. 160, n. 68).

Comparison: ("3" : "3" :: D)
(lpr : lpr :: D)
a : a :: B (List)
2pn : 2-s :: B (PN-PW)
+ 3-
+ -C-s

Result: Formula: B B (D D)
Del.-Comp.: - lpr + -C-s
- "3" + 3-
Semantic parallelism: List; PN-PW
Transformation: none

Ps.89

Text: v.12 lkh šmym // 'p lkh 'rṣ
tbl wml'h // 'th ysdtm

Translation: Yours are the heavens; yours the earth;
The world and its fullness, you established them.

Met. units: 4:4(2:2::2:2)

Gram. units: 4:4(2:2::2:2)

Syll. symmetry: 4:4::6:5 (A and B Lines externally asymmetrical)

Gram. structure: P(3)-s S // ptcl P(3)-s S
2 &2-s // lpr a-s

Transformation: 1. 2 &2-s lpr a-s --→ 2 &2-s Spr P(part.a)-s
2. 2 &2-s Spr P(part.a)-s --→ 2 &2-s Spr P (part.a)

Comment: The first transformation transforms the B Line from a verbal sentence into a nominal sentence:

tēbēl ûm^{ə}lō'āh 'attā(h) yōs^{ə}dām

The second transformation removes the casus pendens:

tēbēl ûm^{ə}lō'ā(h) 'attā(h) yōsēd

Addition: + P(3)-s
+ S

Reconstr. sent.: lkh šmym 'p / lkh 'rṣ
'th ysd tbl wml'h

Comparison: (P(3)-s : P(3)-s :: D)
(S : S :: D)
ptcl-P(3)-s : Spr P(part.a) :: /A (Epith)
S : 2 &2-s :: /A (Syn)
+ compensation

Result: Formula: /A /A (D D)
Del.-Comp.: - P(3)-s + compensation
- S
Semantic parallelism: Epith; Syn
Transformation:
1. 2 &2-s Spr P(part.a) --→ 2 &2-s Spr P (part.a)-s
2. 2 &2-s Spr P(part.a)-s --→ 2 &2-s lpr a-s

Comment: The chief difficulty in the above analysis is made apparent by the lack of grammatical parallelism between the semantically parallel terms 'rṣ and tbl wml'h (S : 2 &2). This difficulty can be eliminated by treating the casus pendens as the nominal sentence it is in its underlying structure:

S(2 &2-s) P(lpr a-s)
"The world and its fullness is (what) you created them.

In this case, no transformation is necessary, even that of 'th ysdtm to a nominal clause, since it is already part of the structure of a nominal sentence. Analysis would proceed as follows:

Comparison: (P(3)-s : P(3)-s :: D)
(S : S :: D)
ptcl-P(3)-s : P(lpr a-s) :: /A (Epith)
S : S(2 &2-s) :: /A (Syn)

The resulting formula (/A /A (D D)) is the same produced by the first method.

It may be noted that matters would be simpler if one takes 'th ysdtm as a relative clause. The grammatical analysis of the unit would then be:

P(3)-s S // ptcl P(3)-s S

,S &S-s // ,-R(lpr a-s)

"Yours are the heavens; yours the earth;

(Yours) the world and its fullness, which you established."

Analysis proceeding along these lines would produce the formula /A (D D D). However, it seems that the semantic relationship between the terms lkh ("yours") and 'th ysdtm ("you established them"), though unusual, is too close to allow such a simple analysis. Note, however, the comments on the following unit.

Ps.89

Text: v.13 — ṣpn wymn // 'th br'tm

tbr wḥrmn // bšmkh yrnnw

Translation: Saphon and Amanus, you created them,

Tabor and Hermon, which shout for joy at your name.

Comment: Dahood may be correct in identifying ymn here as Amanus (Psalms, ad locem); (cf. Cross, CMHE, p. 161, n. 70).

Met. units: 4:4(2:2::2:2)

Gram. units: 4:4(2:2::2:2)

Syll. symmetry: 5:5::5:8 (A and B Lines asymmetrical; B Line internally asymmetrical)

Gram. structure: lpn &lpn // lpr a-s

, lpn &lpn // ,-R(3-s b)

Comment: It is necessary to treat bšmkh yrnnw (or 'th ysdtm) as a relative clause to make it analyzable. The identity of structure of the A Line of this unit with the B Line of the previous one makes it clear that we are dealing with a quatrain. However, its structure is not so tightly bound that it requires analysis as a primary unit (cf. Ps.29:1-2).

Transformation: none

Addition: + lpr
+ a-s

Reconstr. sent.: ṣpn wymn
bšmkh yrnnw 'th br'tm
tbr wḥrmn

Comparison: (lpr : lpr :: D)
(a-s : a-s :: D)
lpn &lpn : lpn &lpn :: A≠A (List(PN))
+ ,-R(3-s
+ b)

Result: Formula: A≠A (D D)
Del.-Comp.: - lpr + ,-R(3-s
- a-s + b)
Semantic parallelism: List(PN)
Transformation: none

Ps.114

Text: v.1 bṣ't yśr'l mmṣrym
bt y^{c}qb / m^{c}m l^{c}z

Translation: When Israel went out of Egypt,
The house of Judah from a stammering nation,

Met. units: 3:4(2:2)

Gram. units: 3:4(2:2)

Syll. symmetry: 8::3:4 (symmetrical)

Gram. structure: 3(inf.const.b-Cpn 3pn
,-C-Cpn 3 ,-3)

Transformation: none

Addition: + 3(inf.const.b-

Reconstr. sent.: yśr'l mmṣrym
bṣ't
bt y^{c}qb m^{c}m l^{c}z

Comparison: (3(inf.const.b- : 3(inf.const.b- :: D)
-Cpn : -C-Cpn :: /A (Epith(PN))
3pn : 3 ,-3 :: /A (PN-Epith)
+ compensation

Result: Formula: /A /A (D)
Del.-Comp.: -3(inf.const.b- + compensation
+ compensation
Semantic parallelism: Epith(PN); PN-Epith
Transformation: none

<u>Ps.114</u>

Text: v.2 hyth yhdh lqdšh
yśr'l mmšltw

Translation: Judah became his holy possession,
Israel, his dominion.

Met. units: 3:3

Gram. units: 3:2

Syll. symmetry: 9:7 (asymmetrical)

Comment: Note that the asymmetry is removed if one reads <u>lmmšltw</u> (dittography).

Gram. structure: "b" Spn P("3")-s
,Spn P-s

Transformation: none

Addition: + "b"

Reconstr. sent.:

	yhdh	lqdšh
hyth		
	yśr'l	mmšltw

Comparison: ("b" : "b" :: D)
Spn : Spn :: A (List-PW)
P("3")-s : P-s :: A* (Syn)
+ compensation

Result: Formula: A A* (D)
Del.-Comp.: - "b" + compensation
Semantic parallelism: List-PW; Syn
Transformation: none

<u>Ps.114</u>

Text: v.3 (h)ym r'h wyns
(h)yrdn ysb l'ḥr

Translation: Sea saw and fled;
Jordan turned back.

Met. units: 3:3

Gram. units: 3:3

Syll. symmetry: 6:7 (symmetrical)

Gram. structure: lpn a &b
lpn b 3

Transformation: none

Addition: + a

Reconstr. sent.:
(h)ym wyns
r'h
(h)yrdn ysb l'ḥr

Comparison: (a : a :: D)
lpn : lpn :: A WP(PN)
&b : b 3 :: /A (Syn)
+ compensation

Result: Formula: A /A (D)
Del.-Comp.: -a + compensation
Semantic parallelism: WP(PN); Syn
Transformation: none

<u>Ps.114</u>

Text: v.4 (h)hrm rqdw k'lm
gb^{c}t kbny ṣ'n

Translation: Mountains danced like rams,
Hills like sheep.

Met. units: 3:3

Gram. units: 3:3

Syll. symmetry: 8:6 (asymmetrical)

Gram. structure: l b "3"
,l "3-C"

Transformation: none

Addition: + b

Reconstr. sent.:
hrm k'lm
rqdw
gb^{c}t kbny ṣ'n

Comparison: (b : b :: D)
1 : 1 :: A (Syn)
"3" : "3-C" :: /A (PW)
+ Ø compensation

Result: Formula: A /A (D)
Del.-Comp.: - b + Ø compensation
Semantic parallelism: Syn; PW
Transformation: none

Ps.114

Text: v.7 mlpny 'dn / ḥly 'rṣ
mlpny 'lh y^cqb

Translation: Tremble, O earth, before the Lord,
Before the God of Jacob!

Met. units: 4(2:2):3

Gram. units: 4(2:2):3

Syll. symmetry: 5:3::7 (A Line internally asymmetrical)

Gram. structure: 3-Cpn / b! l!
,3-C-C-pn

Transformation: none

Addition: + b!
+ l!

Reconstr. sent.: mlpny 'dn / 'lh y^cqb ḥly 'rṣ

Comparison: (b! : b! :: D)
(l! : l! :: D)
3-Cpn : 3-C-Cpn :: D/A̸ (D; Epith(PN))
+ compensation

Result: Formula: D/A̸ (D D)
Del.-Comp.: - b! + compensation
-l!
Semantic parallelism: D; Epith(PN)
Transformation: none

Comment: Cross' reading kl h'rṣ would simplify analysis considerably; see CMHE, p. 138, n. 41.

Ps.114

Text: v.8 — (h)hpky (h)ṣr / 'gm mym
ḥlmš lm^{c}ynw mym

Translation: Who turned the rock into a pond of water,
The flint into a fountain of water.

Met. units: 4(2:2):3

Gram. units: 4(2:2):3

Syll. symmetry: 4:3::7 (symmetrical)

Gram. structure: ,= -C(part.a) 2 / "3-C"
,= 2 "3-C"

Comment: hpky is in apposition to 'dn and 'lh y^{c}qb of the previous unit.

Transformation: none

Addition: + ,= -C(part.a)

Reconstr. sent.:
(h)ṣr 'gm mym
(h)hpky
ḥlmš lm^{c}ynw mym

Comparison: (,= -C(part.a) : ,= -C(part.a) :: D)
2 : ,= 2 :: A (Syn)
"3-C" : "3-C" :: A/D (List)
+ compensation

Result: Formula: A A/D (D)
Del.-Comp.: - ,= -C(part.a) + compensation
Semantic parallelism: Syn; List; D
Transformation: none

PART III

Unit Formulae

The unit formulae represent a summary in symbolic form of the relationship between each B Line and its A Line. This section contains a list of all the unit formulae along with a number of analyses of topics related to them. The unit formulae may be classified in several ways according to various criteria:

1. From the point of view of the frequency of their representation in the Corpus, formulae may be classified as major and minor. The former are those represented by at least five examples. Many of the minor formulae may be considered variations of a major one, as, indeed, some major formulae may be viewed as variations of another major formula.

2. From the point of view of the type of semantic relationship they represent, formulae may be classified as parallel or repetition formulae. The relationship between B and A Lines may be represented by the neutral symbol x, along with its variations (/x, x*, etc.). In parallel formulae, the relationship of semantic parallelism between units of B and A Lines is represented by the semantic signs A B and C; in repetition formulae, only by the signs D and "D". However, in this section, both types will be treated together, since they may both appear in some formulae patterns. A later section will deal with repetition formulae specifically.

3. As regards grammatical congruence between A and B Lines, formulae may be classified as "replacement" and "non-replacement." Replacement formulae are those in which one or more grammatical units of the A Line are deleted and are "replaced" in the B Line by various types of compensation, or "compensatory lengthening." Compensation will form the object of analysis in a later section. Depending on the number of deletions from the A Line, replacement formulae may be further classified as single, double or triple. Non-replacement formulae are those in which no such process of deletion and compensation takes place (with the exception of a very few examples which display replacement, i.e., compensation, without deletion).

4. From the point of view of the relationship between metrical units, the unit formulae fall into two major categories: three metrical unit formulae and four metrical unit formulae. The latter also include those formulae that display a metrical unit pattern of three-four and four-three. If one combines this classification with those discussed under (1) and (3) above, one obtains the categories of three and four metrical unit non-replacement formulae, and three and four metrical unit single and double replacement formulae. Triple replacement formulae can, of course, occur only in units with at least four grammatical units. Each of these categories may then be classified as major or minor. The possible relationships are represented in the following chart (MU = metrical units):

	Non-replacement		Replacement					
			Single		Double		Triple	
	Major	Minor	Major	Minor	Major	Minor	Major	Minor
3 MU	x	x	x	x	x	x		
4 MU	(x)	x	(x)	x	x	x	(x)	x

The number of possible combinations is 14; however, the four metrical unit categories are poorly represented in the Corpus and contain only one major formula (x x (D D)). Therefore, only 11 categories actually appear in the following lists.

5. In addition, formulae may be classified by the criterion of syllabic symmetry, that is, the syllabic regularity of the units they symbolize. The metrical aspect of the formulae is represented in this study by the "metrical units" on the one hand, and the attention paid to syllabic symmetry on the other. A later section will discuss this difficult problem from the point of view of overall metrical regularity in the unit formulae. Here the focus is more restricted. Of primary interest is the regularity of formulae from the point of view of certain types of syllabic relationships they must display. For example, formulae characterized by the parallelism of a simple grammatical unit in the A Line with a compound in the B Line can be considered syllabically satisfactory only if the B Line compound exceeds the simple A Line unit by two or more syllables. Formulae which require this or other syllabic patterns may be classified as syllabically satisfactory or unsatisfactory

as they meet, or do not meet, respectively, the specific syllabic pattern characteristic of that formulae. Details on the latter will be given at the beginning of the section dealing with each formulae for which a pattern of syllabic compensation is relevant. Major formulae will be listed in the order in which they approximate the syllabic "ideal" of their pattern.

The lists of unit formulae are followed by totals and statistics, and by two topics related to the unit formulae. A brief description of these analyses is included in the outline for this section.

The nature of some formulae requires special treatment, particularly as regards the order of their presentation. Such formulae will be prefaced by an explanation of the special procedure to be followed.

I. LIST OF THE UNIT FORMULAE
   A. Three metrical unit formulae
      1. Non-replacement formulae
         a. Major formulae
         b. Minor formulae
            (1) List according to the major formulae of which they are a variation
            (2) Unclassified formulae
      2. Replacement formulae
         a. Single replacement formulae
            (1) Major formulae, listed according to syllabic soundness of the pattern characteristic to each
            (2) Minor formulae, arranged according to the major formulae of which they are a variation

               Syllabic regularity is indicated; however, since most such formulae are represented by only a few examples, a syllabic arrangement would be inconvenient.
         b. Double replacement formulae
            (1) Major formulae, listed as the single replacement formulae, above
            (2) Minor formulae, listed as single replacement minor formulae, above
   B. Four metrical unit formulae (The principle of arrangement is stated at the beginning of this list)
      1. Non-replacement formulae
      2. Replacement formulae

a. Single replacement formulae

b. Double replacement formulae

(1) Major formulae

(2) Minor formulae

(a) minor formulae which are variations of the major formulae

(b) additional minor formulae

c. Triple replacement formulae

II. TOTALS AND STATISTICS

III. DISCUSSION OF THE MINOR FORMULAE

This segment contains a summary of the ways in which some minor formulae differ from the major formulae of which they are variations, accompanied by appropriate lists.

IV. ARRANGEMENT OF THE FORMULAE BY GRAMMATICAL UNITS

This section contains a suggestion for an alternative, purely grammatical, approach to the unit formulae with a list of the formulae according to this interpretation.

LIST OF THE UNIT FORMULAE

Three Metrical Unit Formulae

Non-replacement Formulae

Major Formulae

There are four major three metrical unit non-replacement formulae:

1. x x x (14 examples)
2. x x/x (9 examples)
3. x x≠x (10 examples)
4. x/ /x (6 examples)

The following is a full list and brief description of each of these formulae:

x x x

This is the simplest of all formulae in that a single metrical unit of the B Line corresponds to one such unit in the A Line:

Dt.32:2a y^c^rp kmṭr lqḥy "Let my teaching drop like rain;
   tzl kṭl 'mrty Let my word drip like dew!"

The examples of this formulae occurring in the *Corpus* are:

1. Gen.49:6a A A B
2. Gen.49:27b-c A A A
3. Num.23:8 A A A
4. Num.23:21a A A A
5. Dt.32:2a A A A
6. Dt.32:18 A A A
7. Dt.32:23 A A B
8. Dt.32:30a A A A
9. Dt.32:39b D A A
10. Dt.33:28a A A A
11. Dt.33:29c A A C
12. Hab.3:3b A A A
13. Hab.3:5 A A A
14. Hab.3:12 A A A

x x/x

This formula is produced by the parallelism between a grammatical compound in A and B Lines. In fact, it is a grammatical variation of x x x:

II Sam.22:43: 'ṣḥqm k^{c}pr 'rṣ "I crushed them like the dust of the ground;

ktṭ ḥṣt 'dqm Like the dirt of the streets I pulverized them."

1. Num.24:17a A D/A
2. Dt.32:2b A D/A
3. Dt.32:15b A A/A
4. II Sam.22:5 B A/A
5. II Sam.22:6 B A/A
6. II Sam.22:45 A A/A
7. Hab.3:2a A A/A
8. Ps.29:4 A D/D
9. Ps.68:18 A A/A

x x≠x

This formula differs from x x/x in that the compounds are of the type which this system labels "semantic":

II Sam.22:16a: yr'w 'pqm ym "The bed of the sea became visible;

yglw msdt tbl The foundations of the world were revealed."

The following examples of this formula occur in the Corpus:

1. Gen.49:6b B B≠B
2. Gen.49:25a A D≠A
3. Dt.32:9 A A≠A
4. Dt.32:13a B A≠A
5. Dt.32:42a A A≠A
6. II Sam.22:9a-b A A≠A
7. II Sam.22:9b-c A A≠A
8. II Sam.22:15 A C≠C
9. II Sam.22:16a A A≠A
10. Hab.3:2a A A≠A

x/ /x

This formula represents a special rhetorical device which may briefly be described as follows: a compound in the A Line parallels a simple unit in the B Line and, conversely, a simple term in the A Line parallels a compound in the B Line. The overall relationship is, then, one of chiastic compensation:

A Line		B Line
Simple	//	Compound
Compound	//	Simple

However, this formula presents some special problems. In fact, examples of the type of balance described above are few in the Corpus. Strict examples of x/ /x must contain not only a grammatical balance of simple and compound parallel units but also a syllabic balance which, in conformity with the general rule followed in this study, must be not less than two syllables. However, some examples contain a dichotomy of less than two syllables in one or even both of the parallel pairs; still others, further removed from the ideal, display only grammatical chiasm with no discernible syllabic chiasm. Due to the limited number of units in the Corpus, it is impossible to determine whether such looser examples are legitimate variations of the formula x/ /x or anomalies produced by defective texts and errors.

In the following list, examples of x/ /x (and its variations) will be presented in a manner which displays their approximation to the ideal of this formula, as described above. This will also be the case with other formulae which require specific patterns of syllabic compensation.

1. Grammatical chiasm and syllabic chiasm

This is the ideal form of x/ /x: a balance of at least two syllables between parallel simple and compound grammatical units.

a. Dt.32:20a B/ /C

'strh pny mhm "I shall hide my face from them;
'r'h mh 'ḥrtm I shall see what their end will be."

A Line		B Line
'strh pny	compound 5 // 2 simple	'r'h
mhm	simple 2 // 4 compound	mh 'ḥrtm

b. II Sam.22:8a A/ /A

tg^{c}š wtr^{c}š 'rṣ "The earth trembled and shook;

msdy hrm yrgzw The supports of the mountains trembled."

A Line		B Line
tg^{c}š wtr^{c}š	compound 5 // 3 simple	yrgzw
'rṣ	simple 1 // 5 compound	msdy hrm

c. II Sam.22:23 A/ /B

ky kl mspṭw lngdy "All his rules are before me;

ḥqtw l' 'sr mmny I do not remove his laws from myself."

A Line		B Line
ky kl mšpṭw	compound 5 // 3 simple	ḥqtw
lngdy	simple 3 // 6 compound	l' 'sr mmny

2. Grammatical chiasm; partial syllabic chiasm

Dt.32:8a A/ /A

bhnḥl ^{c}lyn gym "When Elyon gave the inheritance of the nations,

bhprdh bny 'dm When he set the divisions of mankind."

A Line		B Line
bhnḥl ^{c}lyn	compound 5 // 4 simple	bhprdh
gym	simple 2 // 4 compound	bny 'dm

3. Grammatical chiasm; insufficient or no syllabic chiasm

a. II Sam.22:17 B/ /B

yšlḥ ydh mmrm "He stretched out his hand from the heights;

ymšny mmm rbm He drew me from the mighty waters."

A Line		B Line
yšlḥ ydh	compound 4 // 3 simple	ymšny
mmrm	simple 3 // 4 compound	mmm rbm

b. Ps.24:7a-b A/ /A

ś' š^{c}rm r'škm "Raise your heads, O gates;

(w)hnś' ptḥ ^{c}lm Raise yourselves, O ancient doors."

A Line		B Line
ś'...r'škm	compound 5 // 4 simple	hnś'
š^{c}rm	simple 3 // 4 compound	ptḥ ^{c}lm

Minor Formulae

Variations of x x x

1. x x /x Dt.32:1 A A/A

h'znw (h)šmym w'dbrh — "Heed, O heavens, what I shall speak;

(w)tšm^c (h)'rṣ 'mry py — Hear, O earth, the words of my mouth!"

Comment: This formula is produced by a grammatical structure of 3:4 in a metrical framework of 3:3.

2. x x x/ Num.23:7b D A A/

lk 'r ly y^{c}qb — "Go curse Jacob for me;

lk z^{c}m yśr'l — Go execrate Israel!"

Comment: This formula is produced by a grammatical structure of 4:3 in a metrical framework of 3:3.

Variations of x x/x

1. x x/x Dt.32:7a A A/A

zkr ymt ^{c}lm — "Remember the days of old;

bnh šnt dr wdr — Consider the years of antiquity!"

Comment: This formula is produced by a grammatical structure of 3:4 in a metrical framework of 3:3.

2. x/x/x

a. Dt.33:14 D/A/A

mmgd tb't šmš — "From the abundance of the crops of the sun,

mmgd grš yrḥ — From the abundance of the produce of the moon."

b. Dt.33:15 D/A/A

mmgd hrr qdm — "From the abundance of the ancient mountains,

mmgd gb^{c}t ^{c}lm — From the abundance of the eternal hills."

Comment: Both units form part of the same chain. The formula perhaps is more a variation of x x/x than simple x x x and is produced by the parallelism of double constructs.

3. x/x x/x

a. Num.23:10a D/A A/A

m mn ^{c}pr y^{c}qb — "Who has counted the dust of Jacob;

(w)m spr trb^{c}t yśr'l — Who has numbered the dust cloud of Israel?"

b. II Sam.22:32 <u>D/A</u> A/A

ky my 'l mbl^{c}dy yhwh "Who except YHWH is God;

(w)my ṣr zlty 'lhnw Who except our God is a rock?"

<u>Comment</u>: This formula is produced by a grammatical structure of 4:4 in a metrical framework of 3:3.

<u>Variations of x x≠x</u>

1. x x̸

Characteristic of this formula is the presence of an indivisible compound. The degree of semantic attraction is high enough so that it seems preferable to treat it as a variation of x x≠x rather than of x x/x. Of course, the relationship between all three patterns is very close.

a. Dt.32:3 A A̸

ky šm yhwh 'qr' "I proclaim the name of YHWH;

hbw gdl l'lhnw Ascribe greatness to our God!"

b. Dt.32:22b A A̸

t'kl 'rṣ wyblh "It devours the earth and its produce;

(w)tlhṭ msdy hrm It sets aflame the foundations of the mountains."

c. Dt.32:35b A A̸

ky qrb ym 'dm "The day of their destruction is near;

(w)ḥš ^{c}tdt lmw That which will happen to them hastens."

2. x/x≠x Gen.49:12a A/A≠A

ḥkll ^{c}nm myn "(His) darkness of eyes is more (than that) of wine:

lbn šnm mḥlb (His) whiteness of teeth is more (than that) of milk."

<u>Comment</u>: This formula seems to be a simple variant of x x≠x and x x/x.

3. <u>x</u>/ x≠x Num.23:10b <u>C</u>/ A≠A

tmt npš mt yšrm "May I die an upright man's death;

th 'ḥrt kmh May my end be like his!"

<u>Comment</u>: This formula is produced by a grammatical framework of 4:3 in a metrical pattern of 3:3.

4. x///ẋ Dt.32:35a A///B̸

lym nqm wšlm "For the day of vengeance and recompense,

l^ct tmṭ rglm For the time when their foot stumbles."

Comment: This rather involved formula represents the parallelism of double compounds, the latter members of which are indivisible.

5. x≠x≠x Dt.32:38a A≠A≠A

ḥlb zbḥmw y'klw "Who ate the fat of their sacrifices;

yštw yn nskmw Who drank the wine of their libations?"

Comment: This formula results from the parallelism of double semantic compounds.

6. x≠≠≠x Dt.33:28b A≠≠≠A

^cl 'rṣ dgn wtrš "On his land are grain and wine;

'p šmw y^crp ṭl His heavens drip dew."

Comment: This formula exhibits much the same pattern as no. 4, above, except that the compounds are semantic.

Variations of x/ /x

1. *x /x Ex.15:2b *A /A

z 'l w'rmmnh "This is my God whom I exalt,

'lh 'b w'nwh The God of my fathers whom I admire."

A Line		B Line
z 'l	simple 3 // 5 compound	'lhy 'by
w'rmmnh	simple 6 // 4 simple	w'nwh

Comment: This unit presents several problems, but seems to be classifiable as a variation of x/ /x. The text has been rearranged (see the Corpus). The grammatical chiasm between simple and compound units characteristic of x/ /x is only partially present. Nevertheless, the metrical pattern is clearly chiastic and meets the requirement of a two-syllable contrast between parallel terms.

2. x/ x* Dt.32:41b A/ A*

'šb nqm lṣry "I shall punish my foes;

(w)lmśn'y 'šlm I shall pay back my enemies."

A Line		B Line
'šb nqm	compound 4 // 3 simple	'šlm
lṣry	simple 3 // 3 simple	lmśn'y

Comment: Like the preceding example, this unit contains several problems, but seems to be a variation of x/ /x. It contains only partial grammatical chiasm, and even its metrical chiasm is incomplete: both lṣry and lmśn'y contain three syllables. Moreover, the grammatical pattern 3:2 is characteristic of the formula x x* (D), a replacement formula.

3. x/ /x̲ Jud.5:29 C/ /A̲

ḥkmt śrth t^{c}nn "The wisest of her ladies answers her;

'p h' tšb 'mrh lh She responds with words to her."

A Line		B Line
ḥkmt śrth	compound 6 // 2 simple	'p h'
t^{c}nn	simple 3 // 6 compound	tšb 'mrh lh

Comment: This variation of x/ /x is unproblematic and is produced by a grammatical parallelism of 3:4 in a 3:3 metrical framework.

Unclassified Formulae

This section contains formulae which cannot be related simply to one of the major formulae. Rather than force them into one of the common formulae, it seems best to treat them as independent patterns. In most cases suggestions may be made regarding their relationship to one of the major formulae. This will also be the procedure in the similar sections dealing with unclassified replacement formulae.

1. *x x*

a. Gen.49:7b *A A*

'ḥlqm by^{c}qb "I shall divide them among Jacob;

(w)'pṣm byśr'l I shall scatter them among Israel."

b. Num.23:23a *A A*

k l' nḥš by^{c}qb "There is no divining against Jacob;

(w)l' qsm byśr'l There is no conjuring against Israel."

Comment: This formula results from a grammatical parallelism of 2:2 in a metrical framework of 3:3. Its closest relative among the major formulae may be x/ /x, although both examples lack any grammatical chiasm and syllabic chiasm is limited to one syllable:

Gen.49:7b:

A Line		B Line
'ḥlqm	simple 4 // 3 simple	'pṣm
by^{c}qb	simple 3 // 4 simple	byśr'l

Num.23:23a:

A Line		B Line
k l' nḥš	simple 4 // 3 simple	l' qsm
by^{c}qb	simple 3 // 4 simple	byśr'l

2. x *x Ex.15:5 A *B

thmt yksym — "The deeps covered them;
yrd bmṣlt km 'bn — They went down into the depths like stone."

Comment: This formula is produced by a grammatical parallelism of 2:2 in a metrical framework of 3:3. It does not seem to be related to any of the major non-replacement formulae. One of the aspects, the non-parallel addition to the B Line (km 'bn), is characteristic of the replacement formula x x (D). Note that the unit is syllabically asymmetrical.

3. x *x* Num.24:10 A *A*

mbrkk brk — "Blessed is everyone who blesses you;
'rrk 'rr — Cursed is everyone who curses you."

Comment: This formula is produced by a grammatical structure of 2:2 in a metrical framework of 3:3. Its pattern seems to be most closely related to either x x/x or x x̸.

4. *x/x̸ Dt.32:25b *A/A̸

gm bḥr gm btlh — "Both young men and women,
ynq ^{c}m 'š śbh — Infants along with old men."

Comment: On the difficulties posed by this unit, see the Corpus. Its affiliation with a major formula is quite uncertain.

5. x x/* Jud.5:17c-d A A/*

yšb lḥp ymm — "He dwells at the coast of the sea;
(w)^{c}l mprṣw yškn — He encamps along its bays."

Comment: This formula results from a grammatical structure of 3:2 in a metrical framework of 3:3, a pattern typical of the replacement formula x x* (D). This unit seems to be most closely related to either x x/x or, better, x x̸.

6. x */x II Sam.22:11 A */A

yrkb ^{c}l krbm — "He was mounted on the Cherubim;
(w)yd'h ^{c}l knpy rḥ — He swooped on the wings of the wind."

Comment: This formula results from a grammatical structure of 2:3 in a grammatical framework of 3:3. From this point of view, it is the reverse of the preceding unit and, like it, is probably most closely related to x x/x or x x̸.

7. x x/ II Sam.22:44b-c A A/

tśmny lr'š gym — "You set me at the head of nations;
^{c}m l' yd^{c}ty y^{c}bdny — A people I did not know serve me."

Comment: This formula displays certain peculiar characteristics, if the analysis of the unit is correct. Chief among these is the fact that there is no deletion from the A Line, but there is a nonparallel addition to the B Line (l' yd^{c}ty), a feature which is characteristic of the replacement formula x x (D) and its variations. The unit also contains metrical peculiarities; see the Corpus.

Replacement Formulae

Replacement formulae occurring in the *Corpus* will be listed in accordance with their approximation to the syllable compensation appropriate to their specific pattern.

Single Replacement Formulae

Major Formulae

There are four major single replacement formulae in the three metrical unit class:

1. x /x (D) (24 examples)
2. x x* (D) (23 examples)
3. x/x̸ (D) (8 examples)
4. x x (D) (12 examples)

The following is a list and brief description of each of these formulae:

x /x (D)

Characteristic of this formula is a replacement of the A Line deletion by a compound in the B Line. Since all examples must contain a grammatical contrast between simple and compound parallel terms in A and B Lines, respectively, it is necessary to list the units only according to their approximation to the ideal syllable compensation. Two aspects of the latter are of interest at this stage (a later section will deal with the nature and placement of deleted and compensatory elements):

1. The syllabic relationship between the simple metrical unit in the A Line and its parallel compound in the B Line. Only examples which display a compensation of two or more syllables can be considered ideal examples of x /x (D).

2. The relationship in syllables between the metrical unit deleted from the A Line and its B Line replacement. One expects the total number of syllables of (a) the deleted A Line plus (b) the metrical unit in the A Line paralleled by the B Line compound to equal, or approximate by one syllable, the number of syllables in the B Line compound. The absence of such approximation may indicate metrical problems, in the form of syllabic asymmetry, in the unit under consideration. This is true for all replacement formulae.

Examples of x /x (D) will be listed in a manner which will register the syllabic relationships discussed above.

1. Compensation of at least two syllables

These examples fulfill the requirements of the ideal pattern of x /x (D).

a. Gen.49:10a A /A (D)

l' ysr špṭ myhd "Judah will never lack a ruler,
(w)mḥqq mbn dglw Its standards, a leader."

A Line				B Line
Parallel units:	myhd	3 //	5	mbn dglw
Deletion:	l' ysr	3		
Total:		6	5	

b. Gen.49:11a A /A (D)

'sr lgpn ^{c}r "He ties his ass to a vine,
(w)lśrq bn 'tn His purebred, to a choice vine."

A Line				B Line
Parallel units:	^{c}r	2 //	5	bn 'tn
Deletion:	'sr	3		
Total:		5	5	

c. Gen.49:11b A /A (D)

kbs byn lbš "He washes his garments in wine,
(w)bdm ^{c}nbm st In the blood of grapes, his mantle."

A Line				B Line
Parallel units:	byn	2 //	5	bdm ^{c}nbm
Deletion:	kbs	2		
Total:		4	5	

d. Dt.32:4a A /A (D)

(h)ṣr tmm p^{c}lh "The Rock's work is perfect;
ky kl drkw mšpṭ All his ways are right."

A Line				B Line
Parallel units:	p^{c}lh	2 //	5	ky kl drkw
Deletion:	(h)ṣr	2		
Total:		4	5	

e. Dt.32:22a A /B (D)

ky 'š qdḥh b'py "A fire has ignited from my nostrils;
(w)tqd ^{c}d š'l tḥtt It burns down to lowest Sheol."

A Line				B Line
Parallel units:	b'py	3 //	5	^{c}d š'l tḥtt
Deletion:	ky š	2		
Total:		5	5	

f. Dt.32:27b B /B (D)

pn y'mrw ydnw rmh "Lest they say, 'Our hand is powerful;
l' yhwh p^{c}l kl z't It was not YHWH who did all this.'"

A Line				B Line
Parallel units:	rmh	2 //	4	p^{c}l kl z't
Deletion:	pn y'mrw	5		
Total:		7	4	

g. Jud.5:26a A /A (D)

ydh lytd tšlḥn "She stretched out her hand to a peg,
(w)ymnh lhlmt ^{c}mlm Her right hand, to a worker's mallet."

A Line				B Line
Parallel units:	lytd	3 //	6	lhlmt ^{c}mlm
Deletion:	tšlḥn	4		
Total:		7	6	

h. II Sam.1:27 B /A (D)

'k npl gbrm "How have the warriors fallen,
(w)y'bd kl mlḥm The weapons of war perished!"

A Line				B Line
Parallel units:	gbrm	3 //	5	kl mlḥm
Deletion:	'k	1		
Total:		4	5	

i. II Sam.22:7b A /A (D)

yšm^{c} mhklh qly "He heard my voice from his palace;
šw^{c}ty tb' b'znw My cry for help entered his ears."

A Line				B Line
Parallel units:	yšm^{c}	2 //	6	tb' b'znw
Deletion:	mhklh	4		
Total:		6	6	

j. II Sam.22:12 B /A (D)

yšt ḥšk sbbtw "He placed darkness around him,
skth ḥšrt mm The rain cloud as his covering."

A Line			B Line
Parallel units: ḥšk	1 // 3		ḥšrt mm
Deletion: yšt	2		
Total:	3	3	

k. II Sam.22:14 A /A (D)

hr^{c}m bšmm yhwh — "YHWH thundered from heaven;
(w)^{c}lyn ytn qlh — Elyon set forth his voice."

A Line			B Line
Parallel units: yr^{c}m	2 // 4		ytn qlh
Deletion: bšmm	3		
Total:	5	4	

l. II Sam.22:29 A /A (D)

ky 'th nry yhwh — "You are my lamp, O YHWH;
'lhy tgh ḥšky — My God, you brighten my darkness."

A Line			B Line
Parallel units: nry	2 // 4		tgh ḥšky
Deletion: ky 'th	3		
Total:	5	4	

m. Ps.29:6 A /A (D)

yrqdm km ^{c}gl lbnn — "He makes Lebanon dance like a calf,
(w)śryn km bn r'mm — Sirion like a wild ox."

A Line			B Line
Parallel units: km ^{c}gl	3 // 6		km bn r'mm
Deletion: yrqdm	3		
Total:	6	6	

n. Ps.114:3 A /A (D)

(h)ym r'h wyns — "Sea saw and fled;
(h)yrdn ysb l'ḥr — Jordan turned back."

A Line			B Line
Parallel units: wyns	3 // 5		ysb l'ḥr
Deletion: r'h	2		
Total:	5	5	

2. Compensation of two syllables in parallel units, but syllabic asymmetry between A and B Lines

Dt.32:13b A /A (D)

ynqhw dbš msl^{c} — "He let him suck honey from rock,
(w)šmn mḥlmš ṣr — Oil from flinty stone."

A Line / B Line

Parallel units: msl^c 2 // 4 mḥlmš ṣr

Deletion: ynqhw 4

Total: 6 4

3. Compensation of only one syllable between parallel units

a. Gen.4:24 A /"D" (D)

k šb^{c}tm yqm qn "Cain was avenged sevenfold;
(w)lmk šb^{c}m wšb^c Lamech seventy and sevenfold!"

A Line / B Line

Parallel units: k šb^{c}tm 4 // 5 šb^{c}m wšb^c

Deletion: yqm 2

Total: 6 5

b. Dt.32:7b A /A (D)

š'l 'bkh wygdkh "Ask your father to tell you,
zqnkh wy'mrw lkh Your elders to relate to you."

A Line / B Line

Parallel units: wygdkh 5 // 6 wy'mrw lkh

Deletion: š'l 2

Total: 7 6

c. Dt.32:21b A /A (D)

'ny 'qn'm bl' ^{c}m "I shall make them jealous with a non-people;
bgy nbl 'k^{c}sm I shall anger them with a brutish nation."

A Line / B Line

Parallel units: bl' ^{c}m 3 // 4 gby nbl

Deletion: 'ny 2

Total: 5 4

d. Dt.33:2b-c A /A (D)

zrḥ mś^{c}r lm "He shone from Seir to them;
hp^c mhr pr'n He beamed forth from Mount Paran."

A Line / B Line

Parallel units: ms^{c}r 3 // 4 mhr pr'n

Deletion: lm 2

Total: 5 4

e. Dt.33:11a A /A (D)

brk yhw ḥl "Bless, O YHWH, his strength;
(w)p^{c}l ydw trṣ Accept the work of his hands!"

A Line			B Line
Parallel units: ḥl	2 //	3	p^{c}l ydw
Deletion: yhw	2		
Total:	4	3	

f. Dt.33:13b-c A /A (D)

mmgd šmm m^{c}l "From the abundance of the heavens above,

mthm rbṣt tḥt From the deep crouching below."

A Line			B Line
Parallel units: m^{c}l	2 //	3	rbṣt tḥt
Deletion: mmgd	2		
Total:	4	3	

g. Hab.3:3a A /A (D)

'lh mtmn yb' "God came from Teman,

(w)qdš mhr pr'n The Holy One from Mount Paran."

A Line			B Line
Parallel units: mtmn	3 //	4	mhr pr'n
Deletion: yb'	2		
Total:	5	4	

4. Compensation of only one syllable between parallel units; A and B Lines syllabically asymmetrical

Dt.32:12 A /A (D)

yhwh bdd ynḥnw "YHWH alone led him;

(w)'n ^{c}mh 'l nkr No strange god was with him."

A Line			B Line
Parallel units: yhwh	2 //	3	'l nkr
Deletion: ynḥnw	3		
Total:	5	3	

5. No syllable compensation in parallel units; A and B Lines syllabically asymmetrical

Ps.114:4 A /A (D)

(h)hrm rqdw k'lm "Mountains danced like rams,

gb^{c}t kbny ṣ'n Hills like sheep."

A Line			B Line
Parallel units: k'lm	3 //	3	kbny ṣ'n
Deletion: rqdw	3		
Total:	6	3	

<u>x x* (D)</u>

A single A Line metrical unit parallels a B Line unit

longer by, ideally, two or more syllables. Examples must have the grammatical structure 3:2; that is, three grammatical units in the A Line, two in the B Line. The following is a list of the examples of x x* (D) in the Corpus. The presentation is the same as that for x /x (D).

1. Compensation of at least two syllables

a. Gen.4:23b A A* (D)

k 'š hrgt lpṣ^c "I have killed a man for striking me,
(w)yld lḥbrt A youth for wounding me."

A Line			B Line
Parallel units: lpṣ^c	3 //	5	lḥbrt
Deletion: hrgt	3		
Total:	6	5	

b. Gen.49:7a A A* (D)

'rr 'pm k ^{c}z "Cursed is their wrath which is (so) powerful,
(w)^{c}brtm k qšt Their anger, which is (so) harsh."

A Line			B Line
Parallel units: k ^{c}z	2 //	4	k qšt
Deletion: 'rr	2		
Total:	4	4	

c. Gen.49:15a A A* (D)

yr' mnḥ k ṭb "When he saw that his resting place was (so) good,
'rṣ k n^{c}m His land was (so) pleasant."

A Line			B Line
Parallel units: k ṭb	2 //	4	k n^{c}m
Deletion: yr'	2		
Total:	4	4	

d. Num.23:9a A A* (D)

k mr'š ṣrm 'r'n "From the peak of the mountains I see;
(w)mgb^{c}t 'šrn From the hills I look."

A Line			B Line
Parallel units: ṣrm	2 //	4	mgb^{c}t
Deletion: k mr'š	3		
Total:	5	4	

e. Num.23:19b A A* (D)

hh' 'mr wl' y^{c}ś "Does he promise, but not do,
dbr wl' yqmn Speak, but not perform?"

A Line		B Line
Parallel units: wl' y^{c}ś	4 // 6	wl' yqmn
Deletion: hh'	2	
Total:	6 6	

f. Num.24:8b A A* (D)

y'kl gym ṣrw "He devours the nations, his enemies;
(w)^{c}ṣmthm ygrm He crushes their bones."

A Line		B Line
Parallel units: gym	2 // 4	^{c}ṣmthm
Deletion: ṣrw	2	
Total:	4 4	

g. Dt.32:11a A B* (D)

knšr y^{c}r knh "Like an eagle which protects its nest,
^{c}l gzlw yrḥp Which hovers over its chicks."

A Line		B Line
Parallel units: qnh	2 // 4	^{c}l gzlw
Deletion: knšr	2	
Total:	4 4	

h. Dt.32:25a A A* (D)

mḥṣ tškl ḥrb "Outside the sword will bereave,
(w)mḥdrm 'mh Inside, terror."

A Line		B Line
Parallel units: mḥṣ	2 // 4	mḥdrm
Deletion: tškl	3	
Total:	5 4	

i. Dt.32:29 A C* (D)

lw ḥkmw yśklw z't "If they were wise they would comprehend this;
ybnw l'ḥrtm They would have concern for their end."

A Line		B Line
Parallel units: z't	1 // 4	l'ḥrtm
Deletion: lw ḥkmw	4	
Total:	5 4	

j. Dt.32:34 A C* (D)

hl' h' kms ^{c}mdy "Is this not laid up with me,
ḥtm b'ṣrty Sealed in my treasuries?"

A Line		B Line
Parallel units: ^{c}mdy	3 // 5	b'ṣrty
Deletion: hl' h'	3	
Total:	6 5	

k. Dt.32:36a B A* (D)

ky ydn yhwh ^{c}mh "YHWH will judge his people;
(w)^{c}l ^{c}bdw ytnḥm He will consider mercy for his servants."

A Line			B Line
Parallel units: ^{c}mh	2 //	4	^{c}l ^{c}bdw
Deletion: yhwh	2		
Total:	4	4	

l. II Sam.22:22 A A* (D)

ky šmrty drky yhwh "I have kept the ways of YHWH;
(w)l' pš^{c}ty m'lhy I have not rebelled against my God."

A Line			B Line
Parallel units: yhwh	2 //	4	m'lhy
Deletion: drky	2		
Total:	4	4	

m. II Sam.22:37 A B* (D)

trḥb ṣ^{c}dy tḥtny "You lengthen my stride under me;
(w)l' m^{c}dw qrsly My ankles do not stumble."

A Line			B Line
Parallel units: trḥb	2 //	4	l' m^{c}dw
Deletion: tḥtny	3		
Total:	5	4	

n. Ps.77:17b-c A A* (D)

r'kh mym yḥlw "The waters saw you and shook;
'p yrgzw thmt The deeps trembled."

A Line			B Line
Parallel units: mym	1 //	3	thmt
Deletion: r'kh	3		
Total:	4	3	

2. Compensation of only one syllable

a. Gen.49:17a A A* (D)

dn nḥš ^{c}l drk "Dan is a snake on the road,
šppn ^{c}l 'rḥ A horned snake on the path."

A Line			B Line
Parallel units: nḥš	2 //	3	šppn
Deletion: dn	2		
Total:	4	3	

b. Dt.32:11b A A* (D)

yprś knpw yqḥhw "He spread his wings, took him up;
yś'hw ^{c}l 'brth He lifted him on his pinions."

A Line			B Line
Parallel units: knpw	3 // 4		^{c}l 'brth
Deletion: yprś	2		
Total:	5	4	

c. Dt.32:21a A A* (D)

hm qn'ny bl' ^{c}m "They made me jealous with a non-god;
k^{c}sny bhblhm They angered me with their nothings."

A Line			B Line
Parallel units: bl' ^{c}m	3 // 4		bhblhm
Deletion: hm	1		
Total:	4	4	

d. Dt.33:18 A B* (D)

śmḥ zbln bṣ'tk "Rejoice, O Zebulon, in your going forth,
(w)yśśkr b'hlk Issachar, in your tents!"

A Line			B Line
Parallel units: bṣ'tk	4 // 5		b'hlk
Deletion: śmḥ	2		
Total:	6	5	

3. Compensation of only one syllable; A and B Lines asymmetrical

a. Num.24:5 A A* (D)

mh ṭb 'hlk y^{c}qb "How beautiful are your tents, O Jacob,
(w)mškntk yśr'l Your encampments, O Israel!"

A Line			B Line
Parallel units: 'hlk	4 // 5		mškntk
Deletion: mh ṭb	3		
Total:	7	5	

b. Num.24:7b "D" A (D)

yrm m'gg mlk "May his kingship be higher than Agag's;
(w)ttnś' mlkt May his kingship be exalted!"

A Line			B Line
Parallel units: yrm	2 // 3		ttnś'
Deletion: m'gg	3		
Total:	5	3	

c. Ps.114:2 A A* (D)

hyt yhd lqdš "Judah became his holy possession,
yśr'l mmšltw Israel, his dominion."

A Line			B Line
Parallel units: lqdš	3 //	4	mmšltw
Deletion: hyt	3		
Total:	6	4	

4. No syllable compensation; A and B Lines asymmetrical

a. Dt.32:30b A A* (D)

'm l' ṣrm mkrm "Unless their rock turn them over,
(w)yhwh hsgrm YHWH deliver them up."

A Line			B Line
Parallel units: mkrm	3 //	3	hsgrm
Deletion: 'm l'	2		
Total:	5	3	

b. II Sam.22:38 B A* (D)

'rdp 'yby w'šmdm "I pursued my enemies and destroyed them;
l' 'šb ^{c}d kltm I did not desist until I had annihilated them."

A Line			B Line
Parallel units: w'šmdm	4 //	4	^{c}d kltm
Deletion: 'yby	3		
Total:	7	4	

x/x̸ (D)

Characteristic of this formula is the parallelism between a compound in the A Line and a double compound in the B Line, which, in three metrical unit formula, comprises the whole of that line. The presentation is the same employed for x /x (D) and x x* (D).

1. Compensation of at least two syllables

a. Num.24:17c A/A̸ (D)

mḥṣ p't m'b "It smites the temples of Moab,
(w)qdqd kl bn št The pate of all the Sons of Sheth."

A Line			B Line
Parallel units: p't m'b	4 //	6	qdqd kl bn št
Deletion: mḥṣ	2		
Total:	6	6	

b. Dt.32:32b A/Ⱥ (D)

^{c}nbmw ^{c}nby rš "Their grapes are venomous grapes,
'šklt mrrt lmw Which have bitter clusters."

A Line			B Line
Parallel units: ^{c}nby rš	4 //	8	'šklt mrrt lmw
Deletion: ^{c}nbmw	4		
Total:	8	8	

c. Dt.33:16b A/Ⱥ (D)

th lr'š ysp "Let it be on the head of Joseph,
(w)lqdqd nzr 'ḥw On the pate of the leader of his brothers."

A Line			B Line
Parallel units: lr'š ysp	4 //	7	lqdqd nzr 'ḥw
Deletion: th	2		
Total:	6	7	

d. Dt.33:23a-b

nptl śb^{c} rṣn "Naphtali is sated with favor,
(w)ml' brkt yhw Full of the blessings of YHWH."

A Line			B Line
Parallel units: śb^{c} rṣn	4 //	6	ml' brkt yhw
Deletion: nptl	3		
Total:	7	6	

e. Hab.3:11b A/Ⱥ (D)

l'r ḥṣk yhlkw "They go forth by the light of your arrows,
lngh brq ḥntk By the radiance of your flashing spear."

A Line			B Line
Parallel units: l'r ḥṣk	5 //	8	lngh brq ḥntk
Deletion: yhlkw	4		
Total:	9	8	

2. Compensation of only one syllable

a. Dt.32:20b A/Ⱥ (D)

ky dr thpkt hmh "They are a rebellious generation,
bnm l' 'mn bm Children who have no faith."

A Line			B Line
Parallel units: ky dr thpkt	5 //	6	bnm l' 'mn bm
Deletion: hmh	2		
Total:	7	6	

b. Dt.32:33 A/A̸ (D)

ḥmt tnnm ynm "Their wine is the poison of serpents,
(w)r'š ptnm 'kzr The harsh venom of vipers."

A Line			B Line
Parallel units: ḥmt tnnm	5 //	6	r'š ptnm 'kzr
Deletion: ynm	2		
Total:	7	6	

c. Dt.33:24a-b A/A̸ (D)

brk mbnm 'šr "Asher is the most blessed of the sons;
yhy rṣy 'ḥw He is the most favored of his brothers."

A Line			B Line
Parallel units: brk mbnm	5 //	6	yhy rṣy 'ḥw
Deletion: 'šr	2		
Total:	7	6	

x x (D)

The B Line has a grammatical unit not parallel to any unit of the A Line. Only the syllabic relationship between deletion and replacement need be noted.

1. B Line replacement equals the A Line deletion, plus or minus one syllable

a. Gen.49:19 C "D" (D)

gd gdd ygdn "Gad is a band which raids;
(w)h' ygdn 'ḥr He raids from the rear."

A Line Deletion: ygdn 3
B Line Replacement: ^{c}qbm 3

b. Ex.15:8b-c B A (D)

nṣb km nd nzlm "The floods stood like a heap;
qp' thmt blb ym The deeps churned in the midst of the sea."

A Line Deletion: km nd 3
B Line Replacement: blb ym 3

c. Dt.33:2a-b A C (D)

yhw mśn b' "YHWH came from Sinai;
(w)zrḥ mś^{c}r lm He shone forth from Seir to them."

A Line Deletion: yhw 2
B Line Replacement: lm 2

d. Jud.5:19a D "D" (D)

b' mlkm nlḥm "The kings came; they fought;

'z nlḥm mlk kn^{c}n Then the kings of Canaan fought."

A Line Deletion: b' 2

B Line Replacement: kn^{c}n 2

e. Jud.5:20 A D (D)

mn šmm nlḥm (h)kkbm "From heaven the stars fought;

mmzltm nlḥm ^{c}m ssr' From their courses they fought with Sisera."

A Line Deletion: kkbm 3

B Line Replacement: ^{c}m ssr' 4

f. Jud.5:24 D D (D)

tbrk mnšm y^{c}l "May Jael be most blessed of women;

mnšm b'hl tbrk May she be most blessed of women in the tent!"

A Line Deletion: y^{c}l 2

B Line Replacement: b'hl 2

g. II Sam.22:18 A A (D)

yṣlny m'yby ky ^{c}zw "He saved me from my enemies when they were powerful,

mśn'y ky 'mṣw mmny From my foes when they were stronger than I."

A Line Deletion: yṣlny 3

B Line Replacement: mmny 3

h. Hab.3:6a B A (D)

^{c}md wymdd 'rṣ "He stood and shook the earth;

r'h wytr gym He looked and made the nations leap."

A Line Deletion: ^{c}md 2

B Line Replacement: r'h 2

i. Ps.24:8b-c D "D" (D)

yhw ^{c}zz wgbr "YHWH, mighty and war-like:

yhw gbr mlḥm YHWH, the hero in warfare!"

A Line Deletion: ^{c}zz 2

B Line Replacement: mlḥm 3

j. Ps.29:3b-c "D" D (D)

ql yhw ^{c}l (h)mym "The voice of YHWH over the waters;

yhw ^{c}l mym rbm YHWH, over the mighty waters."

A Line Deletion: ql 1

B Line Replacement: rbm 2

k. Ps.77:17a-b D D (D)

r'kh mym yhwh "The waters saw you, O YHWH,
r'kh mym yḥlw The waters saw you and trembled."

A Line Deletion: yhwh 2
B Line Replacement: yḥlw 3

2. B Line replacement exceeds the A Line deletion by more than one syllable

Ex.15:16b D "D" (D)

ᶜd yᶜbr ᶜmk yhw "While your people crossed over, O YHWH,
ᶜd yᶜbr ᶜm z qnt While the people you created crossed over."

A Line Deletion: yhw 2
B Line Replacement: z qnt 4

Comment: Note that the unit itself displays overall syllable symmetry.

Minor Formulae

Examples will be listed according to the major formulae of which they seem to be a variation. There are no unclassified formulae in this group.

Variations of x /x (D)

1. /x /x (D)

a. Ex.15:14 /A /A (D)

šmᶜ ᶜmm yrgzn "When the peoples heard, they trembled;
ḥl 'ḥz yšb plšt Pangs seized the inhabitants of Philistia."

b. Num.23:7a /A /A (D)

mn 'rm ynḥn blq "Balak has brought me from Aram,
mlk m'b mhrr qdm Moab's king, from the mountains of Qedem."

c. II Sam.22:21 /A /A (D)

ygmlny yhwh kṣdqy "YHWH rewarded me according to my righteousness;
kbr ydy yšb ly He recompensed me according to my blamelessness."

Comment: All three examples of this formula are characterized by a grammatical framework of 3:4 in a metrical framework of 3:3 (although Ex.15:14 might better be assigned to the metrical framework 3:4). Two of the examples meet the requirements of soundness in x /x (D):

Ex.15:14

A Line			B Line
Parallel units: ^{c}mm	2 //	5	yšb plšt
Deletion: šm^{c}	3		
Total:	5	5	

Num.23:7a

A Line			B Line
Parallel units: mn 'rm	3 //	5	mhrr qdm
Deletion: ynḥn	3		
Total:	6	5	

One example displays a compensation of only one syllable:

II Sam.22:21

A Line			B Line
Parallel units: kṣdqy	3 //	4	kbr ydy
Deletion: yhwh	2		
Total:	5	4	

2. x x/x (D) II Sam.22:28 A B/B (D)

'th ^{c}m ^{c}ny tš^{c} "You save the lowly people;
(w)^{c}nm rmt tšpl But you humble haughty eyes."

Comment: This formula results from a grammatical framework of 4:3 in a metrical framework of 3:3. The unit displays a syllable compensation of one syllable:

A Line			B Line
Parallel units: ^{c}m ^{c}ny	3 //	4	^{c}nm rmt
Deletion: 'th	2		
Total:	5	4	

The unusual feature of this unit is, of course, the parallelism of two compounds, of which the one in the A Line has been awarded the value of only one metrical unit.

3. x /x (D/D) II Sam.22:47 A /A (D/D)

ḥy yhwh brk ṣry "As YHWH lives, may my rock be blessed;
yrm 'lhy yš^{c}y Exalted be my saving God!"

Comment: This formula is produced by a grammatical parallelism of 4:3 in a metrical framework of 3:3. The double replacement consists of two grammatical units to which the value of only one metrical unit has been assigned. The unit displays a degree of syllable compensation required of sound examples of x /x (D):

A Line			B Line
Parallel units: ṣry	2 //	5	'lhy yš^{c}y
Deletion: ḥy yhwh	3		
Total:	3	5	

<u>Variations of x x* (D)</u>

1. x/x* (D) Dt.32:32a A/A* (D)

ky mgpn sdm gpnm "Their vine is from the vines of Sodom,
(w)mšdmt ^{c}mrh From the terraces of Gomorrah."

<u>Comment</u>: This formula is a simple variant of x x* (D) produced by the construct relationship between parallel terms. It displays, however, no syllable compensation:

A Line			B Line
Parallel units: ky mgpn	3 //	3	mšdmt
Deletion: gpnm	2		
Total:	5	3	

However, the 3:2 grammatical structure is sufficient to include it as a variation of x x* (D).

2. x x* (<u>D/D</u>)

a. Num.23:9b A B* (<u>D/D</u>)

hn ^{c}m lbdd yškn "Here is a people that dwells apart,
(w)bgym l' ytḥšb That does not reckon itself to the nations!"

A Line			B Line
Parallel units: yškn	2 //	4	l' ytḥšb
Deletion: hn ^{c}m	2		
Total:	4	4	

b. II Sam.22:7a A A* (<u>D/D</u>)

bṣr ly 'qr' yhwh "When in distress I called out, 'YHWH!';
(w)'l 'lhy 'šw^c I cried for help to my God."

A Line			B Line
Parallel units: yhwh	2 //	4	'l 'lhy
Deletion: bṣr ly	3		
Total:	5	4	

Comment: This formula results from a grammatical structure of 4:2 in a metrical framework of 3:3. Both examples display the degree of syllable compensation required of x x* (D).

Variations of x/x̸ (D)

1. /x/ (D) Ex.15:2a /A/ (D)

   ^{c}z wzmrt yhw — "YHWH is my strength and my protection;
   (w)yh ly lyš^{c} — He has become my help."

   Comment: This complex formula, in which the symbolic representation is, as occasionally, arbitrary, results from the parallelism of a compound in the A Line to a double compound in the B Line. Unlike the major formula x/x̸ (D), however, the compounds are indivisible in the framework of the reconstructed sentence. An additional problem is posed by the fact that the unit is syllabically asymmetrical and displays no degree of syllable compensation:

A Line			B Line
Parallel units: ^{c}z wzmrt	6 //	6	yh ly lyš^{c}
Deletion: yhw	2		
Total:	8	6	

2. x-/x̸ (D)

   a. Num.23:24b A-/A̸ (D)

   l' yškb ^{c}d y'kl ṭrp — "He does not lie down until he devours prey,
   (w)dm ḥllm yšt — Drinks the blood of the slain."

A Line			B Line
Parallel units: y'kl ṭrp	3 //	5	dm ḥllm yšt
Deletion: l' yškb	3		
Total:	6	5	

   b. Dt.32:10a A-A̸ (D)

   ymṣ'hw b'rṣ mdbr — "He found him in the desert,
   (w)bthw yll yšmn — In the desolation of a howling wilderness."

A Line			B Line
Parallel units: b'rṣ mdbr	4 //	8	bthw yll yšmn
Deletion: ymṣ'hw	4		
Total:	8	8	

Comment: This formula resembles the preceding one, except

that the parallel compounds are semantic. Syllabic compensation is satisfactory.

3. /x̲/ (D) Dt.32:28 /A̲/ (D)

ky gy 'bd ^c^ṣt hmh "They are a nation without counsel,
(w)'n bhm tbnh In whom there is no understanding."

Comment: This unit resembles the preceding examples, except that its formula is produced by a grammatical parallelism of 4:3 in a metrical framework of 3:3. The unit is asymmetrical and displays no degree of syllable compensation:

A Line			B Line
Parallel units: ky gy 'bd ^c^ṣt	6 //	6	'n bhm tbnh
Deletion: hmh	2		
Total:	8	6	

4. x/̸x̸ (D̲/D̲) Dt.32:24b A/̸A̸ (D̲/D̲)

šn bhmt 'šlḥ bm "The fang of beasts I shall send against them,
^c^m ḥmt zḥly ^c^pr Along with the venom of gliders in the dust."

Comment: This formula is produced by a grammatical structure of 4:3 in a metrical framework of 3:3. It displays satisfactory syllabic compensation although the unit contains serious metrical problems.

A Line			B Line
Parallel units: šn bhmt	4 //	8	^c^m ḥmt zḥly ^c^pr
Deletion: 'šlḥ bm	4		
Total:	8	8	

5. */x̸ (D)

a. Dt.32:38b */A̸ (D)

yqmw wy^c^zrkm "Let them arise to help you;
yhyw ^c^lkm strh Let them be your protection!"

b. II Sam.22:16b */C̸ (D)

bg^c^rtkh yhwh "At your rebuke, O UHWH,
mnšmt rḥ 'pkh At the blast of the breath of your nostrils."

Comment: This formula results from a grammatical structure of 2:3 in a metrical framework of 3:3. In both cases a single term in the A Line, which has been awarded the value of two metrical units, parallels a double compound in the B Line. Both examples display adequate syllable compensation:

Dt.32:38b

A Line			B Line
Parallel units: wy^{c}zrkm	5 //	7	yhyw ^{c}lkm strh
Deletion: yqmw	3		
Total:	8	7	

II Sam.22:16b

A Line			B Line
Parallel units: bg^{c}rtkh	5 //	7	mnšmt rḥ 'pkh
Deletion: yhwh	2		
Total:	7	7	

<u>Variations of x x (D)</u>

1. x≠x (D)

a. II Sam.22:42 A≠A (D)

yšw^{c}w w'n mš^{c} "They cried for help, but there was none to save,

'l yhwh wl' ^{c}nm To YHWH, but he did not answer them."

A Line Deletion: yšw^{c}w 4

B Line Replacement: wl' ^{c}nm 4

b. Ps.29:3a-b

'l (h)kbd hr^{c}m "The God of glory thunders,

ql yhwh ^{c}l (h)mym The voice of YHWH, over the waters."

A Line Deletion: hr^{c}m 2

B Line Replacement: ^{c}l (h)mym 2

<u>Comment</u>: This simple variation of x x (D) results from the parallelism of semantic compounds. No. 4, below, is similar, except for the fact that the compounds are grammatical ones. Syllabic compensation is satisfactory.

2. x <u>x/x</u> (D) Ex.15:11a-b A <u>D/D</u> (D)

m kmk b'lm yhw "Who like you among the gods, O YHWH,

m kmk n'dr bqdš Who like you is terrible among the holy ones."

<u>Comment</u>: This formula is a simple variation of x x (D) produced by the grammatical structure 4:4 in a metrical framework of 3:3. The syllable compensation is appropriate to x x (D):

A Line Deletion: yhw 2

B Line Replacement: n'dr 3

3. x /x (D) Num.23:18 A /A (D)

qm blq wšm^{c} — "Get up Balak and hear;

h'zn ^{c}d bn ṣpr — Listen to my testimony, O son of Sippor!"

Comment: This formula results from a grammatical structure of 3:4 in a metrical framework of 3:3. Syllable compensation is satisfactory:

A Line Deletion: qm 1

B Line Replacement: ^{c}d 2

4. x/x (D) Jud.5:23b D/D (D)

k l' b' l^{c}zrt yhw — "For they did not come to the aid of YHWH,

l^{c}zrt yhw bgbrm — To the aid of YHWH with their warriors."

Comment: This simple variation is produced by the construct relationship between the parallel (here, repetition) units. The unit displays adequate syllable compensation:

A Line Deletion: k l' b' 4

B Line Replacement: bgbrm 4

The following formulae are more loosely connected with x x (D):

1. *x (D)

a. Dt.32:10b *B (D)

ysbbnhw ybnnhw — "He surrounded him, cared for him;

yṣrnhw k'šn ^{c}nh — He guarded him as the apple of his eye."

b. II Sam.22:39 *B (D)

'mḥṣm wl' yqmn — "I smashed them so that they could not rise,

yplw tḥt rgly — So that they fell under my feet."

Comment: This formula is produced by a grammatical parallelism of 2:3 in a metrical framework of 3:3. In both cases a simple term (so also wl' yqmn in this system with the metrical value of two units parallels a single metrical unit in the B Line. In both cases the syllable compensation meets the requirements for sound examples of x x (D):

Dt.32:10b

A Line Deletion: ysbbnhw 5

B Line Replacement: k'šn ^{c}nh 5

II Sam.22:39

A Line Deletion: 'mḥṣm 3

B Line Replacement: tḥt rgly 3

2. x/* (D) II Sam.22:34 A/* (D)

mšwh rgly k'ylt "He makes my feet like the does';

(w)^{c}l bmtw y^{c}mdny He lets me stand on his heights."

Comment: This formula is produced by a grammatical structure of 3:2, characteristic of the formula x x* (D), within a metrical framework of 3:3. In this case a compound in the A Line parallels a simple term in the B Line; however, the latter has been awarded the value of two metrical units. Syllable compensation is satisfactory although the unit displays metrical problems:

A Line Deletion: k'ylt 4

B Line Replacement: ^{c}l bmtw 4

Unclassified Formulae

There are no unclassifiable formulae in this category.

Double Replacement Formulae

Major Formula

x (D D)

There is only one major formula in the three metrical unit double replacement category. The method of presentation follows that of x x (D).

1. B Line replacement equals the A Line deletion plus or minus one syllable

a. Gen.49:9b A (D D)

kr^{c} rbṣ k'ry "He crouches, lies down like a lion,

(w)klb' m yqmn Like a lion which none would dare arouse."

A Line Deletion: kr^{c} rbṣ 4

B Line Replacement: m yqmn 4

b. Num.24:6b A (D D)

k'rzm nṭ^{c} yhw "Like cedars YHWH has planted,

k'hlm ^{c}l mm rbm Like aloes by abundant waters."

A Line Deletion: nṭ^{c} yhwh 5

B Line Replacement: ^{c}l mm rbm 4

c. Dt.32:37 A (D D)

'mr 'y 'lhmw "He will say, 'Where is their god,
ṣr ḥsyw bh The rock in whom they trusted,'"

A Line Deletion: 'mr 'y 3
B Line Replacement: ḥsyw bh 3

d. Dt.33:11b A (D D)

mḥṣ mtnm qmw "Smite the loins of his adversaries,
(w)mśn'w mn yqmn Of his enemies, whoever attacks him!"

A Line Deletion: mḥṣ mtnm 4
B Line Replacement: mn yqmn 5

2. B Line replacement exceeds the A Line deletion by more than one syllable

Num.23:23b A (D D)

k ^{c}t y'mr ly^{c}qb "Now shall be said to Jacob,
(w)lyśr'l mh p^{c}l 'l To Israel, 'What God has accomplished!'"

A Line Deletion: k ^{c}t y'mr 6
B Line Replacement: mh p^{c}l 'l 4

<u>Minor Formulae</u>

Since the category of double replacement formulae is small, the minor formulae will be divided into variations of the only major formula in the class, x (D D), and all other formulae.

<u>Variations of x (D D)</u>

1. x (<u>D/D</u> D) II Sam.22:41 A (<u>D/D</u> D)

'yby ntth ly ^{c}rp "You have given me the neck of my enemies,
mśn'y w'ṣmtm Of my foes, whom I exterminate."

<u>Comment</u>: This formula is a simple variation of x (D D) produced by a grammatical structure of 4:2 in a metrical framework of 3:3. Syllable compensation is satisfactory:

A Line Deletion: ntth ly ^{c}rp 5
B Line Replacement: w'ṣmtm 4

2. <u>x/x</u> (D D) II Sam.22:45 <u>A/D</u> (D D)

bny nkr ytkhsw ly "Foreigners fawn upon me;
lšm^{c} 'zn yšm^{c}w ly At the report (of me) they obey me."

<u>Comment</u>: This formula also is a simple variation of x (D D), resulting from a grammatical structure of 4:4 in a 3:3

metrical framework. However, the unit displays problems in its overall syllabic structure (see the Corpus). Still, the syllable compensation is adequate for the pattern of x (D D):

A Line Deletion: bny nkr 4

B Line Replacement: lšm[c] 'zn 3

Additional Formulae

1. /x̸ (D D)

a. Gen.49:15b /A̸ (D D)

yṭ škm lsbl "He bent his shoulder to carry;

(w)yh lms [c]bd He became a corvée worker."

b. Dt.33:6 /B̸ (D D)

yḥ r'bn w'l ymt "May Reuben live and not die;

(w)yhy mtw mspr May his men not be few!"

Comment: Both examples reflect the parallelism of a simple term in the A Line with a double compound in the B Line. In both cases the double compound happens to be a "quasi-verbal" sentence. Dt.33:6 is asymmetrical, but its compensation is adequate, inadequate for Gen.49:15b:

Gen.49:15b

A Line Deletion: yṭ škm 4

B Line Replacement: yh lms [c]bd 6

Dt.33:6

A Line Deletion: yḥ r'bn 5

B Line Replacement: yhy mtw mspr 6

2. /x̸ (D D) II Sam.22:19 /B̸ (D D)

(This formula is included here out of sequence due to its close similarity to the preceding one.)

yqdmny bym 'dy "They confronted me on the day of my disaster,

(w)yhy yhwh mš[c]n ly But YHWH was my support."

Comment: This formula reflects the same situation as /x̸ (D D) except that the grammatical structure is 3:4. Note that the B Line also forms a "quasi-verbal" sentence. The unit contains metrical problems (see the Corpus) and displays overall syllable asymmetry. Syllabic compensation is also unsatisfactory:

A Line Deletion: yqdmny 5

B Line Replacement: yhy yhwh mš[c]n ly 7

3. /x (D D)

a. Gen.49:16 /A (D D)

dn ydn ᶜm	"Dan judges his people,
k'ḥd šbṭ yśr'l	Together, the tribes of Israel."

b. Gen.49:27a-b /A (D D)

bnymn z'b yṭrp	"Benjamin is a wolf which preys,
bbqr y'kl ᶜd	In the morning devours prey."

Comment: This formula is a complex one. It displays, like the major replacement formula x /x (D), a contrast between simple and compound terms in A and B Lines, respectively. Its primary relationship, however, is with x (D D), since it contains the type of non-parallel replacement in the B Line characteristic of that formula (also x x (D), etc.):

Gen.49:16

A Line			B Line
Parallel units: ᶜm	2 //	5	šbṭ yśr'l
A Line Deletion: dn ydn	3		
B Line Replacement:		3	k'ḥd
Total:	5	8	

Comment: In this example, the contrast between simple and compound terms is satisfactory, as is the syllabic relationship between the A Line deletion and the B Line replacement. Note that the unit as a whole is syllabically asymmetrical.

Gen.49:27a-b

A Line			B Line
Parallel units: yṭrp	2 //	3	y'kl ᶜd
A Line Deletion: bnymn z'b	4		
B Line Replacement:		2	bbqr
Total:	6	5	

Comment: This unit displays syllable compensation of only one syllable between simple and compound units. Moreover, the relationship between deletion and replacement is unsatisfactory.

Four Metrical Unit Formulae

There are no major formulae in this class except for the double replacement formula x x (D D). This category is represented by relatively few examples in the Corpus. Moreover, the number of possible combinations greatly exceeds that of three metrical unit formulae. Hence it is not surprising that even the small number of examples which occur in the Corpus are divided among a large number of separate formulae, many of which occur only once. Note that formulae with the patterns 3:4 and 4:3 are also to be classified as four metrical unit formulae.

The arrangement of formulae will follow this pattern in the lists:

1. Examples in each category (non-replacement, single replacement, double replacement and triple replacement) will be listed by their grammatical structure: first, 3:4; then 4:3; and, finally, 4:4 proper. Within each class, the examples will be listed in the order in which they occur in the Bible (except for examples occurring more than once). However, the major formula x x (D D) will be arranged in the manner employed for major three metrical unit formulae, i.e., according to the approximation to the syllabic compensation proper to the formula. The grammatical structure (3:4; 4:3; 4:4; 4:5) will be indicated in parentheses after each example.

2. Many formulae are clearly related to one or more of the major three metrical unit formulae. Such examples will be accompanied by a brief summary of their approximation to the proper syllabic form of those formulae.

Non-Replacement Formulae

3:4

Only one formula in this category occurs in the Corpus:

/x x/x Ex.15:15a-b /A A/A

'z nbhl 'lp 'dm	"The leaders of Moab were terrified;
'l m'b // y'ḥzm r^{c}d	Trembling seized the mighty men of Edom."

4:3

One formula of this type occurs in the Corpus:

x/x x/ Ex.15:15b-c A/A A/

'l m'b // y'ḥzm r^{c}d "Trembling seized the mighty men of Moab;

nmg kl yšb kn^{c}n All the inhabitants of Canaan melted away."

Comment: These two formulae occur in the same unit and are opposites in structure. Each can occur in syllabically sound units only in the grammatical structure 3:4 and 4:3, respectively.

4:4

1. x x x̸

a. Gen.4:23a A A A̸

^{c}d wṣl // šm^{c}n ql "Adah and Zillah, hear my voice;

nš lmk // h'zn 'mrt Wives of Lamech, heed my word!"

b. Ex.15:4 B D A̸

mrkbt pr^{c} / yr bym "He cast the chariots of Pharaoh into the sea;

(w)mbḥr šlšw / ṭb^{c} bym sp His best troops drowned in the Reed Sea."

Comment: This formula is produced by a grammatical structure of 4:5 in a metrical framework of 4:4 (2:2::2:2).

2. x/̸x x/̸x Ex.15:9b-c B/̸B B/̸B

'ḥlq šll // tml'm npš "I shall divide the spoil; my greed will be sated;

'rq ḥrb // tršm yd I shall whet my sword; my hand will destroy."

3. x/ /x x Ex.15:17b-c A/ /A D

mkn lšbtk / p^{c}lt yhw "The dais of your throne which you made, O YHWH,

mqdš yhw // knn ydk The shrine, O YHWH, which your hands established."

A Line		B Line
mkn lšbtk	compound 6 // 2 simple	mqdš
p^{c}lt	simple 3 // 6 compound	knn ydk

Comment: This unit, which contains the three metrical unit formula x/ /x, displays a degree of syllabic chiasm between simple and compound terms required of sound examples of that formula.

4. x x x/x

a. II Sam.1:20b D A D/A

pn tśmḥn / bnt plštm — "Lest the daughters of the Philistines rejoice;

pn t^c lzn / bnt (h)^c rlm — Lest the daughters of the uncircumcised exult."

b. Ps.68:3b-c C C D/C

khms dng / mpn 'š — "As wax melts before flame,

y'bd rš^c m / mpn yhw — The wicked shall melt before YHWH."

c. Ps.89:10 D A A/A

'th mšl / bg't (h)ym — "You are the one who rules over Sea's pride;

bnś' glw // 'th tšbḥm — When his waves rose up, you subdued them."

5. x/x x/x

a. II Sam.1:22b-c A/A A/A

qšt yntn / l' nśg 'ḥr — "Jonathan's bow did not turn back;

(w)ḥrb š'l / l' tšb rqm — Saul's sword did not return empty."

b. Ps.68:16 D/B D/D

hr 'lhm // hr bšn — "O mighty mountains, mountains of Bashan,

hr gbnnm // hr bšn — O jagged (?) mountains, mountains of Bashan!"

<u>Comment</u>: This formula and nos. 1 and 5, above, are simple variations.

6. x ~~x~~/ Ps.29:2 D ~~A~~/

hb lyhw / kbd šm — "Give YHWH the glory due his name;

hšthw lyhw / bhdrt qdš — Bow to YHWH in his holy appearance!"

<u>Comment</u>: Note that this unit displays a non-parallel grammatical addition to the B Line, although it is not a replacement; cf. II Sam.22:44b-c in the three metrical unit category.

Replacement Formulae

Single Replacement Formulae

3:4

1. x x (D) Ps.29:10 D D (D)

   yhw lmbl yšb — "YHWH sits enthroned on the Flood-dragon;

   (w)yšb yhw / mlk l^{c}lm — YHWH sits enthroned forever."

   A Line Deletion: lmbl 3

   B Line Replacement: mlk l^{c}lm 3

   Comment: This is the only formula which appears in both the three and four metrical unit categories. The syllabic relationship between deletion and replacement terms is satisfactory.

2. x///x (D) Ps.68:3a-b A///A (D)

   khndp ^{c}šn tndp — "They shall be dispersed as smoke is dispersed,

   khms dng / mpn 'š — As wax melts away before flame."

A Line				B Line
Parallel units:	khndp ^{c}šn	6 //	9	khms dng mpn 's
Deletion:	tndp	3		
Total:		9	9	

   Comment: On the treatment of khms dng mpn 'š as a compound, see the Corpus. The unit displays satisfactory syllable compensation.

3. /x /x (D) Ps.114:1 /A /A (D)

   bṣ't yśr'l mmṣrym — "When Israel went out of Egypt,

   bt y^{c}qb / m^{c}m l^{c}z — The house of Jacob from a stammering nation."

A Line				B Line
Parallel units:	yśr'l	3 //	3	bt y^{c}qb
	mmṣrym	3 //	4	m^{c}m l^{c}z
Deletion:	bṣ't	2		
Total:		8	7	

   Comment: The unit displays overall syllable symmetry, but a deficient relationship between parallel simple and compound units.

<u>4:3</u>

1. x/ /x (D) Ps.68:14b A/ /A (D)

knp yn // nḥp bksp — "The wings of the dove are covered with silver,

(w)'brth byrqrq ḥrṣ — Its pinions with yellow gold."

<u>Comment</u>: This unit contains the non-replacement pattern x/ /x and, in addition, as a replacement formula, exhibits the following over-all syllabic patternings:

A Line						B Line
Parallel units:						
	knp yn	compound	4 //	3	simple	'brth
	bksp	simple	2 //	5	compound	byrqrq ḥrṣ
Deletion:	nḥp		2			
Total:			8	8		

Note that only partial syllabic chiasm is present in this unit.

2. x x/x (D) Ps.114:8 A A/D (D)

(h)hpky (h)ṣr / 'gm mym — "Who turned the rock into a pond of water,

ḥlmš lm^{c}ynw mym — The flint into a fountain of water."

A Line				B Line
Parallel units:	(h)ṣr	2 //	3	ḥlmš
	'gm mym	3 //	5	lm^{c}ynw mym
Deletion:	(h)hpky	3		
Total:		8	8	

<u>4:4</u>

1. x x x (D)

a. Ps.29:1b-2a D D "D" (D)

hb lyhw / kbd w^{c}z — "Give YHWH glory and strength;

hb lyhw / kbd šm — Give YHWH the glory due his name."

A Line Deletion:	w^{c}z	2
B Line Replacement:	šm	2

b. Ps.29:5 "D" "D" "D" (D)

ql yhw / šbr 'rzm — "The voice of YHWH breaks the cedars

(w)yšbr yhw / 'rz (h)lbnn — YHWH shatters the cedars of Lebanon."

A Line Deletion:	ql	1
B Line Replacement:	(h)lbnn	3

c. Ps.29:8 "D" D "D" (D)

ql yhw / yḥl mdbr — "The voice of YHWH makes the desert tremble;

yḥl yhw / mdbr qdš — YHWH makes the desert of Qadesh tremble."

A Line Deletion: ql 1

B Line Replacement: qdš 2

Comment: Ps.29:5 exhibits unsatisfactory syllabic compensation.

2. x x /x (D)

a. Jud.5:28b D A /A (D)

md^{c} bšš / rkb lb' — "Why does his chariotry delay in coming;

md^{c} 'ḥr / p^{c}m mrkbtw — Why do the hooves of his chariots tarry?"

A Line			B Line
Parallel units: rkb	2 //	6	p^{c}m mrkbtw
Deletion: lb'	2		
Total:	4	6	

Comment: The unit displays satisfactory compensation between parallel simple and compound units, but syllable asymmetry between A and B Lines.

b. Ps.89:7 D A /A (D)

ky my bšḥq / y^{c}rk lyhwh — "Who in the sky can compete with YHWH;

ydmh lyhwh / bbny 'lm — Can compare to YHWH among the lesser gods?"

A Line			B Line
Parallel units: bšḥq	2 //	4	bbny 'lm
Deletion: ky my	2		
Total:	4	4	

Comment: Syllabic compensation is satisfactory.

3. x/x /x (D) II Sam.1:21b D/A /A (D)

k šm ng^{c}l / mgn gbrm — "There the heroes' shield was defiled;

mgn š'l / bl mšḥ bšmn — The shield of Saul was not anointed with oil."

A Line			B Line
Parallel units: ng^{c}l	2 //	5	bl mšḥ bšmn
Deletion: k šm	2		
Total:	4	5	

Comment: Syllabic compensation is satisfactory.

4. x≠x /x (D) Ps.89:8 A≠A /A (D)

'l n^{c}rṣ / bsd qdšm	"God is terrible in the assembly of the holy ones,
rb wnr' / ^{c}l kl sbbw	Great and feared over all those who surround him."

A Line		B Line
Parallel units: n^{c}rṣ	2 // 4	rb wnr'
Deletion: 'l	1	
Total:	3 4	

Comment: Syllabic compensation is satisfactory.

Double Replacement Formulae

This category contains the only major formula in the entire four metrical unit class, x x (D D). Examples will be listed in the manner employed for three metrical unit formulae: first, major formulae arranged by their approximation to the appropriate syllabic compensation, followed by minor formulae and additional formulae. With each example its adherence to the categories 3:4, 4:3 and 4:4 will be noted in parentheses.

Major Formulae

The sole major formula is x x (D D).

x x (D D)

1. B Line replacement equals the A Line deletion plus or minus one syllable

a. Ex.15:6 D D (D D) (4:4)

ymnk yhw // n'dr bkḥ	"Your right hand, O YHWH, is fearful in strength;
ymnk yhw // tr^{c}ṣ 'yb	Your right hand, O YHWH, smashes the enemy."

A Line Deletion: n'dr bkḥ 5

B Line Replacement: tr^{c}ṣ 'yb 4

b. Ex.15:13 A A (D D) (4:4)

nḥt bḥsdk / ^{c}m z g'lt	"By your faithfulness you led the people you redeemed;
nhlt b^{c}zk / 'l nw qdšk	With your strength you guided them to your holy encampment."

A Line Deletion: ^{c}m z g'lt 5

B Line Replacement: 'l nw qdšk 6

c. Num.10:35 A A (D D) (4:3)

qm yhw // (w)ypṣ 'ybk "Rise, O YHWH, let your enemies be scattered;

(w)yns mśn'k mpnk Let your foes flee before you!"

A Line Deletion: qm yhwh 4

B Line Replacement: mpnk 4

d. Jud.5:3b-c D A (D D) (4:4)

'nk lyhw // 'nk 'šr "I to YHWH, I shall sing;

'zmr lyhw // 'lh yśr'l I shall hymn YHWH, the God of Israel!"

A Line Deletion: 'nk...'nk 6

B Line Replacement: 'lh yśr'l 6

e. Ps.89:11 B B (D D) (4:4)

'th dk'th / kḥll rhb "You crushed Rahab like a corpse;

bzr^c ^{c}zkh // pzrth 'ybkh With your mighty arm you scattered your foes."

A Line Deletion: 'th...kḥll 5

B Line Replacement: bzr^c ^{c}zkh 5

2. B Line replacement exceeds the A Line deletion by more than one syllable

a. Jud.5:25 A A (D D) (4:4)

mm š'l // ḥlb ntn "He asked for water; she gave him milk;

bspl 'drm / hqrb ḥm' She offered curds in a noble bowl."

A Line Deletion: mm š'l 3

B Line Replacement: bspl 'drm 5

b. Ps.68:17b-c A A (D D) (4:3)

hr ḥmd / 'lhm lšbt "O mountains which God desired for his habitation,

'p yhw yškn lnṣḥ YHWH, to dwell forever."

A Line Deletion: hr ḥmd 4

B Line Replacement: lnṣḥ 2

Minor Formulae

x x (D/D)

a. Ex.15:8a-b A A (D/D) (4:3)

brḥ 'pk / n^{c}rm mm "At the blast of your nostrils the waters piled up;

nṣb km nd nzlm The floods stood like a heap."

A Line Deletion: brḥ 'pk 5

B Line Replacement: km nd 3

b. Ps.29:1 D D (D/D) (4:4)

hb lyhw // bn 'lm "Give YHWH, O lesser gods,
hb lyhw // kbd w[c]z Give YHWH glory and strength!"

A Line Deletion: bn 'lm 4

B Line Replacement: kbd w[c]z 4

<u>Comment</u>: Only the second example displays a satisfactory syllabic relationship between deletion and replacement units. The formula is, of course, a simple variation of x x (D D) produced by the construct relationship between deletion elements.

<u>Additional Formulae</u>

1. /x (D <u>D/D</u>) Ex.15:11b-c /A (D <u>D/D</u>) (3:4)

m kmk n'dr bqdš "Who like you is terrible among the holy ones,
nr' thlt // [c]ś pl' Feared for praiseworthy acts, performing wonders?"

A Line			B Line
Parallel units: n'dr	2 //	5	nr' thlt
A Line Deletion: m kmk	4		
bqdš	2		
B Line Replacement:		3	[c]ś pl'
Total:	8	8	

<u>Comment</u>: A combination of x /x (D) and x x (D) in a metrical framework 3:4. The grammatical ratio is, however, 4:4.

2. x/ (D/D) Ps.68:6 A/ (D/D) (4:3)

'b ytmm // (w)dyn 'lmnt "The father of orphans, the judge of widows;
yhw bm[c]n qdš YHWH is in his holy abode."

A Line			B Line
Parallel units: dyn 'lmnt	5 //	2	yhw
A Line Deletion: 'b	2		
ytmm	3		
Total:	10	4	bm[c]n qdš

<u>Comment</u>: Also a combination of x /x (D) and x x (D), but unlike the preceding (and following) example, in a 4:3 metrical framework. The syllabic asymmetry is extreme.

3. x /x (D D)

a. Ex.15:10 B /A (D D) (4:4)

nšpt brḥk // ksm ym "You blew with your wind; Sea covered them;

ṣll k^c^prt / bmm 'drm They sank like a lead weight in the terrible waters."

A Line			B Line
Parallel units: ym	1 //	5	bmm 'drm
A Line Deletion: nšpt brḥk	7		
B Line Replacement:		3	
Total:	8	8	

b. Ps.68:5a B /A (D D) (4:3)

šr lyhw // zmr šm "Sing to YHWH; hymn his name;

sl lrkb b^c^rbt Make a road for the rider in the clouds!"

A Line			B Line
Parallel units: šm	2 //	7	lrkb b^c^rbt
A Line Deletion: šr lyhw	5		
B Line Replacement:			none
Total:	7	7	

Comment: This formula is, in the case of the 4:4 example, Ex.15:10, a combination of the three metrical unit formula x /x (D) and x (D D); i.e., it displays a contrast between simple and compound terms in A and B Lines, respectively, and also a non-parallel B Line replacement. Ps.68:5a, however, is a simple variation of x /x (D) in a 4:3 metrical framework.

4. x≁x (D D)

a. Ex.15:17a-b A≁A (D D) (4:4)

tb'm tṭ^c^m / bhr nḥltk "You brought them, you planted them in the mountain of your possession,

mkn lšbtk / p^c^lt yhw The dais of your throne which you made, O YHWH."

A Line Deletion: tb'm tṭ^c^m 8

B Line Replacement: p^c^lt yhw 5

b. Ps.68:19 A≁A (D D)

^c^lt lmrm // šbt šb "You went north (or: to the heights); you took captives;

lqḥt mtnt b'rm You received gifts from Aram."

A Line Deletion: ^c^lt lmrm 5

B Line Replacement: b'rm 3

c. Ps.89:13 A/A (D D) (4:4)

ṣpn wymn // 'th br'tm — "Saphon and Amanus, you created them;

tbr wḥrmn / bšmkh yrnnw — Tabor and Hermon, which shout for joy at your name."

A Line Deletion: 'th br'tm 5

B Line Replacement: bšmkh yrnnw 8

Comment: None of these examples exhibits satisfactory syllabic compensation.

5. x* /x (D D) Ps.89:6 A* /A (D D) (4:3)

ydw šmym / pl'kh yhwh — "In the heavens they praise your wonderful deeds, O YHWH,

'p 'mntkh / bqhl qdšm — Your faithfulness, in the asbly of the holy ones."

A Line			B Line
Parallel units:	šmym	2 // 5	bqhl qdšm
	pl'kh	3 // 6	'p 'mntkh
Deletion:	ydw...yhwh	4	
Total:		9 11	

Comment: The compensatory relationship between simple and compound terms in A and B Lines, respectively, and also between the simple A Line term (pl'kh) and its B Line parallel ('p 'mntkh) is satisfactory. However, the unit as a whole is syllabically asymmetrical.

6. /x /x (D D) Ps.89:12 /A /A (D D) (4:4)

lkh šmym 'p lkh 'rṣ — "Yours are the heavens; yours the earth;

tbl wml'h // 'th ysdtm — The world and its fullness, you established them."

A Line			B Line
Parallel units:	'p lkh	3 // 5	'th ysdtm
	'rṣ	1 6	tbl wml'h
Deletion:	lkh šmym	4	
Total:		8 11	

Comment: This unit has two relationships between simple and compound terms; in both cases the syllabic relationship is satisfactory. However, the contrast is so great between 'rṣ and tbl wml'h (1:6) that the unit is syllabically asymmetrical in its overall structure.

7. x/x̸ (D D) Ps.114:7 D/D̸ (D D) (4:3)

mlpny 'dn / ḥly 'rṣ "Tremble, O earth, before the Lord,
mlpny 'lh y^{c}qb Before the God of Jacob!"

A Line			B Line
Parallel units: mlpny 'dn	5 //	7	mlpny 'lh y^{c}qb
Deletion: ḥly 'rṣ	3		
Total:	8	7	

Comment: This formula is a variation of the three metrical unit formula x/x̸ (D) in a 4:3 metrical framework. Syllabic relationships are satisfactory.

Triple Replacement Formulae

This category can occur, of course, only with four unit formulae and is represented in the Corpus by only two formulae, each with one example. Both are 4:4.

1. /x (D D D) Jud.5:30 /A (D D D)

hl' ymṣ' // yḥlq šll "Have they not found, divided the spoil,
rḥm rḥmtm / lr'š gbr One girl, two girls for each warrior?"

A Line			B Line
Parallel units: šll	2 //	4	rḥm rḥmtm
A Line Deletion: hl' ymṣ' yḥlq	9		
B Line Replacement:		3	
Total:	11	7	

Comment: The syllabic relationship between simple and compound units is satisfactory; however, the syllabic asymmetry between A Line deletion and B Line replacement terms is extreme.

2. x (D D D) Ps.68:17a-b "D" (D D D)

lm trṣdn // hrm gbnnm "Why do you look (?), O jagged (?) mountains,
hr ḥmd / 'lhm lšbt O mountains which God desired for his habitation."

A Line Deletion:	lm trṣdn...gbnnm	9
B Line Replacement:	ḥmd 'lhm lšbt	8

Comment: The syllabic relationship between A Line deletion and B Line replacement terms is satisfactory.

TOTALS AND STATISTICS

Total number of units in the _Corpus_: 240

Parallel units: 212 (88%)

Non-parallel units: 28 (12%)

Total number of unit formulae in the _Corpus_: 80

Non-replacement formulae: 34

Replacement formulae: 45

Total number of major formulae in the _Corpus_: 10

Number of units: 118 (49% of _Corpus_; 56% of parallel units)

Number of formulae occurring once: 50 (21% of _Corpus_; 24% of parallel units)

Three Metrical Unit Formulae

Total number of formulae: 51

Total number of examples: 167 (70% of total examples in _Corpus_; 79% of parallel examples)

Major formulae: 9

Number of examples: 111 (66% of three metrical unit parallel examples)

Non-replacement formulae

Number of formulae: 25

Number of examples: 65 (39% of three metrical unit examples)

Major formulae: 4

Number of examples: 39 (60% of the class)

Replacement formulae

Number of formulae: 26

Number of examples: 102 (61% of three metrical unit examples)

Major formulae: 5

Number of examples: 72 (71% of the class)

Single replacement

Number of formulae: 20

Number of examples: 90 (88% of replacement examples)

Major formulae: 4

Number of examples: 67 (75% of the class; 66% of three metrical unit replacement formulae)

<u>Double replacement</u>

Number of formulae: 6

Number of examples: 12 (12% of replacement examples)

Major formulae: 1

Number of examples: 5 (42% of the class)

<u>Four Metrical Unit Formulae</u>

Total number of formulae: 30

Total number of examples: 45 (19% of total examples in <u>Corpus</u>; 21% of parallel examples)

Major formulae: 1

Number of examples: 7 (16% of four metrical unit parallel formulae)

<u>Non-replacement formulae</u>

Number of formulae: 9

Number of examples: 12 (27% of four metrical unit examples)

Major formulae: none

<u>Replacement formulae</u>

Number of formulae: 20

Number of examples: 33 (73% of four metrical unit examples)

Major formulae: none

<u>Single replacement</u>

Number of formulae: 9

Number of examples: 12 (36% of replacement examples)

Major formulae: none

<u>Double replacement</u>

Number of formulae: 9

Number of examples: 19 (58% of replacement examples)

Major formulae: 1

Number of examples: 7 (37% of the class)

<u>Triple replacement</u>

Number of formulae: 2

Number of examples: 2 (6% of replacement examples)

Major formulae: none

No attempt has been made to supply full statistics on all the possible relationships displayed by formulae in the *Corpus*. Parallel and repetition formulae are not differentiated in the list; a later section will deal with the latter specifically. The statistics on four metrical unit formulae can hardly be considered conclusive in light of the poor representation of the class in the *Corpus* and the greater number of possible combinations which such examples present.

The most significant data in the above list seem to be, firstly, the percentage of parallel formulae (88%), and, secondly, the fact that the major formulae represent just under half of the *Corpus* and 56% of the parallel units. In other words, half the *Corpus* is composed of examples that are non-parallel or parallel formulae that occur less than five times. One notes the domination of three metrical unit formulae and, within that class, of single replacement formulae, which account for almost one-third of the whole *Corpus*. A larger sample might affect these proportions but is unavailable within the chronological span and textual requirements imposed on the examples of the *Corpus*. The relatively large number of minor formulae, especially in the four metrical unit category, attests to the versatility of the ancient poets, on the one hand, and, on the other, to the general strictness with which the system of analysis has been applied. For example, by combining the 10 major formulae with very closely related minor formulae, one obtains perhaps more significant figures. Then the major formulae would account for about 160 examples or 68% of the *Corpus* and 76% of the parallel examples. Similarly, in the three metrical unit class, the 9 major formulae would account for ca. 150 units or 92% of the examples. The procedure might be continued (see the following section). However, it seems more consistent with the methodology of this study to allow for the maximum amount of variation in the results.

THE MINOR FORMULAE: ADDITIONAL REMARKS

This system of analysis has been designed to register in the formulae all features of parallel verse isolated by the method of analysis. Within the framework of these criteria, the formulae represent the maximum number of variations. As stated above, no attempt will be made to reduce the number of formulae. However, it is clear that many minor formulae and some major ones differ from others only in relatively simple ways, for example, x/x/x = x x x + construct relationship between parallel units. The same applies to the relationship between x x x and x x/x among the major formulae. In many cases where a minor formula has been produced by the incongruence of grammatical and metrical structure, the discordant grammatical element is one which, with a slight change of the rules stated in Part I, would not have produced a minor formula. For example, the grammatical element in question is often a monosyllable, either a noun which forms an idiomatic unit with another noun (so 'mry py of Dt.32:1), or a monosyllabic form of a preposition (so ly of yšb ly in II Sam.22:21). It will be useful to have a list of such and similar cases, which will demonstrate the relatively simple way in which many minor formulae differ from the major formulae of which they are variations. One is left with a hard core of examples which resist such analysis and represent true metrical variations which, if the *Corpus* contained more examples, might become major formulae.

The following lists contain:

1. Minor formulae produced by simple grammatical variation, i.e., grammatical compounds;
2. Minor formulae produced by the incongruence between metrical and grammatical structure. This will be subdivided further into:
   a. Examples where the discordant grammatical element is a monosyllabic noun. Note will be taken of those examples that seem to form an idiomatic unit with another noun.
   b. Examples that contain a monosyllabic form of a preposition with suffix or another monosyllabic grammatical element, exclusive of nouns, which,

according to the principles stated in Part I, have been treated as full grammatical units. Reference is, as will be seen from the lists, primarily to the prepositions _l_ and _b_ in the former case, and the pronouns _my_ and _zh_, in the latter. Note that in some cases the difference between grammatical and semantic compounds has been ignored.

1. Grammatical variation
   - a. The major formulae x x/x (9) = x x x
   - b. x/x/x (2) = x x x
     - Dt.33:14
     - Dt.33:15
   - c. x//x̸ (1) = x x̸
     - Dt.32:35a
   - d. x/x* (D) (1) = x x* (D)
     - Dt.32:32a
   - e. x/x (D) (1) = x x (D)
     - Jud.5:23b
   - f. x x (D/D) (2) = x x (D D)
     - Ex.15:8a-b
     - Ps.29:1

2. Incongruence between grammatical and metrical elements
   - a. Monosyllabic nouns
     1. x x /_x_ (1) = x x x
        - Dt.3_2_:1 (_'mry py_)
     2. x x/_x̸_ (1) = x x/x
        - Dt.32:7a (_dr wdr_)
     3. _x_/ x⁄x (1) = x x⁄x
        - Num.23:10b (_mt yšrm_)
     4. /_x_ /x (D) (3; one below under b. 3) = x /x (D)
        - Ex.15:14 (_ḥl 'ḥz_)
        - Num.23:7a (_mlk m'b_)
     5. x _x_⁄x (D) (1) = x /x (D)
        - II Sam.22:28 (_^{c}m ^{c}ny_)
     6. x /x (_D/D_) (1) = x /x (D)
        - II Sam.22:47 (_ḥy yhwh_)
     7. x /_x_ (D) (1) = x x (D)
        - Num.23:18 (_bn ṣpr_)

b. Monosyllabic prepositions and pronouns

1. x x x/ (1) = x x x
   Num.23:7b ('r ly)
2. x/ /x (1) = x/ /x
   Jud.5:29 ('mrh lh)
3. /x /x (D) (3; two above in a. 4) = x /x (D)
   II Sam.22:21 (yšb ly)
4. x x* (D/D) (2) = x x* (D)
   Num.23:9b (hn 'm)
   II Sam.22:7a (bṣr ly)
5. x/x (D/D) (1) = x/x (D)
   Dt.32:24b ('šlḥ bm)
6. x (D/D D) (1) = x (D D)
   II Sam.22:41 (ntth ly)
7. x/x (D D) (1) = x (D D)
   II Sam.22:45 (ytkḥšw ly // yšm^{c}w ly)
8. /x (D D) (1) = /x (D D)
   II Sam.22:19 (mš^{c}n ly)

---

1. x/x x/x (2) = x x/x
   Num.23:10a (m mn // m spr)
   II Sam.22:32 (my 'l // my ṣr)
2. *x /x (1) = x /x
   Ex.15:2b (z 'l)
3. x x/x (D) (1) = x x (D)
   Ex.15:11a-b (m kmk // m kmk)

The removal of the respective criteria assimilates the minor formula to a major one, except in four cases: Dt.32:35a, Ex.15:2b, Dt.32:35a, and II Sam.22:19. By this reckoning, the major formulae would account for 62% of the Corpus and 70% of the parallel (and repetition) units. In the category of monosyllabic nouns, a clearly idiomatic unit is formed, again, with with some exceptions: Num.23:10b (mt yšrm), which is, however, a "cognate accusative," and II Sam.22:28 (^{c}m ^{c}ny); possibly also Ex.15:14 (ḥl 'ḥz).

One grammatical criterion, the construct relationship, must be retained as an important aspect of the system of analysis. As regards the monosyllabic prepositions and pronouns, and possibly also those monosyllabic nouns which form idiomatic units, a different procedure may be advisable. Perhaps the criteria for grammatical and metrical units stated in Part I should, as suggested there, be revised to allow for the treatment of such elements as grammatically and metrically "*anceps*"; that is, elements capable of being awarded or denied the value of a metrical and grammatical unit depending on the structure of the poetic unit in which they occur and the environment of the poem as a whole. Note that prepositions and particles have already been treated in this manner, primarily in units with the grammatical structure 3:2 where the B Line contains a prepositional phrase; so, for example, in the formula x x* (D) in several instances (see the section on deletion and compensation).

THE UNIT FORMULAE: ARRANGEMENT BY GRAMMATICAL UNITS

Many minor formulae were produced, primarily in three metrical unit formulae, by the oncongruence of grammatical and metrical structure (so, also, the major formula x x* (D)). It is useful, however, to have a list of the formulae arranged solely by grammatical structure. This may be obtained by eliminating the signs indicating metrical addition and subtraction, * and _, respectively. Thus x/ x* = x/ x; x x x̲/ = x x x/. The following list does not itself perform this operation, but presents the formulae as they appear in the *Corpus* and preceding lists, arranged, however, only by grammatical structure; i.e., three metrical unit formulae with the grammatical structure 2:2; 2:3; 3:2; 3:3; 3:4; 4:2; 4:3; and 4:4; and four metrical unit formulae with the grammatical structure 3:4; 4:2; 4:3; 4:4; 4:5. Since this system allows the metrical structures 3:4, 4:3, and 4:4, only units with the grammatical structure 4:2 and 4:5 can be considered as metrical variations in the four metrical unit class, aside from x x* (D D).

The large number of formulae with the metrical signs * and _ in the three metrical unit class reflect the manner in which such units have been treated in this study. In texts in which a metrical structure of 3:3 seems to dominate throughout (Num.23; Num.24; Dt.32; Dt.33; II Sam.22; etc.), examples with grammatical structures other than 3:3 have been assigned to the three metrical unit pattern. Texts which display 4:4 patterns or clear alternation between 3:3 and 4:4 (including 3:4 and 4:3) (Ex.15; Jud.5; Ps.68; etc.) have not required the mechanical application of metrical rules. In other words, the use of the metrical signs * and _, as well as their frequent appearance in the three metrical unit class, represents the workings of *Systemzwang*. A purely syllabic interpretation of Hebrew verse would eliminate the necessity for the metrical signs. A totally grammatical approach to the patterns represented by the formulae, along the lines suggested above, would then also be possible. One might proceed further and include as grammatical units those grammatical elements which were excluded in Part I, i.e., particles, etc. Of course, syllable counts have been an important factor in classifying the formulae. It must be noted that even with a solely syllabic approach, one would still be required to take into account the types of patterning represented by the formulae as an important aspect of poetic structure.

Two aspects of the following lists call for special comment. Firstly, the metrical sign * must occur in three metrical unit formulae when one of the lines contains a grammatical structure of less than three grammatical units, i.e., 2:2, 2:3 or 3:2. Similarly, the metrical sign _ can occur in three metrical unit formulae only when one line contains more than three grammatical units, i.e., 3:4, 4:3, and 4:4. The appearance of the sign * in a unit with the grammatical structure 3:3 marks a special problem: *x /x (Ex.15:2b). Here the grammatical unit z has been treated as a grammatical element without metrical value. This departs from the procedures outlined in Part I, but seems called for by the overall structure of the unit.

Due to the manner in which four metrical unit formulae are treated in this study, the metrical signs appear only once in connection with them: * in Ps.89:6 (x* /x), a unit which should perhaps be classed as 4:3.

A second aspect of the lists should also be noted. The elimination of metrical criteria means that some formulae would fall together. Most notably the large three metrical unit formula x x* (D) would merge with x x (D). In four metrical unit formulae mergings would occur on a smaller scale. Thus x/x x/x = x/x x/x (Num.23:10a and II Sam.22:32) would join x/x x/x (Ps.68:16); /x /x (D) = /x /x (D) (Ex.15:14; Num.23:7a, and II Sam.22:21) fall together with /x /x (D) (Ps.114:1); and, in the four metrical unit category, x* /x (D D) = x /x (D D) (Ps.89:6) merges with x /x (D D) (Ex.15:10 and Ps.68:5a). However, many of these mergings would throw together formulae with quite different grammatical structures. For example, all examples of x x* (D) are grammatically 3:2, while x x (D) is a 3:3 class. This means that what has been allowed for four metrical unit formulae would have to be extended, after the removal of the metrical aspect, to grammatically 3:3 units also; namely, the same formula could occur in different grammatical categories. Only the details of deletion and compensation would clarify the difference in structure.

Three Metrical Unit Non-Replacement Formulae

Grammatical Units: 2:2

x x (2)

Gen.49:7b

Num.23:23a

x *x* (1)

Num.24:9

Grammatical Units: 2:3

x *x (1)

Ex.15:5

*x⌿x̸ (1)

Dt.32:25b

x */x (1)

II Sam.22:11

Grammatical Units: 3:2

x/ x* (1)

Dt.32:41b

x x/* (1)

Jud.5:17c-d

Grammatical Units: 3:3

x x x (14)

x x/x (9)

x x⌿x (10)

x/ /x (6)

x/x/x (2)

Dt.33:14

Dt.33:15

x x̸ (3)

Dt.32:3

Dt.32:22b

Dt.32:35b

x/x⌿x (1)

Gen.49:12a

x//x̸ (1)

Dt.32:35a

x⌿x⌿x (1)

Dt.32:38a

x⌿⌿x̸ (1)

Dt.33:28b

*x /x (1)

Ex.15:2b

x x/ (1)

II Sam.22:44b-c

Grammatical Units: 3:4

x x /x̲ (1)

Dt.32:1

x x/x̸̲ (1)

Dt.32:7a

x/ /x̲ (1)

Jud.5:29

Grammatical Units: 4:3

x x x̲/ (1)

Num.23:7b

x/ x⌿x (1)

Num.23:10b

Grammatical Units: 4:4

x̲/x̲ x/x (2)

Num.23:10a

II Sam.22:32

Three Metrical Unit Replacement Formulae (Single and Double)

Grammatical Units: 2:3

*/x̸ (D) (2)

Dt.32:38b

II Sam.22:16b

*x (D) (2)

Dt.32:10b

II Sam.22:39

Grammatical Units: 3:2

x x* (D) (23)

x/x* (D) (1)

Dt.32:32a

x/* (D) (1)

II Sam.22:34

Grammatical Units: 3:3

x /x (D) (24)

x/x̸ (D) (8)

x x (D) (10)

x (D D) (5)

/x/ (D) (1)

Ex.15:2a

x⁄x̸ (D) (2)

Num.23:24b

Dt.32:10a

x⁄x (D) (2)

II Sam.22:42

Ps.29:3a-b

x/x (D) (1)

Jud.5:23b

/x̸ (D D) (2)

Gen.49:15b

Dt.33:6

/x (D D) (2)

Gen.49:16

Gen.49:27a-b

Grammatical Units: 4:2

x x* (D̲/D̲) (2)

Num.23:9b

II Sam.22:7a

Grammatical Units: 3:4

/x̲ /x (D) (3)

Ex.15:14

Num.23:7a

II Sam.22:21

x /x̲ (D) (1)

Num.23:18

/x̸̲ (D D) (1)

II Sam.22:19

Grammatical Units: 4:3

x x̲⁄x (D) (1)

II Sam.22:28

x /x (D̲/D̲) (1)

II Sam.22:47

/x̲/ (D) (1)

Dt.32:28

x⁄x̸ (D̲/D̲) (1)

Dt.32:24b

x (D̲/D̲ D) (1)

II Sam.22:41

Grammatical Units: 4:4

x x̲/x̲ (D) (1)

Ex.15:11a-b

x̲/x̲ (D D) (1)

II Sam.22:45

Four Metrical Unit Non-Replacement Formulae (3:4, 4:3 and 4:4)

Metrical Units: 3:4; Grammatical Units: 3:4

/x x/x (1)

Ex.15:15a-b

<u>Metrical Units</u>: <u>4:3</u>; <u>Grammatical Units</u>: <u>4:3</u>

x/x x/ (1)

Ex.15:15b-c

<u>Metrical Units</u>: <u>4:4</u>; <u>Grammatical Units</u>: <u>4:4</u>

x x ✗ (1)

Gen.4:23a

x/x x/x (1)

Ex.15:9b-c

x/ /x x (1)

Ex.15:17b-c

x x x/x (3)

II Sam.1:20b

Ps.68:3b-c

Ps.89:10

x/x x/x (2)

II Sam.1:22b-c

Ps.68:16

x ✗/ (1)

Ps.29:2

<u>Metrical Units</u>: <u>4:4</u>; <u>Grammatical Units</u>: <u>4:5</u>

x x ✗ (1)

Ex.15:4

<u>Four Metrical Unit Replacement Formulae</u>:
(<u>Single</u>, <u>Double</u> and <u>Triple</u>)

<u>Metrical Units</u>: <u>3:4</u>; <u>Grammatical Units</u>: <u>3:4</u>

x///x (D) (1)

Ps.68:3a-b

/x /x (D) (1)

Ps.114:1

x x (D) (1)

Ps.29:10

<u>Metrical Units</u>: <u>3:4</u>; <u>Grammatical Units</u>: <u>4:4</u>

/x (D <u>D/D</u>) (1)

Ex.15:11b-c

<u>Metrical Units</u>: <u>4:3</u>; <u>Grammatical Units</u>: <u>4:3</u>

x/ /x (D) (1)

Ps.68:14b

x x/x (D) (1)

Ps.114:8

x x (D/D) (2; one also 4:4)

Ex.15:8a-b

x /x (D D) (2; one also 4:4)

Ps.68:5a

x/✗ (D D) (1)

Ps.114:7

x/ (D/D) (1)

Ps.68:6

<u>Metrical Units</u>: <u>4:4</u>; <u>Grammatical Units</u>: <u>4:3</u>

x* /x (D D) (1)

Ps.89:6

<u>Metrical Units</u>: <u>4:4</u>; <u>Grammatical Units</u>: <u>4:4</u>

x x x (D) (3)

Ps.29:1b-2a

Ps.29:5

Ps.29:8

x x /x (D) (2)

Jud.5:28b

Ps.89:7

x/x /x (D) (1)

II Sam.1:21b

x⁄x /x (D) (1)

Ps.89:8

x x (D D) (7)

x x (D/D) (2; one also 4:3)

Ps.29:1

x /x (D D) (2; one also 4:3)

Ex.15:10

x⁄x (D D) (3)

Ex.15:17a-b

Ps.68:19

Ps.89:13

/x /x (D D) (1)

Ps.89:12

/x (D D D) (1)

Jud.5:30

x (D D D) (1)

Ps.68:17a-b

Non-parallel Units

The approximately 11% of the examples of the *Corpus* which are non-parallel fall into the following basic grammatical categories:

1. Verbal sentence-verbal sentence (VS-VS)
   - a. Ex.15:1b
   - b. Ex.15:7
   - c. Ex.15:9a-b
   - d. Ex.15:16a
   - e. Jud.5:3a-b
   - f. II Sam.22:40
   - g. Ps.24:7b-c
2. Nominal sentence-nominal sentence (NS-NS)
   - a. Gen.49:5
   - b. Gen.49:14
   - c. Num.23:21b
   - d. Num. 23:22
   - e. Dt.33:20b
3. Verbal sentence-nominal sentence (VS-NS)
   II Sam.22:10
4. Nominal sentence-verbal sentence (NS-VS)
   - a. Gen.49:9a
   - b. Gen.49:17b
   - c. Gen.49:20
   - d. Dt.33:22
   - e. Dt.33:23b-c
5. "Quasi-verbal" sentence-nominal sentence (QVS-NS)
   Dt.33:24b-c
6. Verbal sentence-"quasi-verbal" sentence (VS-QVS)
   Dt.32:39d-e
7. Enjambed lines
   - a. Dt.32:6a
   - b. Dt.32:8b
   - c. Dt.33:13a-b
   - d. Dt.33:16a
   - e. Jud.5:19b
   - f. II Sam.1:22a-b
   - g. Ps.24:8a-b

With so limited a number of examples, it would be hazardous to proceed beyond the most general remarks. On the position of non-parallel lines, see Part I. It must be noted that the relatively small number of non-parallel units in the *Corpus* may be due to the fact that epic is not represented in biblical poetry. In Ugaritic poetry the proportion of non-parallel lines is substantially higher (ca. 25%), as also in other literatures in which epic is well represented. Of course, one of the most common positions for non-parallel units is as an introduction to speeches, so common in epic (cf. Steinitz's *Sagte* verses).

In non-parallel units one may distinguish between enjambed units and all the other categories. In enjambed units either the A or B Line is, of necessity, joined to its partner by grammatical dependency to form a single sentence. Of course, enjambment is also common in parallel units; however, in these cases the semantic parallelism between lines dominates. The enjambed line may be related in a number of ways to its partner, which in all cases is an independent sentence. In the examples of the _Corpus_ one finds adverbial relationships (Dt.32:8b; Dt.33:13a-b; Jud.5:19b, and II Sam.1:22a-b; in each case the enjambed line forms a prepositional phrase); the vocative relationship (Dt.32:6a); a question-answer relationship (Ps.24:8a-b); and a relationship formed by a "chain" (Dt.33:16a).

Non-enjambed units are capable of expressing certain kinds of general semantic relationships between the member lines, of the types which occur between any two coordinated prose sentences. The clearest to isolate is one which may be described as metaphorical. In several examples, the A Line states a comparison and the B Line provides a _tertium comparationis_; so Gen.49:9a; Gen.49:14; Dt.33:20b, and Dt.33:22. This category is, of course, not limited to non-parallel units; cf. Gen.49:27a-b. The device is appropriate to the _genre_ of blessings, to which it is limited in the _Corpus_.

Another clearly recognizable category is one in which the relationship between A and B Lines is one of purpose; so, Ps.24:7b-c. In several cases the relationship may be one of either purpose or result: Gen.49:17b; Gen.49:20; Ex.15:1b; Ex.15:7, Ex.15:9a-b; Ex.15:16b; Dt.33:23b-c; Jud.5:3a-b, and II Sam.22:40.

In some examples the relationship between the lines may be described as circumstantial: Num.23:21b; Num.23:22; II Sam.22:10; or descriptive: Gen.49:5; Dt.33:24b-c, and, perhaps, Dt.32:39d-e. It must be stated that in some cases one is perhaps dealing with "loose" parallelism of the type so common in later poetry; so, for example, II Sam.22:40.

Repetition Units

Total or partial repetition has long been recognized as a significant aspect of the earliest Hebrew verse, and one of the features it shares with Canaanite and even early Akkadian verse (see, especially, Albright's Yahweh and the Gods of Canaan). Repetition units are, of course, represented in the Corpus. Approximately 18% of the examples exhibit repetition in their unit formulae; the percentage would be higher if one included repetition of grammatical elements below the level of grammatical units, which are not recorded by the formulae.

One must distinguish between repetition formulae, proper, and those parallel formulae which display repetition of one or more parallel members. Repetition formulae are, strictly speaking, non-parallel units. In the reconstructed sentence they form one continuous syntagmatic sequence, just as non-parallel units would do if one formed a reconstructed sentence for them. By nature, all must fall into the category of the major formula x x (D), and its variations. The examples that occur in the Corpus are:

a. Ex.15:6 D D (D D)
b. Ex.15:16b D "D" (D)
c. Jud.5:19a "D" D (D)
d. Jud.5:23b D/D (D)
e. Jud.5:24 D D (D)
f. Ps.24:8b-c D "D" (D)
g. Ps.29:1a-b D D (D/D)
h. Ps.29:1b-2a D D "D" (D)
i. Ps.29:3b-c "D" D (D)
j. Ps.29:5 "D" "D" "D" (D)
k. Ps.29:8 "D" D "D" (D)
l. Ps.29:10 D D (D)
m. Ps.68:17a-b "D" (D D D)
n. Ps.77:17a-b D D (D)

Included in this list are also examples with "D" = virtual repetition. These repetition units account for ca. 6% of the Corpus.

A larger number of units (12% of the Corpus) display partial repetition within a variety of parallel formulae. The following is a reference list:

Single Repetition

Gen.4:24	Num.23:7b
Gen.49:19	Num.23:10a
Gen.49:25a	Num.24:7b
Ex.15:4b-c	Num.24:17a
Ex.15:17b-c	Dt.32:2b

Dt.32:39c-d
Dt.33:14
Dt.33:15
Dt.33:17c
Jud.5:3b-c
Jud.5:20
Jud.5:28b
II Sam.1:21b
II Sam.22:32
II Sam.22:45
Ps.29:2
Ps.68:3b-c
Ps.89:7
Ps.89:10
Ps.114:7
Ps.114:8

Double Repetition

Ex.15:11a-b
II Sam.1:20b
Ps.29:4

Triple Repetition

Ps.68:16

Note the cases of internal repetition between short lines: Ex.15:3; Jud.5:3b, and Ps.82:12.

All of the above repetitions are recorded by the unit formulae. Mention should be made of those types of grammatical elements which do not appear in the formulae, but whose repetition plays a great role, particularly in the acoustical patterning of Hebrew verse. Reference is especially to particles and prepositions; so, for example, *ky*: Gen.49:7a; Gen.49:15a; II Sam.22:18; *l'*: Gen.49:6a; Num.23:8; Num.23:19b; Num.23:21a; Num.23;23a; II Sam.1:22b-c; *^{c}l* and *^{c}ly*: Gen.49:17a; II Sam. 22:11; Ps.29:3; *^{c}d*: Ex.15:16b; *kmw*: Ps.29:6. Note also *mh* in Num.23:8. One might also include the frequent repetition of elements like pronominal suffixes, etc.

Deletion-Compensation

An essential feature of all replacement formulae is compensation, that is, compensatory lengthening. Syllabic compensation is, of course, the purpose of replacement in such formulae. A grammatical element having been deleted from the A Line, its approximate number of syllables should be replaced in the B Line to maintain the general syllable symmetry which most couplets display. There are two major types of compensation, the first of which may be further subdivided into two categories:

1. A B Line unit, parallel to a unit in the A Line, may be lengthened by the addition of syllables. This may be accomplished in two ways:

    a. Syllables may be added to a simple B Line term; that is, a simple term may be employed in the B Line which is (ideally) longer by two or more syllables than its simple parallel in the A Line. This type of compensation is characteristic of the major three metrical unit formula x x* (D).

    b. A simple A Line term may be paralleled by a compound, or a compound by a double compound, in the B Line. In effect, new grammatical elements have been added, but the compound as a whole is semantically parallel and occupies the same rank in the reconstructed sentence as its A Line parallel. This type of compensation is characteristic of the major three metrical unit formulae x /x (D) and x/x̸ (D).

2. One or more grammatical elements may be added to the B Line which form a separate rank in the reconstructed sentence; i.e., are not parallel to any term in the A Line and do not form a compound with any term in the B Line. These replacement terms must, however, be grammatically and semantically compatible with the A Line in the reconstructed sentence. This type of compensation is typical of the major three metrical unit formulae x x (D) and x (D D) and the four metrical unit formula x x (D D).

Variations and four metrical unit formulae display the same patterns and fall into one or another of the major types of compensation. A few complex examples display more than one type of compensation. Also notable are a very few non-replacement formulae which show compensation in the B Line although nothing has been deleted from the A Line.

This section will list and briefly analyze the major aspects of deletion and compensation. Examples will be listed according to a pattern which is based on a number of principles. Of interest are two major aspects of deletion and compensation which have to do with the position and the grammatical nature of deletion and replacement elements.

1. Position: Three metrical unit formulae have three positions, or ranks, in both A and B Lines. These may be referred to as A, B, and C positions, using the standard terminology. However, since these letters have been used for other purposes also in this study, it seems preferable to employ some more distinctive terminology. Therefore the three positions will be referred to as initial, medial, and final, abbreviated in the lists to I, M, and F, respectively. Metrical variations may, in fact, have more positions (i.e., examples with a grammatical structure of 4:4 in a metrical framework of 3:3, etc.), but this fact need not be reflected in the lists and analyses. Four metrical unit formulae have a maximum of four positions, which will be abbreviated as I, M1, M2, and F. Variations will be treated in the same manner as those of three metrical unit formulae.

The type of compensation displayed by a given formula determines how many of these positions are relevant for analysis. Specific details will be presented at the beginning of each list. In general, however, the following aspects of position will be monitored:

a. The position of the grammatical unit deleted from the A Line.

b. The position in the A Line of the unit to be paralleled by the B Line compensation.

c. The position in the B Line of the compensation unit.

Some formulae are prevented by their nature from being analyzed for certain aspects of position. This also will be presented at the beginning of each list. For example, formulae which display the type of compensation characteristic of x /x (D) can be analyzed for all three positions; formulae of the pattern x x (D), only for a. and c., above.

2. <u>Grammar</u>: The lists will register the following:
   a. The grammatical unit deleted from the A Line.
   b. The grammatical aspect of the B Line replacement that forms the compensation, according to the pattern characteristic of each formula. This, again, will be described at the beginning of each list.

Due to the limited number of examples in the <u>Corpus</u>, and the further necessity of dividing many formulae into sub-categories, the final statistics and the conclusions based on them are tentative. Moreover, the syllabic regularity of each unit must also be taken into account. Examples of the major formulae are listed in the order in which they appear in the lists of the section on unit formulae which begins Part III; i.e., in order of their approximation of the "ideal" syllabic pattern of each formula. In the lists in this section these sub-categories will simply be divided by a horizontal line which represents a decreasing degree of syllabic soundness, as appropriate to each formula. For details one must consult the section on the unit formulae. However, since it is necessary to list minor formulae and variations according to the type of compensation they display, they cannot, of course, be listed in the order they appear in the section on unit formulae. Such examples do not, in this section, contain a reference to their syllabic acceptability. For this important aspect, one must, again, refer to the unit formulae lists. These complications seem unavoidable, nor need they affect the validity of the general statements. Note that some examples, labelled "complex," exhibit characteristics of two types of compensation and appear in two lists.

<u>Lists</u>

1. Compensation by the parallelism of a simple unit in the A Line and a compound unit in the B Line

This type of compensation is characteristic of the major three metrical unit formula x /x (D), its variations, the minor formulae related to it, and the formulae displaying the same characteristics in the four metrical unit category. Examples of each of these will be listed in turn. The pattern of presentation is the following:

a. A Line: The first column, marked Del. (= deletion), indicates the position in the A Line of the deleted grammatical unit as I (initial), M (medial), and F (final). Four metrical unit formulae sub-divide M into M1 and M2, as explained above.

The second column, marked Comp. (= compensation), indicates the position in the A Line of the simple unit paralleled by the compound in the B Line.

b. B Line: The third column, headed simply B Line, indicates the position in that line of the compound unit. Since the characteristic of this type of compensation is the parallelism of a simple unit and a compound, the B Line can contain only two relevant positions: the compound can form the initial and medial units (IM) or the medial and final ones (MF).

c. The fourth and fifth columns deal with grammar. The fourth column, headed Gram.Del. (= grammatical deletion), lists the grammatical units omitted from the A Line. The fifth column, headed Gram.Comp. (= grammatical compensation), lists the grammatical units forming the B Line compound. These will be indicated both by the signs employed for grammatical notation and, in addition, a brief description, in parentheses, of the type of structure represented by the compound.

Three Metrical Unit Formulae

x /x (D) and Its Variations

x /x (D)

	A Line				
Passage	Del.	Comp.	B Line	Gram.Del.	Gram.Comp.
Gen.49:10a	I	F	MF	neg-b	3(prep)-C-s (construct)
Gen.49:11a	I	F	MF	a(inf.abs.)	2-C-s (construct)
Gen.49:11b	I	M	IM	a	3-C (construct)
Dt.32:4a	I	F	IM	-C	ptcl-"S"-C-s (construct with kl)
Dt.32:22a	I	F	MF	ptcl-1	3 ,-3 (attributive)
Dt.32:27b	I	F	MF	ptcl-a	a "2"-Cpr (verbal compound)

Passage	A Line Del.	A Line Comp.	B Line	Gram.Del.	Gram.Comp.
Jud.5:26a	F	M	MF	a	3-C (construct)
II Sam.1:27	I	F	MF	ptcl!	1-C (construct)
II Sam.22:7b	M	F	MF	3-s	a 3-s (verbal compound)
II Sam.22:12	I	M	MF	a	2-C (construct)
II Sam.22:14	M	I	MF	3	a 2-s (verbal compound)
II Sam.22:29	I	M	MF	ptcl-Spr	a 2-s (verbal compound)
Ps.29:6	I	M	MF	a-encl.<u>mem</u>	"3-C" (construct)
Ps.114:3	M	F	MF	a	b 3 (verbal compound)

Dt.32:13b	I	F	MF	a-s	3-C (construct)

Gen.4:24	M	I	MF	c	3 &3 (numerical compound)
Dt.32:7b	I	F	MF	a!	&a 3-s (verbal compound)
Dt.32:21b	I	F	IM	lpr	3 ,-3 (attributive)
Dt.33:2b-c	F	M	MF	3-s	3-Cpn (construct)
Dt.33:11a	M	F	IM	lpn!	2-C-s (construct)
Dt.33:13b-c	I	F	MF	3-	,-R(part.b 3)
Hab.3:3a	F	M	MF	b	3-C (construct)

Dt.32:12	F	I	MF	a-s	S ,-S (attributive)

Ps.114:4	M	F	MF	b	"3-C" (construct)
Minor Formulae					
/<u>x</u> /x (D)					
Ex.15:14	I	M	MF	a	2-C (construct)
Num.23:7a	M	I	MF	a-s	3-C (construct)
II Sam.22:21	M	F	IM	lpn	3-C-s (construct)
x <u>x</u>/x (D)					
II Sam.22:28	I	M	IM	lpr	2 ,-2 (attributive)
x /x (<u>D/D</u>)					
II Sam.22:47	I	F	MF	1-Cpn!	1-C-s (construct)

Passage	A Line Del.	A Line Comp.	B Line	Gram.Del.	Gram.Comp.
Complex Formulae					
/x (D D) (also listed under grammatical replacement formulae (no. 5, below))					
Gen.49:16	IM	F	MF	1pn a	2-Cpn (construct)
Gen.49:27a-b	IM	F	MF	Spn P	a 2 (verbal compound)
Four Metrical Unit Formulae					
3:4					
/x /x (D)					
Ps.114:1	I	M	IM1	3(inf.	-C-Cpn (construct)
		F	M2F	const.b-	3 ,-3 (attributive)
4:3					
x/ /x (D)					
Ps.68:14b	M2	F	MF	c	3-C (construct)
x x/x (D)					
Ps.114:8	I	M2F	M2F	,=-C(part.a)	3-C (construct)
4:4					
x x /x (D)					
Jud.5:28b	F	M2	M2F	3(inf. const.b)	1-C-s (construct)
Ps.89:7	I	M1	M2F	ptcl-1pr	3-C (construct)
x/x /x (D)					
II Sam.1:21b	I	M1	M2F	ptcl-3	neg-c 3 (verbal compound)
x/x /x (D)					
Ps.89:8	I	M1	IM1	Spn	P(part.b) &P (part.b)(compound)
/x /x (D D)					
Ps.89:12	IM1	M1	IM1	P(3)-s	1pr a-s (verbal compound)
		F	M2F	S	2 &2-s (compound)

Passage	A Line Del.	A Line Comp.	B Line	Gram.Del.	Gram.Comp.
Complex					
x /x (D D) (also listed under grammatical replacement formulae (no. 5, below))					
Ex.15:10	IM1	F	M1...F	b 3-s	3 ,-3 (attributive)
Ps.68:5a	IM1	F	MF	-a -3pn	3 3
x* /x (D D) (also listed under syllabic compensation formulae (no. 4, below))					
Ps.89:6	I...F	M1 M2	M2F	a 1pn!	3-C (construct)
/x (D D/D) (also listed under grammatical replacement formulae (no. 5, below))					
Ex.15:11b-c	I...F	M	IM1	Spr?-"3-s" 3	P(part.c)-C (construct)
/x (D D D) (also listed with grammatical replacement formulae (no. 5, below))					
Jud.5:30	IM1M2	F	IM1	ptcl? a a	2 2 (numerical compound)

---

2. Compensation by the parallelism of a compound in the A Line with a double compound in the B Line

This type of compensation is characteristic of the three metrical unit formula x/✗ (D), its minor formulae, variations, and the four metrical unit formulae related to it. For this formulae only the A Line position columns can be listed, since a double compound forms the whole of the B Line. Only in four metrical unit formulae can a B Line column theoretically appear. However, the sole four metrical unit example of this pattern in the Corpus (Ps.114:7) happens to be 4:3. Since the A Line must contain a compound, only two positions are available for the A Line compound paralleled in the B Line by the double compound: initial-medial (IM) and medial final (MF). Four metrical unit formulae may distinguish between M1 and M2.

Three Metrical Unit Formulae

x/✗ (D) and Its Variations

x/✗ (D)

Passage	A Line Del.	Comp.	Gram.Del.	Gram.Comp.
Num.24:17c	I	MF	a	2-"C"-C-C (construct)
Dt.32:32b	I	MF	S-s	S ,-S P(3)-s (nominal sentence compound)
Dt.33:16b	I	MF	"b!"	P(3)-C-Cpn (construct)
Dt.33:23a-b	I	MF	Spn	P(part.b) 2-Cpn (compound)
Hab.3:11b	F	IM	b	3-C-C-s (construct)

Dt.32:20b	F	IM	Spr	P ,-R(neg-S P(3)-s) (compound (noun + relative clause))
Dt.32:33	F	IM	S-s	P-C ,-P (construct; attributive)
Dt.33:24a-b	F	IM	Spn	"b" P(part.c)-C-s ("quasi-verbal" sentence)
/x/ (D)				
Ex.15:2a	F	IM	Spn	"b" 3-s P(3) ("quasi-verbal" sentence)
x≁✗ (D)				
Num.23:24b	I	MF	neg-b	2-C a (verbal sentence compound)
Dt.32:10a	I	MF	a-s	3-C-C (construct)
/x̲/ (D)				
Dt.32:28	F	IM	ptcl-P	,-R("neg-b"-P(3)-s 1) (relative clause= "quasi-verbal" sentence)
x/✗ (D/D)				
Dt.32:24b	F	IM	a-3-s	&(prep)-2-C-C (construct)
*/✗ (D)				
Dt.32:38b	I	MF	b!	"b!" 3-s P ("quasi-verbal" sentence)
II Sam.22:16b	F	I(M)	lpn!	3-C-C-s (construct)

Passage	A Line Del.	Comp.	Gram.Del.	Gram.Comp.
Four Metrical Unit Formulae				
4:3				
x/x̸ (D D)				
Ps.114:7	M2F	IM1	b! l!	3-C-C (construct)

3. Parallelism of a simple unit in the A Line with a double compound in the B Line

This small category blends features of x /x (D) and x/x̸ (D).

Passage	A Line Del.	Comp.	Gram.Del.	Gram.Comp.
/x̸ (D D)				
Gen.49:15b	IM	F	a 2-s	"b" P(3) ,-P((3) part.a) ("quasi-verbal" sentence; attributive)
Dt.33:6	IM	F	b! lpn	"b!" S-s P ("quasi-verbal" sentence)
/x̲ (D D)				
II Sam.22:19	MF	I	3 -C-s	"b" Spn P-3-s ("quasi-verbal" sentence)

4. Compensation by the parallelism of a simple unit in the A Line with a syllabically longer simple unit in the B Line, which may include a grammatical element below the level of a grammatical unit

This type of compensation is characteristic of the three metrical unit formula x x* (D), its minor formulae and variations, and the four metrical unit formulae related to it. In fact, only one example of the latter category is present in the <u>Corpus</u> (Ps.89:6), and it itself is a complex example which is also related to x /x (D). Three metrical unit formulae of this type display the grammatical structure 3:2. Therefore, only two B Line positions are available for compensation, initial (I) and final (F). No grammatical compensation column is possible for this formula. However, if the simple unit contains a sub-unit grammatical element (particles or prepositions), that fact will be recorded.

Three Metrical Unit Formulae

x x* (D) and Its Variations

x x* (D)

	A Line				
Passage	Del.	Comp.	B Line	Gram.Del.	Gram.Comp.
Gen.4:23b	M	F	F	a	(syllables)
Gen.49:7a	I	F	F	P(part.c)	(syllables)
Gen.49:15a	I	F	F	a	(syllables)
Num.23:9a	I	M	I	ptcl-3-	(syllables)
Num.23:19b	I	F	F	ptcl?-lpr	(syllables)
Num.24:8b	F	M	I	,=2-s	(syllables)
Dt.32:11a	I	F	I	"3"	(syllables: prep-noun)
Dt.32:25a	M	I	I	a	(syllables)
Dt.32:29	I	F	F	ptcl-b	(syllables)
Dt.32:34	I	F	F	ptcl?-Spr	(syllables)
Dt.32:36a	M	F	I	lpn	(syllables: prep-noun)
II Sam.22:22	M	F	F	2-	(syllables)
II Sam.22:37	F	I	I	3-s	(syllables: neg-a)
Ps.77:17b-c	I	M	F	a-s	(syllables)

Gen.49:17a	I	M	I	Spn	(syllables)
Dt.32:11b	I	M	F	a	(syllables: prep-noun)
Dt.32:21a	I	F	F	lpr	(syllables)
Dt.33:18	I	F	F	b!	(syllables)

Num.24:5	I	M	I	ptcl!-b	(syllables)
Num.24:7b	M	I	I	3pn	(syllables)
Ps.114:2	I	F	F	"b"	(syllables)

Passage	A Line Del.	Comp.	B Line	Gram.Del.	Gram.Comp.
Dt.32:30b	I	F	F	ptcl-neg	(syllables)
II Sam.22:38	M	F	F	2-s	(syllables: prep-inf.const.)
Minor Formulae					
x/x* (D)					
Dt.32:32a	F	I	I	S-s	(syllables)
x x* (D/D)					
Num.23:9b	I	F	F	P!-S	(syllables: neg-c)
II Sam.22:7a	I	F	I	3-3-s	(syllables: prep-noun)
Four Metrical Unit Formulae					
Complex (listed also under single // compound (no. 1, above))					
x* /x (D D)					
Ps.89:6	I...F	M1 M2	IM1	a lpn!	(syllables: ptcl-noun)

---

5. Compensation by the addition of a non-parallel grammatical unit or units

This type of compensation is typical of the three metrical unit formulae x x (D) and x (D D), the major four metrical formula x x (D D), their minor formulae and variations. For this pattern it will be necessary to distinguish between single, double, and triple replacement formulae in the lists. No column indicating the A Line term semantically parallel to the B Line compensation is possible with this category, since compensation is effected by a non-parallel grammatical element or elements added to the B Line.

Three Metrical Unit Formulae

Single Replacement

x x (D) and Its Variations

x x (D)

Passage	A Line Del.	B Line	Gram.Del.	Gram.Comp.
Gen.49:19	F	F	,-R(a)	3
Ex.15:8b-c	M	F	"3"	3-C
Dt.33:2a-b	I	F	lpn	3-s
Jud.5:19a	I	F	b́	-Cpn
Jud.5:20	F	F	l	3pn
Jud.5:24	F	M	lpn	,-R(3)
II Sam.22:18	I	F	a-s	3-s
Hab.3:6a	I	I	b	a
Ps.24:8b-c	M	F	,=S	-C
Ps.29:3b-c	I	F	S-	,-3
Ps.77:17a-b	F	F	lpn	b

Ex.15:16b	F	F	lpn	,-R(rel.pr.-a)

Minor Formulae

x/x (D)

Passage	A Line Del.	B Line	Gram.Del.	Gram.Comp.
II Sam.22:42	I	I	a	3pn
Ps.29:3a-b	F	F	b	3

x x/x (D)

Passage	A Line Del.	B Line	Gram.Del.	Gram.Comp.
Ex.15:11a-b	F	M	lpn!	P(part.c)

x /x (D)

Passage	A Line Del.	B Line	Gram.Del.	Gram.Comp.
Num.23:18	I	M	b!	2-s

x/x (D)

Passage	A Line Del.	B Line	Gram.Del.	Gram.Comp.
Jud.5:23b	I	F	ptcl-neg-b	3

*x (D)

Passage	A Line Del.	B Line	Gram.Del.	Gram.Comp.
Dt.32:10b	I	(M)F	a-s	"3-C-s"
II Sam.22:39	I	(M)F	a-s	3(prep)-C-s

x/* (D)

Passage	A Line Del.	B Line	Gram.Del.	Gram.Comp.
II Sam.22:34	F	I	"3"	3-s

Double Replacement Formulae

x (D D) and Its Variations

x (D D)

Passage	A Line Del.	B Line	Gram.Del.	Gram.Comp.
Gen.49:9b	IM	MF	b	,-R(1pr?
			b	a-s)
Num.24:6b	MF	MF	,-R(a	3
			1pn)	,-3
Dt.32:37	IM	MF	a	,-R(b
			P(3?)	3-s)
Dt.33:11b	IM	MF	a!	,-R(1pr?
			2-encl.*mem*	a-s)

Num.23:23b	IM	MF	ptcl-3	1(2pr!-a
			c	1pn)

Minor Formulae

x (D/D D)

II Sam.22:41	MF	(M)F	a-3-s	,-R(&a-s)
			2-	

x/x (D D)

II Sam.22:45	IM	IM	1-	3-
			-C	-C

Complex

/x (D D) (also listed under simple // compound (no. 1, above))

Gen.49:16	IM	I	1pn	"3"
			a	
Gen.49:27b	IM	I	Spn	3
			P	

Four Metrical Unit Formulae

Single Replacement

3:4

x///x (D)

Ps.68:3a-b	F	F	c	3(prep)-
				-C

x x (D)

Ps.29:10	M	M2F	3	"3"
				3

Passage	A Line Del.	B Line	Gram.Del.	Gram.Comp.
4:4				
x x x (D)				
Ps.29:1b-2a	F	F	&2	-C-s
Ps.29:5	I	F	S-	-Cpn
Ps.29:8	I	F	1-	-Cpn
Double Replacement Formulae				
x x (D D)				
Ex.15:6 (4:4)	M2F	M2F	b(inf.abs.)	a
			3	2
Ex.15:13 (4:4)	M2F	M2F	2	3
			,-R(rel. pr.-a)	-C-s
Num.10:35 (3:4)	IM1	F	b!	3-s
Jud.5:3b-c (4:4)	I...M2	M2F	1pr	,=3-
			1pr	-Cpn
Ps.89:11 (4:4)	I...M2	IM1	1pr	3-
			"3"	-C-s

Jud.5:25 (4:4)	IM1	IM1	2	3
			a	-C
Ps.68:17b-c (4:3)	IM1	F	,=1!- a	3
Minor Formulae				
x x (D/D)				
Ex.15:8a-b	IM1	M	3-C-s	"3"
Ps.29:1	M2F	M2F	1-Cpn!	2
				&2
/x (D D/D) (also listed under simple // compound (no. 1, above))				
Ex.15:11b-c	I...F	M2F	Spr?-"3-s"	,=P(part.a)-
			-3	-C
x/ (D/D)				
Ps.68:6	IM1	MF	S-C	P(3)-
				-C
x /x (D D)				
Ex.15:10	IM1	M1...F	b	"3"
			3-s	

Passage	A Line Del.	B-Line	Gram.Del.	Gram.Comp.
x/x (D D)				
Ex.15:17a-b	IM1	M2F	a-s	,-R(a)
			a-s	1 pn!
Ps.68:19	IM1	F	b	3pn
			3	
Ps.89:13	M2F	M2F	1pr	,-R(3-s
			a-s	b)
Triple Replacement Formulae				
x (D D D)				
Ps.68:17a-b	IM1...F	M1M2F	3?	a
			b	1pn
			,-1!	3(inf.const.b)-s
Complex				
/x (D D D) (also listed under simple // compound (no. 1, above))				
Jud.5:30	IM1M2	M2F	a	3-
			a	-C

Totals and Statistics

Statistical information is based on the columns of the preceding lists. However, some simplifications will promote the revealing of significant contours by enabling an economical presentation of the results. The small class of parallelism of a simple unit in the A Line with a double compound in the B Line (no. 3) will be included with the larger class of parallelism of a compound with a double compound (no. 2). This leaves four major categories, which, for brevity's sake, may be referred to by the types of deletion-compensation characteristic of the major formulae x /x (D), x/✗ (D), x x* (D), and x x (D) (nos. 1, 2(3), 4, and 5 in the preceding lists). Included in each class are the minor and four metrical unit formulae. Moreover, certain of the placement ranks may conveniently be combined:

1. In four metrical unit formulae (3:4, 4:3, 4:4):
   IM1 = I
   M2F = F
   M1 = M
   M2 = M
   IM1M2 = I (only in triple replacement formulae)
   M1M2F = F (only in triple replacement formulae)
2. In three metrical unit formulae with the grammatical structure 2:3 and 3:2:
   I(M) = I
   (M)F = F
3. Since no. 1 (x /x (D)) contains only two positions in the B Line compensation column, and nos. 2 and 3 (x/✗ (D), //x (D) and //✗ (D)) only two positions in deletion and compensation columns, it is convenient to equate:
   IM = I
   MF = F

   Note that complex examples must be listed twice in the totals; so, of course, units which appear in two categories:
   /x (D D) Gen.49:16 and Gen.27:a-b (listed under (1) x /x (D) and (5) x x (D))
   x /x (D D) Ex.15:10 (listed under (1) x /x (D) and (5) x x (D))
   x* /x (D D) Ps.89:6 (listed under (1) x /x (D) and (4) x x* (D))
   /x (D D D) Ps.68:17b-c (listed under (1) x /x (D) and (5) x x (D))
   /x (D D/D) Ex.15:11b-c (listed under (1) x /x (D) and (5) x x (D))

In addition, the formulae /x /x (D) (Ps.114:1), which has two positions in the A Line compensation and B Line columns, must appear twice in the totals, as also those formulae which have two non-contiguous deletion positions in the A Line:

x* /x (D D) Ps.89:6: I...F
x x (D D) Jud.5:3b-c and Ps.89:11: I...M2
x (D D D) Ps.68:17a-b: IM1...F
/x (D D/D) Ex.15:11b-c: I...F

So also Ex.15:10 x /x (D D) which has two such positions in the B Line compensation column: M1...F.

The statistics are divided into three categories: position, and the grammatical aspects of deletion and compensation units.

<u>Position</u>

The following is a list of the total number of examples in each category presented in the master list, above, with the combination of categories described previously:

	A Line		
Category	Del.	Comp.	B Line
(1) x /x (D)	I 30	I 4	I 11
	M 9	M 17	
	F 6	F 25	F 35
(2)(3) x/✗ (D)	I 9	I 10	
	F 10	F 9	
(4) x x* (D)	I 18	I 4	I 12
	M 6	M 7	M 0
	F 4	F 16	F 15
(5) x x (D)	I 32		I 8
	M 5		M 6
	F 18		F 39
Total	I 89	I 18	I 31
	M 20	M 24	M 6
	F 38	F 50	F 89

Without straining the limits of information that such a relatively small amount of examples imposes, it is safe to say that these figures display a general pattern in all three columns:

1. Deletion tends to be toward the beginning of the A Line.
2. Correspondingly, the unit parallel to the B Line compensated unit tends to be toward the end of the A Line.
3. Compensation in the B Line also tends to be toward its end.

These tendencies are displayed in all categories except the smallest, (2-3); and are most pronounced in the largest class, (1). Note that in the only class for which a medial position is truly available in the A Line, (5) x x (D), the tendency for compensation at the end of the B Line is very clear.

Grammatical Deletion

The grammatical deletion column may be summarized briefly. Here, again, it seems advisable to simplify the results, since a breakdown in detail of the various grammatical categories would be pointless with so few examples. Therefore, two major categories, verbal and nominal, as well as a small group of particles will suffice. The former includes verbs proper (a b c) as well as participles, infinitives, and relatives which consist of a verb. Nouns may be subdivided into the following basic classes: subject (1), object (2), adverb (3), vocatives (1!), the subject (S) and predicate (P) of the nominal sentence (excluding participles), the *nomen rectum* of the construct relationship (-C). The figures are as follows:

Verbal Sentence	
Verbs: (all categories)	82
Nouns:	
Subject (1):	24
Object (2):	9
Adverb (3):	27
Vocative (1!):	11
Construct (-C):	1
Nominal Sentence	
Subject (S):	20
Predicate (P):	6
Particles (ptcl):	3

Omitted from the list is a unit which forms a complete nominal sentence, Num.23:9b (hn ^{c}m). Constructs which exhibit a double deletion metrically (1-C, 3-C, etc.) have been listed as simple units. The number of particles is, of course, small, because most particles are treated in this study as simple grammatical elements without the value of a full grammatical and metrical unit.

In the grammatical deletions nouns exceed verbs somewhat (82:101). More detailed statistical interpretation would be hazardous. With a larger body of data it would be interesting to know what percentage of each category is deleted.

Grammatical Compensation

The topic of compensation is taken up again in the section on sub-line units. There the examples are arranged according to grammatical criteria and are scattered. Here it is possible briefly to present examples of compensation together as a group. However, it is not necessary to enter into a thorough discussion of each type of compensation from a grammatical point of view. The general characterizations of the types of compensation presented in the preceding lists will suffice for this section.

(1) x /x (D)

- *Constructs*: 28
- *Attributives*: 6
- *Compounds*:
  - *Verbal Compounds*: 9
  - *Other Compounds*: 6

(2) x/x̸ (D)

- *Constructs*: 7
- *Construct and Attributive*: 1
- *Compounds*:
  - *"Quasi-verbal"*: 4
  - *Other Compounds*: 4

(3) /x̸ (D) and /x̸̲ (D)

- *"Quasi-verbal" Compounds*: 2
- *"Quasi-verbal" Compound and Attributive*: 1

(4) x x* (D)

- *Syllabic Compensation*: 19
- *Syllabic Compensation by Preposition + Noun*: 5
- *Syllabic Compensation by Negative Particle + Verb*: 2
- *Syllabic Compensation by Particle + Noun*: 1

(5) x x (D) (Non-parallel grammatical replacement)

- *Verbs* (all types): 14
- *Nouns*:
  - *Subject (1)*: 4
  - *Object (2)*: 3
  - *Adverb (3)*: 36

Vocatives (l!): 1
Construct (-C): 5

In category (4), x x* (D), the differentiation of syllabic compensation, proper, from syllabic compensation by the addition of prepositions or particles plus noun, or negative particle plus verb, reflects the principle of this study assigning most particles and prepositions to the status of grammatical elements without metrical weight. Therefore units containing them must be classified as 3:2, the typical pattern of the formula x x* (D), if only one other grammatical (and metrical) unit is present in the B Line.

Here, again, it seems best to let the figures speak for themselves. However, it does seem noteworthy that in category (5) x x (D), adverbial relationships (prepositional phrases, etc.) dominate the class, accounting for over half of the examples.

Additional Remarks

A small number of non-replacement units display compensation without deletion:

Three Metrical Units

*x /x Ex.15:2b

x x ✗ Ex.15:4

x *x Ex.15:5

x /x II Sam.22:44b-c

Four Metrical Units

x ✗/ Ps.29:2

Such examples, along with units with the structures 2:3, 3:2, 3:4, 4:3, raise a wider issue. A full statement of the relationship between the lines of the couplet would require not only the unit formula, which includes deletion, but also compensation: for example, x /x (D) = x x - Deletion + Replacement (Compensation); x x (D D) might be restated as x x - 2 Deletions + 2 Replacements. The issue is significant only if one wishes a full statement of the structure of the B Line for units in which the number of deletions does not correspond to the number of replacements, or in cases such as those listed above.

Sub-Line Units

This section is concerned with the building blocks of the unit formulae, the relationship between semantically parallel grammatical and metrical units. The complexity and richness of parallelism in Hebrew verse is displayed in the multiplicity of grammatical relationships possible between such units.

A necessary prerequisite to analysis of grammatical parallelism is a complete list of parallel sub-line units, to which the first half of this section is devoted. Following the list are the relevant statistics and a series of brief analyses based on the data contained in the list. No attempt is made to write a grammar of the language of biblical poetry. Such an undertaking, important as it is, can hardly have as its base a Corpus of examples so restricted in number as the one presented in this study. In any case, a poetic grammar would be meaningful only in relationship to a grammar of prose materials contemporary with the poetic data and much of the poetry of the Corpus is earlier than any sizable portion of biblical prose. The analyses in this study may at least be considered preliminary steps in the composition of such a poetic grammar, but are limited to those aspects of grammatical parallelism which can be considered significant in terms of the data available in the examples of the Corpus.

List of Sub-Line Units

This list, which may be considered a master list for the analyses which follow, is arranged by a strictly grammatical pattern. Metrical variations are not ignored as a category, but are appended to the type of grammatical structure they represent and play no role in the analyses. In addition, no separate status is given to grammatical elements below the level of the grammatical units (chiefly proclitic particles and pronominal suffixes); that is, in the list no account is taken of the difference between the parallelism of, for example, l // l and l-s // l-s or l-s // l, etc. However, these grammatical elements are treated as a class in one of the analyses. Compounds formed by grammatical and semantic criteria are treated as such; so, for example, x/x/x is classified as a double compound and is not broken down into its constituent units x + x + x.

The list of sub-line units follows the outline presented below. This is also the order in which examples will be presented in the successive analyses. A breakdown by grammatical categories will be offered only for the longer lists.

- Verbal Sentence
  - Nouns and Particles
    - Simple // Simple
      - Subject (1) (including vocatives)
        - Metrical Variations
      - Object (2)
        - Metrical Variations
      - Adverb (3)
        - Metrical Variations
      - Construct (-C)
        - Metrical Variations
      - Particles (ptcl)
    - Simple // Compound and Compound // Simple
      - Subject (1)
        - Metrical Variations
      - Object (2)
        - Metrical Variations
      - Adverb (3)
        - Metrical Variations
      - Construct (-C)
    - Compound // Compound
      - Subject (1)
      - Object (2)
      - Adverb (3)
      - Particles (ptcl)
    - Compound // Double Compound
      - (All grammatical categories)
    - Double Compound // Double Compound
      - (All grammatical categories)
      - Metrical Variations
        - (All grammatical categories)

Verbs

Simple // Simple

Metrical Variations

Simple // Compound and Compound // Simple

Metrical Variations

Simple // Double Compound and Double Compound // Simple

Metrical Variations

Compound // Compound

Metrical Variations

Compound // Double Compound

Double Compound // Double Compound

Compound // Triple Compound

Nominal Sentence

Subject

Simple // Simple

Metrical Variations

Simple // Compound and Compound // Simple

Compound // Compound

Metrical Variations

Double Compound // Double Compound

Predicate

Simple // Simple

Metrical Variations

Simple // Compound and Compound // Simple

Metrical Variations

Compound // Compound

Compound // Double Compound

Double Compound // Double Compound

Examples not grammatically parallel are listed according to the category of the A Line member. However, all units containing verbs are in that section. Units in sentences that have been transformed are indicated by (T).

Verbal Sentence

Nouns and Particles

Simple // Simple

Passage	Gram. Par.	Formula	Sem. Par.	Parallel Terms
Subject (1) (including vocatives)				
Gen.4:24	lpn // lpn	A	List(PN)	qn // lmk
Gen.49:6a	l-s! // l-s!	A	List	npš // kbd
Gen.49:10a	l // l	A	Syn	špṭ // mḥqq
Ex.15:5	l // 3 --→ l (T)	A	Syn	thmt // bmṣlt
Ex.15:6	l-s // l-s	D	D	ymnk // ymnk
Ex.15:6	lpn! // lpn!	D	D(PN)	yhw // yhw
Ex.15:8a-b	l // l	A	Syn	mm // nzlm
Ex.15:8b-c	l // l	A	Syn	nzlm // thmt
Ex.15:16b	l-s // l	"D"	"D"	ᶜmk // ᶜm
Ex.15:17b-c	lpn! // lpn!	D	D(PN)	yhw // yhw
Num.10:35	l-s // l-s	A	Syn	'ybk // mśn'k
Num.23:8	lpn // lpn	A	Syn(PN)	'l // yhw
Num.23:21a	l // l	A	Syn	'n // ᶜml
Num.24:5	lpn! // lpn!	A	Syn(PN)	yᶜqb // yśr'l
Num.24:7b	l-s // l-s	"D"	"D"	mlk // mlkt
Dt.32:1	lpn! // lpn!	A	Mer	(h)šmym // (h)'rṣ
Dt.32:2a	l-s // l-s	A	Syn	lqḥy // 'mrty
Dt.32:25a	l // l	A	Concr.-Abstr.	hrb // 'mh
Dt.32:27b	l-s // neg-lpn	B	WP-PN	ydnw // l'yhwh
Dt.32:30a	l // l	A	Num	'ḥd // šnym
Dt.32:30b	l-s // lpn	A	Epith-PN	ṣrm // yhw
Dt.32:39c-d	lpr // &lpr	D	D	'ny // w'ny
Dt.33:18	lpn! // lpn!	A	List(PN)	zbln // yśškr
Dt.33:28a	lpn // lpn	A	Syn(PN)	yśr'l // yᶜqb
Dt.33:29c	l-s // 3-s --→ l-s (T)	A	WP	'ybk // ᶜl bmtm
Jud.5:19a	l // l-	"D"	"D"	mlkm // mlk
II Sam.22:14	lpn // lpn	A	Syn(PN)	yhwh // ᶜlyn
II Sam.22:29	lpn! // l-s!	A	PN-Syn	yhwh // 'lhy
Hab.3:2a	lpn! // lpn!	D	D(PN)	yhw // yhw
Hab.3:3a	l // l	A	Epith	'lh // qdš

Passage	Gram. Par.	Formula	Sem. Par.	Parallel Terms
Hab.3:3b	1-s // 1-s	A	List	hdh // thlth
Hab.3:5	1 // 1	A	Syn	dbr // ršp
Ps.29:10	1pn // 1pn	D	D(PN)	yhw // yhw
Ps.68:17a-b	1! // ,=1!-	"D"	"D"	hrm // hr
Ps.68:17b-c	1pn // ptcl-1pn	A	PN	'lhm // 'p yhw
Ps.114:3	1pn // 1pn	A	WP(PN)	(h)ym // (h)yrdn
Ps.114:3	1 // 1	A	Syn	hrm // gb^{c}t

Metrical Variations

Passage	Gram. Par.	Formula	Sem. Par.	Parallel Terms
Num.24:5	1-s // 1-s	A*	Syn	'hlk // mškntk
Ps.77:17b-c	1 // 1	A*	Syn	mym // thmt

Object (2)

Passage	Gram. Par.	Formula	Sem. Par.	Parallel Terms
Gen.4:23a	2-s // 2-s	A	Syn	ql // 'mrt
Gen.4:23b	ptcl-2 // 2	A	List	k 'š // yld
Gen.49:11b	2-s // 2-s	A	Syn	lbš // swt
Gen.49:15a	2-s // 2-s	A	Syn	mnḥ // 'rṣ
Gen.49:27b-c	2 // 2	A	Syn	^{c}d // šll
Num.23:7b	2pn // 2pn	A	Syn(PN)	y^{c}qb // yśr'l
Dt.32:7b	2-s // 2-s	A	Syn	'bkh // zqnkh
Dt.32:13b	2 // 2	A	List	dbš // šmn
Dt.32:18	2 // 2	A	Epith-Syn	ṣr // 'l
Dt.32:23	2 // 2-s	A	Abstr.-Concr.	r^{c}t // hṣy
Dt.32:30a	2 // 2	A	Num	'lp // rbbh
Dt.32:42a	2-s // 1-s ---→ 2-s (T)	A	List	ḥṣy // ḥrby
Jud.5:25	2 // 2	A	List	ḥlb // ḥm'
Jud.5:26a	2-s // 2-s	A	WP	ydh // ymnh
II Sam.22:7b	2-s // 1-s ---→ 2-s (T)	A	Syn	qly // šw^{c}ty
II Sam.22:12	"2-s" // "2-s"	B	List	sbbtw // skth
II Sam.22:37	2-s // 1-s ---→ 2-s (T)	A	List	ṣ^{c}dy // qrsly
Hab.3:3b	2 // 2	A	Mer	šmym // 'rṣ
Hab.3:6a-b	2 // 2	A	WP	'rṣ // gym
Hab.3:12	2 // 2	A	WP	'rṣ // gym
Ps.29:2	2 // 2-	"D"	"D"	kdb // kbd

Passage	Gram. Par.	Formula	Sem. Par.	Parallel Terms
Ps.29:5	2 // 2-	"D"	"D"	'rzm // 'rz
Ps.29:6	2pn // 2pn	A	List(PN)	lbnn // śryn
Ps.29:8	2 // 2-	D	D	mdbr // mdbr
Ps.89:11	2pn // 2-s	B	PN-PW	rhb // 'ybkh
Ps.114:8	2 // 2	A	Syn	(ḥ)ṣr // ḥlmš

Metrical Variations

Passage	Gram. Par.	Formula	Sem. Par.	Parallel Terms
Num.24:8b	2 // 2-s	A*	WP	gym // ^{c}ṣmthm
Dt.32:11a	2-s // 3-s	A*	List	qnh // ^{c}l gzlw
Dt.32:11b	2-s // 3-s	A*	Syn	knpw // ^{c}l 'brth
Dt.32:36a	2-s // 3-s	A*	Syn	^{c}mh // ^{c}l ^{c}bdh
II Sam.22:7b	2(lpn!) // 3-s	A*	PN-Syn	yhwh // 'l 'lhy
Ps.89:6	2-s // ptcl-2-s	A*	Syn	pl'kh // 'p 'mntkh

Adverb (3)

Passage	Gram. Par.	Formula	Sem. Par.	Parallel Terms
Gen.49:6a	3-s // 3-s	A	Syn	bsdm // bqhlm
Gen.49:6b	ptcl-3-s // 3-s	B	Syn	k b'pm // brṣnm
Gen.49:9b	"3" // "3"	A	Syn	k'ry // klḇ'
Gen.49:11a	3 // 3	A	List	lgpn // lśrq
Gen.49:17a	3 // 3	A	Syn	^{c}l drk // ^{c}l 'rḥ
Ex.15:4	3 // 3-	"D"	"D"	bym // bym
Ex.15:11a-b	3 // 3	A	Epith	b'lm // bqdš
Ex.15:13	3-s // 3-s	A	List	bḥsdk // b^{c}zk
Num.23:9b	3 // 3	A	Ant	lbdd // bgym
Num.23:21a	3pn // 3pn	A	Syn(PN)	by^{c}qb // byśr'l
Num.23:23b	3pn // 3pn	A	Syn(PN)	ly^{c}qb // lyśr'l
Num.24:6b	"3" // "3"	A	List	k'hlm // k'rzm
Dt.32:2a	"3" // "3"	A	List	kmṭr // kṭl
Dt.32:2b	"3" // "3"	A	Syn	kś^{c}rm // krbbm
Dt.32:12	3 // "neg-b"-P (3)-s	A	Syn	bdd // 'n ^{c}mh
Dt.32:23	3-s // 3-s	A	Syn(PR)	^{c}lmw // bm
Dt.33:2a-b	3pn // 3pn	A	List(PN)	mśn // mś^{c}r
Dt.33:28a	3 // 3	A	Syn	btḥ // bdd
Dt.33:29c	3-s // 1-s --→ 3-s (T)	C	Syn(PR)	lk // 'th

Passage	Gram.Par.	Formula	Sem.Par.	Parallel Terms
Jud.5:3b-c	3pn // 3pn	D	D(PN)	lyhw // lyhw
Jud.5:20	3 // 3-s	A	WP	mn šmm // mmzltm
Jud.5:29	3 // 3	D	D	mnšm // mnšm
II Sam.22:9 a-b	3-s // 3-s	A	List	b'pw // mphw
II Sam.22:9 b-c	3-s // 3-s	A*	PW-PR	mphw // mmnw
II Sam.22:18	3-s // 3-s	A	Syn	'yby // mśn'y
Hab.3:5	3-s // 3-s	A	Syn	lpnw // lrglw
Hab.3:12	3 // 3	A	Syn	bz^{c}m // b'p
Ps.29:1	3pn // 3pn	D	D(PN)	lyhw // lyhw
Ps.29:1-2	3pn // 3pn	D	D(PN)	lyhw // lyhw
Ps.29:2	3pn // 3pn	D	D(PN)	lyhw // lyhw
Ps.89:7	3pn // 3pn	D	D(PN)	lyhwh // lyhwh

Metrical Variations

Passage	Gram.Par.	Formula	Sem.Par.	Parallel Terms
Gen.4:23b	3-s // 3-s	A*	Syn	lpṣ^c // lḥbrt
Gen.49:7b	3pn // 3pn	A*	Syn(PN)	by^{c}qb // byśr'l
Num.23:23a	3pn // 3pn	A*	Syn(PN)	by^{c}qb // byśr'l
Dt.32:21a	3 // 3	A*	Syn	bl' 'l // bhblhm
Dt.32:25a	3 // 3	A*	Ant	mḥṣ // mḥdrm
Dt.32:34	3-s // 3-s	C*	PR-Syn	^{c}mdy // b'ṣrty
Dt.32:41b	3-s // 3-s	A*	Syn	lṣry // lmśn'y
Dt.33:18	3(inf.constr. b)-s // 3-s	B*	Ant	bṣ'tk // b'hlk

Construct (-C)

Passage	Gram.Par.	Formula	Sem.Par.	Parallel Terms
Dt.32:12	-Cpn // 3-s	A	Epith	yhwh // l'lhnw
Dt.33:11b	-C-s // -C-s	A	Syn	qmw // mśn'w
Dt.33:13b-c	-C // 3	A	Mer	šmm // mthm
II Sam.22:41	-C-s // -C-s	A	Syn	'yby // mśn'y
II Sam.22:44 b-c	-C // 1 --→ 2 (T)	A	Syn	gym // ^{c}m
Ps.29:3b-c	-Cpn // Spn	"D"	"D"(PN)	yhw // yhw
Ps.29:5	-Cpn // lpn --→ 2 (T)	"D"	"D"(PN)	yhw // yhw
Ps.29:8	-Cpn // lpn	"D"	"D"(PN)	yhw // yhw
Ps.68:3b-c	-C // 1	C	Met	dng // rš^{c}m

Passage	Gram. Par.	Formula	Sem. Par.	Parallel Terms
Metrical Variations				
Num.23:9a	-C // 3	A*	Syn	ṣrm // mgb^{c}t
II Sam.22:22	-C // 3-s	A*	PN-Syn	yhwh // m'lhy

Particles (ptcl)

Passage	Gram. Par.	Formula	Sem. Par.	Parallel Terms
Jud.5:28b	ptcl? // ptcl?	D	D	md^c // md^c
II Sam.1:20b	neg // neg	D	D	pn // pn

Simple // Compound
Compound // Simple

Subject (1)

Passage	Gram. Par.	Formula	Sem. Par.	Parallel Terms
Ex.15:10	1 // 3 ,-3 --→ 1 ,-1 (T)	/A	Epith	ym // bmm 'drm
Ex.15:14	1 // 2-Cpn --→ 1-Cpn (T)	/A	WP-PN	^{c}mm // yšb plšt
Dt.32:12	1pn // S ,-S	/A	PN-Ant	yhwh // 'l nkr
Jud.5:28b	1-s // 1-C-s	/A	WP="D"	rkb // p^{c}m mrkbtw
Jud.5:29	1-C-s // ptcl-1pr	C/	PR	ḥkmt śrth // 'p h'
II Sam.1:27	1 // 1-C	/A	List	gbrm // kl mlḥm
II Sam.22:8a	1 // 1-C	/A	List	'rṣ // msdy hrm
II Sam.22:47	1-s // 1-C-s	/A	Syn(Epith)	ṣry // 'lhy yš^{c}y
Ps.24:7a-b	1! // 1-C!	/A	Epith	š^{c}rm // ptḥ ^{c}lm
Ps.68:14a-b	1-C // 1-s	A/	Syn	knp yn // 'brth
Metrical Variations				
Num.23:7a	1pn // 1-Cpn	/A̲	Epith(PN)	blq // bn ṣpr
Num.23:18	1pn! // 1-Cpn!	/A̲	Epith(PN)	blq // bn ṣpr

Object (2)

Passage	Gram. Par.	Formula	Sem. Par.	Parallel Terms
Gen.49:11a	2-s // 2-C-s	/A	Epith	^{c}r // bn 'tn
Gen.49:16	2-s // 2-Cpn	/A	PN	^{c}m // šbṭ yśr'l
Dt.32:8a	2 // 2-C	/A	Syn	gym // bny 'dm
Dt.33:11a	2-s // 2-C-s	/A	Abstr.-Concr.	ḥl // p^{c}l ydw

Passage	Gram. Par.	Formula	Sem. Par.	Parallel Terms
Jud.5:30	2 // 2 2	/A	WP	šll // rḥm rḥmtm
II Sam.22:12	2 // 2-C	/A	WP	ḥšk // ḥšrt mm
Ps.68:5a	2-s // 3 3	/A	Epith	šm // lrkb b^{c}rbt

Metrical Variations

Passage	Gram. Par.	Formula	Sem. Par.	Parallel Terms
Num.23:10b	"2-C" // P ("3")-s	C/	PR	mt yšrm // kmh
Dt.32:1	2(,-R(&a)) // 2-C	/A	Syn	w'dbrh // 'mry py

Adverb (3)

Passage	Gram. Par.	Formula	Sem. Par.	Parallel Terms
Gen.4:24	ptcl-3 // 3 &3	/"D"	"D"=Num	k šb^{c}tm // šb^{c}m wšb^{c}
Gen.49:10a	3pn // 3-C-s	/A	PN-WP	myhd // mbn dglw
Gen.49:11b	3 // 3-C	/A	Epith	byn // bdm ^{c}nbm
Ex.15:17b-c	3 3-s // 3	A/	Epith-Syn	mkn lšbtk // mqdš
Num.23:7a	3pn // 3-Cpn	/A	S(PN)	m'rm // mhrr qdm
Dt.32:13b	3 // 3-C	/A	Syn	msl^{c} // mḥlmš ṣr
Dt.32:20a	3-s // 2(Ppr? S-s)	/C	PR-WP	mhm // mh 'ḥrtm
Dt.32:21b	3 // 3 ,-3	/A	Syn	bl' ^{c}m // bgy nbl
Dt.32:22a	3-s // 3 ,-3	/B	Mer	b'py // ^{c}d š'l tḥtt
Dt.33:2b-c	3pn // 3-Cpn	/A	List(PN)	mś^{c}r // mhr pr'n
Dt.33:13	,-R(3) // ,-R (part.b 3)	/A	Ant	m^{c}l // rbṣt tḥt
Jud.5:26a	3 // 3-C	/A	List	lytd // lhlmt ^{c}mlm
II Sam.22:17	3 // 3 ,-3	/B	Mer	mmrm // mmm rbm
II Sam.22:21	"3-s" // "3-C-s"	/A	Syn	kṣdqy // kbr ydy
Hab.3:3a	3 // 3-Cpn	/A	WP(PN)	mtmn // mhr pr'n
Ps.29:6	"3" // "3-C"	/A	List	km ^{c}gl // km bn r'mm
Ps.68:14b	3 // 3-C	/A	List	bksp // byrqrq ḥrṣ
Ps.89:6	3 // 3-C	/A	Syn	šmym // bqhl qdšm
Ps.89:7	3 // 3-C	/A	Syn	bšḥq // bbny 'lm

Passage	Gram. Par.	Formula	Sem. Par.	Parallel Terms
Ps.114:1	3pn // 3 ,-3	/A	PN-Epith	mmṣrym // m^{c}m l^{c}z
Ps.114:4	"3" // "3-C:	/A	PW	k'lm // kbny ṣ'n

Metrical Variations

Passage	Gram. Par.	Formula	Sem. Par.	Parallel Terms
Jud.5:17c-d	3-C // 3-s	A/*	Syn	lḥp ymm // ^{c}l mprṣw
II Sam.22:11	3 // 3-C	*/A	Epith	^{c}l krbm // ^{c}l knpy rḥ

Construct (-C)

Passage	Gram. Par.	Formula	Sem. Par.	Parallel Terms
Ps.114:1	-Cpn // -C-Cpn	/A	Epith(PN)	yśr'l // bt y^{c}qb

Compound // Compound

Subject (1)

Passage	Gram. Par.	Formula	Sem. Par.	Parallel Terms
Gen.4:23a	lpn! &lpn! // 1-Cpn	A̸	PN-Epith	^{c}d wṣl // nš lmk
Ex.15:15a-b	1-Cpn // 2-Cpn --→ 1-Cpn(T)	A/A	List; List(PN)	'lp 'dm // 'l m'b
II Sam.1:20b	1-Cpn // 1-C	D/A	PN-Epith	bnt plštm // bnt (h)^{c}rlm
II Sam.1:21b	1-C // 1-Cpn	D/A	WP-PN	mgn gbrm // mgn š'l
II Sam.1:22 b-c	1-Cpn // 1-Cpn	A≠A	List; List(PN)	qšt yntn // ḥrb š'l
II Sam.22:5	1-Cpn // 1-Cpn	A/A	List; Syn(PN)	mšbry mt // nḥly bly^{c}l
II Sam.22:6	1-Cpn // 1-Cpn	A/A	List; List(PN)	ḥbly š'l // mqšy mt
II Sam.22:16a	1-encl.<u>mem</u>-C // 1-C	A≠A	List	'pqm ym // msdt tbl
Hab.3:6c-d	1-C // 1-C	A/A	Syn	hrry ^{c}d // gb^{c}t ^{c}lm
Ps.29:3a-b	1-C // S-Cpn --→ 1-Cpn(T)	A≠A	Epith-WP-PN	'l (h)kbd // ql yhw
Ps.68:16	1-Cpn! // ,=1-Cpn!	D/B	D; Syn	hr 'lhm // hr gbnnm

Passage	Gram. Par.	Formula	Sem. Par.	Parallel Terms
Ps.68:16	,=1-Cpn! // ,=1-Cpn!	D/D	D; D(PN)	hr bšn // hr bšn
Ps.89:13	1pn &1pn // 1pn &1pn	A≠A	List(PN)	spn wymn // tbr wḥrmn

---

Object (2)

Passage	Gram. Par.	Formula	Sem. Par.	Parallel Terms
Ex.15:4	2-Cpn // 1-C-s ---→ 2-C-s(T)	Ⱥ	List	mrkbt pr^{c} // mbḥr šlšw
Ex.15:15b-c	2-Cpn // "1"-C-Cpn ---→ "2"-C-Cpn (T)	A/A	List(PN); PW	'l m'b // kl yšb kn^{c}n
Num.23:10a	2-Cpn // 2-Cpn	A/A	Syn; Syn(PN)	^{c}pr y^{c}qb // trb^{c}t yśr'l
Dt.32:15b	2 ,-R(a-s) // 2-C-s	A/A	Epith; List	'lh ^{c}śhw // ṣr yš^{c}th
Dt.32:22b	2 &2-s // 2-C	Ⱥ	List	'rṣ wyblh // msdy hrm

Adverb (3)

Passage	Gram. Par.	Formula	Sem. Par.	Parallel Terms
Gen.49:25a	3-C-s // 3pn ,=3pn	D≠A	Epith-PN	m'l 'bk // 'l šdy
Ex.15:17a-b	3-C-s // 3 3-s	Ⱥ	Epith	bhr nḥltk // mkn lšbtk
Dt.32:2b	3-C // 3-C	D/A	Syn	^{c}ly dš' // ^{c}ly ^{c}śb
Dt.32:13a	3-C // 2-C	A≠A	WP; Syn	bmty 'rṣ // tnbt śdy
Jud.5:23b	3-Cpn // 3-Cpn	D/D	D; D(PN)	l^{c}zrt yhw // l^{c}zrt yhw
II Sam.22:32	3-Cpn // 3-C-s	A/A	Syn; PN	mbl^{c}dy yhwh // zlty 'lhnw
II Sam.22:43	"3-C" // "3-C"	A/A	Syn; List	k^{c}pr 'rṣ // kṭṭ ḥṣt
Ps.68:3b-c	3-C // 3-Cpn	D/D	D; Met-PN	mpn 'š // mpn yhw
Ps.89:8	3-C // "3"-C-s	A≠A	Epith	bsd qdšm // ^{c}l kl sbbw
Ps.89:10	3-Cpn // 3(inf. const.b)-C-s ---→ 2(inf.const.b) -C-s (T)	A/A	Met; WP	bg't (h)ym // bnś' glw
Ps.114:8	"3-C" // "3-C"	A/D	List	'gm mym // m^{c}ynw mym

Passage	Gram. Par.	Formula	Sem. Par.	Parallel Terms

Particles (ptcl)

Passage	Gram. Par.	Formula	Sem. Par.	Parallel Terms
Num.24:17a	&neg 3 // &neg 3	D/A	Syn	wl' ^{c}t // wl' qrb

Compound // Double Compound

(All grammatical categories)

Passage	Gram. Par.	Formula	Sem. Par.	Parallel Terms
Num.24:17c	2-Cpn // 2-"C"-C-Cpn	A/A̸	List(PN)	p't m'b // qdqd kl bny št
Dt.32:10a	3-C // 3-C-C	A≠A̸	Epith	b'rṣ mdbr // bṭhw yll yšmn
Dt.32:24b	2-C // &(prep) -2-C-C	A≠A̸	List	šn bhmt // ^{c}m ḥmt zḥly ^{c}pr
Hab.3:11b	3-C-s // 3-C-C-s	A/A̸	Syn; List	l'r ḥṣk // lngh brq ḥntk
Ps.114:7	3-Cpn // 3-C-Cpn	D/A̸	D; Epith (PN)	mlpny 'dn // mlpny 'lh y^{c}qb

---

Double Compound // Double Compound

(All grammatical categories)

Passage	Gram. Par.	Formula	Sem. Par.	Parallel Terms
Dt.32:25b	& 2 & 2 // 2 &(prep.) 2-C	*A≠A̸	List	gm bḥr gm btlh // ynq ^{c}m 'š śbh
Dt.32:35a	3-C &-C // 3 ,-R(b l-s)	A//B̸	Syn; Met	lym nqm wšlm // l^{c}t tmṭ rglm
Dt.33:14	3-C-C // 3-C-C	D/A/A	Syn; List	mmgd tb't šmš // mmgd grš yrḥ
Dt.33:15	3-C-C // 3-C-C	D/A/A	Syn	mmgd hrr qdm // mmgd gb^{c}t ^{c}lm

---

Metrical Variations (All grammatical categories)

Passage	Gram. Par.	Formula	Sem. Par.	Parallel Terms
Dt.32:7a	2-C // 2-C &-C	A/A̲	Syn	ymt ^{c}lm // šnt dr wdr
II Sam.22:16b	3-s // 3-C-C-s	*/C̸	Met	bg^{c}rtkh // mnšmt rḥ 'pkh
II Sam.22:28	2 ,-2 // 2 ,-2	B̲≠B	Ant=WP	^{c}m ^{c}ny // ^{c}nm rmt

Verbs (a b c)

Simple // Simple

Passage	Gram.Par.	Formula	Sem.Par.	Parallel Terms
Gen.4:23a	a! // a!	A	Syn	šm^{c}n // h'zn
Gen.49:6a	neg-b! // neg-b!	B	Syn	'l tb' // 'l tḥd
Gen.49:25a	,-R(&a-s) // ,-R(&a-s)	A	Syn	wy^{c}zrk // wybrrk
Gen.49:27b-c	a // a	B	Syn	y'kl // yḥlq
Ex.15:4	a // c --→ a (T)	B	Syn	yr // ṭb^{c}
Ex.15:8a-b	c // c	A	Syn	n^{c}rm // nṣb
Ex.15:8b-c	c // b	B	Syn	nṣb // qp'
Ex.15:10	a-s // b --→ a-s (T)	B	Syn	ksm // ṣll
Ex.15:13	a // a	A	Syn	nḥt // nhlt
Ex.15:16b	prep-b // prep-b	D	D	^{c}d y^{c}br // ^{c}d y^{c}br
Num.10:35	b! // b!	A	Syn	ypṣ // yns
Num.23:7b	b! // b!	D	D	lk // lk
Num.23:8	3?-a // 3?-a	A	Syn	mh 'qb // mh 'z^{c}m
Num.23:8	neg-a-s // neg-a-s	A	Syn	l' qbh // l' z^{c}mh
Num.23:9a	a // a	A	Syn	'r'n //'šrn
Num.23:18	&a // a!	A	Syn	wšm^{c} // h'zn
Num.23:19b	a // a	A	Syn	'mr // dbr
Num.23:21a	neg-c // neg-c	A	Syn	l' hbṭ // l' r'
Num.24:8b	a // a	A	List	y'kl // ygrm
Num.24:17a	a // a	A	Syn	'r'n // 'šrn
Dt.32:1	a! // a!	A	Syn	h'znw // wtšm^{c}
Dt.32:2a	a! // a!	A	Syn	y^{c}rp // tzl
Dt.32:7a	a! // a!	A	Syn	zkr // bnh
Dt.32:11a	a // b	B	Syn	y^{c}r // yrḥp
Dt.32:11b	a-s // a-s	A	List	yqḥhw // yś'hw
Dt.32:13a	a-s // a-s	B	WP	yrkbhw // y'klhw
Dt.32:15b	a // a	A	List	yṭš // ynbl
Dt.32:18	a // a	A	Syn	tšh // tškḥ
Dt.32:18	,-R(a-s) // ,=2(part.a)-s	A	Syn	yldkh // mḥllkh

Passage	Gram.Par.	Formula	Sem.Par.	Parallel Terms
Dt.32:21a	a-s // a-s	A	Syn	qn'ny // k^{c}sny
Dt.32:21b	a-s // a-s	A	Syn	'qn'm // 'k^{c}sm
Dt.32:22a	b // b	A	Syn	qdḥh // tqd
Dt.32:22b	a // a	A	Syn	t'kl // tlhṭ
Dt.32:23	a // a	B	List	'sph // 'klh
Dt.32:29	a // a	A	Syn	yśklw // ybnw
Dt.32:30a	ptcl?-a // a	A	Syn	'kh yrdp // ynsw
Dt.32:36a	ptcl-a // c	B	Syn	ky ydn // ytnḥm
Dt.32:39c-d	a // a	A	Syn	'mt // mḥṣty
Dt.32:39c-d	&a // a	A	Syn	w'ḥyh // 'rp'
Dt.33:2a-b	b // b	C	Met	b' // zrḥ
Dt.33:2b-c	b // b	A	Syn	zrḥ // hp^{c}
Dt.33:11a	a! // a!	A	List	brk // trṣ
Dt.33:28a	b // b	A	Syn	yškn // ^{c}n
Dt.33:29c	c // b → c (T)	A	List	ykḥš // tdrk
Jud.5:3b-c	a // a	A	Syn	'šr // 'zmr
Jud.5:17c-d	b // b	A	Syn	yšb // yškn
Jud.5:19a	a // 3-c	D	D	nlḥm // 'z nlḥm
Jud.5:20	c // c	D	D	nlḥm // nlḥm
Jud.5:24	c! // c!	D	D	tbrk // tbrk
Jud.5:25	a // a	A	Syn	ntn // hqrb
Jud.5:28b	b // b	A	Syn	bšš // 'ḥr
II Sam.1:20b	b // b	A	Syn	tśmḥn // t^{c}lzn
II Sam.1:27	b // b	B	Syn	npl // y'bd
II Sam.22:5	a-s // a-s	B	Syn	'ppny // yb^{c}tny
II Sam.22:6	a-s // a-s	B	Syn	sbbny // qdmny
II Sam.22:7a	a // b	A	Syn	'qr' // 'šw^{c}
II Sam.22:11	b // b	A	List	yrkb // yd'h
II Sam.22:15	&a-s // &a-s	A	Syn	wypṣm // wyhmm
II Sam.22:16a	c // c	A	Syn	yr'w // yglw
II Sam.22:18	ptcl-b // ptcl-b	A	Syn	ky ^{c}zw // ky 'mṣw
II Sam.22:22	ptcl-a // neg-b	A	Syn	ky šmrty // l' pš^{c}ty
II Sam.22:28	a // a	B	Ant	tš^{c} // tšpl
II Sam.22:38	b // neg-b	B	Syn	'rdp // l' 'šb
II Sam.22:43	a-s // a-s	A	Syn	'śḥqm // 'dqm
Hab.3:3b	a // a	A	List	ksh // ml'h

Passage	Gram. Par.	Formula	Sem. Par.	Parallel Terms
Hab.3:5	b // b	A	Syn	ylk // yṣ'
Hab.3:6a-b	&a // &a	B	Syn	wymdd // wytr
Hab.3:6c-d	c // b	A	List	ytpṣṣw // šḥw
Hab.3:12	a // a	A	Syn	tṣ^{c}d // tdš
Ps.29:1	a! // a!	D	D	hb // hb
Ps.29:2	a! // a!	D	D	hb // hb
Ps.29:8	a // a	D	D	yḥl // yḥl
Ps.29:10	b // b	D	D	yšb // yšb
Ps.68:3b-c	"3"(inf.const. c-) // b	C	Met	khms // y'bd
Ps.68:5a	a // a	B	Syn	zmr // sl
Ps.77:17a-b	a-s // a-s	D	D	r'kh // r'kh
Ps.77:17b-c	b // ptcl-b	A	Syn	yḥlw // 'p yrgzw
Ps.89:7	b // b	A	Syn	y^{c}rk // ydmh
Ps.89:11	a // a	B	List	dk'th // pzrth

Metrical Variations

Passage	Gram. Par.	Formula	Sem. Par.	Parallel Terms
Gen.49:7a	,-R(ptcl-b) // ,-R(ptcl-b)	A*	Syn	k ^{c}z // k qšt
Gen.49:7b	a-s // a-s	*A	Syn	'ḥlqm // 'pṣm
Gen.49:15a	ptcl-b // ptcl-b	A*	Syn	k ṭb // k n^{c}m
Ex.15:2b	,-R(&a-s) // ,-R(&a-s)	*A	Syn	w'rmmnh // w'nwh
Ex.15:5	a-s // b --→ a-s (T)	*B	Syn	yksym // yrd
Num.23:9b	b // neg c	B*	Ant	yškn // l' ytḥšb
Num.23:19b	&neg-a // &neg-a-s	A*	Syn	wl' y^{c}ś // wl' yqmn
Num.23:23a	ptcl-neg-c // neg-c	*A	Syn	k l' nhš // l' qṡm
Num.24:7b	b! // c!	A*	Syn	yrm // ttnś'
Dt.32:10b	a-s // a-s	*B	Syn	ybnnhw // yṣrnhw
Dt.32:30b	a-s // a-s	A*	Syn	mkrm // hsgrm
II Sam.22:37	a // neg b --→ neg a (T)	B*	Syn	trḥb // l' m^{c}dw
II Sam.22:38	&a-s // 3(inf. const.a)-s	A*	Syn	w'šmdm // ^{c}d kltm
II Sam.22:39	&neg b // b	*B	Syn	wl' yqmn // yplw

Simple // Compound
Compound // Simple

Passage	Gram.Par.	Formula	Sem.Par.	Parallel Terms
Gen.49:27a-b	,-R(a) // ,-R(...a 2)	/A	List	yṭrp // y'kl ^{c}d
Ex.15:15a-b	3-c // a-s 1 --→ c 3 (T)	/A	Syn	'z nbhl // y'ḥzm r^{c}d
Ex.15:15b-c	a-s 1 // c --→ a-s (T)	A/	Syn	y'ḥzm r^{c}d // nmg
Ex.15:17b-c	,-R(a) // ,-R(a 1s)	/A	Syn	p^{c}lt // knn ydk
Dt.32:7b	&a-s // &a 3-s	/A	Syn	wygdkh // wy'mrw lkh
Dt.32:8a	3(inf.const.a -Cpn) // 3(inf. const.a-s ...)	A/	PN-Syn	blnḥl ^{c}lyn // bhprdh
Dt.32:20a	a 2-s // a	B/	Ant	'strh pny // 'r'h
Dt.32:27b	b // a "2"-Cpn	/B	Syn	rmh // p^{c}l kl z't
Dt.32:41b	a 2 // a	A/	Syn	'šb nqm // 'šlm
II Sam.1:21b	c // neg-c 3	/A	Syn	ng^{c}l // bl mšḥ bšmn
II Sam.22:7b	a // b 3-s --→ a 3-s (T)	/A	Syn	yšm^{c} // tb' b'znw
II Sam.22:8a	b &b // b	A/	Syn	tg^{c}š wtr^{c}š // yrgzw
II Sam.22:14	b // a 2-s	/A	Epith	yr^{c}m // ytn qlh
II Sam.22:17	a 2-s // a-s	B/	Ant	yšlḥ ydh // ymšny
II Sam.22:44 b-c	a-s 3- // a-s --→ a 3-s (T)	A/	Syn	tśmny lr'š // y^{c}bdny
Ps.24:7a-b	a...2-s // c	A/	Syn	ś'...r'škm // hnś'
Ps.114:3	&b // b 3	/A	Syn	wyns // ysb l'ḥr

Metrical Variations

Passage	Gram.Par.	Formula	Sem.Par.	Parallel Terms
Ex.15:14	b // 1 a --→ 3 c T)	/A	Syn	yrgzn // ḥl 'ḥz
Num.23:7b	a!-3-s // a!	A/	Syn	'r ly // z^{c}m
II Sam.22:21	a-s // a-3-s	/A	Syn	ygmlny // yšb ly

Simple // Double Compound
Double Compound // Simple

Passage	Gram.Par.	Formula	Sem.Par.	Parallel Terms
Gen.49:15b	3(inf.const.a) // "b" P(3) ,-P ((3)part.a)	/A̸	WP	lsbl // yh lms ^{c}bd
Dt.33:6	&neg-b! // "b!" S-s P	/B̸	Syn	w'l ymt // yhy mtw mspr
Ps.29:2	a!...2-C-s // c	A̸/	Syn	hb...kbd šm // hštḥw

Metrical Variations

Passage	Gram.Par.	Formula	Sem.Par.	Parallel Terms
Dt.32:38b	&a!-s // "b!" 3-s P	*/A̸	Syn	wy^{c}zrkm // yhyw ^{c}lkm strh
Jud.5:29	a-s // a 2-s- 3-s	/A̸̲	Syn	t^{c}nn // tšb 'mrh lh
II Sam.22:19	a-s // "b" Spn P-3-s	/A̸̲	Ant	yqdmny // yhy yhwh mš^{c}n ly

---

Compound // Compound

Passage	Gram.Par.	Formula	Sem.Par.	Parallel Terms
Gen.49:6b	a 2 // a 2	B⌿B	List	hrg 'š // ^{c}qr šr
Ex.15:9b-c	2(a 2 // 2(a 2-s	B⌿B	List	'ḥlq šll // 'rq ḥrb
Ex.15:9b-c	b-encl.<u>mem</u> 1-s // a-encl.<u>mem</u> 1-s	B⌿B	List	tml'm npš // tršm yd
Num.23:10b	b! 1-s // "b"! S-s	A⌿A	Syn	tmt npš // th 'ḥrt
Dt.32:3	ptcl-2...a // a! 2	A̸	Syn	ky šm...'qr' // hbw gdl
Dt.32:42a	a 3 // a 2 --→ a 2 (T)	A⌿A	Syn	'škr mdm // t'kl bśr
II Sam.1:22 b-c	neg-b 3 // neg-b 3	A/A	Syn	l' nśg 'ḥr // l' tšb rqm
II Sam.22:9 a-b	b 1 // 1...a	A⌿A	List	^{c}lh ^{c}šn // 'š...t'kl
II Sam.22:9 b-c	1...a // 1 b	A⌿A	List	'š...t'kl // gḥlm b^{c}rw
II Sam.22:15	a 2 // 2 a	C⌿C	Met	yšlḥ ḥṣm // brqm ybrq

Passage	Gram. Par.	Formula	Sem. Par.	Parallel Terms
II Sam.22:42	&"neg-b" P (part.a) // &neg a-s	A⌿A	Syn	w'n mš^{c} // wl' ^{c}nm
Hab.3:2a	a 2-s // a... 2-s	A⌿A	List	šm^{c}ty šm^{c}kh // r'ty...p^{c}lkh
Ps.68:19	a 2 // a 2	A⌿A	List	šbt šb // lqḥt mtnt

Metrical Variations

Passage	Gram. Par.	Formula	Sem. Par.	Parallel Terms
Num.23:10a	lpr?-a // lpr?-a	D/A	Syn	m mn // m spr
II Sam.22:45	c-3-s // c-3-s	A/D	Syn	ytkḥšw ly // yšm^{c}w ly

Compound // Double Compound

Passage	Gram. Par.	Formula	Sem. Par.	Parallel Terms
Num.23:24b	prep-a 2 // 2-C a	A⌿Ⱥ	List	^{c}d y'kl ṭrp // dm ḥllm yšt

---

Double Compound // Double Compound

Passage	Gram. Par.	Formula	Sem. Par.	Parallel Terms
Dt.32:38a	a 2-C-s a // a 2-C-s	A⌿A⌿A	List	ḥlb zbḥmw y'klw // yštw yn nskmw

---

Compound // Triple Compound

Passage	Gram. Par.	Formula	Sem. Par.	Parallel Terms
Ps.68:3a-b	"3"(inf.const. c-C) // "3" (inf.const.c-C 3-C)	A⌿⌿⌿A	Syn; List	khndp ^{c}šn // khms dng mpn 'š

Nominal Sentence

Subject

Simple // Simple

Passage	Gram.Par.	Formula	Sem.Par.	Parallel Terms
Gen.49:7a	S-s // S-s	A	Syn	'pm // ^{c}brtm
Gen.49:19	Spn // lpr --→ Spr (T)	C	PR	gd // h'
Dt.32:37	S-s // S	A	Epith	'lhmw // ṣr
Ps.24:8b-c	Spn // ,=Spn	D	D(PN)	yhw // yhw
Ps.24:8b-c	,-&S // ,-S-	"D"	"D"	wgbr // gbr
Ps.89:10	Spr // Spr	D	D	'th // 'th
Ps.114:2	Spn // Spn	A	List-PW (PN)	yhdh // yśr'l

Metrical Variations

Passage	Gram.Par.	Formula	Sem.Par.	Parallel Terms
Num.24:10	S-s // S-s	*A*	Ant	mbrrk // 'rrk

Simple // Compound
Compound // Simple

Passage	Gram.Par.	Formula	Sem.Par.	Parallel Terms
Dt.32:4a	S-s // ptcl-"S"-C-s	/A	Syn	p^{c}lh // ky kl drkw
II Sam.22:23	ptcl-"S"-C-s // 2-s --→ S-s (T)	A/	Syn	ky kl mšpṭw // ḥqtw
Ps.68:6	,=S-C // ,=Spn	A/	Epith-PN	dyn 'lmnt // yhw
Ps.89:12	S // 2 &2-s --→ 2 &2 (T)	/A	Syn	'rṣ // tbl wml'h

Compound // Compound

Passage	Gram.Par.	Formula	Sem.Par.	Parallel Terms
Dt.32:9	ptcl-S-Cpn // S-C-s	A/A	PN-Syn	ky ḥlq yhwh // ḥbl nḥlth
Dt.32:35b	S-C-s // S 3-s	B̸	PW	ym 'dm // ^{c}tdt lmw
Dt.33:17c	S-Cpn // S-Cpn	A/A	Num; List(PN)	rbbt 'prm // 'lp mnš
Ps.29:4	S-Cpn // S-Cpn	D/D	D; D(PN)	ql yhw // ql yhw
Ps.68:18	S-Cpn // S-Cpn	A/A	List; PN-Epith	rkb yhw // šnn 'dny

Passage	Gram.Par.	Formula	Sem.Par.	Parallel Terms
Metrical Variations				
Ex.15:11a-b	Spr?="3"-s // Spr?-"3"-s	D/D	D	m kmk // m kmk
II Sam.22:32	ptcl-Spr?-P // Spr?-P	D/A	D; Epith	ky my 'l // my ṣr

Double Compound // Double Compound

Passage	Gram.Par.	Formula	Sem.Par.	Parallel Terms
Gen.49:12a	S-C P(3) // S-C P(3)	A/A≠A	Ant; List	ḥkll ^{c}nm myn // lbn šnm mḥlb

Predicate

Simple // Simple

Passage	Gram.Par.	Formula	Sem.Par.	Parallel Terms
Gen.49:19	P // a --→ P(part.a) (T)	"D"	"D"	gdd // ygd
Num.24:9	P // P	A	Ant	brk // 'rr
Dt.32:4a	P // P	A	Syn	tmm // mšpṭ
Dt.32:9	P-s // Ppn	A	PN	^{c}mh // y^{c}qb
Dt.32:34	P(part.c) // P(part.c)	A	Syn	kms // ḥtm
Dt.32:35b	ptcl-P(part.b) // P(part.b)	A	Syn	ky qrb // ḥš
Dt.33:17a	P(ptcl!) // P(ptcl!)	D	D	hm // hm
II Sam.22:47	P(part.c)! //b!	A	List	brk // yrm
Ps.29:3b-c	P(3) // P(3)	D	D	^{c}l (h)mym // ^{c}l mym
Ps.29:4	P(3) // P(3)	A	Syn	bkḥ // bhdr
Ps.29:5	P(part.a) // a --→ P (part.a) (T)	"D"	"D"	šbr // yšbr
Ps.68:18	P // P	A	Num	rbtm // 'lpm
Ps.89:10	P(part.a) // a-s --→ P (part.a) (T)	A	Syn	mšl // tšbḥm

Passage	Gram.Par.	Formula	Sem.Par.	Parallel Terms
Metrical Variations				
Gen.49:17a	P // P	A*	WP	nḥš // šppn
Ps.114:2	P("3")-s // P-s	A*	Syn	lqdšh // mmšltw

Simple // Compound
Compound // Simple

Passage	Gram.Par.	Formula	Sem.Par.	Parallel Terms
Ex.15:2b	Ppr-S-s // S-C-s	/A	Epith-"D"	z 'l // 'lh 'b
Ex.15:11b-c	P(part.c) // P(part.c)-C	/A	Syn	n'dr // nr' thlt
II Sam.22:23	P(3)-s // neg-a 3-s --→ "neg-b"-P (part.c) 3-s(T)	/B	Syn	lngdy // l' 'sr mmny
II Sam.22:29	P-s // a 2-s --→ P(part.a) (T)	/A	Epith	nry // tgh ḥšky
Ps.89:8	P(part.c) // P(part.b) &P (part.c)	/A	Syn	n^c^rṣ // rb wnr'
Ps.89:12	ptcl-P(3)-s // lpr a-s --→ Spr P(part.a) (T)	/A	Epith	'p lkh // 'th ysdtm
Metrical Variations				
II Sam.22:34	P(part.a) 2-s // a-s --→ P(part.a)-s (T)	A/*	Syn	mšwh rgly // y^c^mdny

Compound // Compound

Passage	Gram.Par.	Formula	Sem.Par.	Parallel Terms
Metrical Variations				
Dt.32:28	,-P(part.b)-C -Spr // ,-R ("neg-b"-P(3) -s 1)	/A/	Syn	'bd ^c^ṣt hmh // 'n ḃhm tbnh
Dt.32:32a	ptcl-P(3)-Cpn // P(3)-Cpn	A/A*	List; List(PN)	ky mgpn sdm // mšdmt ^c^mrh

Passage	Gram.Par.	Formula	Sem.Par.	Parallel Terms
	Compound // Double Compound			
Ex.15:2a	P-s &P-s // "b" 3-s P(3)	/A/	List	^{c}z wzmrt // yh ly lyš^{c}
Dt.32:20b	ptcl-P-C // P ,-R(neg-S P(3)-s)	A/A̸	Syn	ky dr thpkt // bnm l' 'mn bm
Dt.32:32b	P-C // S ,-S P(3)-s	A/A̸	List; Syn	^{c}nby rš // 'šklt mrrt lmw
Dt.32:33	P-C // P-C ,-P	A/A̸	Syn	ḥmt tnnm // r'š ptnm 'kzr
Dt.33:16b	P(3)-Cpn // P(3)-C-C-s	A/A̸	WP; PN-Epith	lr'š ysp // lqdqd nzr 'ḥw
Dt.33:23a-b	P(part.b)-C // P(part.b) 2-Cpn	A/A̸	Syn; PN	śb^{c} rsn // ml' brkt yhw
Dt.33:24a-b	P(part.c) 3 // "b" P(part.c) -C-s	A/A̸	Syn	brk mbnm // yhy rṣy 'ḥw

Passage	Gram.Par.	Formula	Sem.Par.	Parallel Terms
	Double Compound // Double Compound			
Dt.33:28b	P(3)-s S &S // ptcl-l a 2 ⟶ ptcl-3-s P(part.c) l	A//A̸	Mer; List	^{c}l 'rṣ dgn wtrš // 'p šmw y^{c}rp ṭl

Totals and Statistics

The pattern follows that of the list of sub-line units, but with a subdivision into subject, object, and adverb in the compound categories.

Verbal Sentence

Nouns and Particles

Simple // Simple	
Subject (1) (including vocatives)	37
Metrical Variations:	2
Object (2):	26
Metrical Variations:	6
Adverb (3):	31
Metrical Variations:	8
Construct (-C):	9
Metrical Variations:	2
Particles (ptcl):	2
Simple // Compound	
Compound // Simple	
Subject (1):	10
Metrical Variations:	2
Object (2):	7
Metrical Variations:	2
Adverb (3):	21
Metrical Variations:	2
Construct (-C):	1
Simple // Double Compound	
Object (2):	
Metrical Variations:	1
Compound // Compound	
Subject (1):	13
Object (2):	5
Metrical Variations:	1
Adverb (3):	11
Particles (ptcl):	1
Compound // Double Compound	
Object (2):	2
Metrical Variations:	1
Adverb (3):	3

Double Compound // *Double Compound*	
Object (2):	1
Adverb (3):	3
Verbs	
Simple // *Simple*:	79
Metrical Variations:	14
Simple // *Compound* *Compound* // *Simple*:	17
Metrical Variations:	3
Simple // *Double Compound* *Double Compound* // *Simple*:	3
Metrical Variations:	3
Compound // *Compound*:	13
Metrical Variations:	2
Compound // *Double Compound*:	1
Double Compound // *Double Compound*:	1
Compound // *Triple Compound*:	1

Nominal Sentence

Subject	
Simple // *Simple*	7
Metrical Variations:	1
Simple // *Compound* *Compound* // *Simple*	4
Compound // *Compound*:	5
Metrical Variations:	2
Double Compound // *Double Compound*	1
Predicate	
Simple // *Simple*:	13
Metrical Variations:	2
Simple // *Compound* *Compound* // *Simple*	6
Metrical Variations:	1
Compound // *Compound*	
Metrical Variations:	2
Compound // *Double Compound*:	7
Double Compound // *Double Compound*:	1

Total number of sub-line units: 398

<u>Verbal Sentence</u>

Nouns and nominal relationships (including particles):		209
Verbs and verbal relationships:		137
	Total	346

<u>Nominal Sentence</u> (S and P): 52

Total number of metrical variations: 56 (14% of total sub-line units)

<u>Totals by category</u> (including metrical variations)

Simple // Simple:		239
Nouns	124	
Verbs	92	
S	8	
P	15	
Simple // Compound:		59
Compound // Simple:		17
Compound // Compound:		55
Simple // Double Compound:		5
Double Compound // Simple:		1
Compound // Double Compound:		14
Double Compound // Double Compound:		7
Compound // Triple Compound:		1

With such a relatively small number of examples, it would be pointless to list the totals and percentages for all the categories represented in the preceding lists. The statistics given above deal with what are probably the most significant features of sub-line parallelism. Note that the categories which display an imbalance in favor of the B Line (simple // compound ; simple // double compound; compound // double compound ; and compound // triple compound) are far more numerous than units which display the opposite situation (compound // simple and double compound // simple); 79:18, respectively. Also note that the balanced units (simple // simple (239); compound // compound (55); and double compound //

double compound (7) stand in a ratio of 3:1 to the imbalanced units (301:97, respectively), but that outside the simple // simple category, the imbalanced groups exceed (97:62).

Sub-Line Units: Analyses

The purpose of this section is to present a number of analyses of significant aspects of the relationship of sub-line parallel units. These analyses are limited in scope, restricted to conclusions which may be drawn from the preceding master list. A major distinction must be made between units which are fully parallel grammatically and those which are not. The latter category may be subdivided into those units in which the grammatical incongruence consists of an added grammatical element below the level of the grammatical unit (particles, and here, also, pronominal suffixes) and units which contain more extensive grammatical incongruence. Also to be classified are units which contain a grammatical imbalance between parallel semantic units; that is, units of the type simple // compound, compound // double compound, etc.

The materials in this section consist of lists and brief analyses presented in the following format:

1. Units fully parallel grammatically
2. Parallel units plus an additional grammatical element
3. Grammatically compatible units
4. Grammatically incongruent units

Details will be given at the beginning of each section.

Fully Parallel Units

Only units with the structure simple // simple, compound // compound, and double compound // double compound, i.e., which display grammatical symmetry, can be fully parallel. The list follows the order of the preceding list. The minor modifications for pn and pr are omitted. In addition, metrical variations are included within their larger categories. Only examples which occur once will be cited by passage.

Grammatical Units	Number of Examples
Verbal Sentence	
Noun	
Simple // Simple	
Subject (1)	
1 // 1	16
1-s // 1-s	6
1! // 1!	6
1-s! // 1-s! (Gen.49:6a)	1
Object (2)	
2 // 2	12
2-s // 2-s	5
"2-s" // "2-s"	1
Adverb (3)	
3 // 3	19
3-s // 3-s	10
"3" // "3"	4
Construct (-C)	
-C-s // -C-s (Dt.33:11b)	1
-C-s // -C-s (II Sam.22:41)	1
Particles	
ptcl? // ptcl? (Jud.5:28b)	1
neg // neg (II Sam.1:20b)	1
Compound // Compound	
Subject (1)	
1-C // 1-C	6
1-Cpn! // 1-Cpn!	2
1pn &1pn // 1pn &1pn (Ps.89:13)	1
Object (2)	
2-Cpn // 2-Cpn (Num.23:10a)	1
2-C-s // 2-C-s (Dt.32:38a)	1
2 ,-2 // 2 ,-2 (II Sam.22:28)	1
Adverb (3)	
3-C // 3-C	3
"3-C" // "3-C"	2

Grammatical Units	Number of Examples
Particles (ptcl)	
&neg 3 // &neg 3 (Num.24:17a)	1
Double Compound // Double Compound	
The only category is:	
3-C-C // 3-C-C	2
Verb (the intransitive categories represented by the signs b and c are listed together)	
Simple // Simple	
a // a	18
b-c // b-c	17
a-s // a-s	10
a! // a!	7
b/c! // b/c!	4
,-R(ptcl-b) // ,-R(ptcl-b)(Gen.49:7a)	1
ptcl-b // ptcl-b	2
neg-b! // neg-b! (Gen.49:6a)	1
,-R(&a-s) // ,-R(&a-s)	2
prep-b // prep-b (Ex.15:16b)	1
3?-a // 3?-a (Num.23:8)	1
neg-a-s // neg-a-s (Num.23:8)	1
neg-c // neg-c (Num.23:21a)	1
&a // &a (Hab.3:6a-b)	1
,-R(&a-s) // ,-R(&a-s) (Ex.15:2b)	1
&a-s // &a-s (II Sam.22:15)	1
Compound // Compound	
neg-b 3 // neg-b 3 (II Sam.1:22b-c)	1
a 2 // a 2 (2 a)	3
lpr?-a // lpr?-a (Num.23:10a)	1
c-3-s // c-3-s (II Sam.22:45)	1
a-2-s // a...2-s (Hab.3:2a)	1
Double Compound // Double Compound	
2-C-s a // a 2-C-s (Dt.32:38a)	1

Grammatical Units	Number of Examples
Nominal Sentence	
Subject (S)	
Simple // Simple	
S // S	3
S-s // S-s	2
Compound // Compound	
S-C // S-C	3
Spr?-"3"-s // Spr?-"3"-s (Ex.15:11a-b)	1
Double Compound // Double Compound	
S-C P(3) // S-C P(3) (Gen.49:12a)	1
Predicate	
Simple // Simple	
P // P	4
P(3) // P(3)	2
P(part.c) // P(part.c) (Dt.32:34)	1
P(ptcl!) // P(ptcl!) (Dt.33:17c)	1

The total number of fully parallel units is 196 or almost exactly one-half of the parallel sub-line units. In addition, most of the parallel units in the following list may be added to this total, since they differ from fully parallel ones only by the addition of a minor grammatical element (particles, pronominal suffixes, etc.).

Parallel Units with Additional Element

Listed here are those units in which the A or B Line unit differs from its parallel only by the addition of a grammatical element which, of course, cannot comprise a full grammatical unit. Therefore, in effect, the grammatical elements consist of particles and prepositions, also pronominal suffixes and the adverb _'az_. Strictly speaking, this list must be restricted to grammatical units which are otherwise fully congruent in grammatical structure; that is, the categories simple // simple, compound // compound, and double compound // double compound. However, it seems expedient to include here also a second list of grammatical additions, similar to those described above, attached to the A or B Line member of grammatically compatible units of the categories simple // compound, compound // simple, etc. These compatible units are characterized by the addition of a grammatical unit to an A or B Line rank in the reconstructed sentence. Such units will be listed in detail in the following section. Of interest in the second list presented here are only those minor grammatical elements, below the level of the grammatical unit, added either to A or B Line compound; i.e., 1-s // 1-C; 1 // 1-C-s, etc.

Since the scope of this section is restricted to the nature of added elements, it is not necessary to indicate the structure of the parallel units.

Grammatically Congruent Units

1. Addition of a pronominal suffix (-s)

Verbal Sentence	A Line	B Line
Noun		
Simple // Simple	Ex.15:16b	II Sam.22:29
	Dt.32:27b	Dt.32:23
	Dt.32:30b	Ps.89:11
		Num.24:8b
		Num.23:19b
		Jud.5:20
		Dt.32:12
		II Sam.22:22
Compound // Compound	Dt.32:22b	Ex.15:4
	Gen.49:25a	II Sam.22:32
		Ps.89:8
		Ps.89:10
Verb		
Simple // Simple	Ex.15:10 (T)	
	Ex.15:5 (T)	
Compound // Compound		Ex.15:9b-c

	A Line	B Line
Nominal Sentence		
Subject		
Simple // Simple	Dt.32:37	
Compound // Compound: none		
Predicate		
Simple // Simple: none		
Compound // Compound		Dt.32:9

---

2. Addition of a particle

	A Line	B Line
Verbal Sentence		
Noun		
Simple // Simple	Gen.4:23b (ky)	Dt.32:27b (l')
	Gen.49:6b (ky)	Dt.32:39c-d (w)
		Ps.68:17b-c ('p) ('p)
		Ps.89:6 ('p)
Compound // Compound	II Sam.22:16a (encl.mem in construct)	
Verb		
Simple // Simple	Num.23:18 (w)	Jud.5:19a ('z)
	Dt.32:30a('kh) (ptcl?)	Ps.77:17b-c ('p)
	Dt.32:39c-d (w)	II Sam.22:38 (l')
	Dt.32:36a(ky)	Num.23:9b (l')
	II Sam.22:38 (w)	II Sam.22:37 (l')
	Num.23:23a (ky)	
	II Sam.22:39 (wl') (ptcl-neg)	
Compound // Compound	Dt.32:3 (ky)	
Nominal Sentence		
Subject		
Simple // Simple	Dt.32:9 (ky)	
Compound // Compound	II Sam.22:32 (ky)	
Predicate		
Simple // Simple	Dt.32:35b (ky)	
Compound // Compound	Dt.32:32a (ky)	

Grammatically Compatible Units

1. Addition of a pronominal suffix (-s)

	A Line	B Line
Verbal Sentence		
Noun		
Simple // Compound Compound // Simple	Jud.5:29	Ps.68:14b
	Gen.49:16	Num.23:10b
	Ps.68:5a	Gen.49:10a
	Ex.15:17b-c	Jud.5:17c-d
	Dt.32:22a	
Verb		
Simple // Compound	Dt.32:20a	Ex.15:17b-c
Compound // Compound		II Sam.22:42
Nominal Sentence		
Subject		
Simple // Compound Compound // Simple		Ps.89:12
Predicate		
Compound // Double Compound	Dt.33:16b	

---

2. Addition of a particle, preposition, or the adverb 'z

	A Line	B Line
Verbal Sentence		
Noun		
Simple // Compound Compound // Simple	Gen.4:24 (ky)	Jud.5:29 ('p)
Compound // Double Compound	Num.23:24b (^{c}d)	Dt.32:24b (^{c}m)
Verb		
Simple // Compound Compound // Simple	Ex.15:15a-b ('z)	II Sam.1:21b (bl)
	Ps.114:3 (w)	
Simple // Double Compound Double Compound // Simple	Dt.33:6 (w'l)	
	Dt.32:38b (w)	

	A Line	B Line
Nominal Sentence		
Subject		
Simple // Compound		
Compound // Simple	II Sam.22:23 (ky) Ps.89:12 ('p)	Dt.32:4a (ky)
Predicate		
Simple // Compound		II Sam.22:23 (l')
Compound // Double Compound	Dt.32:20b (ky)	

Of the pronominal suffixes, both possessive and object, 15 are added to A Line units and 21 to B Line units; of the particles, 24 to A Line and 14 to B Line units. All the particles are proclitics except, of course, enclitic mem. Their distribution is as follows:

	A Line	B Line
ky	12	1
w	5	1
'p	1	4
l'		5
bl		1
wl'	1	
w'l	1	
'kh	1	
'z	1	1
^{c}m		1
^{c}d	1	
encl.mem	1	

As expected, one finds that ky is primarily an A Line added element and 'p a B Line one. The majority of negative particles (6:2) also occur in the B Line; a situation which reflects what must be considered a special rhetorical device: the parallelism of a positive term in the A Line with a negative one in the B Line.

The preceding list has mechanically registered the presence or absence of pronominal suffixes or particles in units of the type described (not in all examples of the Corpus). As regards the former, it is clear that a pronominal suffix as an added element is truly significant only when it bears some relationship to the suffixless form. This is especially true with "double-duty" suffixes: Ex.15:16b: *^{c}mk* // *^{c}m*; Ex.15:17b-c: *mkn lšbtk* // *mqdš*; Num.23:19b: *wl' y^{c}ś* // *wl' yqmn*; Dt.32:23: *r^{c}t* // *ḥṣy*. So also when the suffix replaces an A Line term: Gen.49:10a: *myhd* // *mbn dqlw*; Ex.15:4: *mrkbt pr^{c}* // *mbḥr šlšw*; Num.24:8b: *qym* // *^{c}ṣmthm*; Jud.5:17c-d: *lḥp ymm* // *^{c}l mprṣw*; Ps.68:5a: *rkb b^{c}rbt* // *šm* (*šᵊmô*); and Ps.68:14b : *knp yn* // *'brth*. Note also the cases where a transformation produces a form which requires a pronominal suffix (Ex.15:5 and 10).

Grammatically Compatible Units

A basic principle of this system of analysis is that semantically parallel units must also be grammatically parallel or, failing that, grammatically compatible in the framework of the reconstructed sentence. However, a large number of couplets exhibit partial or total grammatical incongruence; for example, nominal sentences parallel to verbal sentences, or parallelism between transitive and intransitive verbs, etc. In some cases it is necessary to remove this incongruence by subjecting the sentences in question to grammatical transformation to allow the direct comparison of such lines and the units of which they are composed. In many cases, however, structures may be considered simply compatible within the reconstructed sentence. They exhibit no true incongruence but merely the annexion of a grammatical unit to one which itself is grammatically parallel. The most common such patterns are compound structures like constructs or combinations of verb + noun forming idiomatic units; i.e., semantic or indivisible compounds. Since the reconstructed sentence determines grammatical parallelism and compatibility, it is possible for structures of considerable length within its boundaries to be directly compared, even if one or more constituents are actually incongruent; so, for example, the parallelism of *yr^{c}m* and *ytn qlh* (intransitive verb // transitive verb + object) in II Sam.22:14.

This section deals first with compatible structures formed by simple annexion. The most frequent of these is the construct relationship, but also compounds formed by coordinated nouns or, in a single example (II Sam.22:8a), verbs, or similar constructions. This will be followed by a list of compounds which involve verbal constructs. Most of these involve the parallelism of a simple unit parallel to an idiomatic expression or, in the case of the parallelism of two compounds, two such idioms (or semantic compounds). A special category is formed by parallelism in which one member forms part or the whole of a "quasi-verbal" sentence.

Parallelism of Compounds Formed by Annexion

Characteristic of these compounds is that they are formed by two or more grammatical elements, usually nouns, all but the first of which represent no progressive syntactic rank in the sentence; that is, nouns in construct, attributives, nouns in apposition, coordinated nouns (or verbs), and relative phrases. Such annexed elements may be considered grammatically compatible from the point of view of parallelism, provided that the unit to which they are appended is itself grammatically parallel. This segment contains only what may be considered such simpler patterns; more complex types are discussed in the appropriate sections, below.

The first category consists of constructions formed by nouns (except for II Sam.22:28a):

Verbal Sentence

Simple // Compound

Compound // Simple

Nouns

Subject (1)

Jud.5:28b
Jud.5:29
II Sam.1:27
II Sam.22:8a
II Sam.22:47
Ps.24:7a-b
Ps.68:14b

Metrical Variations

Num.23:7a
Num.23:18

Object (2)

Gen.49:11a
Gen.49:16
Dt.32:8a
Dt.33:11a
II Sam.22:12

Adverb (3)

Gen.49:10a
Gen.49:11b
Dt.32:13b
Dt.33:2b-c
Dt.33:13
Jud.5:26a
II Sam.22:21
Hab.3:3a
Ps.29:6
Ps.68:14b
Ps.89:6
Ps.89:7
Ps.114:4

(Metrical Variations)

Jud.5:17c-d
II Sam.22:11
Ps.114:1

Construct (-C)

Ps.114:1

Compound // Double Compound (all grammatical categories)

Num.24:17c
Dt.32:10a
Dt.32:24b
Hab.3:11b
Ps.114:7

Simple // Double Compound

(Metrical Variations)

II Sam.22:16b

Verbs (applicable only to nominal forms)

Compound // Simple

Dt.33:8a: 3(inf.const.a-Cpn) // 3(inf.const.a-s...)
(bhnḥl ᶜlyn // bhprdh)

Nominal Sentence

Subject

Simple // Compound

Compound // Simple

Dt.32:4a (pᶜlh // ky kl drkw)
Ps.68:6
II Sam.22:23 (ky kl mšpṭw // ḥqtw) (T)

Predicate

Simple // Compound

Ex.15:11b-c

Compound // Double Compound
Dt.33:16b

This class contains 43 examples. Note that in the cases of Dt.32:4a and II Sam.22:23 the construct consists of a compound with kl, strengthened by ky (and in the latter case, transformed). Neither of these grammatical elements is itself awarded the value of a metrical unit in this system; the combination ky kl + noun, however, must be considered the equivalent of a full construct relationship; cf. Part I.

Also to be assigned to this category is the following example which represents a grammatical structure compatible with constructs:

Ex.15:17b-c: 3 3-s // 3 (mkn lšbtk // mqdš)

The prepositional phrase is a common periphrastic construction for the simple construct; without, however, any of the additional nuances this construction generally has in prose (G.K. 129aff.); cf. also Ps.68:5a (lrkb b^c^rbt).

A much smaller class consists of nouns followed by an attributive:

Dt.32:21b (bl' ^c^m // bgy nbl)
Dt.32:22a (b'py // ^c^d š'l tḥtt)
II Sam.22:17 (mmrm // mmm rbm)
Ps.114:1 (mmṣrym // m^c^m l^c^z)

All of the examples listed above are Simple // Compound. The only unit of this type in the category of Compound // Double Compound also contains a notable feature in that, if the text is correct, the attributive is separated from its noun by a construct:

Dt.32:33: P-C // P-C ,-P (ḥmt tnnm // r'š ptnm 'kzr)

Another small class is composed of units in which the longer parallel consists of two coordinated nouns or verbs.

Gen.4:24 (šb^c^tm // šb^c^m wšb^c^)
Dt.32:7a (ymt ^c^lm // šnt dr wdr)
II Sam.22:8a (tg^c^š wtr^c^š // yrgzw)
Ps.89:8 (n^c^rṣ // rb wnr')
Ps.89:12 ('rṣ // tbl wml'h) (T)

In each of these examples the compound contains the coordinating conjunction waw. Also to be included in this group is a unit which does not:

Jud.5:30 (šll // rḥm rḥmtm)

Verbal Compounds

These units are formed by idiomatic, i.e., semantic compounds. Grammatically they consist of verb // verb + noun, or the reverse, or verb + noun // verb + noun. The predicate of a nominal sentence may also be involved. Note that some units have been transformed.

Simple // Compound (including double compounds)

Compound // Simple

Gen.49:27a-b: ,-R(a) // ,-R(a...2) (yṭrp // y'kl ^{c}d)

Ex.15:14: b // 1 a --→ 3 c (T) (yrgzn // ḥl 'ḥz)

Ex.15:15a-b: 3-c // a-s 1 --→ c 3 (T) ('z nbhl // y'ḥzm r^{c}d)

Ex.15:15b-c: a-s 1 // c --→ a-s (T) (y'ḥzm r^{c}d // nmg)

Ex.15:17b-c: ,-R(a) // ,-R(a 1-s) (p^{c}lt // knn ydk)

Dt.32:20a: a 2-s // a ('strh pny // 'r'h)

Dt.32:41b: a 2 // a ('šb nqm // 'šlm)

Jud.5:29: a-s // a 2-s 3-s (t^{c}nn // tšb 'mrh lh)

II Sam.1:21b: c // neg-c 3 (ng^{c}l // bl mšḥ bšmn)

II Sam.22:7b: a // b 3-s --→ a 3-s (T) (yšm^{c} // tb' b'znw)

II Sam.22:14: b // a 2-s (yr^{c}m // ytn qlh)

II Sam.22:17: a 2-s // a-s (yšlḥ ydh // ymšny)

II Sam.22:23: P(3)-s // neg-a 3-s --→ "neg-b"-P(part.c) 3-s (T) (lngdy // l' 'sr mmny)

II Sam.22:29: P-s // a 2-s --→ P(part.a) 2-s (T) (nry // tgh ḥšky)

II Sam.22:34: P(part.a) 2-s // a-s --→ P(part.a)-s (T) (mšwh rgly // y^{c}mdny)

II Sam.22:44b-c: a-s 3- // a-s --→ a 3-s (T) (tśmny lr'š // y^{c}bdny)

Ps.24:7a-b: a...2-s // c (ś'...r'škm // hnś')

Ps.29:2: a!...2-C-s // c (hb...kbd šm // hšthw)

Ps.114:3: &b // b 3 (wyns // ysb l'ḥr)

Compound // Compound

Ex.15:9b-c: b-encl.mem l-s // a-encl.mem l-s (tml'm npš // tršm yd)

Dt.32:3: ptcl-2-...a // a! 2 (ky šm...'qr' // hbw gdl)

II Sam.1:22b-c: neg-b 3 // neg-b 3 (l' nśq 'ḥr // l' tšb rqm)

II Sam.22:9a-b: b 1 // 1...a (^{c}lh ^{c}šn // 'š...t'kl)

II Sam.22:9b-c: 1...a // 1 b ('š...t'kl // gḥlm b^{c}rw)

II Sam.22:15: a 2 // 2 a (yšlḥ ḥṣm // brqm ybrq)

Hab.3:2a: a 2-s // a...2-s (šm^{c}ty šm^{c}kh // r'ty...p^{c}lkh)

Twenty-six units fall into this category, of which 13 are simply compatible and 8 involve units in lines which have been transformed. Six units exhibit parallelism of units which are grammatically incongruent: II Sam.22:14; Ps.24:7a-b; Ps.29:2; Ex.15:9b-c; II Sam.22:9a-b; II Sam.22:9b-c. All, of course, are compatible in terms of their position in their respective reconstructed sentences. It may be noted that three examples contain transitive verbs without object; so t'kl of II Sam.9a-b and b-c. The suffix of tršm in Ex.15:9b-c is taken, with Cross and Freedman, to be enclitic mem (cf. the Corpus). However, it must be pointed out that the parallel tml'm involves the verb ml', whose position as regards transitivity-intransitivity is ambiguous. If the suffixes are pronominal, the effect on analysis would be minimal.

Compounds Involving a "Quasi-Verbal" Sentence

In some units, elements of a nominal sentence (only Ex.15:2a and Dt.33:24a-b) or verbal sentence are parallel to part or all of a "quasi-verbal" sentence. In this system of analysis, such units may be directly compared without recourse to grammatical transformation. In any case, most of the examples involve a semantic compound which, in the framework of the reconstructed sentence, may be considered grammatically compatible along the lines of the units discussed in the preceding sections.

Simple // Compound

Dt.32:12: lpn // S ,-S (yhwh // 'l nkr)

Simple // Double Compound

Gen.49:15b: 3(inf.const.a) // "b" P(3) ,-P((3)part.a) (lsbl // yh lms ^{c}bd)

Dt.32:38b: &a!-s // "b!" 3-s P (wy^{c}zrkm // yhyw ^{c}lkm strh)

Dt.33:6: &neg-b! // b! S-s P (w'l ymt // yhy mtw mspr)

II Sam.22:19: a-s // "b" Spn P-3-s (yqdmny // yhyh yhwh mš^{c}n ly)

Compound // Compound

II Sam.22:42: &"neg-b" P(part.a) // &neg a-s (w'n mš^{c} // wl' ^{c}nm)

Compound // Double Compound

Ex.15:2a: P-s &P-s // "b" 3-s P(3) (^{c}z wzmrt // yh ly lyš^{c})

Dt.33:24a-b: P(part.c) 3 // "b" P(part.c)-C-s (brk mbnm // yh rṣy 'ḥw)

One unit does not involve a compound (as analyzed in the Corpus), but seems best included at this point:

Dt.32:12: 3 // "neg-b"-P(3)-s (bdd // 'n ^{c}mh)

Grammatically Incongruent Units

There remain a number of units which cannot be simply assigned to any of the categories discussed above, but involve structures which must be considered truly incongruent. None requires a grammatical transformation; indeed, the nature of most of them is such that no transformation is possible. However, in most cases, the incongruence can be removed by reference to what may be termed the "deep structure" of the sentence in which they occur. In the context of this study "deep structure" refers to the structure of a sentence which differs from the traditional grammatical interpretation of its syntactic relationships, which may be called its "surface structure." The terminology is that employed in transformational grammar, applied here somewhat casually. Of course, all sentences which have been transformed belong in this category. However, such cases are treated as a body in the following section. Under consideration here are sub-line units which may be considered grammatically compatible by reason of the deep structure of their sentence, although they are, as regards surface structure, grammatically incongruent; individual cases which also invólve a transformation are noted as such.

First, examples will be treated which are represented by several examples in the Corpus and may be taken to be more common types of deep structure parallelism; then, less frequent types will be considered. Some cases of the latter involve grammatical analysis of deep structures quite at variance with the surface structure. For fuller discussion one must in some cases refer to the analysis of these units in the Corpus.

1. The most common type of incongruence between semantically parallel units is represented by those cases which involve a compound verb. The surface structure of such units is verb + prepositional phrase (preposition + noun); the deep structure must be considered to be compound verb (verb + preposition) + noun; that is, those verbs which regularly or optionally combine with prepositions must be treated as the equivalent of transitive active verbs and the second member of the prepositional phrase, the noun, is the equivalent of a direct object; cf. Joüon, 125b. Note that the verbs themselves may be transitive or intransitive "inherently."

Most cases of the parallelism of a direct object (2) and an adverbial (= prepositional) phrase (3), and some examples of the parallelism of transitive (a) and intransitive (b/c) verbs in non-idiomatic phrases can be accounted for in this way:

Dt.32:11a: 2-s // 3-s (qnh // ᶜl gzlw)
a // b (yᶜr // yrḥp) (compound verb: yrḥp ᶜl)

Dt.32:11b: 2-s // 3-s (knpw // ᶜl 'brth) (compound verb: yś'hw ᶜl)

Dt.32:13a: 3-C // 2-C (bmty 'rṣ // tnbt śdy) (compound verb: yrkbhw ᶜl)

Dt.32:36a: 2-s // 3-s (ᶜmh // ᶜl ᶜbdw)
ptcl-a // c (ky ydn // ytnḥm) (compound verb: ytnḥm ᶜl)

Ps.68:5a: 2-s // 3 3 (šm // lrkb bᶜrbt) (compound verb: sl l)

In Ps.89:10 the characteristic 2 // 3 parallelism is the result of a transformation:

3-Cpn // 3(inf.const.b)-C-s ---> 2(inf.const.b)-C-s
(bg't (h)ym // bnś' glw ---> nś' glw (T))
(compound verb: mšl b)

In several examples more complex structures are involved; so:

II Sam.22:7a: 2(lpn!) // 3-s (yhwh // 'l 'lhy)
a // b ('qr' // 'šw^{c}) (compound verb: 'šw^{c} 'l)

Dt.32:20a: 3-s // 2(Ppr? S-s) (mhm // mh 'hrtm)
(compound verb: 'strh pny m)

The vocative of the former example and the clause of the latter are both the objects of verbs (2). Note that the verbal compound of Dt.32:20a is also an idiomatic unit.

Two examples belong both to this category and the following one, the parallelism of units involving a construct: Dt.32:3 (compound verb: hbw gdl l) and II Sam.22:22 (compound verb: pš^{c} m; verbal parallelism: ptcl-a // neg-b (ky šmrty // l' pš^{c}ty)). These examples are described in more detail in the next section. Related to this class, and also described in the following section, is II Sam.22:44b-c, where the 3 // 2 structure is the result of a transformation.

2. Another category of parallelism between non-congruent grammatical units is that represented by parallelism between a noun and the second element of the construct relationship (-C). Since the nomen rectum can represent subjectival and objectival, as well as properly genitival deep level structures, the parallelism of, for example, 1 // -C can be considered grammatically compatible if the genitive is subjective. When the nomen rectum's underlying structure is truly that of a genitive, since it is tangential to the progressive syntactic positions of the sentence, it may be considered to share the syntactic rank of its regens. The following examples of these types of relationship occur in the Corpus:

In eight examples the relationship between regens and rectum is truly genitival from the point of view of its deep structure. Three of these also display the type of deep level structure discussed above in (1); that is, each contains a compound verb.

Dt.32:3 -Cpn // 3-s

ky šm yhwh 'qr' ptcl 2-Cpn a

hbw gdl l'lhnw a! 2 3-s

The underlying structure of -Cpn // 3-s is 2 // 3-s. The compound verb, which also forms an idiomatic unit, is hbw gdl l.

II Sam.22:22 -Cpn // 3-s

ky šmrty drky yhwh ptcl a 2-Cpn

(w)l' pš^{c}ty m'lhy neg b 3-s

Here also the deeper structure of -Cpn // 3-s is 2 // 3-s. The compound verb is pš^{c}ty m.

II Sam.22:44b-c -C // 1 --→ 2 (T)

tśmny lr'š gym a-s 3-C

^{c}m l' yd^{c}ty y^{c}bdny 1 ,-R(neg a) a-s

This example is more complicated than the preceding ones in that it requires a transformation in the B Line (see the *Corpus*). Otherwise, the situation is similar to that of the other two examples: the deeper structure of the parallelism -C // 2 is 3 // 2. A further, though slight, complication is the fact that the compound verb is tśmny l, but the phrase parallel to the B Line unit (y^{c}bdny) is tśmny lr'š = a-s 3-.

Three other examples are simpler: Ps.29:3b-c; 5; and 8. Each represents the parallelism of -C // 1, where -C is truly genitival and is the *nomen rectum* of a noun which is the subject of the sentence. The structure is, therefore, the equivalent of 1 // 1. In each case the parallel units are yhw // yhw.

The *Corpus* contains two similar examples with adverbial structure. Both cases contain in the A Line a construct where the *rectum*'s relationship to the *regens* is properly genitival, and both present the parallelism -C // 3:

Dt.33:13b-c mmgd šmm m^{c}l

(w)mthm rbṣt tḥt

Num.23:9a k mr'š ṣrm 'r'n

(w)mgb^{c}t 'šrn

No special grammatical problems are presented by these units.

In one example the relationship between _regens_ and _rectum_ is subjectival:

Ps.68:3b-c -C // 1

khms dng mpn 'š   "3"(inf.const.c-C) 3-C

y'bd rš^c m mpn yhw b l 3-Cpn

The construct is the functional equivalent of the subject, and, therefore, from the point of view of the underlying structure, the grammatical parallelism may be said to be the equivalent of l // l.

In two examples constructs are parallel to relative clauses:

Dt.32:1: 2(,-R(&a)) // -C (_w'dbrh_ // _'mry_ _py_)

Dt.32:35a: -C &-C // ,-R(b l-s) (_nqm_ _wšlm_ // _tmṭ_ _rqlm_)

The former example also displays the type of structure described above: the relative clause is the object (2) of a transitive verb, as is the _regens_ of the construct which forms its parallel.

As noted in the section on nominal compounds, two units exhibit structures which are the equivalent of the construct relationship: Ex.15:17b-c (_mkn_ _lšbtk_) and Ps.68:5a (_lrkb_ _b^c rbt_). In both cases an objectival genitive has been replaced by a prepositional phrase.

Special comment is required for II Sam.22:47 and Num.23:10b:

II Sam.22:47: P(part.c)! // b! (_brk_ // _yrm_)

In this example the passive participle _bāruk_ is certainly precative in its force (it follows _ḥy_ _yhwh_). Technically, the system of analysis requires a transformation of _yrm_ to a nominal form. However, the application of _Systemzwang_ seems inappropriate in a unit where the precative force of the verbs dominates.

Num.23:10b: "2-C" // P("3")-s (_mt_ _yšrm_ // _kmh_)

The adverbial predicate is in a "quasi-verbal" sentence and is parallel to a direct object (in this case a "cognate accusative"). The parallelism of a direct object with a prepositional phrase does not seem objectionable when the latter contains the "preposition of equivalence" _k_.

Two units involve more serious problems, and may be refractory. The first, at least, shows a type of relationship which is perhaps best understood in terms of the deep structure of its sentence:

1. Ps.89:12: The parallel sub-line units are:

ptcl-P(3)-s // lpr a-s ---→ Spr P(part.a) (T)
(lkh // 'th ysdtm)

S // 2 &2-s ---→ 2 &2-s (T) ('rṣ // tbl wml'h)

Even after transformation the parallel semantic units are grammatically incongruent; although they are, of course, compatible in terms of their hypothetical reconstructed sentence. As suggested in the Corpus, the simplest way of analyzing the grammatical parallelism in these units is from the point of view of the deep structure of sentences with casus pendens, as types of nominal sentences. In effect, then, the parallelism ptcl-P(3)-s // lpr a-s is ptcl-P(3)-s // P(lpr a-s); and that of S // 2 &2-s is S // S(2 &2-s). The transformation would be unnecessary.

2. Dt.33:28b: P(3)-s // ptcl-1-s ---→ ptcl-3-s (T)
(ᶜl 'rṣ // 'p šmw)

After the transformation, a hypothetical prepositional phrase has been produced in the B Line: mšmw. The predicate of the B Line after transformation is a participle: P(part.c) (nᶜrp). There is, then, a real incongruence between semantic and grammatical parallelism, since the semantic parallels are ᶜl 'rṣ and the transformed unit mšmw. The simplest explanation is to say that in this case a secondary grammatical feature dominates; here, the adverbial (3) relationship.

Transformations

Nineteen examples (8%) of the units of the Corpus require a transformation to produce grammatical parallelism between the B Line and its A Line. Six of these examples involve two transformations: Ex.15:15a-b and b-c; Dt.33:28b; II Sam.22:23; Ps.89:10; and Ps.89:12. The proportion of units requiring a transformation is relatively small because many examples of grammatical incongruence fall into categories which, in this system, do not require transformations; see the preceding section on sub-line units.

The following are the categories of transformation involving transitivity and intransitivity which appear in the Corpus:

1. Intransitive --→ Transitive

   This transformation produces a sentence with transitive verb which is, in fact, causative:

Ex.15:4	Ex.15:15b-c (first transformation)
Ex.15:5	II Sam.22:7b
Ex.15:10	II Sam.22:37

2. Causitive

   Two examples display a transformation from transitive active verbs to causative:

   Dt.32:42a
   II Sam.22:44b-c

3. Transitive --→ Intransitive

   The verbal transformation produces a passive or reflexive verb (c):

Ex.15:14	Dt.33:29c
Ex.15:15a-b (second transformation)	II Sam.22:23 (second transformation)
Dt.33:28b (second transformation)	

   Note that in the case of Dt.33:29c the transformation on the surface is b --→ c; however, the verb is, as regards its "deep structure," the equivalent of a transitive verb (a), since it is a compound (drk ᶜl).

Another group of transformations produces a nominal sentence from a verbal one:

Gen.49:19

Dt.33:28b (first transformation)

II Sam.22:23 (first transformation)

II Sam.22:29

II Sam.22:34

Ps.29:5

Ps.89:10 (first transformation)

Ps.89:12 (first transformation)

Only one example of transformation from nominal sentence to verbal sentence is attested in the _Corpus_: Ps.29:3. Interesting in this case is that the predicate P(3) becomes simple 3 by the transformation.

The system of analysis recognizes only one additional type of obligatory transformation; namely, that which removes the structure of _casus pendens_: Ex.15:15a-b (first transformation); Ps.89:10 (temporal clause with resumptive suffix which, since the latter's antecedent is the former, may be classified as a type of _casus pendens_); and Ps.89:12. One example requires a transformation to generate a sentence with _casus pendens_ structure: Ex.15:15b-c (second transformation).

Final Remarks

The patterns represented by the unit formulae and the sub-line units of which they are composed certainly played a significant role in the composition of early Hebrew verse. However, they are, of course, only one of a number of interlocking devices. It has become increasingly apparent that many of these have their origin in and owe their nature to the type of composition characteristic of an oral poetic tradition. The parallel word pairs and general use of formulaic language which have been the object of much recent study must be discussed in terms of the metrical patterns, whether of a syllabic or accentual nature, or both, and the numerous categories of grammatical parallelism. The number of the latter is quite large, ranging from the types of grammatical congruence and compatibility between the lines of the couplet which have been studied in this work to the larger patterns of quatrains and other strophic structures. Devices involving sequence must also be taken into account: alternating and internal parallelism and, especially, chiasm (a pleasing example of which occurs in the *Corpus* in II Sam.22:5-6, a triple chiasm). Of course, phonetic factors, rhyme, assonance in general, alliteration, and, above all, repetition are significant. The poet had a large stock of devices at his command. It is perhaps impossible to arrange them in a hierarchical order; however, meter must certainly have ranked high in the list, if not at the top, with semantic parallelism and grammatical parallelism perhaps next in order. As noted at the beginning of Part I, a study of the ways in which all the poetic devices interplay within the structure of a poem is beyond the scope of this study. We can no more than glimpse the over-all structure until the basic building blocks are better understood. However, it may be noted in general that any understanding of a poetic system is most difficult unless the prose system of the language is fully comprehended, since one of the most important aspects of poetic analysis is the perpetual contrast between prose ("casual speech") and poetry ("non-casual speech"). One must be aware of the many ways in which the poet is frustrating prosaic expectations.

A detailed application of these general statements is impossible in this work. However, a few interesting examples of the interplay between the types of patterns characteristic of some of the unit formulae and other devices may be offered as relatively simple illustrations.

In many cases, the pattern of the unit formula is obscured by other devices which cut across it, so to speak. The following are two examples of units with the same formula, but whose over-all effect is quite different.

Jud.5:28b

md[c] bšš / rkb lb'	"Why does his chariotry delay in coming;
md[c] 'ḥr / p[c]m mrkbtw	Why do the hooves of his chariots tarry?"

Ps.89:7

ky my bšḥq / y[c]rk lyhwh	"Who in the sky can compete with YHWH,
ydmh lyhwh / bbny 'lm	Can compare to YHWH among the lesser gods?"

In both cases the unit formula is the same: x x /x (D), and has the same pattern of semantic grades: D A /A (D), that is, both display one deletion from the A Line, the parallelism of two metrical units in A and B Lines, one of which is repetition. Both examples are questions. However, the unit formula is here little more than a relatively insignificant abstract pattern. More meaningful as regards the poetic effect of the units are the differences: Ps.89:7 displays chiasm; repetition occurs in the initial position in Jud.5:28b, and the deletion is in the initial position of Ps.89:7 but in the final one of Jud.5:28b. Repetition and sequence have here, as in many units, served to vary the basic parallel pattern, partially obscuring it at the same time.

Especially interesting are examples in which one can observe interplay between different unit formulae, that is, units that the system assigns to one formula but that, because of the workings of other devices, produce a poetic effect which is similar to that of another formula. Chiasm is, as noted above, a very potent device. Characteristic of the unit formula x/ /x and its variations (x/ /x (D), x x/ /x, etc.) is double chiasm which, in its ideal form, is both syntactic, in the contrast between a simple unit in the A Line parallel to a compound in the B Line and, conversely, between a compound in the A Line and a simple unit in the B Line; and also syllabic, in that the units should display a contrast of at least two syllables. Several units exhibit patterns similar to that of x/ /x, although the unit formula is, in fact, different. For example, Dt.32:39c-d:

'ny 'mt w'ḥyh	"I kill and make well;
mḥṣty w'ny 'rp'	I smite and I heal."

The unit formula is x x x (D A A), itself a common pattern. However, syntax and repetition tend to make one view <u>'ny</u> <u>'mt</u> and <u>w'ny</u> <u>'rp'</u> chiastically, in the pattern of x/ /x (although clear syllabic chiasm is lacking):

<u>A Line</u>			<u>B Line</u>
'ny 'mt	compound 4	// 3 simple	mḥṣty
w'ḥyh	simple 4	// 5 compound	w'ny 'rp'

A similar example is Dt.32:21b:

'ny 'qn'm bl' ^{c}m	"I shall make them jealous with a non-people;
bgy nbl 'k^{c}sm	I shall anger them with a brutish nation."

Here the chiastic effect is reinforced by partial syllabic contrast:

<u>A Line</u>			<u>B Line</u>
'ny 'qn'm	compound 5	// 3 simple	'k^{c}sm
bl' ^{c}m	simple 3	// 4 compound	bgy nbl

The unit formula, however, is x /x (D).

In Ex.15:15b-c only partial syntactic chiasm is present; the double chiasm is produced mainly by syllabic contrast, and the effect is reinforced by the <u>casus</u> <u>pendens</u> in the A Line:

'l m'b / y'ḥzm r^{c}d	"Trembling seized the mighty men of Moab;
nmq kl yšb kn^{c}n	All the inhabitants of Canaan melted away."

<u>A Line</u>			<u>B Line</u>
'l m'b	compound 4	// 6 compound	kl yšb kn^{c}n
y'ḥzm r^{c}d	compound 5	// 3 simple	nmg

The unit formula in this case is x/x x/.

The most striking series of units displaying this phenomenon is in Ps.29, vv.3b-c, 5, and 8, which are similar in other respects also. In each case a simple term parallels a compound (_(h)mym_ // _mym_ _rbm_; _'rzm_ // _'rz_ _(h)lbnn_; and _mdbr_ // _mdbr_ _qdš_, respectively); and a compound parallels a simple unit (_ql_ _yhw_ // _yhw_, in each case). However, the system of analysis assigns these units to a formula pattern quite unlike x/ /x; namely x x (D) for v.3b-c and x x x (D) for vv.5 and 8. Clearly, repetition and climactic parallelism are significant devices in these units, and perhaps dominate from the point of view of poetic effect.

These examples highlight an important general conclusion: the unit formulae can be employed to display contrasts with other patterns. In fact, this may be their most significant function as regards literary analysis. Only through an understanding of the way these basic compositional units work in their larger context can one arrive at a true appreciation of the art of the ancient Hebrew poet.

APPENDIX A

Observations on Meter

The system of analysis has demanded that the unit formulae record the relationship between the number of grammatical units and what are termed metrical units. The latter, of course, reflect an accentual interpretation of Hebrew verse. Incongruence between the number of grammatical and metrical units is faithfully reflected by the unit formulae, producing what have been labelled the "metrical variations," marked by the signs * and _. On the other hand, note has been taken of syllabically symmetrical and asymmetrical units and the lists of major formulae have been arranged in order of syllabic "soundness." Clearly, this study has taken a middle ground between an accentual and a purely syllabic interpretation of the nature of Hebrew meter for the examples of the Corpus. A totally grammatical interpretation of the formulae is also possible, and was briefly described in Part III. However, this system aims at an over-all understanding of the major relationships between A and B Lines; therefore, meter could not be ignored. Until the matter of the true nature of Hebrew meter is settled, even for poetry in the chronological limits of the Corpus, it seems safer to walk the middle line between competing accentual and syllabic interpretations.

However, it is appropriate that consideration be given to the evidence that supports a syllabic or accentual interpretation of Hebrew meter as represented by the examples of the Corpus.

In general, couplets that display syllable asymmetry support an accentual understanding of meter; conversely, examples in which the assignment of stresses according to any regular pattern is difficult, tip the scales toward a syllabic interpretation. However, syllable counts also play a role in interpreting the accentual evidence, since the assigning of one stress to both a word of one syllable and a word or compound of, say, five syllables is most problematic.

Approximately 24% of the couplets in the Corpus are syllabically asymmetrical, that is, exhibit an imbalance of two or more syllables. The following is a list of these units, arranged by the degree of syllable disparity they exhibit:

1. Imbalance of four syllables

Dt.32:1

Jud.5:30

Ps.68:6

(Note also Ex.15:2b, whose rearrangement was prompted by syllabic imbalance)

2. Imbalance of three syllables

Gen.49:16
Ex.15:17a-b
Num.23:18
Dt.33:6
Jud.5:20
Jud.5:25
Ps.24:7b-c
Ps.68:17b-c
Ps.89:12
Ps.89:13

3. Imbalance of two syllables

Gen.4:23b
Gen.49:5
Gen.49:11a
Gen.49:27b-c
Ex.15:2a
Ex.15:3-4b-c
Ex.15:5
Ex.15:7
Ex.15:9a-b
Ex.15:16a
Num.23:21a
Num.23:21b
Dt.32:13b
Dt.32:22a
Dt.32:22b
Dt.32:23
Dt.32:27b
Dt.32:28
Dt.32:30b
Dt.32:37
Dt.32:39
Dt.33:22
Jud.5:19b
Jud.5:28b
II Sam.22:5
II Sam.22:8a
II Sam.22:9
II Sam.22:19
II Sam.22:21
II Sam.22:38
II Sam.22:39
Hab.3:3b
Ps.24:8a-b
Ps.29:2
Ps.29:5
Ps.68:3b-c
Ps.68:18
Ps.68:19
Ps.89:6
Ps.89:10
Ps.89:11
Ps.89:13
Ps.114:2
Ps.114:8

In one example, II Sam.1:22, the A and C Lines of a triplet are asymmetrical as regards each other but are syllabically symmetrical in their relationship to their B Line: 10:9:8.

Units exhibiting such a syllable imbalance must be considered a strong argument against a purely syllabic interpretation of the Hebrew verse of the Corpus. This is especially true of the examples asymmetrical by four or three syllables. In some of the couplets in which only two syllables form the imbalance, the adding of waw at the beginning of the B Line (contrary to the practice in this study) would remove the syllable asymmetry by reducing it to one syllable. However, in an almost equal number of cases, the same procedure would actually increase the asymmetry.

A related issue is that of syllabic balance between the two short lines that make up four metrical unit lines. There are about ninety such lines in the Corpus, and 17% are asymmetrical:

1. Imbalance of three syllables

Gen.4:23a	Ps.68:17b
Ex.15:10	Ps.89:13
Num.10:35	

2. Imbalance of two syllables

Ex.15:6	Ps.29:5
Ex.15:11	Ps.89:8
Ex.15:13	Ps.89:10
Ex.15:17a	Ps.89:11
Ex.15:17c	Ps.114:7
II Sam.1:22c	

Arguing for a syllabic approach are units in which the assignment of stresses is difficult. Among these are couplets in which units of equal syllabic length must be assigned three stresses:

Num.23:10b: tmt npš and mt yšrm both 4 syllables
Dt.32:10b: ysbbnhw and ybnnhw both 5 syllables
Dt.32:24b: šn bhmt and 'šlḥ bm both 4 syllables
II Sam.22:34: ᶜl bmtw and yᶜmdny both 4 syllables

Even more significant are examples in which stresses must be assigned to grammatical units with a great disparity in syllabic length:

Gen.49:25a: *m'l* = 2 syllables; *'bk* = 3 syllables; *wy^{c}zrk* = 5 syllables (so also in the B Line: *'l* = 1 syllable; *šdy* = 2 syllables; *wybrkk* = 5 syllables)

II Sam.22:19: *yqdmny* = 5 syllables; *bym* = 2 syllables; *'dy* = 2 syllables

II Sam.22:44b-c: *^{c}m* = 1 syllable; *l' yd^{c}ty* = 4 syllables; *y^{c}bdny* = 4 syllables

II Sam.22:45: A Line: *bny* = 2 syllables; *nkr* = 2 syllables; *ytkḥšw ly* = 5 syllables
B Line: *lšm^{c}* = 2 syllables; *'zn* = 1 syllables; *yšm^{c}w ly* = 5 syllables

A metrical decision based on accents is very difficult to make in the case of Dt.32:25b: *gm bḥr gm btlh* in which one *gm* must be assigned metrical value.

In general, the elimination of accents as a metrically significant factor would remove the necessity of treating certain grammatical elements as "anceps." In fact, the many minor formulae produced by incongruence between the number of grammatical units in a given accentual framework, marked by the metrical signs * and _, would be eliminated as metrical variations. Moreover, it would no longer be necessary to assign lines in accentually unclear environments to the categories of three or four metrical units. Therefore, units like Ps.114:1, 7, and 8, for example, would be less troublesome.

APPENDIX B

<u>Observations on "Synthetic Parallelism"</u>

To a large extent the study of biblical parallelism has suffered from what is probably a cultural prejudice. Scholars have diligently attempted to uncover the well-hidden secrets of biblical meter, but only a small fraction of this effort has been applied to the analysis of parallelism. This disproportionate emphasis on meter is the result of the training in classical literatures which was the background of earlier generations of scholars and which has been perpetuated, at least in theory, up to the present. In classical poetry parallelism is a device of only marginal significance from the point of view of standard prosody.

One of the results of this relative disinterest in parallelism is the survival of certain misconceptions for decades and, indeed, for centuries. The most striking example is so-called "synthetic parallelism," which, as all students of the Bible know, was one of Bishop Lowth's categories of biblical parallelism. Most are also aware that, unlike the other two categories ("synonymous" and "antithetic"), "synthetic parallelism" is problematic, as was admitted by Lowth himself. G. B. Gray discussed the topic authoritatively in his standard <u>Forms of Hebrew Poetry</u> more than sixty years ago. His critique of Lowth should have served to erase the term "synthetic parallelism" from the lexicon of biblical scholarship. However, the basic confusion found in Lowth thrives to some extent in all works on biblical poetry which deal with the topic. The purpose of this brief discussion is to examine the issue by first reviewing Lowth's statements and then surveying the manner in which this topic is treated in a number of later works.

It will become clear that part of the problem is a persistent failure of the literature to distinguish between three aspects of parallelism:

1. The two <u>types</u> of parallelism: semantic and grammatical; i.e., parallelism of meaning and of form;

2. The degree of parallelism; i.e., the inherent "propinquity" of parallel terms to each other in meaning, an aspect represented in this study by the semantic "grades."
3. The rhetorical relationships present in all parallelism.[1]

"Synthetic parallelism" has been taken by different scholars to refer to one or two of these aspects, or to all of them together.

The source of this unclarity is Lowth himself. He introduces "synthetic parallelism" in a manner which suggests that it is intended to refer only to what we would term grammatical parallelism:

> "The third sort of parallels I call synthetic or constructive---where the parallelism consists only in the similar form of construction; in which word does not answer to word, and sentence to sentence, as equivalent or opposite; but there is a correspondence and equality between different propositions, in respect of the shape and turn of the whole sentence, and of the constructive parts---such as noun answering to noun, verb to verb, member to member, negative to negative, interrogative to interrogative."[2]

Now grammatical parallelism is present in most semantic parallelism. Although they are independent in principle and can occur separately,[3] parallelism of meaning usually occurs together with some type of parallelism of form. Therefore, if by "synthetic parallelism" we mean grammatical parallelism, it is incorrect to refer to it as Lowth does, as a "third sort of parallelism" along with "synonymous" and "antithetic." The

---

1. On all three aspects, see Part I.

2. Robert Lowth, Isaiah: A New Translation; with a Preliminary Dissertation and Notes, Critical, Philological and Explanatory[10] (Boston, 1834), p. xvii. This is the edition used in this study; on that employed for the Lectures, see note 7, below. The discussion is based mainly on the Preliminary Dissertation as the most complete exposition of Lowth's views.

3. So, for example, Ex.17:7:

brb g'nk thrs qmk	"By your great majesty you destroyed your adversaries;
tšlḥ ḥrnk y'klm kqš	You sent forth your wrath, which consumed them like chaff."

The central units thrs qmk // tšlḥ ḥrnk are grammatically fully parallel (a 2-s // a 2-s) without being semantically so.

latter are rhetorical relationships between semantically parallel units and are not of the same character or category as "synthetic parallelism."

Even graver complications arise from his very first example of "synthetic parallelism":

> "Praise the Lord from the netherworld,
> Sea monsters and all deeps,
>
> Fire and hail, snow and smoke,
> Storm wind, which performs his command,
>
> Mountains and all hills,
> Fruit trees and all cedars,
>
> Wild animals and all beasts,
> Reptiles and winged birds,
>
> Kings of the earth and all nations,
> Princes and all rulers of the earth,
>
> Young men and also young women,
> Old men together with youths,
>
> Let them praise the name of YHWH,
> For his name alone is exalted,
>
> His glory is above earth and heavens...."
> (Ps.148:7-13)

Now while it is true that the relationship between most of the corresponding terms in this (and Lowth's succeeding) examples is neither "synonymous" nor "antithetic," can one seriously maintain that it is only "constructive," i.e., grammatical? Clearly, the Psalmist is presenting a type of inventory of creation in praise of God. The parallelism is a splendid example of the rhetorical relationship labelled "List" in this study and is quite as complete as if it were "synonymous."[4]

If by "synthetic" Lowth now meant not grammatical ("constructive") parallelism but only the enumerative type of rhetorical relationship characteristic of "List," one would have

---

4. Lowth, <u>ibid</u>., p. xx. He states:

> "The reader will observe in the foregoing examples, that though there are perhaps no two lines corresponding one with another as equivalent, or opposite in terms; yet there is a parallelism equally apparent, and almost as striking, which arises from the similar form and equality of the lines, from the correspondence of the members and the construction...."

Admittedly, he still does not seem to discern any <u>semantic</u> relationship between corresponding terms.

little theoretical objection. "List" is a term of the same category as "synonymous" and "antithetic." Since the latter really are variants of the same type of relationship, Lowth would, in effect, be proposing a basic dichotomy between "synonymous" and "antithetic" on the one hand, and "synthetic" on the other. This is the same basic pattern suggested by Steinitz' "synonymous" and "analogous" parallelism. Only the term "synthetic" itself would have to be replaced as valueless, since it describes no characteristic of the "List" relationship.

However, Lowth becomes involved in yet another complication. He introduces a third aspect of parallelism into the discussion: degree of parallelism:

> "...sometimes the (synthetic) parallelism is more, sometimes less exact; sometimes hardly at all apparent."[5]

It is presumably the last category which leads him to talk of the Masoretic division of verses, as indicated by the system of accents:

> "It requires indeed particular attention, much study of the genius of the language, much habitude in the analysis of the construction, to be able in all cases to see and distinguish the nice rests and pauses which ought to be made, in order to give the period or the sentence its intended turn and cadence, and to each part its due time and proportion...they (the Masoretes) sometimes seem to have more regard in distributing the sentence to the poetical or rhetorical harmony of the period, and the proportion of the members, than to the grammatical construction."[6]

His examples make it clear that he is referring to couplets which conform metrically to the pattern of parallel verse; for example:

> "For the stars of heaven and their constellations
> Will not shed their light." (Isa.13:10)

At the equivalent point in the discussion in his Lectures he gives his most quoted example of this type of "synthetic":

> "I have anointed my king on Zion, my holy mountain" (Ps.2:6)

which he says should be read "as if it were":

> "I have anointed my king;
> I have anointed him in Zion, my holy mountain."[7]

---

5. Ibid. 6. Ibid.

7. Robert Lowth, Lectures on the Sacred Poetry of the Hebrews, tr. by G. Gregory (Boston, 1815), p. 270.

The true metrical division is, of course:

"I have anointed my king
On Zion, my holy mountain."

This couplet is enjambed, and such enjambed units are the very model of the non-parallel. To include them in the category of "synthetic parallelism" is truly misleading. As Gray forcefully objected:

> "Now if the term parallelism, even though it be qualified by prefixing the adjective synthetic, be applied to lines which, though synthetically related to one another, are connected by no parallelism of terms or sense, then this term (synthetic) parallelism, will really conceal an all important difference under a mere semblence of similarity."[8]

In other words, it is nonsensical to call the non-parallel "synthetically parallel." Non-parallel units play an important role in poetic systems which employ pervasive parallelism, and Lowth's pioneering insight that such couplets must be understood metrically in terms of their environment within a poem is valuable; but his inclusion of such units in his "synthetic" has worked much mischief. Gray's incisive comments on this point by no means ended the matter.

This troublesome category of "synthetic parallelism" somehow involves all three aspects of parallelism listed above. Lowth first makes it apply to grammatical parallelism only; but his examples seem to imply that it refers primarily to the rhetorical meaning "List"; and his successive comments clearly indicate that it is to be employed for units with lesser degrees of parallelism down to the level of the truly non-parallel in its most definitive form, the enjambed couplet.

Discussions of parallelism after Lowth are, in general, too laconic to establish even if the problematic nature of his "synthetic" is understood. The confusion of type, degree, and rhetorical meaning of parallelism persists. Even Gray does not deal with the issue in a definitive way. His replacement of "synthetic" by "formal" parallelism is only a slight improvement, since the real objection must be to the application of the term "parallelism" to what is, in fact, metrical

---

8. Gray, Forms of Hebrew Poetry, p. 50.

regularity.[9] Moreover, Gray does not concern himself with "List" parallelism, which was the principle type included in Lowth's "synthetic"; rather, he mixes examples of that rhetorical category promiscuously with definitely "synonymous" units.[10]

The most detailed study of biblical parallelism is Newman and Popper's analysis of Amos and Isaiah, respectively.[11] The former, like Gray, does not distinguish "List" parallelism from from "synonymous."[12] Popper's dissent shows an understanding of the necessity for some discrimination:

> "But it must be noted that in parallelism this term ("synonymous") is applied to series of words other than those cited in the dictionaries as synonyms or antonyms.... More often the terms are synonyms only by synechdoche or some other variety of metonomy....Perhaps, then, a broader term than 'synonyms' should be used, such as 'complements,' denoting terms which as they are used by the author are seen to belong to some one logical category."[13]

Below he says:

> "...the term 'complementary' can be applied to thought units or periods as a whole, to two or more lines each of which expresses an equal part of some one complex idea."[14]

His further discussion of the issue makes it clear that by "complementary" parallelism he has primarily the "List"

---

9. A similar objection must be made to P. Yoder's treatment of this topic in an otherwise judicious summary of biblical poetics, "Biblical Hebrew" in Versification. Major Language Types. Sixteen Essays, ed. W. K. Wimsatt (New York: New York University Press, 1972), p. 53f. His "structural parallelism" includes both syntactic and metrical correspondence. The same comment applies to T. H. Robinson's "numerical parallelism"; see his "Hebrew Poetic Form: The English Tradition" in SVT I (1953), 136. Robinson's approach is, in general, very sound. Especially useful is his defense of parallelism as a major poetic device in biblical poetry.

10. For example, Gen.49:12; Prov.2:4; Jer.6:25; Jer.5:6; Prov.25:6; Prov.3:10. It should be noted that Lowth also includes examples of "List" in his "synonymous" class, which does not help to alleviate the grave complications in his "synthetic" category; so, among others, Isa.51:7-8; Isa.65: 21-22; Joel 3:13.

11. Newman and Popper, Studies in Biblical Parallelism.

12. For example, Amos 8:11b; 5:5a; 6:6a, among others.

13. Newman and Popper, p. 436.

14. Ibid., p. 437.

rhetorical class in mind:

> "Such complements Isaiah is fond of heaping up; e.g., in 1.11-14, terms referring to ritual service (offerings and sacrifices of various kinds, oblations, incense, festivals and feasts; 2.7-8, to riches (silver, gold, horses, chariots); 3.18-23, to dress (21 items)...."[15]

Note, however, that Popper does not think of classifying this "complementary" parallelism as "synthetic," despite the fact that it was perhaps the major constituent of that category in Lowth.

Newman's major contribution to the issue of the clarification of "synthetic" parallelism is only accidental; since he does not deal explicitly with Lowth's categories, it cannot be ascertained if he is aware of the nature and dimensions of the problems. In any case, he defines "synthetic couplets" as those:

> "...wherein neither synonymity nor parallelism is so close, and where the twilight zone between prose and poetry is most evident."

This statement is not without its difficulties. By "parallelism" he presumably means grammatical parallelism; and reference to a "twilight zone between prose and poetry" certainly hints at metrical considerations. Nevertheless, it is clear from the examples he cites that his major criterion for "synthetic" is <u>degree</u> of parallelism. "Synthetic" are those semantic parallels that one might characterize as "loose." So, among others, Amos 4:13:

> "For indeed the one who forms the mountains and is
> the creator of the wind,
> The one who tells man his thoughts."

As Popper points out, one may prefer to assign some of his examples to more clearly semantically parallel classifications (especially Amos 5:11; 5:8c and 9:6b; 8:8a, 1:2b). However, Newman's limitation of "synthetic" to the single criterion of degree of parallelism is at least consistent, and does reflect one aspect of Lowth's category. The major problem is that degree of parallelism is by its nature the most difficult aspect of parallelism to deal with: one person's "loosely" parallel may be another's "clearly" parallel and yet another's "non-parallel." To be useful, this type of classification

---

15. <u>Ibid</u>., p. 436.

will need basic clarification (see below). In any case, Newman's limitation of "synthetic" seems to have had no effect on the subsequent treatment of parallelism.

One of the few later discussions to deal with general issues involved with the topic of the classification of the types of parallelism is Begrich's "Der Satzstil im Fünfer." To be sure, he does not deal explicitly with the term "synthetic parallelism," but a few pages of this important article are devoted to the topics which have played a role in the discussion, as will be seen from what follows. It will be especially clear, also, that Begrich's classification is marred by the same kind of confusion between categories which has obscured this issue since Lowth.

His opening statement is valuable:

> "Es ist merkwürdig, dass man sich bisher mit der allgemeinen Feststellung, dass Parallelismus da und dort vorliege, begnügt hat, aber nie, soweit wir sehen, die Frage aufgeworfen, was denn der Hebräer als parallel empfinde."[16]

He then attempts to establish three categories of parallelism. The first of these consists of close synonymous (and grammatical) parallelism:

> "Der Gedanke läuft in beiden Sätzen parallel und zwar so, dass jeder Satzteil im gleichlaufenden Glied durch ein Synonym ersetzt wird."[17]

He cites as examples Isa.1:10, 1:18 and 44:22. Since the last of these verses contains deletion and compensation, Begrich presumably means that semantic and grammatical parallelism is complete for those members which _are_ parallel. In any case, neither this category nor his third class of parallelism causes any real problems. The latter he defines as follows:

> "Eine dritte Art des Parallelismus ist die, dass man zur Veranschaulichung eines Gedankens verschiedene Einzelzüge zusammenstellt, die weder synonym parallel sind, die auch für sich allein betrachtet, nicht gedanklich gleichlaufen, die aber in ein und dieselbe Situation gehören und von da aus ihr Licht empfangen."[18]

---

16. J. Begrich, "Der Satzstil im Fünfer," _ZSem_, 9 (1933/34), 201.

17. _Ibid_.

18. _Ibid_., 202-3.

This is clearly the rhetorical meaning "List," Lowth's primary type of "synthetic." Among Begrich's examples are Isa.52:2 and 47:13. Presumably he would include also those rhetorical relationships related to "List" (PW, Met, etc.).

It is his second class which is the source of real difficulties:

> "Eine andere Art des Parallelismus ist die, dass die Glieder nur gedanklich gleichlaufen, es aber keine Entsprechung in Synonymen gibt."[19]

It is evident from his examples (Isa.1:14, 38:12 and Ps.27:5) that his criterion is degree of parallelism, since each of the cited passages is characterized by "looser" parallelism (Newman's "synthetic"). Now his first and third classes involve rhetorical meaning (synonymous and "List," respectively), his second category, degree of parallelism. It must be stated that this kind of mixed classification represents a taxonomic laxity not in keeping with the rigor of the grammatical analyses in the main sections of his article.[20]

It should be clear even from this brief survey that Lowth's "synthetic parallelism" includes couplets of such disparate structure as to be the source of much confusion in the later study of parallelism. The term can hardly be employed for all of Lowth's categories. Is there, then, some limitation in its meaning which might justify its continued use?

As noted above, the only reference a term like "synthetic parallelism" could have that would make sense is that proposed by Newman and Popper, who apply it to varying degrees of "looser" parallelism. However, it is necessary to restrict the arbitrariness of such a classification. "Synthetic parallelism" should characterize only those couplets in which at least one unit of A and B Lines are <u>semantically</u> parallel but in which <u>grammatical</u> parallelism is so absent that the formation of a simple reconstructed sentence is impossible, even within the perimeters of adjustment outlined in Part I; so, for example, Ps.23:6:

---

19. <u>Ibid</u>., 202.

20. F. Horst, "Die Kennzeichen der hebräischenPoesie," <u>ThRu</u>, 21 (1953), in his discussion of parallelism follows Begrich, in the main. He suggests calling Begrich's type 2 "coordinating" parallelism and his type 3 "additive" (<u>additionellen</u>) or "summative" parallelism.

"Indeed goodness and lovingkindness will pursue me
all the days of my life;
I will dwell in the house of YHWH for days without end."

It must be noted that the *Corpus* contains few such units. Examples of the parallelism of indivisible compounds, especially those which make up the whole of their respective lines, are clear candidates or, at least, a very long step along the way.[21] However, units of this type are certainly one of the elements diagnostic of later verse, where they are common. A full description and typology of such units must be the object of further study.

However, even such a basic limitation of "synthetic parallelism" by strict semantic and, especially, grammatical criteria would not, in my opinion, justify continued employment of the term. It has been so tainted by the historical carelessness of its use that its potential for confusion remains undiminished. It is best to abandon the term and to replace it by some neutral designation, such as "parallelizing verse," or the like.[22]

In addition, mention must be made of a more general point which emerges from this brief survey of "synthetic parallelism." Earlier scholarly treatment of this topic reveals a certain degree of lassitude which is the result of the relative disinterest in parallelism noted at the beginning of this section. The issues involved in a discussion of "synthetic parallelism" also concern one's over-all understanding of the nature and function of parallelism as a literary phenomenon. The very common practice of lumping whatever is not clearly "synonymous" or "antithetic" into a shapeless category of "synthetic" reveals the same type of carelessness which also characterizes the unwillingness to consider what the Hebrews themselves felt to be parallel that was mentioned by Begrich. Parallelism has its own logic, a fact that has been little appreciated. Popper's comments on this point are worth quoting:

---

21. For example, Dt.32:35a.

22. E. Sellin and G. Fohrer, *Introduction to the Old Testament*, tr. by David E. Green (Nashville: Abingdon, 1968), pp. 45f. Here, however, the term is used in a somewhat different sense.

> "It will be seen, then, that lyric, prophetic, or didactic poetry must not be viewed as would be an historical or geological treatise; in the light of parallelism a list such as that in (Isa.)3:18 is poetical and effective; as archaeology it might be interesting, but it is tedious and defective.
>
> And here, the rule should be enunciated that in a parallelistic setting, i.e., when surrounded by other couplets or strophes in evident parallelism, any two lines must also be read as parallelism if this is in any way possible; just as in the scansion of poetry a doubtful line must be scanned in the light of the dominant meter. For example (Isa.)5:25:
>
> Therefore is the anger of the Lord kindled against his people,
> And he hath stretched forth his hand against them and smitten them.
>
> If this were simple narrative, it might be said that the fact detailed in the second line was subsequent to that described in the first. But Isaiah is not here concerned mainly with writing history or making a psychological analysis; the second line is not only a logical complement of the first, but by implication one is a repetition of the other: from the standpoint of prophetic philosophy God's anger implies of necessity punishment; or at least punishment implies his anger."[23]

In other words, parallelism as a poetic device means that one must always understand a given B Line as much as possible in terms of its A Line, both semantically and grammatically. This point, which is basic to all appreciation of parallelism, is implied in Cross's discussion of the "impressionistic" effect of "List" parallelism,[24] and is clearly implicit in Albright's treatment of Jud.5:26 and Josh.10:12-13.[25]

---

23. Newman and Popper, *op. cit.*, p. 437.

24. See the discussion of semantic parallelism in Part I.

25. See especially, W. F. Albright, *History, Archaeology and Christian Humanism* (New York, Toronto, London: McGraw Hill, 1964), pp. 95f.

WORKS CONSULTED

Albright, William F. "A Catalogue of Early Hebrew Lyric Poems (Psalm LXVIII)," HUCA, 23 (1950-1951), 1-39.

_______. "The Oracles of Balaam," JBL, 63 (1944), 207-233.

_______. "The Psalm of Habakkuk," Studies in Old Testament Prophecy. Edited by H. H. Rowley. Edinburgh: T. and T. Clark, 1950.

_______. Yahweh and the Gods of Canaan. Garden City, N. Y.: Doubleday and Company, 1968.

Andersen, Francis I. The Hebrew Verbless Clause in the Pentateuch. Journal of Biblical Literature Monograph Series, vol. 14. Nashville: Abingdon Press, 1970.

Begrich, Joachim. "Der Satzstil im Fünfer, ZSem, 9 (1933/34), 169-209.

Cross, Frank M. Canaanite Myth and Hebrew Epic. Cambridge, Mass.: Harvard University Press, 1973.

_______. "Prose and Poetry in the Mythic and Epic Texts from Ugarit," HTR, 67 (1974), 1-15.

_______. "The Song of the Sea and Canaanite Myth," JThC, 5 (1968), 1-25.

Cross, Frank M. and Freedman, David N. Early Hebrew Orthography: A Study of the Epigraphic Evidence. American Oriental Society, 1952.

_______. "A Royal Song of Thanksgiving: II Samuel 22=Psalm 18," JBL, 72 (1953), 16-21.

_______. "The Song of Miriam," JNES, 14 (1955), 237-250.

_______. Studies in Ancient Yahwistic Poetry. Baltimore, 1950. Microfilm-reprint, Ann Arbor, 1961.

Culley, Robert C. Oral Formulaic Language in the Biblical Psalms. Toronto: University of Toronto Press, 1967.

_______. "Metrical Analysis of Classical Hebrew Poetry," Essays on the Ancient Semitic World. Edited by J. W. Wevers and D. B. Redford. Toronto: University of Toronto Press, 1970, 12-28.

Dahood, Mitchell. Psalms I, II, III. The Anchor Bible, vols. 16, 17, 17a. Garden City, New York: Doubleday and Company, 1966-1970.

Freedman, David N. "Archaic Forms in Early Hebrew Poetry," ZAW, 72 (1960), 101-107.

_______. Prolegomenon to The Forms of Hebrew Poetry, by George Buchanan Gray, 1915. Reprint, Ktav Publishing House, 1972.

_______. "The Structure of Psalm 137," Near Eastern Studies in Honor of William Foxwell Albright. Edited by H. Goedicke. Baltimore: The Johns Hopkins Press, 1971, pp. 187-205.

Gevirtz, Stanley. Patterns in the Early Poetry of Israel. The Oriental Institute of the University of Chicago, Studies in Ancient Oriental Civilization, no. 32. Chicago: The University of Chicago Press, 1963.

Gordis, Robert. Poets, Prophets, and Sages: Essays in Biblical Interpretation. Bloomington, Ind.: University Press, 1971.

Gray, George Buchanan. The Forms of Hebrew Poetry, 1915. Reprint, Ktav Publishing House, 1972.

Greenstein, Edward L. "Two Variations of Grammatical Parallelism in Canaanite Poetry and Their Psycholinguistic Background," JANES, 6 (1974), 87-105.

Harris, Zellig. Development of the Canaanite Dialects. American Oriental Series, vol. 16. Microfilm-reprint, Ann Arbor, 1965.

Hightower, James R. "Some Characteristics of Parallel Prose" in Studia Serica Bernhard Karlgren Dedicata. Edited by S. Egerod and E. Glahn. Copenhagen: 1959, pp. 60-91.

Honeyman, A. M. "Merismus in Biblical Hebrew," JBL, 71 (1952), 11-18.

Horst, Friedrich. "Die Kennzeichen der hebräischen Poesie," ThRu, 21 (1953), 97-121.

Jacobson, Roman. "Grammatical Parallelism and Its Russian Facet," Language, 42 (1966), 399-429.

Jakobson, Roman and Halle, Morris. Fundamentals of Language. The Hague: Mouton & Co., 1956.

Kiparsky, Paul. "The Role of Linguistics in a Theory of Poetry," Daedalus, 102 (1973), 231-244.

Lambdin, Thomas O. "The Junctural Origin of the West Semitic Definite Article," Near Eastern Studies in Honor of William Foxwell Albright. Edited by H. Goedicke. Baltimore: The Johns Hopkins Press, 1971, 315-333.

Levin, Samuel R. Linguistic Structures in Poetry. The Hague: Mouton & Co., 1962.

Loewenstamm, Samuel F. "The Expanded Colon in Ugaritic and Biblical Verse," JSS, 14 (1969), 176-196.

Lowth, Robert. Lectures on the Sacred Poetry of the Hebrews. Trans. by G. Gregory. Boston, 1815.

______. Isaiah. A New Translation with a Preliminary Dissertation and Notes, Critical, Philological and Explanatory.[10] Boston, 1834.

Moran, William L. "The Hebrew Language in Its Northwest Semitic Background," The Bible and the Ancient Near East. Essays in Honor of William Foxwell Albright. Edited by G. Ernest Wright. Anchor Books, Garden City, New York: Doubleday and Company, 1965, pp. 59-84.

Newman, Louis I. and Popper, William. Studies in Biblical Parallelism. Parts I and II. Berkeley: University of California Press, 1918.

Parry, Adam, ed. The Making of Homeric Verse. The Collected Papers of Milman Parry. Oxford, 1971.

Robinson, T. H. "Hebrew Poetic Form: The English Tradition," SVT I (1953), 128-149.

Schökel, L. A. Estudios de Poética Hebrea. Barcelona, 1963.

Sellin, E. and Fohrer, G. Introduction to the Old Testament. Trans. by David E. Green. Nashville: Abingdon, 1968.

Speiser, E. A. Genesis. The Anchor Bible, vol. 1. Garden City, New York: Doubleday and Company, 1964.

Steinitz, Wolfgang. "Der Parallelismus in der finnisch-karelischen Volksdichtung," FF Communications, no. 115, Helsinki, 1934.

Yoder, Perry R. "Biblical Hebrew" in Versification. Major Language Types. Sixteen Essays. Edited by W. K. Wimsatt. New York: New York University Press, 1972.